GOTHENBURG STUDIES IN ENGLISH. VI
Editor: FRANK BEHRE
PROFESSOR OF ENGLISH IN THE UNIVERSITY OF GOTHENBURG

THE IDEA OF HONOUR IN THE ENGLISH DRAMA
1591—1700

BY

C. L. BARBER

GÖTEBORG
1957

822.309
Bc34i

84956

Distr.:
ALMQVIST & WIKSELL
STOCKHOLM

GÖTEBORG 1957
ELANDERS BOKTRYCKERI AKTIEBOLAG

Acknowledgments

On the completion of this book, my main thanks are due to Professor Frank Behre, without whose help and encouragement I should never have dared to undertake the work. To Dr Alvar Ellegård I am grateful for much acute criticism and constructive advice: without him, it would have been a much worse book.

I should like to thank Mr A. Terry, lecturer in Spanish at the Queen's University, Belfast, for explaining to me the substance of Castro's article on Spanish honour. To Dr Hannes Hyrenius, head of the Statistical Institute of the University of Gothenburg, I am indebted for advice on statistical methods. I should like, finally, to thank the staff of the City and University Library of Gothenburg, for their unfailing courtesy and helpfulness.

It gives me particular pleasure that the book appears in a series published by the English Department of the University of Gothenburg, a university where I spent many pleasant years and met great kindness.

Contents

Chapter 1

Aims, Methods, and Material 11
    A. Aims, p. 11. B. The Choice of Period, p. 12. C. The Choice of Drama, p. 15. D. Limitations caused by the Choice of Drama, p. 16. E. The Changing Audience, p. 28. F. Methods, p. 32. G. Material, p. 38. H. The Dating of the Material, p. 44. I. The Presentation of the Material, p. 45.

Chapter 2

The Head-Meanings Exemplified 46
    Introduction, p. 46. A. The Head-Meaning R, p. 47. B. The Head-Meaning H, p. 49. C. Equivocation: the RH Group, p. 52. D. Chastity, p. 55. E. The Head-Meaning K, p. 58. F. Esteem, p. 59. G. The Head-Meanings M, T, and P, p. 61. H. The Head-Meaning D, p. 70. I. The Head-Meaning S, p. 72. J. Word of Honour, p. 74. K. The Legal Meaning, p. 74. L. Oaths and Asseverations, p. 75. M. Respectful Forms of Address, p. 77. N. Unclassified Examples, p. 77. O. The Complexity of the Word, p. 78. P. Principles of Classification, p. 83.

Appendix to Chapter 2

Summary of Symbols for Head-Meanings 87

Chapter 3

The Head-Meanings through the Century 88

Chapter 4

The Possessors of Honour 101
    A. General, p. 101. B. Possessors of Honour, R/RH/H Group, p. 107. C. Possessors of Honour, Rc/RcC/C Group, p. 121.

Chapter 5

Two Aspects of Reputation 127
    A. Reputation, Positive and Negative, p. 127. B. Mere Reputation, p. 132.

Chapter 6

Virtue and Convention: (I) General 137

Chapter 7

Virtue and Convention: (II) The R Material 148
    A. 1591—1600, p. 148. B. 1601—1610, p. 152. C. 1611—1620, p. 158. D. 1621—1630, p. 165. E. 1631—1640, p. 173. F. 1661—1670, p. 179. G. 1671—1680, p. 184. H. 1681—1690, p. 192. I. 1691—1700, p. 197. J. Summary, R 1591—1700, p. 200.

Chapter 8

Virtue and Convention: (III) The RH Material 201
    A. 1591—1600, p. 201. B. 1601—1610, p. 203. C. 1611—1620, p. 206. D. 1621—1630, p. 208. E. 1631—1640, p. 211. F. 1661—1670, p. 215. G. 1671—1680, p. 218. H. 1681—1690, p. 223. I. 1691—1700, p. 225. J. Summary, RH 1591—1700, p. 227.

Chapter 9

Virtue and Convention: (IV) The H Material 229
    A. 1591—1600, p. 229. B. 1601—1610, p. 231. C. 1611—1620, p. 234. D. 1621—1630, p. 237. E. 1631—1640, p. 239. F. 1661—1670, p. 243. G. 1671—1680, p. 248. H. 1681—1690, p. 255. I. 1691—1700, p. 259. J. Summary, H 1591—1700, p. 262.

Chapter 10

Virtue and Convention: (V) Summary 263
    A. The Changes during the Century, p. 263. B. The k Group, p. 272. C. The v Group, p. 279. D. The growth of n, p. 282. E. Contemporary Comments, p. 283. F. The Possibility of Foreign Influence, p. 291. G. Public Theatre and Private Theatre, p. 295.

Chapter 11

Chastity 299

CONTENTS 7

Chapter 12

Other Head-Meanings 311
    A. The MTP Group, p. 311. B. The Head-Meaning E, p. 319. C. The Head-Meaning S, p. 320. D. The Head-Meaning W, p. 321. E. The Head-Meaning D, p. 323. F. The Head-Meaning K, p. 324. G. The Head-Meaning L, p. 324. H. The Head-Meaning O, p. 324. I. The Head-Meaning Y, p. 326. J. "Man of Honour" and Similar Expressions, p. 327.

Chapter 13

Summary and Conclusions 330
    A. Summary of Changes, p. 330. B. Possible Causes of the Changes, p. 333.

Appendices 338
    Appendix A, Chronological list of plays used as material: (1) The Main Material, p. 338; (2) The Supplementary Material, p. 347. Appendix B, Alphabetical list of plays used as material, p. 349. Appendix C, Editions of plays used as material, p. 353. Appendix D, Other works referred to, p. 355. Appendix E, Supplementary Material, p. 359. Appendix F, Statistical Methods, p. 363. Appendix G, List of Minor Symbols, p. 364.

What is Honour? A word.

(Henry IV Part 1)

CHAPTER 1

Aims, Methods, and Material

A. Aims

Although this book is concerned with meaning and change of meaning, it is not primarily intended as a contribution to semasiology, but as a contribution to cultural history. I hope nevertheless that it will be useful to semasiologists. My object is to show the way in which the word *honour* was used in the seventeenth century (insofar as that usage is revealed in the drama), and especially to show any changes in usage during the century. It is hoped that this will, in a modest way, illuminate some of the cultural changes that took place during the period.

The assumption underlying the book is that the way in which a single word is used can reveal something about the attitudes and the scale of values of the users, especially if the word is concerned with moral and aesthetic judgments.[1]) Words like *virtuous* and *beautiful* may appear in the dictionaries over long periods of time with their definitions unchanged; but different ages and different social groups often have quite different views about what in practice constitutes virtuous behaviour or a beautiful object; they therefore use the words *virtuous* and *beautiful* in different ways, even, it seems reasonable to say, with different meanings, although the dictionary-definitions may remain unchanged. The word *honour* is a word of this type, at any rate in some of its meanings; and it is these meanings, the ones in which honour is a determiner of conduct, which I shall be mainly concerned with, though other meanings will not be neglected entirely, since the word is a complex one and various meanings often occur in combination.[2])

---

[1]) For my methods, the further assumption is required that honour itself as a determiner of conduct remained at the same high point on the gentry's scale of values throughout the period studied. As will be argued later, this seems in fact to have been the case.

[2]) For a brief analysis of one example in *Othello*, see W. Empson, *The Structure of Complex Words*, pp. 228—229.

The changes of meaning that are most important for my purpose are, plainly, of the type which Professor Gustaf Stern classed as "substitution", i. e. semantic changes due to "external, non-linguistic causes".[1] However, one must not overlook the possibility that purely linguistic causes may also be at work causing changes of meaning; this is an additional reason for paying some attention to all the meanings of *honour*, even those that do not bear directly on conduct, since the various meanings of a word may influence one another.[2]

My primary object is not to discover causes of changes, but rather to display the changes themselves, to give a kind of map of usage during the century. However, possible causes of the changes will also be discussed; attempts will be made to distinguish between changes with narrowly linguistic causes and those with wider social causes, and to correlate the latter kind with other cultural changes during the century.[3]

B. The Choice of Period

The seventeenth century was chosen because it seemed likely that interesting changes might be found in it. It was a century of rapid change, political, economic, and cultural, perhaps one of the most decisive periods of change in English history, standing as it did as a kind of watershed between medieval and modern England.[4] It was therefore a time when ideas changed rapidly; for example, changes took place in important ideas like "truth" and "nature";[5] it would not be surprising, therefore, if changes were found in the idea of honour.

---

[1] *Meaning and Change of Meaning*, pp. 166, 192—197.

[2] For evidence that polysemy can cause disturbance of meaning, and perhaps loss of a meaning, see A. Rudskoger, *Fair, Foul, Nice, Proper*, Ch. VIII—XI.

[3] I am not forgetting, of course, that even the "narrowly linguistic" changes must be understood in a social context; see note 1 on p. 333 below.

[4] See e. g. G. M. Trevelyan, *England under the Stuarts*, pp. 225—6; H. J. Laski, *The Rise of European Liberalism*, pp. 86—160; G. N. Clark, *The Seventeenth Century*, pp. ix sqq.; H. Butterfield, *The Origins of Modern Science, passim*; E. M. W. Tillyard, *The Elizabethan World Picture, passim*; S. L. Bethell, *The Cultural Revolution of the Seventeenth Century*, pp. 11—114; D. Bush, *English Literature in the Earlier Seventeenth Century*, pp. 1 sqq., 258 sqq. For a different view, see C. S. Lewis, *De Descriptione Temporum, passim*.

[5] See B. Willey, *The Seventeenth Century Background, passim*; *The Eighteenth Century Background*, Ch. 1; J. F. Danby, *Shakespeare's Doctrine of Nature, passim*.

That the concept of honour was an important one throughout the period, at any rate for some social classes, is clear enough. The evidence for the early part of the century is given by Miss Ruth Kelso,[1] whose material extends up to 1625, and by Mr Bertram Joseph.[2] To the sources adduced by these authors can be added the recently published treatise by Robert Ashley, the manuscript of which is dated by its editor between 1596 and 1603.[3] There appears to be no similar documentation for the later part of the century in England, but the evidence of the literature suggests that, if anything, even more prominence was given to honour than earlier. An opposite view, indeed, is taken by Mr L. N. Chase, who maintains that very little importance is accorded to honour in Restoration heroic drama, since (a) love is usually shown as triumphant over honour, and (b) a number of characters speak contemptuously of honour.[4] But this argument is not convincing. It is true that, in the love-honour conflicts, it is often (though not always) love that wins, but surely the implication is that love is such an overwhelming passion that (in Chase's own words) "it nullifies all other ideals in the lover",[5] even the one that is normally accepted as the absolute guide to heroic conduct, i. e. honour. The importance of honour is clearly shown by the great prominence given to the conflicts between love and honour in the hero's soul. Moreover, the few characters that Chase cites as sneering at honour[6] are plainly intended to be unsympathetic to the audience, or at any rate to be unheroic; the heroes and heroines of Restoration drama always attach great importance to honour. It may be true, as Chase says, that the ideal of honour had become debased,[7] but that is not the same thing as saying that it was not felt to be important. Indeed, it seems rather that, from the time of Beaumont and Fletcher, honour became one of

---

[1] *The Doctrine of the English Gentleman in the 16th Century*, pp. 96—105.
[2] *Conscience and the King*, pp. 37—45
[3] *Of Honour*, ed. V. B. Heltzel, p. 18.
[4] *The English Heroic Play*, pp. 121—8.
[5] *Ibid.*, p. 117.
[6] As a matter of fact, the cases cited by Chase are not even all concerned with *honour*; at least one is concerned with *virtue*; but he seems not to make any distinction. The characters concerned are Dianet (*Aureng-Zebe*), Zempoalla (*Indian Queen*), and Zulema (*Conquest of Granada. 1*).
[7] *Ibid.*, p. 123.

the absolutes of the drama, and remained so for the rest of the century.

That some kind of change in the concept took place during the century, at least in the drama, has also seemed sufficiently plain to cause comment. Commentary, in fact, began in the Restoration period itself. Dryden, for example, struck a complacent note, congratulating his age on its increased refinement:[1])

> If love and honour now are higher raised,
> 'Tis not the poet, but the age is praised.

Shadwell, on the other hand, attacked the "wilde Romantick *Tales* wherein they strein Love and Honour to that Ridiculous height, that it becomes Burlesque";[2]) and in every one of his comedies there are jibes at the "Love and Honour" plays of the time. Later critics have noticed the "straining" rather than the refinement; Alexandre Beljame, for example, remarked of the heroes of Restoration tragedy that "Leur honneur est un mélange de délicatesses et d'élans également incompréhensibles";[3]) and Professor Allardyce Nicoll has pointed out the way in which these heroes "form worlds of honour and morality for themselves".[4]) The "straining" or "raising" of honour has also been noticed in the drama before the Restoration period; Professor Alfred Harbage, who emphasizes the continuity of the English dramatic tradition in the seventeenth century, finds parallels in the "cavalier drama" of the reign of Charles I;[5]) and the casuistical honour-debates of the later drama, and the elevating of honour into an absolute value, are clearly foreshadowed in the plays of Beaumont and Fletcher.[6]) Comments of this kind could be multiplied extensively, but enough has been said to show that there is a *prima facie* case for some kind of change that may be worth investigating.

---

[1]) *Conquest of Granada.2*, Epilogue lines 21—22.
[2]) *Sullen Lovers*, Preface.
[3]) *Le public et les hommes de lettres en Angleterre au dix-huitième siècle*, p. 43.
[4]) *A History of Restoration Drama 1660 to 1700*, p. 117.
[5]) *Cavalier Drama*, p. 54. Note especially the quotation from Suckling, "I will raise honour to a point it never was ...". See too the account on p. 61 of a typical "cavalier" plot, with "the fanciful claims of honour" as an ingredient.
[6]) See U. M. Ellis-Fermor, *The Jacobean Drama*, p. 223; J. F. Danby, *Poets on Fortune's Hill*, pp. 205—6.

C. The Choice of Drama

The drama was chosen as source-material because, besides being reasonably homogeneous,[1]) it gives us large numbers of specific situations, where we can see what honour actually meant in practice. Other kinds of work, such as courtesy-books, essays, and treatises, may give us the dictionary-definitions, but they give us relatively few concrete examples. The drama gives us the specific applications of those definitions, and thus provides us with what I shall call the "content" of the word. For example, one important meaning of honour is "reputation", and loss of honour in this sense was felt as a serious thing for a seventeenth-century gentleman; this much we could learn from many sources, but the drama can show us what things in practice were felt to cause loss of honour, and whether these showed any tendency to change during the century. The number of examples, moreover, is relatively great, much greater than could easily be found in any other kind of source from the period.

Another inducement, naturally, is that the drama was an important medium, and therefore attracted writers who can reasonably claim to speak for the culture of their age, or at any rate for an important section of it. Admittedly the level of the drama declined steeply after about 1615; after the reign of James I, the best work obviously lies outside the theatre; but even in the Restoration period it could attract the most important man of letters of the time, Dryden, who wrote over 25 plays. It is clear that, however sectional the drama may have become during the century, its attitudes cannot simply be dismissed as not having been held by anybody of importance.

At the same time, it must be recognized that the use of the drama as the sole source of material entails certain limitations, and these must now be examined.

---

[1]) There would be obvious dangers in comparing, say, sermons in one half of the century with romances in the other half. It is worth noticing that the incidents treated in the drama change little during the century; what changes is the attitude to them and the method of treating them. Indeed, Restoration dramatists often stole their situations from earlier English drama, especially Beaumont and Fletcher (see J. H. Wilson, *The Influence of Beaumont and Fletcher on Restoration Drama*, pp. 59—74, 79—85).

D. Limitations caused by the Choice of Drama

The most important limitation caused by the use of drama as the source of material is this: that what is true in the drama is not necessarily true in society outside.[1] The usage observed in the drama may be that of an individual character, perhaps an unusual one; it may be deliberately distorted by the author, for example by idealization or by parody; it may represent a literary convention; it may be intended to represent the usage of a different age or country. It cannot simply be assumed, therefore, that a usage or a change of usage in the drama is a direct reflection of the same phenomenon in the speech of the community.

The point about the individual character is probably not serious. People of different characters and temperaments are depicted as using the word *honour*, and a sufficiently large quantity of material should give us an average of usage. If, during the century, there were a marked change in the types of people depicted as using the word, or as having it used of them, this might cause difficulties; if, for example, it came to be used largely of or by affected people, or Machiavellian villains; but I have been able to detect no tendencies of this kind.[2] It therefore seems reasonable to assume that oddities of usage by individual characters will not significantly affect comparisons between usage in different decades of the century.

The second point, about possible distortion by the author, is more fundamental. It is worth remembering, however, that it is a characteristic shared by other possible sources of material. The author of a courtesy-book or of a treatise will obviously have his own ideas about what honour is and what it ought to be, just as much as the author of a play; and if (as often) he is trying to fashion an ideal gentleman, he will probably be even more liable to idealize the code of honour than the dramatist, who at least has to maintain some show of verisimilitude. Moreover, if the treatise-writer is learned, he is just as

---

[1] It is worth noting, however, that many violent and extravagant things depicted in 17th C. drama can be paralleled from contemporary life. For example, Miss E. M. Brennan, in Ch. IX and X of her unpublished thesis *The Theme of Revenge in Elizabethan Life and Drama 1580—1605*, has found examples (mainly from Star-Chamber records) of revenge-murders and attempted revenge-murders, which she compares with those in the revenge-plays.

[2] On the people of whom the word *honour* is used in the 17th century drama, see Chapter 4 below.

likely to reproduce what ancient authors thought about honour as to reflect the usage of his own day. Both the idealization and the reproduction of the ancients can be clearly seen, for example, in Robert Ashley's treatise on honour; he is much concerned to prove that honour is something given to a man "as an approbacion of his vertue", but the very way in which he argues against other meanings (e. g. "glorie" and "renown") shows that these other meanings were current;[1]) moreover, he more than once gives his case away, as when he admits that we give great honour to princes and noblemen "not because we thincke there ys greatest vertue in them, but because these thinges either be or shold be the ornaments of great vertues".[2]) The phrase "or shold be" is characteristic of Ashley's whole approach. Furthermore, as his editor points out, there is nothing in the treatise about Elizabethan England: his examples are drawn from Greek and Roman history; and there is not a single word about duelling.[3]) It is also clear from his editor's notes that the work is based on the classics, in the best contemporary manner, and especially on Aristotle. It is tolerably certain that the drama will give us a more accurate picture of contemporary usage than we can hope to get from Ashley.

However, even if it is recognized that other sources have the same limitation, we are still left with the problem. The head-meanings, or dictionary-definitions, are not likely to be distorted much: a play, after all, must be comprehensible to its audience, and the people on the stage must do and say things which can at least be imagined as possible. But on the other hand there is obviously scope for a fair amount of variation in what I call the content of the word, its specific applications, and this is one of the main elements in my material. The problem becomes simpler when we notice that most distortions are likely to be in the direction of idealization: the code of conduct that honour prescribes is likely to be represented as more magnanimous and more disinterested than it was in practice. The reason for this expectation is that, during the greater part of the century, the dramatists accept the code of honour as a norm for gentlemanly conduct, and accept it uncritically. This emerges clearly from a study of the plays: honour is exalted as an ideal, in comedy and tragedy alike; breaches

---

[1]) *Of Honour*, pp. 36—7.
[2]) *Ibid.*, p. 70.
[3]) *Ibid.*, pp. 15—16.

of the code of honour are expected to be viewed with disfavour by the audience; people who evade or criticize the code are represented as fools or cowards, and are held up to ridicule or contempt. This is seen, for example, in the attitude to duelling, which is an important part of the code of honour: men who evade the obligation to duel, like Bessus in *A King and No King* (1611) or Nickum in *The Volunteers* (1692), are held up to scorn; and examples of this kind abound throughout the century.[1] The dramatists, then, did not desire to satirize or denigrate the honour code. On the other hand, there is every reason to believe that the audience, or an important part of it, would be flattered by an idealization of honour, and that dramatists were willing to oblige.[2] As Johnson said in the following century:[3]

> Ah! let not Censure term our Fate our Choice,
> The Stage but echoes back the public Voice.
> The Drama's Laws the Drama's Patrons give,
> And we that live to please, must please to live.

It may be expected, therefore, that the usage of the word *honour* in the drama will range continuously from a simple reflection of usage in society to an extreme idealization of this usage. That such idealization exists is obvious. Even if we bear in mind the warning not to judge by what seems sensible today, but by what seemed sensible to the contemporary playgoer,[4] it is plain that the demands of honour as represented in many seventeenth-century plays, from Beaumont and Fletcher onwards, are "strained" above the point of credibility: nobody could possibly behave as represented.[5] It was this idealization, and not the code of honour itself, that was jibed at by Shadwell and

---

[1] There are also caricatures of the fire-eating duellist, like Sir Furious Inland in *News from Plymouth*, but these are not a criticism of the practice of duelling as such.

[2] On the audience, and the aristocratic domination of theatrical taste, see pp. 28—31 below.

[3] Prologue at the opening of the Drury Lane Theatre, 1747 (*The Poems of Samuel Johnson*, ed. D. N. Smith and E. L. McAdam, p. 53).

[4] B. Joseph, *op. cit.*, p. 24.

[5] See for example *Valentinian*, III.1, p. 40; *Bloody Brother*, V.1, p. 306; *The Pilgrim*, IV.2, p. 206; *Fair Favourite*, V.1, p. 275 (third example); *Indian Queen*, IV.2, p. 264; *Tyrannic Love*, V.1, p. 459; etc. References are to the editions listed in Appendix C.

parodied by the authors of *The Rehearsal*;[1]) and it is significant that, in his own comedies, Shadwell completely accepted the code of honour.

The important exceptions to the uncritical acceptance of the code of honour occur at the very beginning of the period. Professor E. M. Wilson, in a comparison of "family honour" in English and Spanish plays of the late sixteenth and early seventeenth centuries, concludes among other things that the English dramatists were more critical of the code of honour than the Spaniards, and put more emphasis on the idea that revenge belongs to God.[2]) Wilson bases this view especially on examples cited from Marston, Webster, and Tourneur. It is not difficult to find examples from the same period to show that there was sometimes a critical attitude to other aspects of honour, especially military honour; Falstaff provides both implicit and explicit comment on Hotspur's cult of honour,[3]) and Falstaff's attitudes are too pertinent to the whole theme of the play to be dismissed like Bessus's or Nickum's; Coriolanus's similar cult of honour is not seen in an altogether sympathetic light;[4]) and in *Troilus and Cressida* there is clear dramatic irony when Troilus justifies the retention of Helen on the grounds of honour, and argues by the analogy of a husband, who is bound in honour not to repudiate his wife.[5]) In *Troilus*, too, we see again the method of implicit and explicit comment on the cult of honour (and the related cults of chivalry, courtly love, and military prowess): explicit, for example, in the commentary of Thersites ("Heele ticle it for his concupie")[6]), implicit in such

---

[1]) III.5 (pp. 41—42) and V.1 (p. 70) (M. Summers's edition).

[2]) "Family Honour in the Plays of Shakespeare's Predecessors and Contemporaries", in *Essays and Studies 1953*, pp. 21 sqq. See also L. B. Campbell, "Theories of Revenge in Renaissance England", *passim*, in MP XXVIII.3. E. M. Brennan, *op. cit.* pp. 442—7, concludes that late Elizabethan revenge-dramatists do not usually condone blood-revenge for murder, but (with the exception of Shakespeare) do usually condone it for affronts to honour.

[3]) See L. C. Knights, "Notes on Comedy", pp. 124—30. For other views see J. D. Wilson, *The Fortunes of Falstaff*, pp. 70—73; E. M. W. Tillyard, *Shakespeare's History Plays*, pp. 264—304; W. G. Zeeveld, "'Food for Powder' — 'Food for Worms'", pp. 250—3.

[4]) See G. W. Knight, *The Olive and the Sword*, pp. 62—3; L. C. Knights, "Shakespeare and Political Wisdom", pp. 48—53.

[5]) II.2.61—8. The Trojans, of course, are maintaining by force a situation where Helen is kept from her lawful husband.

[6]) V.2.177.

things as Achilles's extremely unromantic murder of Hector. It is clear that Shakespeare's attitude to the cult of honour is not one of simple acceptance; I think it is an exaggeration to suggest, as Professor L. C. Knights seems to do, that he makes a fundamental attack on it;[1] but there can be no doubt that he is aware of valid possible criticisms of it, and that his own attitude is not simple. This prevents the extreme idealization of honour as found later in the century; but there is no evidence to suggest that he distorts in the other direction, and parodies it; with his subtle methods of commentary this is unnecessary.

In general, then, there is less idealization of honour at the beginning of the century, and a more critical attitude to it; but this passes very quickly, and after about 1615 a critical attitude is exceptional; there are a few interesting exceptions round about 1630,[2] but I have found no certain ones later. Even in the earlier part of the century one can expect some idealization, in view of the courtly element in the audience;[3] and the difference from the later part of the century is probably one mainly of degree.

It is important to emphasize that the idealizations of the code of honour are as important for our purposes as its actual everyday practice. The idealized pictures of themselves that groups hold up for admiration are as revealing as their actual practice, and none the less revealing if there is a large gap between the two, or if the picture is an impossible one. The gap itself is significant for the cultural historian. Our difficulty is to distinguish between those cases where practice on the stage corresponds to real practice, and those that are idealized, especially as there are no doubt many grades of idealization. Common sense is not sufficient as a guide here, since our ancestors often had a different view of common sense from ours; people, for example, did fight duels and kill one another for what we should consider ridiculous reasons. A more hopeful approach seems to be to compare the usage in more realistic with that in less realistic plays: for it is reasonable to assume that plays that correspond to contemporary reality in other respects will also do so in their depiction of honour; and it is of course in the plays that are notoriously unrealistic that we in fact find the clearest examples of incredibly "strained"

---

[1] "Notes on Comedy", pp. 124—6.

[2] See pp. 283—291 below.

[3] There are even examples in Shakespeare that might well be classed as "strained", e. g. *Richard II*, V.3.66—72. Is this *meant* to be comic?

honour.[1]) The division of plays into more and less realistic is a delicate business, however; and there is always the danger of one's assessment being influenced by the "honour" usage in the play, which, if we are to avoid circularity, must be left out of account in making the division. I have therefore adopted a rough but reasonably objective criterion, and have taken comedies to be more realistic and tragedies[2]) to be less realistic. There can be no doubt that this method is effective for the Restoration period; Restoration comedies, says Professor Nicoll, "are but a reflex of real life",[3]) and this view is fairly widely accepted;[4]) on the other hand, "the aspect which first strikes every reader of Restoration tragedy is its unreality",[5]) and on this point there is general agreement.[6]) The distinction is not so clear-cut in the first half of the century, but nevertheless exists: there is a considerable body of realistic comedy, especially by Jonson and Middleton, which is obviously much closer to contemporary life than any of the tragedies of the period (including those of Jonson and Middleton themselves);[7]) the distinction is less clear in Shakespeare, but seems to me to exist;[8]) while in Beaumont and Fletcher, whose tragi-comedy operates in a world of "fairy-tale unreality",[9]) there are comedies with more naturalistic elements; and indeed there is a stream of naturalistic social comedy right through the Jacobean

---

[1]) For example in the tragi-comedies of the Beaumont and Fletcher folio, and in the heroic drama of Dryden.

[2]) Including tragi-comedies; see pp. 41—42 below.

[3]) *Op. cit.*, p. 8.

[4]) See B. Dobrée, *Restoration Comedy*, pp. 26—30; K. M. Lynch, *The Social Mode of Restoration Comedy*, p. 4; J. Palmer, *The Comedy of Manners*, pp. 15—29; J. W. Krutch, *Comedy and Conscience after the Restoration*, pp. 7—9; M. Ellehauge, *English Restoration Drama*, pp. 199 sqq.

[5]) Dobrée, *Restoration Tragedy*, p. 13.

[6]) See Nicoll, *op. cit.*, p. 75; Chase, *op. cit.*, pp. 45—53, 166—71.

[7]) See *C. H. E. L.* VI, pp. 8 sqq., 63—5; Ellis-Fermor, *op. cit.*, pp. 99, 116; Lynch, *op. cit.*, pp. 11 sqq.; F. E. Schelling, *Elizabethan Drama*, Ch. XI; A. H. Thorndike, *English Comedy*, pp. 146—66; T. S. Eliot, *Selected Essays*, p. 169; W. D. Dunkel, *The Dramatic Technique of Thomas Middleton*, pp. 9—12, 102—4. For a different view of Middleton, see L. C. Knights, *Drama and Society in the Age of Jonson*, pp. 257—8.

[8]) Thorndike, while strongly contrasting Shakespeare's romantic comedies with the realistic comedies of Jonson and Middleton, nevertheless observes that "in every play he is drawing from his observation of real life and depicting manners and men as he knew them" (*op. cit.*, p. 137).

[9]) Ellis-Fermor, *op. cit.*, p. 210.

and Caroline periods, which is probably the direct ancestor of Restoration comedy.[1]) There is at any rate enough difference between the two *genres* for them to be used for a working division; and if the distinction between realistic and non-realistic drama is less sharp than in the later period, this is at least partly due to the fact that, in the latter, there was a greater discrepancy between the audience as they liked to imagine themselves and as they really were, between ideals and practice.[2])

On this second possible source of distortion, therefore, it is concluded that the alteration can be expected to be in the direction of idealization, i. e. the representation of the conduct demanded by honour as something more noble and magnanimous than it was in practice; and that the existence, and probably the extent, of the distortion can be gauged by a comparison of comedy with tragedy, the usage of comedy being nearer to that of real life.

The third possible source of distortion, literary convention, is covered by the same kind of considerations as the second, with the additional implication that the distortion is generally accepted by playwrights, and that it is to some extent self-perpetuating; but distortions of reality only perpetuate themselves as long as they are acceptable to the audience, and distortions caused by literary convention can be considered as simply a special case of the distortion already discussed.[3])

Fourthly, we have the possible complication that the dramatist may try to depict the usage of other ages and other countries. More can be said about this after the examination of the material, but a few preliminary points will be made here. First, we must distinguish between two different possibilities. In the first case, the writer attempts to depict alien manners and usages, intending his audience to recognize them as such; he includes elements of "local colour", expecting his audience to see them as specifically characteristic of a different age or country; this I shall call "reproduction". In the second case, the writer adopts alien manners or usages (consciously or unconsciously) without intending his audience to think of them as in any way different from those of his own age and country, or without intending to suggest any specific

---

[1]) See Lynch, *op. cit.*, pp. 19 sqq.; Nicoll, *op. cit.*, p. 79.

[2]) Cf. Nicoll, *op. cit.*, pp. 78—9.

[3]) Purely theatrical conventions of time, place, action, etc., as analysed for example by Miss M. C. Bradbrook in *Themes and Conventions of Elizabethan Tragedy*, can obviously be neglected from our point of view.

age or place by them; this I shall call "influence". Often, of course, it may be difficult to distinguish the effects of the two types. In general, reproduction should appear only in plays with a setting remote in place or time, while influence should appear in all plays by the author influenced; but there is the complication that an author may be influenced by the source of his play, without that influence spreading to his other plays, so that plays derived from foreign sources may show influence while those derived from domestic sources may not (irrespective of the actual setting chosen by the dramatist for each play).[1])

I do not intend to enter on the question of foreign *influence* on the drama; it is extremely probable that the code of honour depicted in the English drama was influenced by foreign ideas (especially Mediterranean), but this does not mean that the usages depicted did not occur in English society; the occurrence of a usage in a naturalistic play with an English setting is strong evidence that the usage existed in English society. Nor does the existence of foreign influence mean that other causes of change can be neglected; people are only influenced by ideas that appeal to them: there must be something in their own situation and their own attitudes which makes the foreign influence acceptable to them, and it is this receptivity that is important. For example, it is credible that Dryden's ideals of conduct might be influenced by the code of honour in a Spanish play that he read, but quite incredible that the same reading would have this effect on Bunyan or Milton. Foreign influence alone is an unsatisfactory explanation for a change of usage in a society, though it may have important effects on the form taken by the change; the underlying causes of the change must be sought in the society itself.

The same is not true, however, of what I have called "reproduction". If the dramatist is deliberately representing the usage of a different time or place, consciously using local colour, then his play may contain usages that do not exist in his own society, or that are rare in it. There is a danger, therefore, that his usages may mislead us. It is therefore of interest to consider to what extent seventeenth-century dramatists attempt to reproduce in detail the life and customs of other times and

---

[1]) For an example of the way in which foreign attitudes demanded by the plot can be combined with the realistic depiction of attitudes familiar to the audience at home, see J. W. Draper, "Desdemona: a Compound of Two Cultures", in *Révue de littérature comparée* 13 (1933), pp. 337—51.

other countries (as distinct from the insertion of mere scraps of local colour, which is hardly likely to be serious from our point of view).

In the drama of the age of Shakespeare there seems little attempt to reproduce in detail the customs and attitudes of other times and places. Professor Mario Praz,[1]) while finding certain authentic local details in Shakespeare's Italian plays, points out how much of the local colour is in reality English, and remarks that "Something approaching a careful study of an historical background can be found only in Ben Jonson".[2]) Jonson, however, seems to have had no intimate knowledge of Italy, as can be seen by comparing the two versions of *Every Man in his Humour*, the first set in Italy and the second in England;[3]) and what was not attempted by the scholarly Jonson was probably not attempted by more popular writers. Admittedly there are critics who take a different view; Dr E. M. W. Tillyard, for example, has argued that *Richard II*, with its emphasis on ceremony, is an attempt to reproduce the spirit of medieval England;[4]) and Schelling thinks that Chapman's French tragedies successfully reproduce the spirit of the French court.[5]) Such cases, however, if admitted, are probably to be regarded as exceptional, and it is noticeable that, if a play does show an undoubted knowledge of foreign customs and ways of thinking, then critics immediately begin looking for special explanations; for example, it is often argued that *Alphonsus Emperor of Germany* (which shows an intimate knowledge of German customs and of the German language) must have been written, or at least revised, by a German.[6])

It may be thought that plays set in classical antiquity present special problems. These plays, not surprisingly, sometimes attribute to their characters at least some ideas and attitudes quite alien to Renaissance England (such as Brutus's republican idealism) taken over from the classical source of the story; but it must be remembered that it is the dramatist who decides whether or not such attitudes are to be depicted in the play as forming part of the code of honour; and a comparison of

---

[1]) "Shakespeare's Italy", in *Shakespeare Survey 7*, pp. 95—105.
[2]) *Ibid.*, p. 100.
[3]) Schelling, *op. cit.*, I, pp. 325—6. Cf. Herford and Simpson: "Jonson knew too little of Italy for effective realism" (*Ben Jonson*, Vol. 1, p. 359).
[4]) *Shakespeare's History Plays*, pp. 251 sqq.
[5]) *Op. cit.*, I, p. 415.
[6]) See *The Tragedies of George Chapman*, ed. Parrott, pp. 683—92.

Shakespeare's Roman plays with their main source, North's *Plutarch*, shows that almost every reference to honour in these plays has been introduced by Shakespeare himself, not taken over from the source.[1])

No doubt authors varied in the extent they strove after accuracy; Jonson annotates his Roman tragedies to prove their authenticity, while Shakespeare is notorious for the way he reinterprets Rome in terms of Renaissance England;[2]) but, at any rate in comedy, even Jonson

---

[1]) These Roman plays are useful for a comparison of this kind, since they are heavily indebted to a single source, and often follow it quite closely. I have therefore made a detailed comparison of these plays and their chief source (North's *Plutarch*) with respect to the use of the noun *honour*. The word occurs quite frequently in North, roughly 20 times in each of the four *Lives* concerned, but the usage in North hardly ever corresponds to that in Shakespeare.

The *Life of Iulius Caesar* refers to the honours heaped on Caesar by the senate, and *The Life of Marcus Brutus* says that Cassius was not comparable to Brutus "for vertue and respect of honor"; these correspond in a general way with some passages in *Julius Caesar*, but not precisely; and the usages in question were in any case common ones in Shakespeare's day. On the other hand, there is nothing in North corresponding to the key-usages of the word in *Julius Caesar*, such as the "Set Honor in one eye, and Death i'th other" passage (I.ii). Nor, incidentally, is there anything corresponding to the "honourable men" of Antony's oration.

In *The Life of Marcus Antonius*, there are three usages corresponding closely to ones in *Antony and Cleopatra* (IV.ii.43, IV.xv.46, and V.ii.161), all quite normal ones for Shakespeare's time. On the other hand there is nothing in North corresponding to such important examples in *Antony and Cleopatra* as I.iii.97, I.iv.68, II.i.26, II.ii.89, II.ii.101, II.vii.78—9, III.iv.22, III.x.23, IV.ii.6, IV.xv.28, V.i.30, and others.

In *The Life of Caius Martius Coriolanus*, considerable emphasis is placed on Coriolanus's early and eager pursuit of honour (military glory), and on the honours proposed for him as rewards; these ideas of course were taken over by Shakespeare (though none of his usages corresponds closely with any passage in North), but they were in any case common usages of Shakespeare's time. On the other hand, there are many examples in *Coriolanus* which have nothing even vaguely corresponding to them in North, e. g. Volumnia's speech about Honour and Policy (III.ii), and Aufidius's reflection that Coriolanus has set his mercy and his honour at difference (V.iii.200).

In conclusion it can be said that, in Shakespeare's three Roman plays, there are only three places where the noun *honour* has precise antecedents in North's *Plutarch* (all three in *Antony and Cleopatra*); there are a number of usages which correspond in a general way with what North says, and these are all quite common usages of Shakespeare's time; but the great majority of examples where Shakespeare refers to honour as a determiner of conduct have nothing corresponding to them in North whatever.

[2]) Cf. M. W. MacCallum, *Shakespeare's Roman Plays*, pp. 81—6, 200—207.

could treat Rome very much as if it were Jacobean London, as can be seen in *Poetaster*. Furthermore, with the rise of tragi-comedy round about 1610, there is an increasing tendency to set plays in a fairyland world of romance that is nowhere earthly;[1]) nominally the scene may be Sicily or Naples or even Russia, but we could change the names without noticing any difference — they are all the same escape-world, and lack local distinctiveness. It may be true that attitudes and ideas, including those about honour, are not what the spectator met in English society outside the theatre, but it is hardly reasonable to attribute this to the reproduction of foreign customs, for the customs are substantially the same whether the scene is set in Paphos (*The Mad Lover*), in Moscow (*The Loyal Subject*), or in ancient Rome (*The Prophetess*). Even in comedies, which are usually more naturalistic than the tragi-comedies and tragedies, it is occasionally difficult to decide where the scene is supposed to be laid; *Monsieur Thomas* is presumably set in England, but there is little positive indication. On the whole, it does not seem likely that, in the Jacobean period, much importance need be attached to the effects of "reproduction".

The same seems true of the Caroline period. Such, at any rate, was the opinion of Shirley's editor, Gifford, who wrote, in his introduction to *Love Tricks*:[2])

> There is nothing in this play to determine where the scene is laid; the only local allusion is in the 2d Scene of the 2d Act, where "this our Fairy-Isle" occurs. The fact is, Shirley thought only of England, the true fairy-isle to him and his contemporaries, who, wherever their Scene is laid, generally make their characters think, and speak, and act, like those that were moving around them.

The tragedies and tragi-comedies of Massinger, Shirley, and Davenant carry on the tradition of Beaumont and Fletcher, and have the same romantic, idealized settings, lacking local distinctiveness. The comedies are more naturalistic, but the most naturalistic ones are nearly always set in England anyway. Ford's tragedies are rather different, looking back to the revenge tradition rather than to Beaumont and Fletcher; but they too show little sign of local colour. How many people could say

---

[1]) Ellis-Fermor, *op. cit.*, pp. 201—7; Schelling, *op. cit.*, II, p. 192. For a subtler analysis of the relation between Beaumont and Fletcher tragi-comedy and contemporary society see J. F. Danby, *Poets on Fortune's Hill*, pp. 152—83.

[2]) Shirley, *Dramatic Works and Poems*, ed. Gifford & Dyce, Vol. 1, p. 7.

offhand where the action of *The Broken Heart* is laid? Apart from the names, and a few religious references, there is little to remind us that we are supposed to be in ancient Sparta.

It is less easy to decide about the Restoration period, and it may be thought that its more sophisticated audience would have demanded a more faithful representation of foreign customs. In my material I have found a few small things that would support this view, but they are not very strong.[1]) And as against this we have to consider the way in which the aura of unreality of earlier tragi-comedy is even further developed in Restoration heroic drama, which takes place in an idealized super-world of its own creation. Professor Nicoll expresses it thus:[2])

> These scenes [of Restoration heroic drama] most frequently had some vague historical basis, but truth to history and truth to local customs was never insisted upon. To fit them in with the prevailing temper of the time, the characters, were they Romans, Arabians, Mexicans, Chinamen, even Englishmen of the earlier Tudor periods, were all warped out of their national characteristics and made to live in one world — the world of heroic ardour and of dauntless courage . . .

From our point of view, it is interesting to note especially that seventeenth-century duelling conventions are frequently depicted as existing in the ancient world, or in Aztec Mexico, or among the Spaniards of the time of Cortez, or in some other equally anachronistic setting.[3]) Since practically all Restoration tragedy and tragi-comedy comes under the description "heroic drama",[4]) we are only left with the problem of the comedy; and the vast majority of comedies are set in England, so that the problem in fact hardly exists. For example, of the fifty Restoration comedies included in my material, no less than thirty-seven are set in England, nearly all of them in London; six are set in Spain, four in Italy, one in Sicily, one in ancient Greece, and one on an enchanted island; and, with only two exceptions, they are all plainly intended to

---

[1]) See pp. 291—295 below.
[2]) *Op. cit.*, p. 121. See also Chase, *op. cit.*, pp. 151—71.
[3]) Duelling, as distinct from judicial combat, did not arise until about the middle of the 16th century. See Kelso, *op. cit.*, p. 101.
[4]) But some writers confine the term to rhymed plays (e. g. Chase, *op. cit.*, pp. 1—6).

represent the contemporary period, not the historical past. Moreover, the plays set in foreign countries often have Englishmen among their characters; this applies, for example, to *An Evening's Love* (set in Spain) and *The Rover* (set in Italy), both of which have Englishmen among their principal characters. The converse is not true: it is unusual for foreigners to appear as major characters in the comedies set in England. On the whole it seems probable that, even if Restoration dramatists sometimes aim at geographical and historical accuracy (which is by no means certain), this will hardly be on such a scale as to have any serious effect on the over-all picture given by the drama.

In summary, it can be said that there appear to be two main probable ways in which usage in the drama may differ from usage in real life in the seventeenth century, as far as honour is concerned. The first is idealization by the dramatist, the representation of the code as finer than it was; some measure of this can probably be obtained by comparing comedy with tragedy, and this comparison is made in all the analyses that follow. The second is the deliberate representation of the usage of other times and places, intended to be recognized by the audience as such; it does not seem probable that this occurred to any great extent; it should be possible to detect it by comparing plays set in England with plays set in other countries; I have carried out a comparison of this kind (with respect to honour) in Restoration comedy; I have compared plays set in England with plays set in Spain, and have found no great difference between the two.[1]

E. The Changing Audience

There is, however, a further and extremely important result of the choice of drama as material. The dramatist and his audience may not represent the whole of society, but only a certain class or certain classes, and the audience may change in social composition during the period studied. The ideas and ideals that appear in the drama will be those of the classes represented in the audience, and will not necessarily coincide with those of the rest of society. It is the social composition of the audience that is important, rather than the social origin of the individual dramatist: it is the "drama's patrons" that call the tune.

It is evident that the social composition of the audience changed greatly during the seventeenth century. The great age of Elizabethan

---

[1] See pp. 291—295 below.

drama sprang from a fusion of the popular and the scholarly traditions, and this implies a fusing of the audiences: the audience of the public theatre in 1600 was a wide one, representing all classes of Elizabethan London.[1]) The audience certainly included courtiers, and moreover the plays performed in the public theatres were often performed at court for the sovereign. It is important to remember that, despite Puritan opposition to the theatres (as seen, for example, in the constant hostility of the city authorities), there were also large middle-class elements in the audience, as has been emphasized by Mr L. B. Wright;[2]) the extreme puritans were only a minority, even at the end of the sixteenth century,[3]) and many well-known literary men (including dramatists) had middle-class parents.[4]) The change in the theatre audience in the first half of the seventeenth century seems to consist largely in the gradual disappearance of the middle classes, as puritanism grows stronger and hostility between court and city increases with the deteriorating political situation. As the gap grows in the middle of the audience, taste becomes stratified: the "private theatres" (which, significantly, disappear during the 1590's) become increasingly the theatres of the upper classes, as do the new enclosed theatres, while certain of the old open-air theatres, like the Fortune and the Red Bull, become more and more popular in taste, with clownery, jigs, spectacle, and noise.[5]) Some of the older dramatists, notably Thomas Heywood, become champions of popular and middle-class ideals, but more and more the new plays come to be written for courtly taste, the lead being given by Beaumont and Fletcher;[6]) and Beaumont and Fletcher are perhaps the most important single influence on the theatrical taste of the rest of the century.[7])

---

[1]) See *C. H. E. L.*, VI, p. 273; Harbage, *Shakespeare's Audience*, pp. 53—91; Schelling, *op. cit.*, I, pp. xxxviii—xxxix.

[2]) *Middle-Class Culture in Elizabethan England*, pp. 603—8.

[3]) *Ibid.*, p. 14.

[4]) *Ibid.*, pp. 17—18.

[5]) See Wright, *op. cit.*, pp. 608—13; *C. H. E. L.*, VI, p. 107; E. K. Chambers, *The Elizabethan Stage*, II, p. 425 and note; L. G. Salingar, "The Decline of Tragedy", in *A Guide to English Literature: 2*, ed. B. Ford, pp. 429 sqq.

[6]) See Wright, *op. cit.*, p. 614; Harbage, *Cavalier Drama*, pp. 7—25; Schelling, *op. cit.*, I, pp. xli—xlii, 523—5; Salingar, *op cit.*, pp. 429—30.

[7]) J. H. Wilson, *The Influence of Beaumont and Fletcher on Restoration Drama*, *passim*; Nicoll, *op. cit.*, pp. 83—4; Salingar, *op. cit.*, p. 430.

Even so, a popular element seems to have persisted in the theatre right up to (and even into) the Commonwealth period, even if attenuated.[1]) But after the Restoration the popular element has disappeared completely, and the theatre is something for the upper classes,[2]) the audience consisting predominantly of "courtiers and their satellites".[3]) Theatrical taste is dominated by the aristocracy,[4]) and even a Whig poet like Shadwell adopts the usual rakish attitudes of the Restoration *roué*, the anti-citizen satire, etc. .

The development, then, is from a very broad audience to an exclusively aristocratic one; there are clear signs of the change from about 1610, with the rise of Beaumont and Fletcher tragi-comedy, the growing importance of the private theatres,[5]) and perhaps even such little things as the growing tendency for gallants to sit on the stage;[6]) and the process is complete when the theatres re-open after the Restoration. Now in the seventeenth century, honour is an exclusively upper-class concept, a prerogative of the gentry;[7]) in tracing its history in the drama of the time, therefore, we are (among other things) seeing what happens to an upper-class ideal among courtly circles as these circles become more and more isolated from the rest of society. This isolation is political as well as cultural, for the change of the theatre from a national to a court institution is obviously part of a wider social dichotomy, seen at its acutest in the civil wars. And not even the whole of the gentry is represented in the later theatre audience. According to Mr G. S. Gordon, a result of the political and religious strife of the seventeenth century was that there arose two conflicting ideals of the gentleman, the cavalier ideal (represented by Peacham) and the puritan ideal

---

[1]) See L. Hotson, *The Commonwealth and Restoration Stage*, pp. 3—59.
[2]) Nicoll, *op. cit.*, pp. 3 sqq.; Beljame, *op. cit.*, pp. 56—7.
[3]) Nicoll, *op. cit.*, p. 8.
[4]) Beljame, *op. cit.*, Ch. 1, esp. pp. 71—113.
[5]) E. g. the Blackfriars became the leading theatre of the King's Men, instead of the Globe. They began to use it in addition to the Globe in 1609, and by Caroline times it was their main theatre. See Chambers, *op. cit.*, II, pp. 425, 509—15.
[6]) In the public theatres, little is heard about the custom before the turn of the century; complaints from dramatists begin in about 1603. See J. C. Adams, *The Globe Playhouse*, pp. 79—80, 95—97; Chambers, *op. cit.* II, pp. 535—7.
[7]) Kelso, *op. cit.*, pp. 96—7; and see pp. 102—126 below.

(represented by Brathwaite).[1]) The ideal depicted in the drama will obviously be the cavalier ideal, at least from the reign of Charles I onwards, and the ideal of honour that we trace will be that of court circles; there was doubtless also a puritan ideal of honour, among puritan gentry, but we learn nothing about it from the plays, in which puritans are not represented as gentry.[2]) We shall therefore be tracing the development of courtly honour, which the cavaliers considered their prerogative, as the court became progressively isolated from the rest of the community, and this fact may reasonably be reckoned as one of the causes of any changes that we find in the use of the word.[3]) There may be many other causes, both cultural and linguistic, but the theatrical and social development that has been sketched adds greatly to the interest of the study.

It is theoretically arguable that any changes found in the drama during the century may be due to the change in the social composition of the audience alone, irrespective of any social changes outside the theatre; this means that, if the theatre in 1600 had catered only for the upper classes, it would have depicted the code of honour in just the way that the Restoration theatre did. It is possible to test this hypothesis by comparing plays written for the Jacobean private theatres (which had an exclusive and high-class audience) with those written for Jacobean public theatres. I have carried out a comparison of this kind for comedies written in the decade 1601 to 1610, and have found that there is no appreciable difference with respect to honour between the private-theatre plays and the public-theatre plays, but that both differ significantly from comedies written for the Restoration theatre.[4]) The hypothesis is therefore untenable; the changes found in the use of the

---

[1]) *Peacham's Complete Gentleman 1634*, p. vi. See also W. L. Ustick, "Changing Ideals ... in Seventeenth-Century England", pp. 154—6.

[2]) In her *Memoirs of Col. Hutchinson*, Lucy Hutchinson refers quite often to her husband's honour (e. g. pp. 20, 28, 30, 31—3, 61—4, etc.)(1846 ed.); she also refers occasionally to her own honour (e. g. pp. 30, 63) and to that of her own and her husband's relatives (e. g. pp. 14, 36—8, 41, 54, 56). Probably the nearest the dramatists get to a character like Col. Hutchinson is Shadwell's Col. Hackwell senior, whose claim to gentry is dubious and who rejects honour (see p. 103 below).

[3]) For the growing divisions in the ranks of the gentry, and isolation of the court, see for example Trevelyan, *op. cit.*, pp. 100—30, 349—50.

[4]) See pp. 295—298 below.

word *honour* in the drama during the century cannot be explained as a result of theatrical change alone; rather the theatrical change (the change in composition of the audience) must itself be seen in the light of wider social changes.

F. Methods

The concept of honour studied is the seventeenth-century one, not that of our own time: I am not concerned with what we mean by the word, but with what they meant by it. It is clear from many sources that what the seventeenth-century gentry called *honour* was something of great importance to them in the regulation of their conduct, and I am trying to see what that something was. I am therefore making my starting-point the actual seventeenth-century usage of the noun *honour*, and only taking into account cases where the word is actually used. Admittedly the idea of honour may be implied in many other places, intended to be understood by the audience as a motive for conduct without being made explicit; but it is impossible to be certain of the cases in which this is so: two apparently identical situations may differ from one another in small ways not easily detected by the modern reader. The safest method is to limit oneself to those cases where the idea of honour is indisputably involved, and that means the cases where the word *honour* is actually used. Other approaches have been used by writers on the subject, the two main variants being the approach from the group of synonyms and the approach from situations. Both methods have disadvantages for my purposes.

The approach from a group of synonyms is exemplified by Professor E. M. Wilson. After remarking that the Spaniards used several words for honour, he refers to the *N. E. D.* to show that this was also the case in England; "reputation", "credit", "fame", and "opinion" are, he says, roughly synonymous and cover the same kind of notion; and he quotes passages from *Othello* and *Law Tricks* to show that two or more of these words could be used in a similar sense in the same passage.[1]) He therefore treats these words as equivalent to one another, and as synonyms of "honour". The fact remains, however, that the determinant of the gentlemanly code of conduct was always denoted by the word *honour*, not by the words *reputation*, etc.; and it is difficult to be

---

[1]) *Op. cit.*, p. 20.

certain that, in any given context, a seventeenth-century speaker would have felt that *honour* could be replaced by one of these other words. The head-meaning of *honour* was often "reputation", but the associations evoked by the two words were different. Moreover, *honour* had other head-meanings besides "reputation", including meanings directly relevant to the code of conduct, as will be seen later. An example of the use of the word *reputation* in a context where, despite all appearances, *honour* might have been felt impossible by the original audience can be seen in *The Merry Wives of Windsor*. Ford, jealous of his wife, soliloquizes: "See the hell of hauing a false woman: my bed shall be abus'd, my Coffers ransack'd, my reputation gnawne at, and I shall not onely receiue this villanous wrong, but stand under the adoption of abhominable termes, and by him that does mee this wrong".[1] This looks like a clear case of *reputation* synonymous with *honour*, for the unchastity of a wife is one of the undoubted causes of loss of honour to a husband in this period. However, it should be noticed that Ford is probably intended to be a citizen, and consequently not a member of the gentry; honour was the prerogative of the gentry, and a citizen would have no honour to lose; but anybody could have reputation. It is quite possible, therefore, that to the original audience the word *honour* would have sounded intolerably pretentious in Ford's mouth. It is noteworthy that in this play neither Ford nor Page ever has honour attributed to him; the only male characters who lay claim to it are Falstaff (a knight) and Pistol (who can be classed as a pretender to gentry, and who in any case is rapped sharply over the knuckles by Falstaff for using the word).[2] This example is a reminder that the dictionary-definition does not tell us all we need to know about a word: we also need to know who can use it, and in what circumstances, and these things are part of the meaning of the word.

The approach through situations can also be seen in Wilson, for example when he describes *Othello* as a tragedy of honour;[3] but it is

---

[1] II.2.241—6.

[2] The word is used of Mistress Ford in the sense "chastity"; but in this meaning the word was not strictly limited to the gentry; see pp. 123—126 below.

[3] *Op. cit.*, p. 21; see also his article "Othello, a Tragedy of Honour", in *The Listener*, June 5th 1952, and criticisms of this article by Miss Janet Spens in a letter to *The Listener*, June 19th 1952. In *Othello* there is only one reference (V.2.296) *explicitly* suggesting honour as the motive for the murder of Desdemona.

more clearly seen in Mr Bertram Joseph's study of *Hamlet*, called *Conscience and the King*. Joseph's thesis is that the main theme of *Hamlet* is a conflict between honour and religion: honour commands Hamlet to revenge the murder of his father by killing his uncle, but religion threatens him with damnation if he does. The play is therefore seen as a conflict between the desire to preserve honour, and the fear of damnation. Joseph's method is to assemble a large quantity of contemporary evidence about the demands made by honour and by religion, and the importance attached to them, and then to apply these to the situation in the play. The striking thing is that he does not consider at all what the play itself says about honour; in over 150 pages of text, including many quotations from *Hamlet*, I have been able to find only two quotations from the play that so much as contain the word *honour*, and one of these is irrelevant. It is plain that Joseph is relying entirely on the actual situation itself in *Hamlet*, and arguing that it is identical with the situations referred to in the treatises, courtesy-books, etc., from which he has compiled his evidence. But here there is a possible source of error: as in the example cited above from *The Merry Wives*, it is difficult to be certain that situations are identical in all relevant respects; and it is hazardous to claim that the idea of honour is involved in a situation before a study has been made of a very large number of situations where honour is undoubtedly involved, i. e. where the word *honour* is actually used. Joseph's material is of great interest, but it hardly supplies such situations in sufficient numbers or sufficient concreteness. Now in fact I think that both Wilson and Joseph are right in believing that the original audiences would have recognized that honour was involved in the central situations of *Othello* and *Hamlet* respectively; and there is in fact slight but nevertheless explicit reference to this involvement in the plays themselves.[1] But the method is dangerous, especially when combined with a neglect of what the play itself says about honour, and it is all too easy for the modern critic to detect honour in situations where the dramatist had no thought of it. It is also liable to lead to an exaggeration of the importance of honour in a given play: it is one thing to say that honour is implicitly involved in the main plot of *Hamlet*, but

---

[1] *Othello* V.2.295—6; *Hamlet* IV.4.56 (and V.2.230 and V.2.245—7 are obviously also relevant). Notice how *late* in the plays all these references come.

quite another to say that it is the main theme of the play; and on this point I cannot agree with Joseph. If honour had been the major theme of *Hamlet*, this would surely have been made abundantly clear, and the word *honour* would not merely have crept in in casual references. This becomes clear if we compare *Hamlet* with *A Fair Quarrel*, which contains exactly the conflict between honour and the fear of damnation which Joseph thinks he sees in *Hamlet*. A great part of *A Fair Quarrel*, especially of the second and third acts, is devoted to the dilemma of Captain Ager. He has been insulted by the Colonel, who has called him the son of a whore, and for a soldier this is clear and imperative grounds for a challenge; but it occurs to Captain Ager, who is an exceptionally scrupulous man, that it is just possible that the Colonel's insult is true: perhaps at some time in her life his mother has been unchaste; in that case he will be duelling in an unjust cause, and this will imperil his soul:

> he should be one, indeed,
> That never heard of heaven's joys or hell's torments,
> To fight this out: I am too full of conscience,
> Knowledge, and patience, to give justice to't;
> So careful of my eternity, which consists
> Of upright actions, that unless I knew
> It were a truth I stood for, any coward
> Might make my breast his foot-pace:
>
> (II.1.7—14)

It is constantly insisted, on the other hand, that honour demands that Ager shall fight; when, imagining his mother unchaste, he refuses to fight, his friends try to persuade him to, urging that no great importance must be attached to mere life, "which in respect /Of life in honour is but death and darkness" (III.1.32—3); and when finally he discovers what he considers to be a just cause for fighting the Colonel, he is delighted, exclaiming "Blessed remembrance in time of need!/ I'd lost my honour else" (III.1.132—3). Indeed, both the damnation theme and the honour theme are amply emphasized, and the reader is never in any doubt about Ager's dilemma. It is reasonable to assume that Shakespeare would have made the theme equally clear in *Hamlet* if he had intended it to be the main subject of the play, as Joseph alleges; it can hardly be argued that, in the fifteen years between the writing of *Hamlet* and the writing of *A Fair Quarrel*, the drama became more naive and explicit, for the tendency seems in fact to have been in the opposite direction;[1]) nor can it be argued that Middleton was a simple-minded writer who had to say in so many words what Shakespeare more artistically left to be deduced: the author of *The Changeling* and *Women beware Women* was no simpleton, and *A Fair Quarrel* is not an early work.[2])

I have therefore rejected both the synonym approach and the situation approach, and worked solely from the usage of the word *honour* itself as a noun. It may perhaps be thought that my objections to synonyms do not apply to other parts of speech related to the noun *honour*, such as the adjective *honourable* and the verb *honour*, which might be expected to give the same kind of information as the noun. This is not necessarily true: the verb *honour* gives no information at all about honour as a determinant of conduct, being used exclusively in the senses "to esteem" and "to confer marks of distinction upon". Other such words, including *honourable*, do relate in some of their meanings to the code of conduct, but their numbers are so small compared with the noun that they are not much help; and a surprisingly small fraction of them give the kind of specific content that I am looking for. As an indication of the relative numbers of the noun *honour* and these related words, it can be mentioned that, in the material I have studied, the sum total of all related words put together, including negative forms like *dishonour* etc., and also including foreign words like French *honneur*, only comes to about a third of the number of examples of *honour* as a noun. Any attempt to take these other forms into account would give rise to almost insoluble problems of classification and weighting; since they provided so little material anyway, I decided to neglect them and to concentrate on the noun.[3]) As a precaution, however, I have examined the other words, and made sure that they do not show trends which would cancel out the changes that I have found in the use of the noun.

Given the noun *honour* as the basic material, I have treated it in a statistical way, by comparing the numbers of different usages that occur in different periods. I have selected a number of plays from each

---

[1]) See Ellis-Fermor, *op. cit.*, pp. 278—83.

[2]) *A Fair Quarrel* is by Middleton and Rowley, but the scenes in question are usually attributed to Middleton. See P. G. Wiggin, *An Inquiry into the Authorship of the Middleton-Rowley Plays*, pp. 29—39.

[3]) Including the few cases where the noun is used adjectivally.

decade[1]) of the century, and excerpted all the examples of the noun *honour* from them. I have then classified these according to head-meaning and content, and have looked for changes from one half of the century to the other, and even from decade to decade. This method should give a lowest common measure of usage in each decade (insofar as this is reflected in the drama). It should therefore give some idea of the changes in the ideals and values of the honour-bearing classes during the century, or at least of those sections of them that patronized the theatre.

The statistics as I have presented them disregard the attitude of the dramatist himself to honour, his implicit and explicit comments on the ideal. As suggested earlier, this comment can appear in many ways: in the pitting of character against character, attitude against attitude (Hotspur and Falstaff); in the contrast between ideal and reality (Troilus's ideals and Achilles' behaviour); in the tragic working-out of an ideal in practice (Brutus's murder of Caesar and its results); in explicit discussion of different attitudes to honour (the king's lecture to Bertram in *All's Well*, II.3); in the very imagery of a play (as in passages in *Henry IV.1* and *Coriolanus* commented on by L. C. Knights[2]) and Wilson Knight[3]) respectively); and so on. My method does not take such things into account; but, as suggested earlier, the attitude of the dramatists becomes increasingly one of simple acceptance, and on the whole it is only in the early Jacobean period (and the Elizabethan period) that we find views of honour that are at all complex. This change is itself of cultural significance, suggesting the growing dominance of the court in drama, the elimination of the popular element, and an increasing tendency for the dramatist to flatter the aristocracy. But it also means that, after the early part of the century, there is not much difference between dramatists in their attitudes to honour, and that their own view of honour is identical with that expressed by the upper-class characters in the plays, who are in fact the predominant users of the word. What I am primarily concerned with, however, is the usage of the period, not the attitudes of the authors towards that usage.

---

[1]) Except the decades 1641—50 and 1651—60, during most of which the public theatres were closed.

[2]) "Notes on Comedy", pp. 124, 127.

[3]) *Op. cit.*, p. 63.

G. Material

Lists of the plays used as the sources of the material will be found in Appendix A (chronological order) and Appendix B (alphabetical order of titles). The editions used are given in Appendix C (in alphabetical order of authors). Cross-reference from appendix to appendix is facilitated by the inclusion of dates in Appendix B and of editions in Appendix A.

I have aimed at taking about twenty to twenty-five plays from each decade of the century (except the decades from 1641 to 1660), and at keeping a rough balance between comedy and tragedy (though this has not always been possible). Since I wished to start from Shakespeare, I have also included the twenty-one of his plays that fall in the last decade of the sixteenth century (1591 to 1600), thus providing material for a ninth decade. Admittedly this decade is not so reliably represented as the others, as it is covered entirely by one author, but on the other hand there can be little doubt that, after the deaths of the "university wits" of the early 1590's, Shakespeare was practically without a serious rival in the theatre until the turn of the century, and is not unnaturally to be regarded as the prime source of material for this period. However, as a check I have collected supplementary material from a number of other authors in this decade, and this has confirmed my original findings based on Shakespeare alone (see Appendix E). I have not been able to reach the desired number of plays in all decades; there was no difficulty in the first half of the century, but the material available is decidedly sparser in the second half; I have eighteen plays from the decade 1661 to 1670, and seventeen from the decade 1681 to 1690; the decade 1691 to 1700 was the most difficult of all, and here I have only twelve plays; on the other hand, there was ample material for the decade 1671 to 1680, and in order to compensate for the deficit in the other decades of the Restoration period I increased the number of plays in this decade to thirty-two. The number of plays taken from each decade, broken down according to type, is shown in Table 1. These figures do not include 29 plays that were examined after the main material had been analysed, to given further light on certain points; for these plays see Appendix E.

Short-length plays have not been admitted, nor have extreme farces (like Aphra Behn's *Emperor of the Moon*). Masques, civic pageants, and dramatic operas have been found to yield little information, and so

TABLE 1. *Number of Plays from each Decade, by Types.*

Period from to	1591 1600	1601 1610	1611 1620	1621 1630	1631 1640	1591 1640	1661 1670	1671 1680	1681 1690	1691 1700	1661 1700	Grand Total
Comedies	9	16	12	15	12	64	10	20	12	8	50	114
Tragedies	3	10	6	4	4	27	1	10	4	1	16	43
Tragi-comedies	0	3	7	6	7	23	7	2	1	2	12	35
Histories	9	0	1	0	1	11	0	0	0	0	0	11
Others	0	1	0	1	0	2	0	0	0	1	1	3
Total	21	30	26	26	24	127	18	32	17	12	79	206

have also been excluded (except for one dramatic opera, *King Arthur*, in an exceptionally lean decade). Only plays written for the public theatre[1]) have been included; closet drama and plays written for private performance have been excluded. Close translations have also been excluded, but "adaptations" have been admitted — it would in any case have been almost impossible to exclude them. Seventeenth-century adaptations tend to be fairly free, whether they are adaptations from foreign or from domestic plays; and even seemingly close adaptations make considerable modifications in key-words like *honour*. This can be seen if one studies the Restoration adaptations of Shakespeare, many of which are recognizably Shakespeare (even though "smoothed" and vulgarized) most of the time. In Shakespeare's *Tempest*, the noun *honour* occurs eight times; in the Dryden/Davenant adaption, it occurs seven times, but only two of these examples correspond to Shakespeare's; so six out of eight have been dropped, and five new ones introduced. Shakespeare's *Troilus and Cressida* contains twenty-six examples, Dryden's adaptation twenty-four; of these, only ten are common to both plays. *Measure for Measure* contains forty-five examples; Davenant's *Law against Lovers*, which is largely an adaptation of it, contains only twenty-two examples, and only three of these correspond to Shakespeare; some parts of *The Law against Lovers*, however, are adapted from *Much Ado about Nothing*, but none of the ten examples in the latter play reappears in Davenant. These adaptations, and especially *Troilus and Cressida*, seem to be fairly close ones by seventeenth-century standards.

---

[1]) The public theatre in the wide sense, including what Shakespeare's contemporaries called "private theatres".

In excerpting the examples, I have usually disregarded prologues and epilogues and lists of *dramatis personae*, since these are usually extraneous and irrelevant; occasionally, however, they form a more integral part of the play, as do for example the prologue to *Troilus and Cressida* and the Chorus of *Henry V*, and the detailed descriptions of characters in many of the lists of *Dramatis Personae* in the plays of Jonson and his disciple Shadwell; and in such cases they have been reckoned as part of the play. Prefaces and dedications have been disregarded in all cases.

In many decades there is very little choice of plays when the unsuitable ones (masques etc., and plays of disputed date) have been eliminated; in others, especially early in the century, there is still a good deal of choice. Where there is choice, I have tried to select first the best dramatists (those of the greatest literary merit), and secondly (other things being equal) those most representative of their period in the theatre. The most important writers are selected first because they seem most likely to reflect the age and its ideals accurately; they should be the most keenly aware of the currents of their age, and the most competent to depict and analyse them. It may perhaps be argued that the greater the writer the more he will transcend his age; but this (if true) will surely give him the greater power to depict it objectively; his own ideals and attitudes will appear in the kind of implicit and explicit comment already noted in Shakespeare, and this kind of comment would be pointless if the things commented on were not current in the age.[1]) After the most important writers, it seems natural to choose the most representative, those that have the most central attitudes of their age and group. However, I have deliberately refrained in the Jacobean period from choosing authors that represent a distinctively middle-class point of view, and that write especially for middle-class elements in the audience: Thomas Heywood, for example.[2]) Since I wanted to follow the development of an aristocratic ideal,[3]) it seemed fairer to limit myself to authors who appealed (though not necessarily exclusively) to the gentry. The changes in usage found during the century might have been greater if I had admitted authors like Heywood

---

[1]) Cf. Knights, *Drama and Society*, Ch. 5, esp. p. 177.
[2]) See Wright, *op. cit.*, pp. 630—51.
[3]) More strictly, an ideal of the gentry; but since there is no convenient adjective for this, I shall sometimes, as here, use the word "aristocratic" without intending to confine my reference to the nobility.

in the early period, but the interpretation of the findings would have been more difficult. Heywood's attitude to honour might have been interesting to study in itself; but it did not develop into anything in the later seventeenth-century theatre, for Heywood's group and their views disappeared from the theatre.

Given these criteria, Shakespeare and Jonson are self-evident choices for the beginning of the period; they are supplemented, in the additional material, by Marlow, Chapman, Marston, Nashe, Peele, Greene, and Dekker (see Appendix E). In the Jacobean period are included a good number of plays by Webster and Middleton; Webster represents the more personal development of revenge tragedy characteristic of the second decade of the century, while Middleton provides highly naturalistic comedy without at the same time writing for the middle classes, and is also responsible for the finest tragedies of the late Jacobean age. The Beaumont and Fletcher folio was an obvious choice, partly because it is so typical of the new courtly trends, and partly because of its great influence (which shows how much it must have appealed to the tastes of the increasingly upper-class audience). It may in fact be thought that too many plays have been chosen from it compared with other authors; but it must be remembered that, though nominally by Beaumont and Fletcher, it is in fact the work of a number of authors,[1] though the hand of Fletcher is admittedly the dominant one. Massinger was chosen as the typical figure of the 1620's; while in the reign of Charles I the only figures of any standing (apart from Jonson, Massinger, and other such older authors) are Ford, Shirley, and Davenant. In the Restoration period, Dryden was self-evident; in tragedy, Otway was a fairly obvious choice, and in comedy, Congreve, Wycherley, and Etherege; but there was in fact little choice, except in one decade; of other authors the best-represented are Shadwell and Mrs Behn, who offer quite a good variety of specimens of Restoration drama; they are complementary, too, in that Mrs Behn is an extreme royalist, while Shadwell is a Whig.

For reasons given earlier, it is desirable to examine comedy and tragedy separately. With tragedy I classify tragi-comedy, which in the seventeenth century is often indistinguishable from tragedy except in its ending. History-plays (i. e. English chronicle plays) form a class

---

[1] See E. H. C. Oliphant, *The Plays of Beaumont and Fletcher, passim.*

by themselves, but for my purposes it is necessary to classify each of them as comedy or as tragedy. They are not very numerous except in the decade 1591 to 1600; the chronicle was only popular for some fifteen years after the Armada, and only two history-plays occur in my main seventeenth-century material (*Henry VIII* and *Perkin Warbeck*), though I made no attempt to avoid them. I have classed the *Henry IV* plays as comedies, and the remaining Shakespeare history-plays as tragedies. *Richard II* and *Richard III* are obviously tragedies, and *Henry VIII* has close affinities with Fletcherian tragi-comedy; the *Henry VI* plays have only very slight comic elements, and bear close resemblances in tone and style to *Richard III*; *King John* and *Henry V* are borderline cases (the Bastard, especially, is a striking comic creation), but their main emphasis is on heroic national feeling, and there is no effective criticism of this feeling, so I class them too with the tragedies and tragi-comedies. It is precisely the all-pervading critical attitude (incarnate in Falstaff) that makes me classify the *Henry IV* plays as comedies.[1]) The only non-Shakespearean history-play is Ford's *Perkin Warbeck*, and I class this as a tragedy, which it quite obviously is. The only other plays falling outside the common categories are *The Faithful Shepherdess* (pastoral), which I group with the tragedies; *A Game at Chess* (a satirical morality-play), which I group with the comedies; and *King Arthur* (a dramatic opera), which I group with the tragedies. We thus arrive at two groups, which for convenience I shall henceforth refer to simply as "tragedy" and "comedy". The number of plays in each of these groups in each decade is shown in Table 2.

TABLE 2. *Number of Plays in each Decade, classed as Comedy or Tragedy*

Period from to	1591 1600	1601 1610	1611 1620	1621 1630	1631 1640	1591 1640	1661 1670	1671 1680	1681 1690	1691 1700	1661 1700	Grand Total
Comedy	11	16	12	16	12	67	10	20	12	8	50	117
Tragedy	10	14	14	10	12	60	8	12	5	4	29	89
Total	21	30	26	26	24	127	18	32	17	12	79	206

---

[1]) In "Notes on Comedy", Knights chooses *Henry IV.1* for analysis as an outstanding example of comedy.

In Appendix A, column (f), is given my narrower classification of each play as comedy, tragi-comedy, history, pastoral, etc., followed by the symbol (C) or the symbol (T) to show whether the play is classified with the comedies or with the tragedies. There were of course a few difficulties of classification; even in the Restoration period, where there is usually a sharp boundary between comedy and tragedy, there are a number a plays that are near the borderline.[1]) In making my classification, I took into account what the author or the original edition called the play, what its editor called it, and my own impression of the play's mood and atmosphere. If I was still doubtful I adopted the classification given by Harbage in his *Annals of English Drama*.

The editions which I have used are given in Appendix C. Where possible, of course, I have used modern scholarly editions, but these do not exist for all authors; for example, the complete plays of Middleton and Davenant exist only in editions from the 1880's and the 1870's respectively, and the complete plays of Shirley have not been printed since 1833. In a few cases, too, I have not been able to get access to the most modern edition, and have had to use earlier or more popular editions. Shakespeare is usually cited from the First Folio (the facsimile edition by Prouty and Kökeritz), but occasionally I have had to quote a Quarto text, and here I have used the Shakespeare Association collotype facsimiles where available, otherwise the Furnivall series of quarto facsimiles. Some plays of multiple or doubtful authorship are printed in more than one of the editions listed in Appendix C; reference should then be made to Appendix A, column (d), which gives a brief indication of the edition used.

References are given by Act, Scene, and Line where possible; but many editions have no line numbering, and in these cases I have cited by Act, Scene, and Page. (Volume numbers are not cited, but can be found if necessary from Appendix A.) I found it inconvenient to take Shakespeare line-numbers from the First Folio, although that was the text used, and instead give the line-numbers from the one-volume collected edition published by the Shakespeare Head Press. The way in which references are given for each play it shown in Appendix A, column (e).

---

[1]) For example Behn's *Amorous Prince* and *Widow Ranter*, Etherege's *Comical Revenge*, Dryden's *Marriage à la Mode* and *Spanish Friar*, and Shadwell's *Libertine*.

I have not knowingly accepted textual emendations involving the introduction of the word *honour* into the text unless they have seemed quite indisputable. So I accept the emendation of *houre* to *honoure* in *The Magnetic Lady* (V.10.140), where the context hardly leaves room for argument, but reject a similar emendation in *Romeo and Juliet* (I.3.68—9) because the original reading makes good sense and is moreover found both in the folio and in the good quarto (Q2); and I reject the insertion of *honour* into a line of *Henry V* (IV.5.11) where a word has dropped out, not because it is not a plausible emendation, but because there are other words that would also fit.

H. The Dating of the Material

The dates I adopt for the plays are shown in Appendix A and Appendix B. For dating I have consulted the editors of the various editions, and the *Cambridge History of English Literature* Volumes V, VI, and VIII. For Shakespeare I have moreover consulted E. K. Chambers's *William Shakespeare*, and for the early Jacobean period his *Elizabethan Stage*. For the complicated problems of the Beaumont and Fletcher plays I have relied a great deal on E. H. C. Oliphant, *The Plays of Beaumont and Fletcher*. On the late Jacobean and Caroline period I have consulted G. E. Bentley, *The Jacobean and Caroline Stage*. The Restoration period offers few problems, and I have merely checked dates given by editors against those given by Nicoll (*Restoration Drama*) and by Dobrée (*Restoration Comedy* and *Restoration Tragedy*). I have, finally, compared my dates with those given by Harbage in his *Annals of English Drama*, and when I have been doubtful, or have had a range of dates to choose from, I have adopted his dating.[1]

In the earlier part of the century, of course, many of the dates are disputable. This does not matter much, provided that the possible limits are not too wide. If the possible error lies entirely within one of my decades, then it has no effect at all. Even an error at the borderline of two decades is not very serious, since changes are hardly likely to occur with startling suddenness; a play written in 1618 or 1619 is not likely to be startlingly different from one written in 1621 or 1622. What is serious is an error of, say, fifteen years or more, and I have tried to

---

[1] The date given by Harbage seems to be that of first performance. This can usually be taken as identical with the date when the writing of the work was completed, which is the date I want, but there are a few cases where this is not so, e. g. Aphra Behn's *The Younger Brother*.

avoid including plays where there is serious disagreement about dating and where the possible error would be of this kind; on these grounds I rejected *Appius and Virginia*, which was originally included in my material. However, I have not been very much worried by a theoretically wide possible variation, provided that there is pretty general agreement about whereabouts in the range the play in fact lies; for example, from strictly objective evidence, it is difficult to date *Coriolanus* exactly, and it might lie in any one of three of my decades, but in fact nobody would think of putting it anywhere except in the decade 1601 to 1610, and most people would agree that it lay within the range 1606 to 1610. When there is a long interval between the dates of composition and of publication, there is the additional risk of revision in the interval; several plays of the Beaumont and Fletcher collection, for example, may have been revised in the reign of Charles I. Unless, however, there is evidence for really extensive rewriting (in which case I reject the play as undatable) this possibility is ignored in my dating, since there is little to be done about it.

I. The Presentation of the Material

There are no purely objective criteria for determining the meaning or the content of an example; these have to be determined by inspection in each particular case, and it is possible for different observers to disagree. It therefore seems desirable to reproduce the material itself, or at least the most important parts of it, so that the reader may be able to judge for himself the reasonableness or otherwise of my classifications. There is, however, a difficulty; the interpretation of an example depends completely on the context, both verbal and situational; in some cases only a few lines are relevant, but in other cases it is impossible to make a decision without studying the whole scene, sometimes even the whole play. It is quite impracticable to reproduce, or even to summarize, as much of the context as is necessary for a decision in every example. For the most important part of the material (important for the regulation of conduct) I have reproduced all my excerpts, and they constitute Chapters 7 to 9 below; but I have made no attempt to reproduce the contexts. Anybody who wishes to check any of my classifications will therefore have to turn up the play in question and study the extract in its context. This is unfortunate, but it seems the only practicable method.

CHAPTER 2

The Head-Meanings Exemplified

I have begun the analysis by classifying all my examples according to their head-meanings. For convenience, I denote each head-meaning by a capital letter, chosen, as far as possible, for mnemonic quality (e. g. R for "reputation"). I have not attempted to use any system of symbolism for denoting implied meanings, "moods", etc., like the one invented by Professor William Empson;[1] for I am mainly concerned with the primary meaning of each example; the consideration of secondary meanings and implications would unduly complicate the statistics. Later, however, I shall need to introduce certain sub-divisions of my head-meanings, and these will be denoted by the attaching of a small letter to the capital letter (e. g. Rm for "military reputation"). These divisions are purely *ad hoc*, and claim no kind of general validity or importance; the head-meanings, in fact, are not all on the same plane, and the classification is made for purely practical purposes.

The history of the word *honour* before the age of Shakespeare is of no importance for our purposes, except insofar as people may have been conscious of that history. We start from a synchronic system,[2] the pattern of usage around 1600; how that pattern arose is a question that can be neglected; the diachronic approach is relevant only inside the period studied.[3] I shall therefore begin by giving examples of my head-meanings and their symbols, taking my examples from the beginning of the period, and as far as possible from Shakespeare, where the contexts will readily be recalled.[4]

---

[1] *The Structure of Complex Words*, pp. 15 sqq.

[2] See F. de Saussure, *Cours de linguistique générale*, pp. 114—43.

[3] Later, I shall attempt to combine the diachronic and synchronic methods by studying the pattern of usage in each decade in turn.

[4] A list of the symbols for head-meanings (capital letters) is given as an appendix at the end of this chapter (p. 87). A list of the symbols for sub-groups (small letters) will be found at the end of the book (Appendix G).

A. The Head-Meaning R

The first head-meaning corresponds to *N. E. D.* meaning 1(c): "Glory, renown, fame; credit, reputation, good name". The *N. E. D.* implies an element of admiration or esteem in this, for 1(c) is a subdivision of 1, which is "High respect, esteem, or reverence, accorded to exalted worth or rank; deferential admiration or approbation . . . (c) As received, gained, held or enjoyed". However, esteem "as received" is not an essential concomitant of "glory" etc., though it is a very common one; and if the main meaning of the word is "esteem as received", I place it in a different category (my E, see pp. 59—61 below). For me, the key idea in this first head-meaning is "reputation", and I give it the symbol R. An example of it can be seen in the opening lines of *Love's Labour's Lost*:

> Let *Fame*, that all hunt after in their liues,
> Liue registred vpon our brazen Tombes,
> And then grace vs in the disgrace of death:
> when spight of cormorant deuouring Time,
> Th'endeuour of this present breath may buy:
> That honour which shall bate his sythes keene edge,
> And make vs heyres of all eternitie.
> (I.1.1—7)

The context shows clearly that we here have a "positive" aspect of R, "glory, fame"; and that the glory will be for having withdrawn from the world and devoted themselves to a monastic life of learning (this is what I call the "content" of the example). A few lines later we have another example, when the king reminds his fellow-devotees that they have already sworn to carry out this programme, and invites them to sign their names to it:

> Your oathes are past, and now subscribe your names:
> That his owne hand may strike his honour downe,
> That violates the smallest branch heerein:
> (I.1.19—21)

Here we have an aspect of R which is "good name" rather than "glory": not something to be gained, but something that may be lost (a distinction I shall return to later); and in this example it will be lost by the breaking of an oath (or, more exactly, by the proof or revelation of the fact that an oath has been broken, the evidence being provided by the signature). The head-meaning R is a very common one, and I shall therefore give a few more examples of different aspects of it. One common cause of R is military achievement; we have it for example in *Henry IV.1*:

> What neuer-dying Honor hath he got,
> Against renowned *Dowglas*?
> (III.2.106—7)

Here it is positive, and means "military glory", the glory won by Hotspur by three times defeating the famous Douglas. There is an example in *Henry IV.2* of the combination of this content with another; Lady Percy is reproaching Northumberland for having broken his word, thus causing Hotspur to lose the battle of Shrewsbury:

> Who then perswaded you to stay at home?
> There were two Honors lost: Yours, and your Sonnes.
> (II.3.15—16)

Northumberland had lost his good name, by breaking his promise to go to Shrewsbury with his forces, and Hotspur had forfeited his military fame by being defeated and killed. Here it will be noticed that the word is a countable, used in the plural; this is obviously because two different people and two different kinds of honour are involved; but *honour* (R) can also be found as a countable in other circumstances. There is a probable example in *Henry V*, when, on the morning of Agincourt, the king rebukes Westmoreland for wishing they had more men with them:

> But if it be a sinne to couet Honor,
> I am the most offending Soule aliue.
> No 'faith, my Couze, wish not a man from England:
> Gods peace, I would not loose so great an Honor,
> As one man more me thinkes would share from me,
> For the best hope I haue.
> (IV.3.28—33)

The context here strongly suggests that "an Honor" means "(a piece of) military glory". It is not safe to use countability as a criterion of meaning, as in this respect the seventeenth-century usage of *honour* is freer than the modern. From *Henry V* can be given another example of R; Pistol soliloquizes after being cudgelled by Fluellen: "Old I do waxe, and from my wearie limbes honour is Cudgeld" (V.1.87—8). Here R is "good name", and is lost by submitting to insult or injury; to regain or repair his honour in these circumstances, Pistol would have to challenge

Fluellen and fight a duel with him, as many parallel examples show. My final example of R also concerns Pistol, this time in *Merry Wives*, when he is being denounced by Falstaff: "goe, you'll not beare a Letter for mee you roague? you stand vpon your honor" (II.2.19—20). Here again it is "good name", and would be lost by performing menial services, the kind of work not befitting a gentleman. It will be seen that there is considerable variety within the R group, but that the idea of reputation is the leading one in all cases.

B. The Head-Meaning H

My second head-meaning corresponds to *N. E. D.* 2: "Personal title to high respect or esteem; honourableness; elevation of character; 'nobleness of mind, scorn of meanness, magnanimity' (Johnson); a fine sense of and strict allegiance to what is due or right (also, to what is due according to some conventional or fashionable standard of conduct)". Primarily it is a quality of character, but this shades off into a mode of behaviour ("strict allegiance"), and into the standard of conduct itself considered as a code. The word *honourableness* covers all these aspects, while not including the idea of reputation, and so I shall denote this head-meaning by the symbol H. Our first example of H can be taken from *Henry VI.3*; Westmoreland is addressing King Henry, who has just alienated his supporters by tamely surrendering to the house of York the succession to the throne:

> Farwell faint-hearted and degenerate King,
> In whose cold blood no sparke of Honor bides.
> (I.1.183—4)

Here there can be no question of R; honour is some quality lacking in Henry, a quality of character; and the kind of quality desired is plainly suggested by "faint-hearted", "cold blood", and "sparke"; the king lacks courage and spirit, he is meek and submissive to his enemies instead of proud and defiant. The next example of H is from *Much Ado*; Benedick is puzzling over the behaviour of Pedro and Claudio, after the rejection of Hero in church:

> Two of them haue the verie bent of honor,
> And if their wisedoms be misled in this:
> The practise of it liues in *Iohn* the bastard,
> Whose spirits toile in frame of villanies.
> (IV.1.186—9)

Here again it is mainly a question of character ("bent"): they are not the kind of men who would deliberately slander and disgrace an innocent lady, but John the Bastard is. Similarly in *Macbeth*, after Malcolm's testing of Macduff:

> Macduff, this Noble passion
> Childe of integrity, hath from my soule
> Wip'd the blacke Scruples, reconcil'd my thoughts
> To thy good Truth, and Honor.
> (IV.3.114—17)

Malcolm's thoughts, clearly, are not "reconciled" to Macduff's reputation, but to his integrity and honesty; he is now sure that Macduff is not a liar and a spy. In Hamlet's apology to Laertes, we again have H as a quality of character, namely sensitivity to injury, eagerness to take revenge:[1]

> what I haue done
> That might your nature, honor, and exception
> Roughly awake, I heare proclaim was madnesse.
> (V.2.229—31)

Obviously it was not Laertes' reputation that was awakened; it might perhaps be his concern for his reputation, which would suffer if he left his father's murder unrevenged; and sensitivity about R is a trait of character, and so to be classified as H. By a slight figurative extension, or by ellipsis, it is very easy to move from "honourableness of character" to "a man of honourable character", and such cases, too, I class as H. There is an example in *King Lear*, when Kent is justifying his bluntness to the king:

> To plainnesse honour's bound,
> When Maiesty falls to folly.
> (I.1.147—8)

"An honourable man must speak bluntly when a king behaves foolishly." Perhaps the same thing is seen in this example from *Troilus*, though here it would be equally possible to read it as a quality of character personified; Troilus, arguing for the continuation of the war, is contemptuously rejecting Helenus's "reasons" for making peace:[2]

---

[1] Quoted from Q2, which has clearer punctuation than F1.
[2] Quoted from Q. F1 reads "hard" for "hare", and "Let's" for "Sets"; it also transposes lines 45 and 46.

THE HEAD-MEANINGS EXEMPLIFIED

> nay if we talke of reason,
> Sets shut our gates and sleepe: man-hood and honour,
> Should haue hare hearts, would they but fat their thoughts
> With this cram'd reason.
> (II.2.46—9)

In either case I classify it as H. The qualities of character involved here are the military ones: courage, fighting spirit, the desire for military glory, etc.. I also class as H many of the examples of the phrases "in honour" and "bound in honour", which I take to mean "in allegiance to the code", or possibly "in uprightness of character". An example can be given from *Henry IV.2*, when the Lord Chief Justice, fearing the worst from the newly-crowned Henry V, justifies his conduct to his fellow-peers:

> Sweet princes: what I did, I did in Honor,
> Led by th'Imperiall Conduct of my Soule.
> (V.2.35—6)

The second line is almost a paraphrase of "in Honor"; he is protesting his moral integrity and the disinterestedness of his motives. The next example, from *Troilus*, shows the character element in the meaning shading off into something like "the demands of morality":

> How may I auoyde
> (Although my will distaste what it elected)
> The Wife I chose, there can be no euasion
> To blench from this, and to stand firme by honour.
> (II.2.65—8)

Here it is possible to think of honour as something within Troilus, or as that quality personified (a fellow-soldier by whom he stands firm); but it is perhaps even more natural to think of honour as a system, a code of conduct, which forbids (among other things) the abandonment of one's wife. This too I classify as H. In the final example, from *Coriolanus*, we see the idea of character shading off into that of conduct, "honourable behaviour"; Volumnia is trying to persuade Coriolanus that political dissimulation is not dishonourable, and is arguing by the analogy of camouflage in warfare:

> If it be Honor in your Warres, to seeme
> The same you are not, which for your best ends
> You adopt your policy: How is it lesse or worse
> That it shall hold Companionship in Peace . . .
> (III.2.46—9)

I paraphrase this "If deception in war is honourable behaviour ...";
but the idea of character is not far away, and one could say "If deceiving
in war is honourableness of character ...", without any undue feeling
of strain in the construction: the verb "to be" is very flexible, after
all. I am aware, however, that an alternative interpretation of this
example is possible: "Honor" could be taken to mean "a source or
cause of R", and then I should put it in a different category (my S,
see pp. 72—74 below). However, the context is in favour of the first
interpretation; it is character and behaviour that are being discussed,
not reputation, and Coriolanus is refusing to be "False to (his) Nature"
(line 15). R is undoubtedly an implication, but I take the head-meaning
to be H.

In general it will be seen that I class together under H all those
examples where "honourableness" rather than "reputation" is the main
meaning, whether the emphasis is on character, behaviour, or the code
itself. In fact the idea of character is the predominant one in the majority
of cases, and is never entirely absent.

C. Equivocation: the RH Group

It will have been noticed, even from the few examples given, that
examples of R and of H often resemble one another in content; H can
mean "military qualities of character", and R "reputation for these
qualities"; H can mean "sensitivity to injury or insult", and R "reputation for this sensitivity"; and so on. Moreover, each of them is often
an implied meaning of the other; if a man gains military glory, we tend
to assume that he possesses military qualities; if we are told that he possesses outstanding military qualities, we shall normally expect him to
have a reputation for this. In addition, one of the qualities of character
often implied by H is "concern about R". It is not surprising, therefore,
that there are many contexts where it is impossible to tell whether the
writer meant R or H, and where in fact he may have meant both, or
not distinguished between them. There may be cases where the sentence is "ambiguous", i. e. where the sense is materially altered by
choosing one meaning rather than the other; but the majority of cases
are rather to be classified as "equivocal", i. e. it makes no material
difference to the "adequate apprehension of the phrase referent"[1])

---

[1]) Stern, *op. cit.*, p. 356, whence I borrow this use of "equivocal".

which of the meanings is selected. Such cases I classify as RH, since both head-meanings are equally present. My first example of RH is from *Titus Andronicus*; Marcus is begging permission to bury Mutius, who has been killed while helping Bassianus to abduct Lavinia, his betrothed, to save her from a forced marriage with the emperor:

> Suffer thy brother *Marcus* to interre
> His Noble Nephew heere in vertues nest,
> That died in Honour and *Lauinia's* cause.
> (I.1.375—7)

Presumably "Honour and *Lauinia's*" is a group-genitive, so Mutius died "in honour's cause"; that is, for the sake of his family's R (which would be sullied by the breaking of Lavinia's engagement), or in the cause of H in the abstract (justice, virtue) — "in a virtuous cause". There is nothing in the context to give the preference to one of these interpretations over the other. If "Honour" is not treated as a genitive, the equivocality remains; "died in Honour" could mean "died in a way that brought him R (or preserved his R)", or "died in an honourable way, behaving honourably". My second example is from *The Merchant of Venice*: Bassanio is explaining to Portia how he had given away her ring to the doctor:

> I was inforc'd to send it after him,
> I was beset with shame and curtesie,
> My honor would not let ingratitude
> So much besmeare it.
> (V.1.216—19)

There is great emphasis on Bassanio's feelings, "shame and curtesie", and so it seems quite natural to interpret "honor" as H; but on the other hand "besmeare" brings in a strong suggestion of R; one could perhaps say that it is H that does the preventing, but R that is besmeared; however, there is a sense in which character itself can be "besmeared" by ingratitude (and not merely "character" in the sense of "reputation"), and it is this duality in the verb that finally makes it impossible to select either of the two meanings as dominant. Another verb that often permits this equivocality is *call*; when "honour calls", it may be an inner sense of duty calling, or it may be personified reputation; sometimes the context tips the balance in favour of one meaning or the other, but not always. Such examples may be equivocal even when *honour* is preceded by a possessive adjective, as in this case from *Antony and Cleopatra*:

> Your Honor calles you hence,
> Therefore be deafe to my vnpittied Folly,
> And all the Gods go with you.
>
> (I.3.97—9)

Antony's R (especially his military reputation) requires that he shall go; and his sense of political duty, and his concern about his reputation, urge him to go. Both aspects are given equal importance. A similar example, but without the possessive adjective, is found in *Henry IV.1*; Vernon is denying Douglas's imputation of cowardice:

> If well-respected Honor bid me on,
> I hold as little counsaile with weake feare,
> As you, my Lord, or any Scot that this day liues.
>
> (IV.3.10—12)

Here again it is the hint of personification given by "bids me on" that enables both meanings to operate freely: "my sense of duty commands me to fight", and "reputation urges me to fight". Onions defines *well-respected* as "well-weighed or considered";[1]) this can apply equally well to R and to H; one can weigh up carefully both the demands of honourableness (one's conscience about honour, the code of honour) and the reputation likely to result from one's actions. This example, too, therefore, I classify as RH. Another construction that often permits equivocality is "with honour", "with mine honour", etc., as in Olivia's

> How with mine honor may I giue him that,
> Which I haue giuen to you.
>
> (*Twelfth Night*, III.2.214—15)

"This behaviour is not consistent with my maintaining my integrity of character", and "If I behave like this I shall lose my reputation". A final example of RH, from *The Maid's Tragedy*, shows the way in which "reputation" and "sensitivity about reputation" tend to occur together; Evadne has revealed to Amintor, on their wedding-night, that she is the king's mistress, and intends to continue so; the "sacred word" of king makes Amintor abandon thoughts of revenge as impious, but he orders Evadne not to reveal to the king his knowledge of her unchastity:

---

[1]) *A Shakespeare Glossary*, s. v. *well-respected*.

THE HEAD-MEANINGS EXEMPLIFIED 55

> Nor let the King
> Know I conceive he wrongs me, then mine honour
> Will thrust me into action . . .
> (II.1, p. 23)

This is a curious example. The meaning R is made possible by the personification given by "thrust", just as in the examples with "call"; on the other hand the H element is very strong, since it will be an inner urge that drives him to attempt revenge ("action") on the king; but the H element is not exactly "sensitivity to injury", for it will operate only if the injury is known; it must rather be "sensitivity about R"; and the R that he is sensitive about is "R for being sensitive about injury"; so the H element is in fact "sensitivity about reputation-for-being-sensitive-about-injury". The Beaumont and Fletcher hero, obviously, is very much concerned about appearances. It is equally striking that the R element is only "R in the eyes of the wronger", since there is no suggestion that the knowledge might go further; and "R in the eyes of Evadne" apparently doesn't matter, or at any rate is insufficient to drive Amintor to take revenge. There is not a trace of irony in the passage, and the audience is obviously meant to sympathize with Amintor.

For the purposes of classification, I treat RH as a separate head-meaning, distinct from R and H; no example, therefore, can appear in more than one of these three groups. It is R, H, and RH that are the important meanings for the determination of conduct, and it is to the content of these that I shall give most attention.

D. Chastity

The next group of head-meanings corresponds to *N.E.D.* 3: "(Of a woman) Chastity, purity, as a virtue of the highest consideration; reputation for this virtue, good name". Reputation for chastity I denote by the symbol Rc, and chastity by the symbol C. There is also the equivocal type, RcC, and this too I treat as an independent head-meaning (like RH). A few examples will be given. In *King John*, the Bastard is rebuked by Queen Elinor for having expressed flippant doubts about his legitimacy:

> Out on thee rude man, $\overset{u}{y}$ dost shame thy mother,
> And wound her honor with this diffidence.
> (I.1.64—5)

This is obviously Rc; there is no question of his mother's chastity being affected, but her good name may be injured. The same applies to the Bastard's pious wish a few lines later:

> Heauen guard my mothers honor, and my Land.
> (I.1.70)

The context shows that he is not all worried about his mother's C (in fact he rather hopes that he is the illegitimate son of Richard I), but that he wishes her Rc to be maintained so that he can inherit his suppposed father's land. Another clear example of Rc can be given from *Measure for Measure*, when the Duke explains why he has permitted Angelo to marry Mariana:

> Consenting to the safe-guard of your honor,
> I thought your marriage fit: else Imputation,
> For that he knew you, might reproach your life,
> And choake your good to come:
> (V.1.417—20)

The Duke does not discuss the question whether Mariana's conduct has been unchaste (though he obviously considers not); the important thing is that no loophole shall be left for scandal. In the following example, on the other hand, I take the head-meaning to be C; we are being told how Bertram is trying to seduce Diana:

> He does indeede,
> And brokes with all that can in such a suite
> Corrupt the tender honour of a Maide:
> (*All's Well*, III.5.71—3)

Diana will very possibly lose Rc if she yields to Bertram, but that is plainly not his object: it is her purity of mind that he is trying to "corrupt", her chastity considered as a quality of character. In some examples, chastity is treated as a physical state rather than as a mental quality, and these too I classify as C. There is an example in *The Two Gentlemen of Verona*; Proteus is addressing Sylvia, whom he has rescued from outlaws:

> Madam, this seruice I haue done for you
> (Though you respect not aught your servant doth)
> To hazard life, and reskew you from him,
> That would haue forc'd your honour, and your loue,
> Vouchsafe me for my meed, but one faire looke:
> (V.4.19—23)

He obviously means that she would have been raped, and purity of mind is irrelevant. Often, of course, both mental purity and the physical state are meant simultaneously, as when a woman is seduced, or resists seduction (losing or preserving her honour). The physical state of chastity is not necessarily identical with virginity; a married woman's C is preserved by faithfulness to her husband, and a married woman who is raped loses physical C. Nor is physical C the same as *N.E.D.* meaning 3 (b), which is a physical organ rather than a physical state; this meaning hardly exists in my material, though there are a few examples in the Restoration period, in bawdy jokes.

The equivocal case, RcC, can be illustrated from *The Comedy of Errors*; Balthazar is persuading Antipholus of Ephesus not to break down the doors of his own house, from which his wife has locked him out:

> Haue patience sir, oh let it not be so,
> Heerein you warre against your reputation,
> And draw within the compasse of suspect
> Th'vnuiolated honor of your wife.
>
> (III.1.85—8)

This may equally well mean "Your wife's hitherto unsullied reputation may come within the range of suspicion" (i. e. may be suspected to have been unmerited), or "Her in fact unsullied chastity may be suspected" (i. e. of not existing, of being a fiction). The following example from *Much Ado* is also fairly clear; Leonato is referring to the accusation of unchastity made against Hero:

> if they speake but truth of her,
> These hands shall teare her: If they wrong her honour,
> The proudest of them shall wel heare of it.
>
> (IV.1.190—2)

The verb *wrong* can fit either interpretation: "if they have an unjust opinion of (are spreading a false story about) her in fact unimpeachable morals", or "if they unjustly injure her reputation".

In my statistics, Rc, RcC, and C are treated as independent head-meanings, so that an example cannot appear in more than one of them. They are also quite independent of R, RH, and H, so an example classified as Rc does not appear under R as well. When R is used with a fairly vague or wide content, it is often possible that R-for-chastity is an element in it; it is not classified as Rc, however, unless the chastity

element is quite specific. It is possible, of course, for the head-meanings
R and Rc to exist side by side in an example, and in that case it is classified RRc, and appears in the statistics for both head-meanings. (In
this respect it is treated just like all other cases where two or more
head-meanings co-exist: see pp. 83—85 below.) The double head-
meaning RRc often occurs when the example refers to two different
people, one a man and the other a woman; an example of this can be
given from Shirley's *Royal Master*: the king is pretending to believe
that his sister is unchaste, and is sounding his favourite about finding
a husband for her, to save her reputation:

> I could wish heartily my sister timely
> Married; — not to the duke, that would betray us,
> But to some one, I know not, who could love
> Us both so well, as [to] be that rare friend,
> And save our honours.
>
> (IV.1, p. 167)

Here "Us" refers to the king and his sister; her honour is Rc, but the
king's is R, that variety of R that is lost when a close female relative
is known to be unchaste; the example is therefore classified as RRc.
The same procedure applies, of course, to H/C and to RH/RcC.

E. The Head-Meaning K

The head-meanings R, RH, and H, especially H, sometimes shade
off into a meaning "the code of honour", considered as a set of un-
written laws. For example, in *The Little French Lawyer*, Sampson has
certain alleged rules of the duello explained to him by his second, and
says "Are these the rules of honour?" (IV.1, p. 428). This can be
classified as H ("honourable behaviour"), but it can also be interpreted
as "the code of honour" ("Are these the rules of the code?"). The distinction between these two interpretations is usually very slight, but
just occasionally there is a case where the latter reading is possible but
the former is not. This is so in the following example from Etherege's
Comical Revenge:

> *Grac.* If to the most deserving I am due,
>   He must resign his weaker claim to you.
> *Bruce.* This is but flatt'ry; for I'm sure you can
>   Think none so worthy as that gen'rous man:
>   By honour you are his.
>
> (V.1.78—82)

Graciana really loves Beaufort, but is pretending to love Bruce out of a sense of duty, because he has been wounded in a duel and his life is in danger. Bruce, however, protests, being certain that she does not love him, and reminds her that "by honour" she is Beaufort's. It is just possible that "honour" here means "promise" (see p. 74 below), but more probably it means "the laws of honour"; Graciana is due to Beaufort because she had already accepted his love (and withdrawal is contrary to the laws of honour) and also because Beaufort had defeated Bruce in a duel about their claims to her. It is hardly possible, however, to interpret the example as meaning "honourableness". I classify it as meaning "the code of honour", and, since there are at any rate a few examples of it that cannot be considered as coming under H, I find it necessary to set up a separate head-meaning for it, which I denote by the symbol K. It is however a rare meaning, and in most cases where the possibility of K exists it is merely as a partner to H or R.

F. Esteem

My next head-meaning corresponds to *N.E.D.* 1 (a): "High respect, esteem, or reverence, accorded to exalted worth or rank; deferential admiration or approbation... As felt or entertained in the mind for some person or thing". I denote it by the symbol E (mnemonic for "esteem"). My first example of E is from *The Two Gentlemen of Verona*; Valentine has been asked by the Duke whether Don Antonio of Verona has a son, and replies:

> I, my good Lord, a Son, that well deserues
> The honor, and regard of such a father.
> (II.4.57—8)

Honour here is a feeling or attitude of Don Antonio's, and could be paraphrased "esteem". The following example from *Julius Caesar* is less certain; it is from Brutus's oration justifying the murder of Caesar:

> As *Caesar* lou'd mee, I weepe for him; as he was Fortunate, I reioyce at it; as he was Valiant, I honour him: But, as he was Ambitious, I slew him. There is Teares, for his Loue: Ioy, for his Fortune: Honor, for his Valour: and Death, for his Ambition.
> (III.2.25—30)

Here "Honor" might mean either "esteem" or "praise, the conferring of marks of esteem and distinction", and the preceding verb "honour" would fit either interpretation; however, what Brutus is emphasizing is that he killed Caesar in spite of his *feelings* about him ("Teares", "Ioy"), and this seems to me to make the "esteem" element slightly more prominent that the "praise" element, and I classify the example as E. Sometimes E occurs in the phrase "in honour", as in the following example from *Winter's Tale*:

> Good *Paulina*,
> Who hast the memorie of *Hermione*
> I know in honor:
>
> (V.1.49—51)

"You hold her memory in reverence." Later in the century, it sometimes occurs as a countable, especially in the phrase "to have an honour for", as in this example from Dryden's *Wild Gallant*:

> Dear Mr. Burr, be pacified; you are a person I have an honour for; and this change of affairs shall not be the worse for you, egad, sir.
>
> (II.1, p. 63)

Esteem can also be considered as received or possessed (by the person for whom esteem is felt), and this is clearly not the same thing as reputation, although the *N. E. D.* identifies the two in its meaning 1(c). I distinguish between R and "esteem as received", and classify the latter as E. Admittedly the two meanings are difficult to separate, and there are few really unmistakable examples of E as received; perhaps the following lines from *Richard II* may serve as an example, however:

> Conuey me to my bed, then to my graue,
> Loue they to liue, that loue and honor haue.
>
> (II.1.137—8)

The dying John of Gaunt is speaking, after his long denunciation of the king and the king's rude and angry reply. Gaunt obviously means that he himself lacks love and honour, and therefore has no zest for life. It is hardly reasonable to interpret "honor" here as R; Gaunt has said nothing to suggest that he himself has lost R, and on the contrary has strongly implied that the king has: the king lies "in reputation sick", and is reproached with the oft-repeated "shame" (lines 93—115); but it is the king who is to go on living, and Gaunt who is to die. The natural thing is to take "honor" to refer to the lack of esteem and respect that the king has just shown towards Gaunt (who after all is his uncle and a venerable old gentleman) in calling him a "lunaticke leane-witted foole" and threatening to execute him (lines 115—123). I therefore interpret the line "Let them love to live (or They love to live) who enjoy the love and esteem of others", and classify the example as E. Another possible example can be seen in *Macbeth*:

> And that which should accompany Old-Age,
> As Honor, Loue, Obedience, Troopes of Friends,
> I must not looke to haue:
>
> (V.3.24—6)

In this case the other possibilities are stronger, especially R and "praise"; but even so I feel that the context makes "esteem" the dominant meaning; what Macbeth here recognizes as lacking in his life is affection: "Loue" and "Troopes of Friends". He can after all enjoy sycophantic praises ("Mouth-honor"): what he regrets is the lack of sincerity in the praise, the absence of genuine love and esteem. He also enjoys reputation of a kind, the reputation arising from high rank, and the reputation of great military prowess; but in effect he recognizes that having reputation is not the same thing as being liked. I therefore classify this example too as E.

G. The Head-Meanings M, T, and P

We next have a group of three head-meanings that overlap a good deal. M is "something conferred as a mark or token of esteem or distinction"; T is "a title of rank"; P is "high rank or position". The "something conferred" in M is often a title, so that the combination MT is common; and "title of rank" and "high rank" are often indistinguishable, so that the combination TP is also very common.

M normally corresponds to *N. E. D.* 5, especially 5(a): "(Usually in *pl.*) Something conferred or done as a token of respect or distinction; a mark or manifestation of high regard; *esp.* a position or title of rank, a degree of nobility, a dignity". (The last portion of the definition also covers my T and P, but T and P are not necessarily something conferred.) However, I should also class as M most of the examples which the *N. E. D.* editors put under their heading 1(b): "High respect, esteem, or reverence, accorded to exalted worth or rank; deferential admiration or approbation . . . (b) As rendered or shown: The expression of high estimation".[1]) For example, I should class as M the quotation that they give from the year 1653: "The Prince was exceedingly pleased with this honour done unto him". I should also class as M many of the phrases that they give under their 9(c), especially those with "in honour of", though not usually those with "to the honour of". My class M is therefore broader than N. E. D. 5, and is by no means "usually in the plural", though it quite often is. In fact I class as M quite a few examples that are plainly uncountables, since in many contexts "to bestow honour on" is quite synonymous with "to bestow an honour on".

My first example of M is from *Sejanus*; Tiberius is praising the senate for rewarding Sejanus:

> But, for the honours, which they haue decreed
> To our SEIANVS, to aduance his statue
> In POMPEI's theatre (whose ruining fire
> His vigilance, and labour kept restrain'd
> In that one losse) they haue, therein, out-gone
> Their owne great wisedomes...
>
> (I.1.518—23)

Although Tiberius says "honours", he in fact only mentions one, the raising of a statue; "to aduance" is presumably in apposition to "honours", so the honours consist in the raising of a statue. It is not at all uncommon in my material for the plural to be used in this way when only one mark of distinction is mentioned; and on the other hand the singular is sometimes used, especially as an uncountable, when several distinctions are involved. In the next example, from *Henry IV.1*, M refers especially to titles of rank, but not exclusively so, and I do not include T in the head-meaning; Falstaff is pretending to have killed Hotspur:

> There is *Percy*, if your Father will do me any Honor, so: if not, let him kill the next *Percie* himselfe. I looke to be either Earle or Duke, I can assure you.
>
> (V.4.41—5)

Here "Honor" could be taken either as a countable or as an uncountable. It would not be impossible to interpret "do . . . . . Honor" as "cause . . . .

---

[1]) The N. E. D. separation of 1(b) from 5 seems to me somewhat artificial. However, some of their examples under 1(b) I should class differently: their example from *Ywaine & Gaw.* I read as E, and that from Stubbs as R.

R", but this is rather forced. The M may obviously consist of a title ("Earle or Duke"), but "title" itself could not possibly function here as the sole head-meaning, so I classify as M, not as MT. In the next example, the word is certainly an uncountable; it is from the opening of *Much Ado*, when Leonato receives the letter giving the news of Don Pedro's victory:

> I finde heere, that Don *Peter* hath bestowed much honor on a yong *Florentine*, called *Claudio*.
> (I.1.8—10)

The nature of the "honor" is not stated, but it presumably refers to such things as orders and distinctions, high military rank, etc. . It would be undesirable to separate an uncountable of this type from a countable like the *Sejanus* example, especially when there are equivocal types like the example from *Henry IV.1*. It is indeed possible to find examples where a countable and an uncountable are used successively to refer to the same thing. In *All's Well*, the Duke of Florence hears that French volunteers are coming to fight for him, and says:

> Welcome shall they bee:
> And all the honors that can flye from vs,
> Shall on them settle:
> (III.1.19—21)

In the next scene, a French gentleman is telling the Countess that her son Bertram is one of these volunteers, and says:

> Such is his noble purpose, and beleeu't
> The Duke will lay vpon him all the honor
> That good conuenience claimes.
> (III.2.71—3)

Presumably both speakers have the same kind of honour in mind.

In *Henry V*, when Fluellen is given the glove to wear by the king, he says:

> Your Grace doo's me as great Honors as can be desir'd in the hearts of his Subiects:
> (IV.7.161—2)

This is a straightforward example of M. Later, when the glove has been challenged by the soldier Williams, and the whole story has come out, the king rewards Williams with the glove filled with crowns:

> Here Vnckle *Exeter*, fill this Gloue with Crownes,
> And giue it to this fellow. Keepe it fellow,
> And weare it for an Honor in thy Cappe,
> Till I doe challenge it.
>
> (IV.8.58—61)

This is also M: the king's glove is conferred on Williams as a mark of distinction; but in this case, in contrast to the previous one, the mark of distinction is the physical emblem itself, a badge. If we go back to the previous scene, we find the king confirming Fluellen's suggestion that he is in the habit of wearing a leek on St David's day:

> I weare it for a memorable honor:
> For I am Welch you know good Countriman.
>
> (IV.7.106—7)

This is again a badge (in fact Fluellen has just called the leek a "padge"), and it is a mark of distinction (the distinction of belonging to the race that did such good service in France under Edward III); but it is not *conferred* on the king. There are other examples of "honour" referring to a physical emblem, and in some of these, too, the idea of conferment is weakened or absent; it is used, for example, of the crown as a physical symbol of sovereignty (*Henry IV.2*, IV.4.176, 322), and of a ring which is a family heirloom (*All's Well*, IV.4.42). It would be possible to set up a separate head-meaning for such examples, but as the question is of negligible importance for honour as a code of conduct, and as the number of examples is small, I have classified them under M.

I also class as M those numerous examples with loss of intensity, where the thing conferred is no great mark of distinction, and is called an honour out of politeness. This is especially common in phrases like "have the honour to", "have the honour of", and "do . . . honour". Two examples can be seen in the following passage from *The Devil is an Ass*; Merecraft introduces to Lady Taylebush an alleged Spanish noblewoman:

> Mer. Here is a noble *Lady, Madame,* come,
>   From your great friends, at *Court,* to see your *Ladiship:*
>   And haue the honour of your acquaintance.
> Tay.   Sir,
>   She do's vs honour.
>
> (IV.3.1—4)

With constructions of this kind there is a continuous range of intensities, from the dukedom conferred by the king down to trivialities like the honour of being invited to dinner by a social equal, and it seems essential to class them all under the same head-meaning.

I also classify as M many of the examples of the phrase "in honour of", which I interpret "as a mark of (my etc.) esteem for", or "as a mark of distinction to"; for example the following two from *The Faithful Shepherdess*:

> And here will I in honour of thy love,
> Dwell by thy Grave, forgeting all those joys...
> (I.1, p. 373)

> Now we have done this holy Festival
> In honour of our great God...
> (I.1, p. 375)

These might be classified E, but the emphasis is on the token (the action) rather than on the feeling, so I prefer to read them as M. I also classify as M the few examples where "in honour of" means "in celebration of" (e.g. a birthday), as in *Pericles*, II.2.5, *The Pilgrim*, V.4, p. 223 ("In honour of the Kings great day"), and *The Maid of Honour*, III.3, p. 239 ("In honour of your birthday").

The token of esteem or distinction sometimes takes the form of words (as in Macbeth's "mouth-honour"), and then M very nearly means "praise". This is seen, for example, in *Volpone*; the mountebank is praising his medicine:

> '*Twill cost you eight crownes. And*, ZAN FRITIDA, '*pray thee sing a verse*, extempore, *in honour of it*.
> (II.2.114—15)

This too I class as M. There is an example in *Coriolanus* where the meaning shifts from R to an M of this type; Coriolanus has gone away to avoid hearing his military exploits publicly praised, and Menenius says:

> He had rather venture all his Limbes for Honor,
> Then on ones Eares to heare it.
> (II.2.81—2)

("Then on ones" is usually taken to mean "Than one on's".) The honour that Coriolanus ventures for is military glory (R), but honour which can be heard must be praise (M).

5

One final type that I classify under M is *N. E. D.* 5(b), "An obeisance; a bow or curtsy". It is a rare meaning in the drama, and when it occurs is often connected with dancing. In my material, I have found only 12 examples in the first half of the century (in seven different plays), and only 6 in the second half (in three plays). No less than eight of the examples occur in four plays by Middleton and his collaborators,[1]) and one of these, in a stage-direction from *A Mad World*, can be given as a specimen:

> [*A strain played by the consort:* SIR BOUNTEOUS *makes a courtly honour to* FOLLYWIT, *and seems to foot the tune.*]
> (II.1.154)

In *The Changeling*, IV.3, in the course of a dancing-lesson, there is a whole series of puns between this meaning and the meaning "rank, title".

The head-meaning T is not often found alone; it is usually a joint meaning with either M or P. However, it occasionally occurs quite unmistakably by itself. There are a couple of good examples in *The Devil is an Ass*; Merecraft, the "projector", is proposing to make Fitz-Dottrell's fortune by a project for the recovery of land from the sea, "drowned land", and they are solemnly discussing what title he shall adopt when his newly acquired wealth shall have enabled him to become a duke; Merecraft makes several suggestions, including the following:

> Mer. I thinke we ha' found a place to fit you, now, Sir.
>   Gloc'ster.
> Fit.   O, no, I'll none!
> Mer.   Why, S^r?
> Fit.   'Tis fatall.
> Mer. That you say right in. *Spenser*, I thinke, the younger,
>   Had his last honour thence. But, he was but *Earle*.
>   (II.4.4—7)

The "thence" shows clearly that the "honour" is not the rank but the style, the name "Earl of Gloucester". After another unsuccessful suggestion, Merecraft suggests the title "Duke of the Drowned Lands", or "Drowned Land", and this is accepted:

---

[1]) This can perhaps be used as a criterion of authorship; see my article on this in *English Studies* (Amsterdam), XXXVIII No. 4, pp. 161—8.

THE HEAD-MEANINGS EXEMPLIFIED 67

> *Fit.*   Ha? that last has a good sound!
>   I like it well. The *Duke of Drown'd-land?*
> *Ing⟨ine⟩*.   Yes,
>   It goes like *Groen-land*, Sir, if you mark it.
> *Mer.*   I,
>   And drawing thus your honour from the worke,
>   You make the reputation of that, greater;
>   And stay't the longer i' your name.
>   (II.4.21—6)

By taking his title from the work of drainage itself, FitzDottrell will enhance the reputation of the work, and it will be remembered longer because his family's dukely title will be a standing reminder of it. The final example, from *Coriolanus*, is less certain, but I also class it as T; Caius Marcius has returned from the successful war against the Volscians, and addresses his wife and mother, who have just welcomed him back:

> Ere in our owne house I doe shade my Head,
> The good Patricians must be visited,
> From whom I haue receiu'd not onely greetings,
> But with them, change of Honors.
>   (II.1.196—9)

The "change of Honors" probably refers to the granting of the cognomen "Coriolanus", and so means "a new title". This title, admittedly, had been conferred on him by the general after the battle, not by the senate, but it had been announced to the people by a herald earlier in the scene; and the word "change" supports the interpretation T: it was his name that had been changed.

The head-meaning P (mnemonic for "position") corresponds to *N. E. D.* 4: "Exalted rank or position; dignity, distinction". It most often occurs in the combination TP, but there are cases where it is the sole head-meaning, as in this example from *Henry V*:

> My Lord of *Cambridge* heere,
> You know how apt our loue was, to accord
> To furnish with all appertinents
> Belonging to his Honour;
>   (II.2.84—7)

The appertinents are those suitable to his high rank; T is hardly relevant, and R is excluded by "Belonging". There is another example in *Macbeth*, when the messenger warns Lady Macduff of approaching disaster:

> Blesse you faire Dame: I am not to you known,
> Though in your state of Honor I am perfect;
>
> (IV.2.64—5)

The Arden editor paraphrases "perfectly acquainted with your rank". Since high rank brings reputation with it, it is sometimes difficult to distinguish P from R, as in the following example from *Henry VI.2*:

> And wilt thou still be hammering Treachery,
> To tumble downe thy husband, and thy selfe,
> From top of Honor, to Disgraces feete?
> Away from me, and let me heare no more.
>
> (I.2.47—50)

The Duke of Gloucester is rebuking his wife for inciting him to treason; the result of treason, he says, will be loss of rank (as in fact turns out: he is dismissed from the Protectorship when his wife's treasonable dabblings are discovered). But the result will also be loss of R: both the reputation arising from high rank and the reputation for loyalty. The R element is emphasized by the contrast with "Disgrace", and it would be possible to classify the example as RP. In fact, in view of the context, I prefer to regard R as a strong secondary meaning, and to take the head-meaning as P. In the lines immediately preceding, the Duke has been pointing out what a fortunate position his wife is in, as second lady of the realm, and it is the fall from this height that attention is directed to; moreover, "disgrace" can refer to loss of rank as well as loss of reputation, as in the common type of example where somebody (e. g. a royal favourite) falls from power and is said to be "disgraced", or "in disgrace"; and the word "top", finally, reinforces the meaning "high rank", which frequently occurs in conjunction with it and with other words suggestive of height.

High rank need not be something conferred, it can be inherited; and so *honour* sometimes means "high birth", "noble blood", "royal blood". There is an example in *Philaster* where it means "royal blood" in more than a figurative sense. Philaster has been released by the king, and has come to pacify the rebels, who have Pharamond prisoner; a rebel captain asks Philaster if he is absolutely free and secure; if he is not, Pharamond will be killed:

> Art thou above thy foemen,
> And free as *Phoebus?* Speak, if not, this stand
> Of Royal blood shall be abroach, atilt, and run
> Even to the lees of honour.
>
> (V.1, p. 140)

The "stand Of Royal blood" is Pharamond, who is a Spanish prince; Pharamond will be like a barrel of wine emptied to the last dregs, and "honour" means "his royal blood". This too I classify as P.

Finally, a few examples will be given of combinations of M, T, and P. The very common combination MT can be seen in the following passage from *Macbeth*, when Ross brings greetings to Macbeth from the king after the victory over the Norwegians:

> And for an earnest of a greater Honor,
> He bad me, from him, call thee *Thane* of Cawdor
> In which addition, haile most worthy *Thane*,
> For it is thine
>
> (I.3.103—6)

Thane of Cawdor is both a title ("addition") and a mark of distinction conferred, and so, presumably, will be the "greater Honor". It may perhaps be thought that P is also a head-meaning here; however, it seems to me that in cases of this type we should regard P as an implication, not as a head-meaning; we think primarily of the conferring of a title, and the rank is something that follows automatically. A second example of MT can also be taken from *Macbeth*; Duncan settles the succession upon Malcolm, and creates him Prince of Cumberland:

> We will establish our Estate vpon
> Our eldest, *Malcolme*, whom we name hereafter,
> The Prince of Cumberland: which Honor must
> Not vnaccompanied, inuest him onely,
> But signes of Nobleness, like Starres, shall shine
> On all deseruers.
>
> (I.4.35—42)

Here again P is an implication rather than a head-meaning; this is felt in the very phrasing, especially in the word "name". The other common combination, TP, can be illustrated from *Henry VI.2*; the Duchess of Gloucester is sentenced by the king for her treasonable dabblings in witchcraft; her four accomplices have just been sentenced to death:

> You Madame, for you are more Nobly borne,
> Despoyled of your Honor in your Life,
> Shall, after three dayes open Penance done,
> Liue in your Countrey here, in Banishment . . .
>
> (II.3.8—11)

"Deprived of rank and title." Of course she cannot be deprived of her P in the sense of "high birth", but she can be deprived of her high position, her rank as second lady in the land. As in many cases of TP, there is also an R element, but only as a secondary meaning. A second example of TP will be given from *Richard III*; the ex-queen, Margaret, is apostrophizing the reigning queen, Elizabeth:

> Thy honor, state, and seate, is due to me.
>
> (I.3.112)

The honour is both the title of queen and the rank of queen. There is also the secondary meaning R, and possibly also E as received.

The combination MP is not normal, since if an M is conferred that brings P, there is almost invariably a T involved; sometimes, however, I classify examples as MTP, for example the following one from *Eastward Ho*; Touchstone, the goldsmith, is addressing his son-in-law Golding, the good apprentice, who, after being taken into the livery of his company on the first day of his freedom, has now, a mere week later, been chosen a Commoner and an Alderman's Deputy in one day:

> Forward, my sufficient *Sonne*, and as this is the first, so esteeme it the least step, to that high and prime honour that expects thee.
>
> (IV.2.58—61)

The honour is not specified, but Touchstone is probably thinking of the rank and title of Lord Mayor of London, the greatest height to which a London citizen could rise in his capacity of citizen. The idea of conferment is not explicit, but it is present to the reader's mind, especially as two other honours have just been conferred on Golding.

H. The Head-Meaning D

There are a few examples that seem to require the interpretation "distinction", not in the sense "mark of distinction" but in the sense of "eminence, condition of being distinguished (i. e. above the ordinary, superior)", and sometimes even "distinctive quality". It is difficult to find absolutely certain examples, but there are a sufficient number of examples where it is the most plausible reading for it to be worth setting up as a separate head-meaning; I denote it by the symbol D. One variety of it can be seen in this example from *The Duchess of Malfi*; Mallateste has spoken to the Cardinal of "the famous *Lanoy*", and the Cardinal seeks to identify him:

> He that had the honour
> Of taking the *French* King Prisoner?
>
> (III.3.7—8)

This could be interpreted R, but then the sentence becomes somewhat ungracious, seeming to suggest that the glory was undeserved, or that it was only a rumour; and this is plainly not the intention. On the other hand it is not M, because the honour did not come to Lanoy from outside, but resided in the action itself. Nor does it quite fit *N. E. D.* 6 (my S: see p. 72 below), "person, thing, action, or attribute that confers honour"; one does not *have* honour in this sense. On the other hand the usage corresponds exactly to that of "distinction" in some of its meanings. A different type can be seen in *The Maid's Tragedy*; the repentant Evadne is speaking:

> I do appear the same, the same *Evadne*,
> Drest in the shames I liv'd in, the same monster.
> But these are names of honour to what I am ...
>
> (IV.1, p. 50)

She means that such words as "monster" are too good for her; "names of honour" possibly means "titles of rank", but even so it seems odd to read "honour" as P, and D is a plausible interpretation. A third type appears in this example from *The Pilgrim*; Alinda is persuading Roderigo, the outlaw, not to kill his enemy Pedro outright, by arguing that this will not be a satisfactory revenge:

> Let him die thus;
> And these that know and love revenge will laugh at ye:
> Here lies the honour of a well-bred anger,
> To make his enemy shake and tremble under him;
> Doubt, nay, almost despair, and then confound him.
>
> (II.2, p. 180)

Here *honour* seems to mean "distinguishing quality", or perhaps "quality that makes it superior", and I class it under D. Cases of M tend to resemble D if the idea of conferment is weakened, but as long as the honour is felt as a *mark* of distinction, and not as a distinction in itself, I class them as M. The following two examples seem to me to be on the D side of the border:

> Why? hee's not come to the honour of a Beard yet, he needs no shaving.
> (*The Fancies*, 1359—61)

> I shall pay soundly for having the honour to give the first wound.
> (*Man's the Master*, V.1, p. 95)

I. The Head-Meaning S

The next head-meaning corresponds to N. E. D. 6: "A person, thing, action, or attribute that confers honour; a source or cause of honour; one who or that which does honour or credit (*to*)". I denote it by the symbol S (mnemonic for "source"). There are two examples of it in this passage from *Poetaster*:

> *Eques.* VIRGIL is now at hand, imperiall CAESAR.
> *Caes.* *Romes* honour is at hand then. Fetch a chaire,
> And set it on our right hand; where 'tis fit,
> *Romes* honour, and our owne, should euer sit.
> (V.1.68—71)

What Virgil confers on Rome is R, and possibly D. In the next example, from *The Alchemist*, honour is conferred by an attribute, not by a person; Face is arguing to Abel Drugger that a bit of notoriety will not injure Dame Pliant's chances of marriage:

> Shee'll be more knowne, more talk'd of, and your widdowes
> Are ne'er of any price till they be famous;
> Their honour is their multitude of sutors:
> Send her, it may be thy good fortune.
> (II.6.46—9)

If the verb *is* is interpreted literally, this must be classed as S; the fact of having a large number of suitors confers R on a woman. It is not D, because the honour is a conferring; it is not M, because what is conferred arises from an attribute of the receiver, not from an external source. It would be possible, however, to interpret *is* as meaning "depends on", and then the example would be classed as R.

The next example is from *All's Well*; Mariana is warning Diana against Bertram, who is attempting to seduce her:

> Well, *Diana*, take heed of this French Earle,
> The honor of a Maide is her name,
> And no Legacie is so rich
> As honestie.
>   (III.5.11—13)

I take "name" to mean "name of maid", and so "reputation for chastity", or perhaps simply "chastity". The whole line therefore means "What confers E on a girl is her (reputation for) chastity".

It is sometimes difficult to decide whether an example should be classified as S or as M, as in this case from *Henry IV.1*:

> For euery Honor sitting on his Helme,
> Would they were multitudes, and on my head
> My shames redoubled.
>   (III.2.142—4)

The honours on Hotspur's helm can be imagined as physical emblems, won in war or awarded to him for prowess in war, and then they will be interpreted as M, like Henry V's glove (p. 63 above). But this seems to be figurative, and the honours are rather to be thought of as the military deeds and military qualities that have conferred R on Hotspur; and in this case the example is to be classified as S. This classification is supported by the fact that the shames on the Prince's head can*not* be imagined as physical emblems, and that, later in the speech, the Prince identifies "euery Honor" with "glorious Deedes" and "euery Glory". I similarly interpret as S an example later in the same play, "all the budding Honors on thy Crest" (V.4.72).

I also include under S *N. E. D.* 6(b): "(Usu. in pl.) An adjunct or part of anything which gives it distinction; a decoration, adornment, ornament (*poetic*)". This indeed follows automatically from my recognition of "distinction" as one of the meanings of *honour*. The examples given by the *N. E. D.*, however, are not entirely convincing. One of them, from *Henry VIII*, occurs in my material:

> This is the state of Man; to day he puts forth
> The tender Leaues of hopes, to morrow Blossomes,
> And beares his blushing Honors thicke vpon him:
> The third day, comes a Frost . . .
>   (III.2.352—5)

I classify this as M rather than as S. The flowers on the tree are admittedly a "decoration, adornment, ornament", but what we are meant to think of, surely, are the titles, orders, and other marks of distinction that Wolsey has lost; we think of the man and the tree simultaneously, whereas the reading S requires us to think only of the tree. "Blushing" refers to the colour of the blossom, but inevitably we think also of the man, "He carries his honours, blushing".

J. Word of Honour

I have found in my material a few examples of *N. E. D.* 2(b): "A statement or promise made on one's honour; word of honour". I denote this by the symbol W. It is a rare usage, and the earliest example quoted by the *N. E. D.* dates from 1658—9. The first quite clear case in my material is in *Epsom Wells* (1672); Rains has made a promise to prevent a duel, and he breaks away from the amorous Mrs Woodly in order to keep his promise:

> Mrs. *Wood.* Stay but one minute; they'll not meet I tell you.
> Rains.   Madam, I pass'd my honour, and dare not venture it.
> (V.1, p. 174)

I have, however, found possible examples much earlier in the century. The *N. E. D.* classification suggests that W is a development of H; it is quite possible, however, that it is a development of R. I shall discuss these points later (pp. 321—323 below).

K. The Legal Meaning

There is a technical, legal sense of *honour*, recorded as *N. E. D.* 7: "A seigniory of several manors held under one baron or lord paramount". I denote it by the symbol L. This (obviously medieval) meaning is very rare in my material, and indeed I have no single example where it is certainly the sole head-meaning, though I have a few (all in the reigns of Elizabeth and James I) where it is a possible co-meaning. There is an example in *Henry V*; Exeter comes as an ambassador to the King of France, and on behalf of Henry lays claim to

> the Crowne,
> And all wide-stretched Honors, that pertaine
> By Custome, and the Ordinance of Times,
> Vnto the Crowne of France.   (II.4.81—4)

This may simply mean MT, but the word "wide-stretched" awakens one's attention to the possibility of L. Indeed, to the Englishman of the Renaissance, with his passion for litigation, L may have been felt as present in many examples where it would not occur to a modern reader: for example, in all cases like the above, where titles are titles to landed property. The Arden editor, following Liddell, finds an example of it in *Macbeth*:

> *Macb.* If you shall cleaue to my consent,
> When 'tis, it shall make Honor for you.
> *Banq.* So I lose none,
> In seeking to augment it, but still keepe
> My Bosome franchis'd and Allegeance cleare,
> I shall be counsail'd.
> (II.1.25—9)

The obvious interpretation is to take the honour that Macbeth offers as MTP, and the honour that Banquo insists on preserving as H; but the Arden editor may well be right in seeing also a reference to free tenure and feudal overlordship.[1]) There is a much clearer case in *A Wife for a Month*, where there is a pun on L and R; Valerio has listened with assumed politeness to the king's plans for making Evanthe (Valerio's wife) his mistress; he then points out, with mock seriousness, that if the king's plan is carried out he himself will be left without a woman, and suggests that he should borrow the queen; to the king's expected reaction Valerio replies:

> Do you start
> At my intrenching on your private liberty,
> And would you force a high-way through mine honour,
> And make me pave it too?
> (IV.1, p. 46)

The main meaning here is R, the R that a man loses when his wife is unfaithful, but there is a play on L, which is the figurative half of the meaning; this is made plain, not only by the highway, but also by the parallel pun on "liberty", which means (1) "freedom", and (2) "a manor within which certain privileges are exercised".

L. Oaths and Asseverations

The word *honour* is often used in phrases like "upon my honour", "by my honour", "on my honour", and even occasionally "of my

---

[1]) The editor of the New Arden edition, however, rejects this possibility.

honour", and similarly also, of course, with the possessive adjective in the second or third person. Sometimes such phrases are used as the solemn confirmation of a statement or a promise, as in this example from *Henry VI.2*:

> *York*. Vpon thine Honor is he Prisoner⟨?⟩
> *Buckingham*. Vpon mine Honor he is Prisoner.
>
> (V.1.42—3)

On other occasions they are used merely as a petty oath or exclamation, as in Olivia's

> By mine honor halfe drunke.
>
> (*Twelfth Night*, I.5.116)

Wyld takes this type of phrase to be an "asseveration that speaker's good name is at stake".[1]) This is the obvious interpretation, and gives a head-meaning R. However, I do not classify such examples as R, because they are not very relevant to honour as a code of conduct, and give us no information of value about the content of R. They form very much a group of their own, so I put them together in a separate class and denote them by the symbol O. Of course O is not a head-meaning in the sense that R and H are; but it is convenient for practical purposes to keep the O examples apart.

I include under O examples like "by the honour of a soldier", where the possessive adjective is replaced by some other genitive, and also the occasional examples like "by honour", where there is no genitive at all.

In a few cases, a definite content is given to an example of O by the context. Phrases like "by the honour of a soldier" are not sufficient to do this; this expression merely asserts that soldiers are above all likely to have honour and to hold it dear, and does not necessarily imply that the honour is, for example, military reputation. But in the following example from *The Traitor* some content is given to O; the Duke has come to Amidea expecting to find a willing mistress, but instead he is held off with a poniard and given a moral lecture, beginning:

> Prince, come not too near me,
> For, by my honour, since you have lost your own,
> Although I bow in duty to your person,
> I hate your black thoughts;
>
> (III.3, p. 142)

---

[1]) *The Universal English Dictionary*, s. v. *honour* (I.), 1a.

The honour that the duke has lost is H; it is dishonourable to attempt to seduce a gentlewoman. This reflects back on "by my honour", and makes it natural to interpret Amidea's honour as C, or perhaps rather RcC. Such cases are not very frequent, but when they occur I classify them under the head-meaning concerned as well as under O.

M. Respectful Forms of Address

Another usage that I put in a group of its own is the respectful form of address or of reference, "your honour", "his honour", "their honours", etc. By far the commonest form is the second person, "your honour", used in addressing people of high rank, and I therefore denote the usage by the symbol Y. An example can be seen in *Hamlet*:

> Good my Lord,
> How does your Honor for this many a day?
> (III.1.90—91)

My Y corresponds to *N. E. D.* 4(b); the *N. E. D.* classification makes it a variant of P, and it is in fact generally used in addressing people of high rank. It is possible, however, that it was felt as a variant of H, and it is worth noticing that the first usages of H and of Y recorded in the *N. E. D.* are from almost exactly the same date (1548 and 1553 respectively). The question is of no great importance for my purposes, but it underlines the desirability of classifying the Y examples in a group of their own.

N. Unclassified Examples

A number of examples have been left unclassified because the meaning is obscure. For example, I leave unclassified the following example from *All's Well*; Helena has come to the king to offer to cure him with her father's prescription:

> And hearing your high Maiestie is toucht
> With that malignant cause, wherein the honour
> Of my deare fathers gift, stands cheefe in power,
> I come to tender it, and my appliance,
> With all bound humbleness.
> (II.1.111—15)

None of the usual meanings fits here without some forcing; the most plausible is S, meaning that it had been an honour to Helena (a source of R) to have been given this prescription by her father; but this does not fit very well with the fact that "honour" is the subject of "stands"; an appropriate meaning for "honour" would be "operation" or "effectiveness". An even obscurer example can be seen in *The Merry Wives*; Falstaff dismisses Nym and Bardolph from his service, retaining only a page:

> Rogues, hence, auaunt, vanish like haile-stones; goe,
> Trudge; plod away ith' hoofe: seeke shelter, packe:
> *Falstaffe* will learne the honor of the age,
> French-thrift, you Rogues, my selfe, and skirted *Page*.
> (I.3.78—81)

The reference is to the fashionable habit of employing French pages and discarding the consequent excess of serving-men.[1]) The most plausible interpretation of "honor" is S: this behaviour is the kind that brings R in (or to) this age. Another possible interpretation is H, taken as "honourable behaviour". But the meaning is so doubtful that I put the example in the unclassified group. Probably the "bad" quarto of 1602 is right here; it reads "humor" instead of "honor".

I normally place the phrase "maid of honour" in the unclassified group, since, while the meaning of the whole expression is clear, it is not easy to assign any separate meaning to the element *honour* in it; originally, probably, it meant P, "high rank". There are a few similar cases like "page of honour", and occasionally even "man of honour"; the latter phrase is not usually left unclassified, but there are some examples, especially in the second half of the century, where it is used so vaguely that it is impossible to be sure what it means.

For the unclassified examples I shall use the symbol U.

O. The Complexity of the Word

It has been seen that the noun *honour* had a large number of possible meanings at the beginning of the seventeenth century. It is nevertheless clear that it was felt as a single word, that the various meanings were all felt to be related to one another. This is seen in the way in which writers move unconsciously from meaning to meaning, or consciously pit one aspect against another, and in which the various meanings occur together in one example, sometimes as subsidiary or implied meanings, creating a distinctive aura round the word. The unconscious

---

[1]) Onions, *op. cit.*, s. v. *French*.

sliding from meaning to meaning is seen in Robert Ashley. He defines honour as "a certeine testemonie of vertue shining of yt self geven of some man by the iudgement of good men",[1]) a definition that can include both R and M (including "praise"); and in fact he never distinguishes between R and M, and moreover often moves off to E, T, P, and even to H, as when he says that "true honour consisteth not in vaine boasting of swelling tytles, but in the moderacion of the minde".[2]) The following is an example of Ashley's tendency to identify R and TP; he is arguing that virtue cannot be hidden, and that even if you seek to avoid honour it will come to you in the name of modesty:[3])

> Therefore great ys the force of vertue which doth not only honour those which do reasonably desire yt but such also as neglect and eschew yt. *Diocletian* refused all honour geving over and renouncing his Empyre, and yet was he desired and praysed of every man. Others contrarilie while they greedelye gripe after too much glorie not hauing any meritt to deserue yt faile of that they hunt after and fall into great hatred, As *Herostratus* who ys said to haue burnt the temple of *Diana at Ephesus* that he might leave a famous memorie of his name behind him.

What Diocletian refused was T and P, what he gained was R and M (praise). The anecdote about Herostratus begins from R ("glorie"), but the opposite of this is called "great hatred", which would be more nearly antithetical to E. (The identification of these things with honour or dishonour is implicit in the whole context, of course.) This movement from meaning to meaning goes on all the time in Ashley, and similar things are found in the drama. For example, the tendency for R and M to be associated, and perhaps not clearly distinguished, can be seen in Massinger's play *The Bondman*, III.4 and IV.1, where there is a series of references to the honour that Leosthenes has won in battle; it is not always clear whether the honour in question is military glory (R) or marks of distinction (M); two of the examples are probably to be taken as M and the rest as R, but most of them can be read either way, and Massinger probably did not distinguish clearly between the two meanings in his own mind.

---

[1]) *Of Honour*, p. 34.
[2]) *Ibid.*, p. 47.
[3]) *Ibid.*, p. 36.

An example of the conscious interplay of different meanings of *honour* can be given from *All's Well*, II.3. Helena has cured the king, and her reward is the choice of a husband from the lords at his court. She moves round among the lords, speaking to them in turn, and to one she says:

> The honor sir that flames in your faire eyes,
> Before I speake too threatningly replies:
> Loue make your fortunes twentie times aboue
> Her that so vvishes, and her humble loue.
>
> (II.3.81—4)

Here we have a combination of P and H; it is a quality of character that flames in his eyes (pride, for example), but the flame is also an expression of his high rank, she sees his noble birth in his face. H is the characteristic of the man of P, and includes pride in his birth, which forbids marrying below his station. Helena finally names Bertram as the man she wants, but he protests violently, scorning to marry "a poore Phisitians daughter"; the king thereupon gives him a lecture on honour; Helena has virtue, and only lacks title, which the king can give her; it is merely a name Bertram is despising:

> Where great additions swell's, and vertue none,
> It is a dropsied honour.
>
> (II.3.129—30)

The dropsied honour is TP without H.

> Shee is young, wise, faire,
> In these, to Nature shee's immediate heire:
> And these breed honour: that is honours scorne,
> Which challenges it selfe as honours borne,
> And is not like the sire: Honours thriue,
> When rather from our acts we them deriue
> Then our fore-goers:
>
> (II.3.133—9)

The honour that is bred by youth, wisdom, and beauty is mainly R, but possibly also TP (a girl with these qualities rises in the world) and E as received; too much stress on TP, however, would introduce a cynical note out of keeping with the tone of the passage (unless we take "breed" to refer literally to the production of children: "if you marry a girl with these qualities your children will have both the rank and the fine qualities of the aristocracy"). The head-meaning, however, I take to be R. In "honours scorne" we have H, and in "honours borne" HTP: the truly honourable man despises the fellow who claims to be born to high rank and title but who lacks the fine qualities of his noble father. The reason for seeing an H element in "honours borne" is that the "sire" is obviously intended to combine TP and H, as suggested by the ambiguous "noble father" of my paraphrase. The "Honours" that are derived from our acts are presumably MT, and those derived from our ancestors are TP: the contrast is between acquired and hereditary rank (a favourite theme of dispute in Shakespeare's day); there is also a secondary meaning R in either case, and the "acts" are presumably to be thought of as those of a person of H.

We must not be deceived by words, the king continues; we see untruthful epitaphs on every tomb, while dust and damned oblivion is the frequent fate of "honour'd bones" indeed. Here, *honoured* cannot mean "esteemed", or "dignified with marks of distinction", because the king is asserting that this is just what the bones lack; it must mean "honourable", "worthy of esteem", and so the bones are those of people of H. He again offers Helena to Bertram:

> If thou canst like this creature, as a maide,
> I can create the rest: Vertue, and shee
> Is her owne dower: Honour and wealth, from mee.
> (II.3.143—5)

Honour is now TP, with no suggestion of H; honour is in fact explicitly contrasted with "Vertue", which Helena already has; to this virtue the king will add rank (title) and wealth. Bertram, however, still refuses, and Helena withdraws her claim to him, but the king will not permit this —

> My Honor's at the stake...
> (II.3.151)

The king's honour here is his R, the good name that is lost if a promise is not fulfilled (his promise to give Helena the husband she wanted), and also the face that a king loses if his wishes are disregarded by his subjects; and so the king asserts his authority, and absolutely commands Bertram to marry Helena:

> Heere, take her hand,
> Proud scornfull boy, vnworthie this good gift,
> That dost in vile misprision shackle vp
> My loue, and her desert: that canst not dreame,
> We poizing vs in her defectiue scale,
> Shall weigh thee to the beame: That wilt not know,
> It is in Vs to plant thine Honour, where
> We please to haue it grow.
>
> (II.3.152—9)

By now the word is so clustered round with associations that it is not easy to assign a head-meaning to this example; I think, however, that the main idea is TP; the king is propagating Bertram's noble stock, and ensuring continuance of his title, by "planting" him in Helena, who is the soil for the noble tree, or for cuttings from it. (Bertram's later refusal to consummate the marriage is therefore a refusal to be "planted" by the king.) Bertram bows to the storm of the king's anger, and agrees to marry Helena:

> Pardon my gracious Lord: for I submit
> My fancie to your eies, when I consider
> What great creation, and what dole of honour
> Flies where you bid it: I finde that she which late
> Was in my Nobler thoughts, most base: is now
> The praised of the King, who so ennobled,
> Is as 'twere borne so.
>
> (II.3.169—75)

The whole problem has centred round Helen's lack of social position, and "honour" here refers primarily to TP; but both R and H are prominent secondary meanings; "base" can refer to character as well as to rank, and so can "ennobled"; and when Bertram says that the king's praises make Helena seem like a born noblewoman instead of a mere created one, he must surely imply that noble blood brings with it certain inherent qualities of character, H as an inborn tendency. Obviously Bertram still thinks poorly of Helena; his very speech of submission implies that the king can give Helena TP but not H: he says that the king's praises make her *seem* like a born noblewoman, not that she really has the qualities of the born noblewoman.

Later in the play there are references to the honour or honours that will be won by the French volunteers, and by Bertram in particular, and these are M. When the countess hears that Bertram has abandoned Helena and gone to the wars, she contrasts the honour that he may gain in war with the honour that he has lost by his treatment of his wife:

> I will intreate you when you see my sonne, to tell him that
> his sword can neuer winne the honor that he looses:
> (III.2.93—6)

The main contrast here is between two kinds of R, military glory and good name for treating your wife well.

The contrasted meanings in these passages have mainly been from the R/H group and the M/T/P group, but examples could easily be found where other head-meanings are deliberately contrasted in a similar way. In this same play, for example, there is a striking passage where an honour meaning "a family heirloom" (M) is contrasted with honour meaning "chastity" (C) (IV.2.42—51). Most of the possible combinations of head-meanings are found in one play or another; even such an improbable combination as RY can be seen in *Volpone*, in a comic phrase used by Lady Would-bee to the court of justice:

> Surely I had no purpose:
> To scandalize your honours, or my sexes.
> (IV.6.8—9)

Here "your honours" means "the judges", but then she goes on to "the honour of my sex".

The sense of the relatedness of the different meanings, the feeling that *honour* is a single word, not a series of homophones, makes it desirable to give at least some attention to all usages of the word, even those that do not bear directly on conduct.

P. Principles of Classification

For purely practical reasons I have based my analysis on head-meanings, and left secondary and implied meanings out of account. To take these subsidiary meanings into consideration would make the work of classification impossibly complicated, and there would also be grave problems in grading the degrees of prominence of subsidiary meanings.[1] This does not mean that I have assigned a single head-meaning to every example: if two or more meanings seem equally pro-

---
[1] To some extent, however, subsidiary meanings are taken into account in my later division of certain groups into sub-groups.

minent in an example, I assign them as joint head-meanings. However, I quite often assign a single head-meaning to an example where other head-meanings are *possible*; frequently, one head-meaning seems to me the most *probable*, even though quite a good case could be made out for others, and then I take this most probable meaning as the sole head-meaning.

I only assign two or more head-meanings to an example if it is possible for the writer to have intended them all; occasionally there is a different kind of case, in which it is difficult for the modern reader to decide between two or more meanings, but where the author cannot possibly have meant more than one of them; in such cases I do not give joint head-meanings, but choose one reading or the other; if it seems quite impossible to decide between them, I leave the example unclassified. An example can be given from *The Magnetic Lady*; Bias is refusing to carry a challenge, on the grounds that it will bring him out of favour with his patron:

> Ile bear no Challenges;
> I will not hazard my Lords favour so;
> Or forfeit mine owne Judgement with his honour,
> To turne a Ruffian:
>
> (III.6.7—10)

This can be interpreted as E: "lose my own judgment and his esteem for me"; or as Y: "lose my good judgment in the eyes of his lordship"; or just possibly as R: "lose my own judgment and cause him to lose reputation (because he has such an irresponsible follower)". The third meaning seems the least probable, but it is very hard to decide between the first two; and it really does not seem possible that Jonson can have intended both meanings. I incline to the interpretation Y, but the important thing is that the example shall not be classified as EY: it must be either E, or Y, or U. Cases of this type are not very common, however; usually, when there is more than one possible meaning, the author may well have meant both, and may not have distinguished clearly between them.

An example that is classified with two head-meanings appears in the tables for both head-meanings; so an example classified RP will be counted in the statistics for R and also in those for P. It should be remembered, however, that RH and RcC count as separate head-meanings, and the examples under RH therefore do not also appear under R and H, nor RcC under Rc and C. An example classified RHE would appear in the RH statistics and in the E statistics. Since M, T, and P overlap a good deal, it is often convenient to treat them as a single head-meaning; I shall then refer to "the MTP group", by which I shall mean "all examples containing M, T, or P, or any combination of them, no example being counted more than once".

It must be remembered that I count only the actual occurrences of the noun *honour*, and that I count every such occurrence. If a repetition occurs by means of a pronoun or a possessive pronoun, like "it" or "yours", this is not counted as an example; so in the phrase "my honour and his", there is only one example, not two. On the other hand, when a character says "His Honor, Oh thine Honor, *Lewis* thine Honor" (*King John*, III.1.316), this is counted as three examples. This purely mechanical rule is adopted for practical convenience.

Sometimes the word *honour* occurs with one meaning, and then later in the speech the meaning changes, intentionally or unintentionally, without the noun being repeated. In this case I count only the first meaning, and leave the second out of account, again as a matter of practical convenience; the point is that changes can continue for many lines, and it would be difficult to know where to stop. There is no clear boundary between this type and the type where two meanings are felt to co-exist simultaneously in the word, since "co-existence" is something that one is made to feel by the context, both before and after the word. I have tried to judge each borderline case on its merits. In the "co-existence" case, of course, I assign two head-meanings, but when I feel that the meaning changes later I assign only one.

The head-meanings have been assigned by an inspection of each example, great attention being paid to context, both verbal and situational. No other method is possible, since no mechanical rule can be given for the determining of a meaning. Such things as the syntactic construction used, and the use of the noun as a countable or an uncountable, have no absolute value, though they are often useful indicators. Even such standard constructions as "to have the honour" permit of a variety of meanings, and there are quite certain examples to prove this. Inevitably, therefore, there is a personal equation involved, the importance of which it is difficult to assess; I have attempted to minimize it by examining every example many times, and on widely separated occasions, but this of course may only make for consistency without eliminating a personal tendency towards certain types of interpretation. This is why I have reproduced as much of my material as practicable, to give every reader the opportunity to disagree. Some readers may be less willing than I have been to select one possible meaning out of several on the basis of relatively small contextual indications; some people, no doubt, would classify a number of my R and H examples as equivocal RH; however, in this kind of case, consistency is probably more important than the exact boundary at which one chooses to begin making distinctions.

APPENDIX TO CHAPTER 2

Summary of Symbols for Head-Meanings

C   = chastity.
D   = distinction, eminence.
E   = esteem, veneration, respect.
K   = the code of honour (considered as a set of laws).
L   = legal meaning, "a seigniory of several manors held under one baron or lord paramount".
M   = something conferred or done as a mark or token of respect or distinction (including the special usages "praise" and "a bow, obeisance, curtsey").
H   = honourableness of character, honourable behaviour.
O   = use in oaths and asseverations.
P   = high position, rank, high birth.
R   = reputation.
Rc   = reputation for chastity.
RcC = equivocal Rc/C.
RH   = equivocal R/H.
S   = a source or cause of honour, something or somebody that does honour (to).
T   = title of rank.
U   = unclassified.
W   = word of honour, statement or promise made on one's honour.
Y   = respectful form of address or reference, "your honour", etc.

CHAPTER 3

The Head-Meanings through the Century

In this chapter an account will be given of the way in which, in my material, the main groups of head-meanings vary in frequency from decade to decade in the period studied. To give some idea of the absolute frequency in each decade, I shall express the results as number of examples per play. This assumes that the average length of plays did not alter materially during the period. It is rather difficult to be sure whether this in fact was so. It is impossible to compare play-lengths by comparing the number of lines, even if the plays are printed in the same format, because prose-lines and verse-lines do not contain the same average number of words, and plays consist of verse and prose in varying proportions. The only safe way of comparing plays for length, therefore, is to count the number of words in each play, and this is impracticable. My own impression, for what it is worth, is that there is no great change during the period; plays vary a good deal in length, but the same range of variation is found in all parts of the century. I shall not, in any case, attempt to apply any corrections to my figures.

In the 206 plays studied, I have found 4,847 examples of *honour* as a noun, the range in single plays being from 0 (*Midsummer Night's Dream*) to 86 (*The Country Wife*). The number of examples in each separate play can be found from Appendix A, column g. The variation in frequency from decade to decade is shown in Table 3; the comedy-group and the tragedy-group are given separately, and in each decade are shown number of examples found, number of plays involved, and the quotient of these two, which gives the number of examples per play.

It is hardly possible to draw any far-reaching conclusions from this table, since all the different head-meanings are here mixed up together, and changes in one head-meaning may be masked by opposite changes in another. However, one or two striking things do emerge from the

TABLE 3. *Total Number of Examples per Decade.*

Period from to		1591 1600	1601 1610	1611 1620	1621 1630	1631 1640	1591 1640	1661 1670	1671 1680	1681 1690	1691 1700	1661 1700	Grand Total
Comedy	(a)	121	229	209	263	279	1101	328	629	392	205	1554	2655
	(b)	11	16	12	16	12	67	10	20	12	8	50	117
	(c)	11.0	14.3	17.4	16.4	23.3	16.4	32.8	31.5	32.7	25.6	31.1	22.7
Tragedy	(a)	167	295	421	296	304	1483	165	326	164	54	709	2192
	(b)	10	14	14	10	12	60	8	12	5	4	29	89
	(c)	16.7	21.1	30.1	29.6	25.3	24.7	20.6	27.2	32.8	13.5	24.5	24.6
All Plays ...	(a)	288	524	630	559	283	2584	493	955	556	259	2263	4847
	(b)	21	30	26	26	24	127	18	32	17	12	79	206
	(c)	13.7	17.5	24.2	21.5	24.3	20.4	27.4	29.8	32.7	21.6	28.7	23.5

(a) Number of examples.
(b) Number of plays.
(c) Number of examples per play.

table. There is a marked increase in the number of examples per play during the century:[1]) for the period 1591 to 1640, there are 20.4 examples per play, while for the period 1661 to 1700 there are 28.7. This increase, however, is entirely due to the comedies, which go up from 16.4 to 31.1, while the tragedies remain stationary (24.7 and 24.5). On the assumption of random sampling, this change in frequency in the comedies is highly significant statistically, i. e. is much greater than could have been expected from chance alone.[2]) The more or less continuous increase during the first half of the century (11.0, 14.3, 17.4, 16.4, 23.3) is also significant: for example, there is a significant difference between the figures for 1591—1610 and those for 1611—1640; and even the difference between the decade 1591—1600 and the decade 1601—1610 is just significant. In comedy, therefore, there is a steady increase in the frequency of the noun *honour* during the first half of the century, whereas in the second half of the century it remains steady, at a higher level than is ever reached in the first half of the century, with a slight fall in the final decade. In the tragedies, there is no difference between

---

[1]) Henceforth, when discussing my tables, I shall refer to the period 1591—1640 as the first half of the century, and to the period 1661—1700 as the second half of the century.

[2]) For statistical methods, see Appendix F.

the two halves of the century, in gross; however, the rising trend seen in the first half of the century is significant, just as in comedy; on the whole, we can say that in the tragedies there is an increase in frequency during the first three decades of our period, after which the figure remains steady at a high level, except perhaps for a fall in the last decade of the century. It will also be noticed that in the first half-century the frequency is higher in tragedy than in comedy, whereas in the second half-century the reverse is the case; these differences are significant.

One must not attempt to read too much into these gross figures. However, it is possible that the increase in frequency, seen especially in the early decades of the period (and there both in comedy and in tragedy), is a reflection of the growing courtliness of the audience, and of the tendency to cater for aristocratic taste. The fact that the change is strongly marked in comedy could be taken as an indication that the increase is a reflection of real life, i. e. that the gentry really began to use the word more frequently. However, part at least of the change is probably due to another reason: a change in ratio between gentle and non-gentle characters represented in the comedies. There are comedies early in the century, especially those of Middleton, where the leading characters come from the middle classes, and where the gentry are definitely in the background;[1]) in the Restoration period, on the other hand, while there are plenty of non-gentle characters in the comedies, these seldom occupy the foreground: the principal characters are nearly always gentlefolk. Not surprisingly, it is precisely these low-life and bourgeois comedies of Middleton that are exceptionally lacking in examples of *honour* (*The Family of Love*, 2 examples; *A Trick to catch the Old One*, 2; *Michaelmas Term*, 2; *Your Five Gallants*, 5; *The Roaring Girl*, 5; *A Chaste Maid in Cheapside*, 1 example). There is no doubt a parallel movement in tragedy: low-life characters are cut out, and tragedy made more "noble" (there is no simple countryman with figs in Dryden's *All for Love*); but in tragedy the change could not be so great as in comedy, simply because the major figures of tragedy were traditionally of high rank anyway, and so the change only affected minor characters. On this view, the change in frequency

---

[1]) See Dunkel, *op. cit.*, pp. 49—52. To depict the middle classes, of course, is not the same thing as to cater for their taste, and Middleton (unlike Heywood) is by no means a pro-citizen writer.

would still be due to the desire to cater for upper-class taste, but would be mediated by the change in the proportions of different social classes depicted in the drama, and would not necessarily be a reflection of any real change in frequency of usage in society. It is possible that both factors operated.

The slight decline in the last decade of the century is confirmed by the supplementary material (see p. 361). It may reflect the change of atmosphere in England after the 1688 revolution. The real turning-point in the theatre, Collier's *Short View*, admittedly did not come until 1698, and it was another decade before the cultural compromise between the aristocracy and the middle classes was crystallized in the essays of Addison and Steele;[1]) but even so there does seem to have

TABLE 4. *Frequencies of Main Groups of Head-Meanings: All Plays*

Period from to	1591 1600	1601 1610	1611 1620	1621 1630	1631 1640	1591 1640	1661 1670	1671 1680	1681 1690	1691 1700	1661 1700	Grand Total
R/RH/H ... (a)	149	212	310	265	286	1222	277	480	216	126	1099	2321
(b)	7.1	7.1	11.9	10.2	11.9	9.6	15.4	15.0	12.7	10.5	13.9	11.3
Rc/RcC/C .. (a)	13	70	85	86	89	343	64	193	99	37	393	736
(b)	0.6	2.3	3.3	3.3	3.7	2.7	3.6	6.0	5.8	3.1	5.0	3.6
MTP group . (a)	63	115	176	161	148	663	95	171	124	36	426	1089
(b)	3.0	3.8	6.8	6.2	6.2	5.2	5.3	5.3	7.3	3.0	5.4	5.3
O .... (a)	33	24	18	5	12	92	37	57	18	14	126	218
(b)	1.6	0.8	0.7	0.2	0.5	0.7	2.1	1.8	1.1	1.2	1.6	1.1
Y .... (a)	26	61	33	21	42	183	2	26	76	26	130	313
(b)	1.2	2.0	1.3	0.8	1.8	1.4	0.1	0.8	4.5	2.2	1.6	1.5
Others ..... (a)	8	22	24	27	18	99	22	24	25	16	87	186
(b)	0.4	0.7	0.9	1.0	0.8	0.8	1.2	0.8	1.5	1.3	1.1	0.9
U .... (a)	6	15	12	19	13	65	13	27	14	13	67	132
(b)	0.3	0.5	0.5	0.7	0.5	0.5	0.7	0.8	0.8	1.1	0.8	0.6

(a) Number of examples.
(b) Number of examples per play.

---

[1]) See Beljame, *op. cit.*, pp. 225—338.

TABLE 5. *Frequencies of Main Groups of Head-Meanings: Comedy*

Period from to	1591 1600	1601 1610	1611 1620	1621 1630	1631 1640	1591 1640	1661 1670	1671 1680	1681 1690	1691 1700	1661 1700	Grand Total
R/RH/H ... (a)	53	71	83	129	124	460	163	262	137	94	656	1116
(b)	4.8	4.4	6.9	8.1	10.3	6.9	16.3	13.1	11.4	11.8	13.1	9.5
Rc/RcC/C .. (a)	8	36	46	34	49	173	57	146	78	30	311	484
(b)	0.7	2.3	3.8	2.1	4.1	2.6	5.7	7.3	6.5	3.8	6.2	4.1
MTP group . (a)	19	48	49	70	72	258	64	131	106	32	333	591
(b)	1.7	3.0	4.1	4.4	6.0	3.9	6.4	6.6	8.8	4.0	6.7	5.1
O .... (a)	21	15	6	1	3	46	30	49	17	14	110	156
(b)	1.9	0.9	0.5	0.1	0.3	0.7	3.0	2.5	1.4	1.8	2.2	1.3
Y .... (a)	15	29	17	17	31	109	2	26	35	23	86	195
(b)	1.4	1.8	1.4	1.1	2.6	1.6	0.2	1.3	2.9	2.9	1.7	1.7

(a) Number of examples.
(b) Number of examples per play.

been some change of mood in the theatre in the 1690's. It can be felt for example, in Shadwell's comedy *The Volunteers*: the hero of this play is the son of one of Cromwell's colonels, and is very much the new Whig gentleman, combining elegance with virtue and fighting for William III in Ireland. (It must be added, however, that this play contains a large number of examples of *honour*.)

Tables 4, 5, and 6 show the frequencies of the main groups of headmeanings in each decade; Table 4 is for all plays, and Tables 5 and 6 for comedy and tragedy respectively. R, RH, and H are shown together as a single group, and so are Rc, RcC, and C; there is of course no overlap within each of these large groups. MTP is treated as a single headmeaning as described on p. 85 above. O and Y are shown separately. In Table 4, the remaining head-meanings are also shown, lumped together; inside this group there is a certain amount of overlapping, and an example classified e. g. as ES will be reckoned twice. The few possible examples of L have not been included. Finally, the number of unclassified examples is given. There is of course an overlap between the main groups; an example classified RHTPE will appear once in the R/RH/H figures, once in the MTP figures, and once in the figures

TABLE 6. *Frequencies of Main Groups of Head-Meanings: Tragedy.*

Period from to	1591 1600	1601 1610	1611 1620	1621 1630	1631 1640	1591 1640	1661 1670	1671 1680	1681 1690	1691 1700	1661 1700	Grand Total
R/RH/H ... (a)	96	141	227	136	162	762	114	218	79	32	443	1205
(b)	9.6	10.1	16.2	13.6	13.5	12.7	14.3	18.1	15.8	8.0	15.3	13.5
Rc/RcC/C .. (a)	5	34	39	52	40	170	7	47	21	7	82	252
(b)	0.5	2.4	2.8	5.2	3.3	2.8	0.9	3.9	4.2	1.8	2.8	2.8
MTP group . (a)	44	67	127	91	76	405	31	40	18	4	93	498
(b)	4.4	4.8	9.1	9.1	6.3	6.8	3.9	3.3	3.6	1.0	3.2	5.6
O .... (a)	12	9	12	4	9	46	7	8	1	0	16	62
(b)	1.2	0.6	0.9	0.4	0.8	0.8	0.9	0.7	0.2	0.0	0.6	0.7
Y .... (a)	11	32	16	4	11	74	0	0	41	3	44	118
(b)	1.1	2.3	1.1	0.4	0.9	1.2	0.0	0.0	8.2	0.8	1.5	1.3

(a) Number of examples.
(b) Number of examples per play.

for other head-meanings. The total number of head-meanings for any decade is therefore greater than the number of examples for the decade given in Table 3; the difference between these two figures is a measure of the extent to which joint head-meanings are assigned to examples in the decade.

It will be seen from these tables that the frequency of the R/RH/H group increases during the century, both in comedy and in tragedy. In comedy, the increase is extremely marked, from 6.9 examples per play in the first half-century to 13.1 in the second (a change that is highly significant); the rising trend seen inside the first half of the century is also real, for the difference between the period 1591—1610 and the period 1611—1640 is significant; the fall from 4.8 to 4.4 in the first two decades of the period is not significant, nor is the difference between the period 1661—1680 and the period 1681—1700; however, the declining tendency in the second half of the century may nevertheless be real, for if the decade 1661—1670 is compared with the decade 1671—1680, the difference is found to be just significant. In tragedy the increase is less marked: from 12.7 per play in the first half-century to 15.3 in the second; but this change is also significant. Inside the first half-century, the difference between 1591—1610 and 1611—1640 is significant, but the other fluctuations are not. In the second half of the century, the falling tendency at the end is possibly significant. Both in comedy and in tragedy, the fall in the final decade of the century is confirmed by the supplementary material.

It may therefore be said that, both in comedy and in tragedy, the R/RH/H group increases in frequency from about 1610 onwards, and reaches a maximum somewhere in the middle of the century; it remains at this high level through the Restoration period, but with a slight decline at the end of the century. The increase in frequency is much more marked in comedy than in tragedy. Since this is the group of head-meanings especially concerned with the regulation of conduct, the increase in numbers presumably reflects an increased interest in honour as a determinant of conduct. The difference in the rate of increase between comedy and tragedy possibly indicates that there really was an increase in the usage in society outside the theatre; partly, however, it may result from the dramatists' emphasizing those aspects of life that would be most pleasing to their increasingly upper-class audience, and especially from an increased emphasis on upper-class characters in the plays.

A somewhat similar development is seen in the Rc/RcC/C group. There is a considerable increase in frequency in comedy, from 2.6 in the first half-century to 6.2 in the second (highly significant); there is however a drop in the final decade of the century (significant). In tragedy, on the other hand, there is no difference at all between the two halves of the century, the figure being 2.8 for each. The reasons for this pattern of development may be the same as for R/RH/H, but to these should perhaps be added an increase in the interest in seduction as a leading theme of comedy after 1661; on the other hand, it must be remembered that the theme of seduction does not in itself necessitate the use of the word *honour* (Rc/RcC/C): for example, it occurs only four times in this meaning in *Measure for Measure*, where the whole play centres round a seduction and an attempted seduction;[1]) the dramatist has many words to choose from (*chastity, fame, modesty, reputation,* etc.), besides a whole range of periphrases (*unstained bed,*

---

[1]) The relatively close Davenant adaptation, *The Law against Lovers,* increases the number to seven.

etc.), and if he chooses the word *honour* he presumably does so because of its other associations.

In the MTP group, opposite trends are seen in comedy and in tragedy. In comedy, the figure rises from 3.9 in the first half-century to 6.7 in the second (highly significant); in fact the figure increases smoothly all the way up to 1690, and this rising trend seems to be real; there is, for example, a significant difference between the figure for 1591—1610 and that for 1611—1640. In tragedy, on the other hand, the frequency falls from 6.8 in the first half-century to 3.2 in the second (highly significant); inside the first half-century, however, there is an increase in frequency after 1610 (significant). As will be seen later, the opposite trends in comedy and tragedy are due to M, which loses intensity and becomes a common courtesy-phrase in comedy, but not in tragedy, for which this usage was probably felt to be insufficiently dignified.

O increases in frequency during the century, but the increase is entirely due to comedy, where the change is from 0.7 to 2.2 (highly significant); the decrease in tragedy, from 0.8 to 0.6, is not significant.

Y remains unchanged in frequency from one half of the century to the other: the observed differences are not significant, either in comedy or in tragedy. However, in Table 6 the figure 8.2 for the decade 1681—1690 is misleading; of the 41 examples in question, no less than 38 are from *The Widow Ranter*; this play is necessarily classed as a tragedy, but in many ways it is an untypical tragedy for its time; for example, it is set in the contemporary period, and most of its characters are English, not the usual unlocalized personages of heroic drama. If this play is excluded, the figure for the decade sinks from 8.2 to 0.75, which is of the same order of magnitude as the figures for the neighbouring decades; the figures for the second half-century then become 6 examples, 0.2 per play, and the difference from the first half-century is highly significant. It is therefore fair to say that in fact Y remains unchanged in comedy, but decreases greatly in tragedy.

The number of unclassified examples increases, from 0.5 to 0.8 per play. This of course is to be expected, since the total number of examples per play increases. In terms of the total number of examples in the material (the number of excerpts, not the number of head-meanings), the U group increases from 2.5% in the first half-century to 2.96% in the second; this increase is not significant.

It will be seen from the tables that, both in comedy and in tragedy, the R/RH/H group is by far the largest, and is so in every decade; in sum it exists in 2321 examples, an average of 11.3 per play; it is more frequent in tragedy than in comedy (13.5 per play against 9.5), the difference being greatest in the first half of the century. The next largest group is MTP, which is less than half the size of the former, with a total of 1089 examples (5.3 per play); in total it is fairly evenly divided between comedy and tragedy, though the ratio varies with time, as has already been seen. The third largest group is Rc/RcC/C, with 736 examples (3.6 per play); in the first half of the century it is about evenly divided between comedy and tragedy, but in the second half it is more frequent in comedy. These three groups provide the bulk of the material, and the remaining head-meanings are relatively infrequent: only O and Y average more than one example per play, and E, S, D, W, and K added together produce only 0.9 examples per play.

More detailed break-downs will be given later, when each group of head-meanings is considered in turn; the object of the present chapter is only to give the broad outlines. However, it will be convenient here to give the figures for R, RH, and H separately; they follow in Tables 7, 8, and 9, which are for All Plays, Comedy, and Tragedy respectively.

The most striking thing in these tables is the increase in the frequency of H; in comedy it rises from 1.4 per play in the first half of the century

TABLE 7. *Frequencies of Head-Meanings R, RH, and H : All Plays.*

Period from to	1591–1600	1601–1610	1611–1620	1621–1630	1631–1640	1591–1640	1661–1670	1671–1680	1681–1690	1691–1700	1661–1700	Grand Total
R .... (a)	103	115	191	178	177	764	97	217	73	46	433	1197
(b)	4.9	3.8	7.4	6.9	7.4	6.0	5.4	6.8	4.3	3.8	5.5	5.8
RH .... (a)	25	33	45	45	46	194	54	87	39	25	205	399
(b)	1.2	1.1	1.7	1.7	1.9	1.5	3.0	2.7	2.3	2.1	2.6	1.9
H .... (a)	21	64	74	42	63	264	126	176	104	55	461	725
(b)	1.0	2.1	2.9	1.6	2.6	2.1	7.0	5.5	6.1	4.6	5.7	3.5

(a) Number of examples.
(b) Number of examples per play.

TABLE 8. *Frequencies of Head-Meanings R, RH, and H : Comedy.*

Period from to	1591 1600	1601 1610	1611 1620	1621 1630	1631 1640	1591 1640	1661 1670	1671 1680	1681 1690	1691 1700	1661 1700	Grand Total
R .... (a)	37	39	48	85	77	286	59	116	41	30	246	532
(b)	3.4	2.4	4.0	5.3	6.4	4.3	5.9	5.8	3.4	3.8	4.9	4.6
RH .... (a)	8	14	14	24	19	79	20	35	21	13	89	168
(b)	0.7	0.9	1.2	1.5	1.6	1.2	2.0	1.8	1.8	1.6	1.8	1.4
H .... (a)	8	18	21	20	28	95	84	111	75	51	321	416
(b)	0.7	1.1	1.8	1.3	2.3	1.4	8.4	5.6	6.3	6.4	6.4	3.6

(a) Number of examples.
(b) Number of examples per play.

TABLE 9. *Frequencies of Head-Meanings R, RH, and H: Tragedy.*

Period from to	1591 1600	1601 1610	1611 1620	1621 1630	1631 1640	1591 1640	1661 1670	1671 1680	1681 1690	1691 1700	1661 1700	Grand Total
R .... (a)	66	76	143	93	100	478	38	101	32	16	187	665
(b)	6.6	5.4	10.2	9.3	8.3	8.0	4.8	8.4	6.4	4.0	6.5	7.5
RH .... (a)	17	19	31	21	27	115	34	52	18	12	116	231
(b)	1.7	1.4	2.2	2.1	2.3	1.9	4.3	4.3	3.6	3.0	4.0	2.6
H .... (a)	13	46	53	22	35	169	42	65	29	4	140	309
(b)	1.3	3.3	3.8	2.2	2.9	2.8	5.3	5.4	5.8	1.0	4.8	3.5

(a) Number of examples.
(b) Number of examples per play.

to 6.4 in the second, and in tragedy from 2.8 to 4.8; these increases are highly significant. In comedy, the rising trend within the first half-century (1591—1610 compared with 1611—1640) is just significant, but the apparent falling trend within the second half-century is not significant. In tragedy, there is no significant trend inside the first half-century; however, if the supplementary material is added in, there emerges a rising trend which is just significant (see Appendix E); the fall in the last decade of the century is significant, and is also confirmed by the supplementary material.

The changes in the frequency of R are much slighter. In comedy there is a rise from 4.3 per play in the first half-century to 4.9 in the second, but this is only possibly significant; however, the increase within the first half-century (1591—1610 compared with 1611—1640) is fully significant, and so is the fall within the second half-century (1661—1680 compared with 1681—1700). In comedy, therefore, the frequency of R increases up to the middle of the century, and then falls back again somewhat. In tragedy, on the other hand, there is a slight fall in frequency from the first half of the century to the second (8.0 to 6.5), and this is just significant; inside the first half-century, however, there is a marked rise in frequency, from 5.9 per play for 1591—1610 to 9.3 for 1611—1640, and this is significant; within the second half-century, however, the apparent fall in the last two decades is not significant.

As might be expected from the marked increase in H and the relative stationariness of R, there is also a clear increase in RH from one half of the century to the other: it goes up from 1.2 to 1.8 per play in comedy, and from 1.9 to 4.0 in tragedy; both these changes are significant.

It will be seen that, in sum, there are as many examples of R as of RH and H put together. However, the pattern is extremely different in the two halves of the century: in the first half of the century, R outnumbers H by nearly three to one (in the first decade by nearly five to one), but in the second half-century there are actually more examples of H than of R. The change in the ratio between R and H occurs both in comedy and in tragedy, but more markedly in the former. RH increases from about a quarter of R to nearly a half, but in this case the change is greater in tragedy than in comedy.

The great increase in the frequency of H during the century is interesting; H was a relatively new meaning of *honour* at the end of the sixteenth century (the earliest example in the N. E. D. is from 1548), and in the seventeenth century we are obviously witnessing the period of its rapid spread. Why, however, did this spread take place, and on such a remarkable scale?[1] In the actual mechanics of the rise of the new meaning, it is to be presumed that the equivocal RH played an important part, the change being of the type that Stern calls "permuta-

---

[1] The change in the *ratio* between R and H cannot, of course, be explained by a change in the social classes depicted in the drama, on the lines discussed in pp. 90—91 above.

tion";[1]) however, the inception of a new meaning and its spread are by no means the same thing,[2]) and the meaning H would hardly have become so common unless a special need had been felt for it. Such a need arose, I suggest, from the development by the gentry (or part of them) of an ethos different from that of the rest of society, and especially from that of the puritans. It has been pointed out by Kelso[3]) that in the sixteenth century a special code of conduct arose which assumed an essential difference in standards between the man of birth and the plebeian; the key to this moral code, she says, was the idea of honour. She suggests that the gentry felt this need of a distinctive code of their own because other distinguishing marks between the classes (dress, ways of living, wealth, armorial bearings, even occupation) were beginning to fail, with the increasing wealth and importance of other classes; and she also quotes a number of authors to show the beginnings of a tendency for *honour* to mean an inner conscience rather than an external reward (i. e. to have the meaning H). In the seventeenth century, I suggest, this trend is accelerated by the growing hostility between court and city, and the increasing tendency of the gentry (at least the courtly gentry who patronised the theatre) to repudiate anything savouring of middle-class morality; this is seen in an extreme form in the Restoration period, when the town aristocracy openly reject traditional morality and exalt libertinism as a way of life.[4]) In this situation they obviously need a word to denote their ideal of character and their code of conduct; traditional ones like *virtue* are repugnant to them, as they refer to bourgeois qualities, so it is very natural for *honour*, with its specifically upper-class associations, to be used more and more, and especially to be used in the sense H, where it can replace the middle-

---

[1]) *Op. cit.*, pp. 168, 351—79. Alternatively, the new meaning may have been due to the influence of the adjective *honourable*, for which the *N. E. D.* records the sense "worthy of being honoured (of persons)" from 1340.

[2]) See S. Ullmann, *Principles of Semantics*, pp. 186—7; G. Matoré, *La méthode en lexicologie*, pp. 43—4.

[3]) *Op. cit.*, pp. 96—9.

[4]) See Beljame, *op. cit.*, pp. 1—9. Ustick, *op. cit.* pp. 154—63, points out that many late 17th century conduct-books urge that gentlemanly ideals are not inconsistent with Christian piety. Such books can hardly have emanated from the smart town-set that patronised the theatre; in part, as Ustick himself suggests, they must have been an attempt to "combat observed tendencies in contemporary life" (p. 160).

class *virtue*. The heroes of Restoration comedy exalt honour, and claim to be men of honour, but often refer to virtue with contempt.

This view of the reasons for the spread of the meaning H is supported by the changes in the content of the word *honour* during the century; in my material, as I shall show later, the ideal of conduct referred to by R, RH, and H becomes increasingly remote from traditional Christian morality, and places increasing emphasis on such things as the revenging of insult, both in comedy and in tragedy.

In view of the importance which the Restoration aristocracy attached to appearances and their preservation, it may be thought a little strange that, while H increases in frequency, R remains virtually stationary. However, RH increases, and if we add R and RH together there is a net increase during the century both in comedy and in tragedy.[1] Moreover, H often refers to a code in which appearances are of great importance: when a Restoration hero is impelled to do something by his H, his inner conscience, the H is often a concern about R, or at any rate includes it. However, as will be seen later, the development of the Rc/RcC/C group is different from that of the R/RH/H group, for the ratio of Rc to C increases in comedy but decreases in tragedy. I do not think that this is incompatible with my explanation of the spread of H, and I shall try to explain it in Chapter 11.

---

[1] The fact that I treat RH and RcC as independent head-meanings does to some extent mask the size of the changes in the head-meanings R, H, Rc, and C. For example, if I had treated RH in the way in which I treat other joint head-meanings (i. e. classified the examples both under R and under H), then R would have increased in frequency during the century both in comedy and in tragedy, and the increase in frequency of H would have appeared even more startling than it does in the present tables (at any rate in tragedy). The method I have adopted is however more convenient for statistical analysis.

CHAPTER 4

The Possessors of Honour

A. General

In my material, honour is most often spoken of as something possessed by a person, or persons; indeed, it is often spoken of as if it were a kind of chattel, like the owner's other wordly goods.[1]) In the case of M, the owner is also a receiver, since honour is here usually considered as something conferred. O and Y conform to the pattern, since they are normally preceded by a possessive adjective. The main exceptions are the minor meanings, E, K, L, and W, which are not usually considered as possessed. In the important groups of head-meanings, the vast majority of examples involve the possession of honour, and nearly always by a person. For example, in the R/RH/H group, less than 7% of the examples fail to specify a possessor; these are the cases where honour is spoken about in a general way, as when the king in *Pericles* says "who hates honour, hates the Gods aboue" (II.3.22). In another 2% of the cases, the possessor is not a person, but, for example, a country, an army, a cause;[2]) thus a character in *Henry VI.2* speaks of the "Honor of this Warlike Isle" (I.1.124), i. e. England. This leaves about 91% of the examples owned by people. In some of these cases, a whole class of persons is specified, e. g. "wives", "soldiers", "the deserving man", or even simply "men", "women"; in other cases, there is an individual owner, but we have little or no information about him; these two types together account for about 8% of the examples. We are therefore left with about 83% of the R/RH/H group where the owner is a specific person (or small group of persons) about whom

---

[1]) There is a chapter with the same title as this one in F. R. Bryson, *The Point of Honor in Sixteenth-Century Italy*. Bryson says that, in 16th century Italy, honour could be possessed by noblemen, soldiers, and simple gentlemen (p. 15); in theory, women were incapable of honour (p. 24), and so were Jews (p. 26).

[2]) But, here and later, I reckon a family as a person for this purpose.

we have some knowledge (e. g. of character, social rank). It is on this 83% that the analysis later in this chapter is based, and similarly for the Rc/RcC/C group.

It is noticeable in my material that, when honour is owned by a person about whom we know anything, the owner is often of very high social rank, and nearly always a member of the gentry. This agrees with Kelso's contention that the idea of honour came to be connected in sixteenth-century England with a specifically gentlemanly code of conduct.[1] My material indicates that, throughout the seventeenth century, honour was considered a prerogative of the gentry, i. e. of a small minority of the population.[2] This was not necessarily true in other European countries: in Spain, according to E. M. Wilson, honour (*opinión*) belonged to all men: if a man's wife was unchaste, he lost honour, whether he was a king or a peasant.[3]

The monopoly of the gentry in the possession of honour in the drama cannot be explained by saying that non-gentle characters are absent; there are in fact many non-gentle characters, in both halves of the century, and they sometimes appear in situations where, if they were possessors of honour, their honour would be involved; and in these situations, moreover, words like "reputation" and "fame" are sometimes used of them. I have already referred to Ford in *Merry Wives*, and to the middle-class and low-life comedies of Middleton; a few examples will now be given from other authors, cases being chosen where R/RH/H would be involved. In Behn's *The Roundheads* there is a hypocritical Lay Elder, Ananias Goggle, who attempts to seduce Lady Desbro, a member of the Roundhead aristocracy; she expresses surprise:

---

[1] *Op. cit.*, pp. 96—9. I follow Kelso in using the word "gentry" in its wide sense, i. e. including the nobility and royalty; some writers restrict it to what I call "the ordinary gentry", i. e. those of lower rank than the nobility.

[2] Harbage suggests 5—10% for Shakespeare's day (*Shakespeare's Audience*, pp. 54—5), but this seems an over-estimate; figures given for 1688 by G. N. Clark suggest that at that time the gentry formed less than 3% of the population (*The Later Stuarts*, p. 25), and figures for 1600 quoted by R. H. Tawney would give an even lower percentage ("The Rise of the Gentry", in *Econ. Hist. Rev.* XI, p. 3).

[3] "Family Honour", p. 19. But a different view is expressed by A. Castro, "Algunas observaciones acerca del concepto del honor en los siglos XVI y XVII", pp. 19—22.

> L. Des. How, this from you, the Head o' th' Church Militant, the very Pope of Presbytery?
> Ana. Verily, the Sin lieth in the Scandal; therefore most of the discreet pious Ladies of the Age chuse us, upright Men, who make a Conscience of a Secret, the Laity being more regardless of their Fame.
> (III.2, p. 385)

She rejects his advances, and threatens to expose him, whereupon he says:

> Ah, Madam! Do not ruin my Reputation; there are Ladies of high Degree in the Commonwealth, to whom we find our selves most comforting; why might not you be one?
> (*Ibid.*)

He does not use the word *honour* either of himself or of her, although *scandal, conscience, fame,* and *reputation* all occur. To a gentleman, it was a point of honour to protect the reputation of a woman that he seduced, as many examples show, but to Ananias it is a point of conscience. Another example of a puritan who will have no truck with honour is Hackwell Senior, the old anabaptist colonel in Shadwell's *The Volunteers*; he only uses the word once — in order to condemn it; Welford is trying to reconcile him to his son, Hackwell Junior, who (Welford urges) has as much virtue and honour as any gentleman living; Hackwell Senior replies:

> Vertue and Honour will bring him but to hell.
> (I.2, p. 175)

Virtue, obviously, is also condemned because Hackwell Senior believes in salvation by grace alone. Hackwell Junior is always represented as a gentleman (and attaches great importance to honour), but there is more than a suspicion that Hackwell Senior (with his rather sharp commercial dealings) is not a gentleman; there are other examples in Restoration comedy of the younger generation being treated as gentry, while the older generation are not, for example in Behn's *Sir Patient Fancy*.[1]

---

[1] In the Restoration period, gentry was perhaps becoming less a matter of birth, and more a matter of breeding. Indeed, Restoration self-consciousness about etiquette may have been due in part to the continued assimilation of recruits from the *bourgeoisie* into the aristocracy: see G. N. Clark, *The Seventeenth Century*, p. 330.

An example of a city type who is not a puritan is Vizard in Farquhar's *The Constant Couple*; honour is not attributed to him, but in one place he expresses great concern about his "reputation". In Dryden's *Amboyna*, which deals with "the cruelty of the Dutch" to English *merchants*, there is very little reference to honour; Beaumont and Collins, who are merchants, never claim honour or have it attributed to them; Towerson does, but he is a "captain", and is represented as the head of the English community. In Shadwell's *Woman Captain*, one of the leading characters is Gripe, a usurer, who is plainly not a gentleman; he never claims honour or has it attributed to him. His wife, on the other hand, seems to be a gentlewoman, for she has a brother who is an army captain, and certainly a gentleman. When the captain[1]) visits Gripe and threatens him with instant death for maltreating Mrs Gripe, Gripe swears that it is not true, and continues:

> Besides, upon the words of a dying man, your Sister run away from me. I lockt her up indeed to save the Honour of your Family; for she is a most salacious Woman — (IV.1, p. 58)

It is amusing and significant that Gripe says *"your* Family"; a gentleman would have kept his wife chaste in order to protect the honour (R) of his own family, but Gripe, not being a gentleman, says that he has been protecting the honour of his wife's family. In Congreve's *Old Bachelor*, Fondlewife the banker never has honour attributed to him, although he is frequently in situations where a gentleman's honour would be concerned (he is cuckolded, for example). Shylock, similarly, never mentions his daughter's honour or his own when Jessica elopes. There are also passages where, implicitly or explicitly, the honour of a gentleman is compared or contrasted with the fame or reputation of a plebeian. In Etherege's *She Would if She Could*, the two young gallants, Courtall and Freeman, are detected breaking their words by two young ladies, and try to laugh it off:

> *Court.* Why should you be so unreasonable, Ladies, to expect that from us, we should scarce have hop'd for from you? fy, fy, the keeping of ones word is a thing below the honour of a Gentleman.
>
> *Free.* A poor shift! fit only to uphold the reputation of a paultry Citizen. (II.2.207—12)

---

[1]) Actually Mrs Gripe in disguise, but we have to see it through Gripe's eyes.

Here the contrast between a gentleman's honour and a citizen's reputation is explicit and striking. In Farquhar's *The Constant Couple*, there is a colonel, Standard, whose regiment has been disbanded, and who is therefore without money or prospects; his mistress's chambermaid, Parly, refuses to carry letters for him if he can no longer pay her; he urges her not to be mercenary, but to take example by her lady and "be honourable", whereupon she replies:

> A lack a day, sir! it shows as ridiculous and haughty for us to imitate our betters in their honour as in their finery; leave honour to nobility that can support it; we poor folks, Colonel, have no pretence to't; and truly, I think, sir, that your honour should be cashiered with your leading-staff.
> (I.2, p. 146)

Honour is a matter for the upper classes; ordinary people have no pretence to it, and can't afford such a luxury, and if the colonel has come down in the world he too should give it up.

When lower-class people are shown posing as noblemen, they are usually made to lay claim to honour (claiming TP involves claiming R and H), but are depicted as in fact lacking H, especially where war and duelling are concerned, and this is considered a huge joke. This theme is found, for example, in three Restoration plays where an imposture of this kind plays a large part (*The Man's the Master*, *Bury Fair*, and *The False Count*), and is probably more popular with dramatists in the second half of the century than in the first. The same kind of thing in a milder form is seen in the bullies, swaggerers, false-captains, etc., who bluster their way through the drama from one end of the century to the other; they too lay claim to gentry and to honour (R and H), and here too the joke lies in the discrepancy between claims and practice. Parvenus are somewhat the same; they may make ridiculous attempts to ape the gentry, or they may show their ignorance by claiming gentry while rejecting the claims of R and H; both types can be seen combined in one character, Cacafogo in Fletcher's *Rule a Wife*; at the beginning of the play he is a ridiculous fire-eater, finding quarrel in less than a straw in the name of honour (I. 1, p. 178), but later in the play he becomes the rich heir who thinks that money is more important than honour (R), and refuses to go to war (III.1, p. 199). Another parvenu shown as notably lacking in honour (H) is Francisco in Behn's *False Count*, but he on the other hand seems to lay no claim to R or H; the only time the word *honour* is applied to him is when somebody denies that he possesses it (H). Among the parvenus are probably to be reckoned many of the knights represented in the plays, especially the grasping and extortionate knights like Sir Giles Overreach in Massinger's *New Way to Pay Old Debts*.

On the other hand, men of noble birth, even if educated obscurely and kept in ignorance of their true origins, are often represented as possessing by nature the qualities that constitute H and that bring R. There is an example in *Cymbeline*; Guiderius and Arviragus, the sons of Cymbeline, have been brought up in the woods by Belarius, and kept in ignorance of their high birth, but they show the high spirit, sensitivity to insult, insistence on their rights, lack of fear, willingness to fight and take revenge, etc., which characterize the man of R and H. Belarius soliloquizes on this:

>'Tis wonder
>That an inuisible instinct should frame them
>To Royalty vnlearn'd, Honor vntaught,
>Ciuility not seene from other:
>
>(IV.2.176—9)

This is a common theme throughout the century, especially perhaps in tragi-comedy, where the lost-child *motif* is popular.

These examples have related to the R/RH/H group, but a similar association with the gentry is found in other groups. This is even true of M, which one might have expected to be conferrable on anybody, whatever their social rank; it is true that there are quite a few cases where M is conferred on non-gentry (citizens, servants, etc.), especially when M loses intensity and becomes part of a mere courtesy-phrase, but these cases form a relatively small fraction of the examples of M (about 6%). P and T, of course, can also be acquired by non-gentry; a man of low birth can be elevated by the king (like Wolsey in *Henry VIII*) or rise through the help of a powerful patron (like Depazzi in *The Traitor*), a woman of low birth can acquire TP by marriage (like Flavia in *The Fancies*), and the word *honour* can be used of the TP thus gained (as it is in the three cases referred to). It is therefore not uncommon in the drama for non-gentry (especially citizens and their daughters, perhaps) to aspire after honour in this sense; in doing so, however, they are in fact aspiring to the status of gentlefolk; no doubt the first-generation nobleman of humble origins will be sneered at by the older gentry as a parvenu: the king, they will say, can confer high rank, but the king cannot make a gentleman;[1]) even so, the family will ultimately be accepted as gentle, for coming of ancient family is only a matter of time. In the plays, therefore, we do find non-gentle characters aspiring after, and sometimes acquiring, T and P; but, as in the case of M, these form a relatively small fraction of the cases.

The closest connection between honour and gentry is found in the groups relating to conduct (R/RH/H and Rc/RcC/C), and, since these are the groups of the greatest interest for my purposes, I shall consider them in a little more detail.

B. Possessors of Honour, R/RH/H Group

In my material, the possessors of honour (R/RH/H) can be either men or women, but are most often men. Women account for about 11% of the examples, and are found more in the H group (about 14%) than in R (about 10%) or in RH (about 8%). This sex difference is no doubt due in part to the fact that men occupy a larger place in the plays than women, but in part to the fact that there is another group (Rc/RcC/C) which applies exclusively to women. There is in fact a double standard of conduct: for women, chastity is of the highest importance; for men, military qualities, sensitivity to insult, insistence on one's rights, etc.; there are other qualities that are prized in both sexes — truthfulness, loyalty to one's rulers, keeping promises, etc. — and it is mainly this area of overlap that gives women a place in the R/RH/H group. The percentage of women is lower in the second half of the century than in the first (about 9.5% against about 12.7%), and this difference is just significant statistically; the change is mostly due to R and RH, while H remains substantially unaltered; in R the decline is from 12.5% to 7% (significant), in RH from 9.5% to 6.1% (not significant), and in H from 14.9% to 13.3% (not significant). This decline in the percentage of women-owners is probably related to the increase in frequency of the Rc/RcC/C group (from 2.7 to 5.0 examples per play) already noted. It rather looks as though the men's and women's codes got farther apart: women's honour tended to relate more exclusively to chastity, and less emphasis was placed on the elements of the code that they had in common with men. As will be seen later,

---

[1]) See Kelso, *op. cit.*, pp. 19—20.

the increase in the Rc/RcC/C group is greatest for Rc and RcC, and least for C, and this fits well with the decline in women's R, RH, and H.

The possessors of honour (R/RH/H) are shown according to social rank in Tables 10, 11, and 12, which are for All Plays, Comedy, and Tragedy respectively. The figures refer to number of examples, not to number of characters: a character to whom R/RH/H is attributed ten times will be reckoned ten times in the tables. The gentry are subdivided into royal, noble, and other;[1]) lesser nobility (knights and baronets) are counted as Other Gentry; cardinals, archbishops, and bishops as nobility; unless there are specific indications to the contrary, generals are also reckoned among the nobility. In plays dealing with the ancient world, characters of senatorial rank are reckoned as nobility, since the dramatists normally treat them as such. Men and women are not shown separately, as there are no marked differences between them. Impostors are reckoned as belonging to the class to which they pretend. The tables do not show the examples without owners, nor those with non-human owners, nor those with human owners about whom nothing is known; these categories account for about 17% of the examples. The tables also omit a score of examples where a good deal is known about the possessors, but where it is doubtful whether or not they are to be reckoned as gentry; these borderline cases will be discussed later. The figures cannot of course be taken as absolute, since it is not always possible to be quite certain about a character's status; it is quite possible that the number of nobility ought to be increased at the expense of other gentry: especially in tragedy, there are plays which operate at such an exalted social level that mere lords are two a penny, and the dramatist does not always bother to specify whether his courtiers are noblemen or simply ordinary gentlemen; this is occasionally true even of quite important characters.

The tables show clearly the tendency for the possessor of R/RH/H to be of high social rank: a third of the owners belong to the nobility, and nearly a fifth are of royal or imperial rank. As could be expected, this tendency is strongest in tragedy, which moves in higher social spheres than comedy: in tragedy there are actually more examples of royal owners than of ordinary gentry, and the royal and noble characters

---

[1]) Noble persons are taken to include the wives and children of noblemen, but not other relatives, and similarly with royal persons. Emperors are reckoned as royal.

TABLE 10. *Social Rank of Possessors of R/RH/H : All Plays.*

Period from to	1591 1600	1601 1610	1611 1620	1621 1630	1631 1640	1591 1640	1661 1670	1671 1680	1681 1690	1691 1700	1661 1700	Grand Total
Royal	21	38	43	29	59	190	41	87	13	19	160	350
Noble	77	73	86	93	70	399	93	97	55	6	251	650
Other Gentry ..	28	53	108	65	93	347	97	215	121	85	518	865
Total Gentry ...	126	164	237	187	222	936	231	399	189	110	929	1865
Non-Gentry	4	5	3	7	6	25	10	11	4	1	26	51

TABLE 11. *Social Rank of Possessors of R/RH/H : Comedy.*

Period from to	1591 1600	1601 1610	1611 1620	1621 1630	1631 1640	1591 1640	1661 1670	1671 1680	1681 1690	1691 1700	1661 1700	Grand Total
Royal	3	2	3	4	11	23	0	11	0	0	11	34
Noble	21	16	5	46	28	116	48	31	29	5	113	229
Other Gentry ..	16	26	59	43	55	199	88	176	90	78	432	631
Total Gentry ...	40	44	67	93	94	338	136	218	119	83	556	894
Non-Gentry	3	5	2	5	4	19	10	6	4	1	21	40

TABLE 12. *Social Rank of Possessors of R/RH/H : Tragedy.*

Period from to	1591 1600	1601 1610	1611 1620	1621 1630	1631 1640	1591 1640	1661 1670	1671 1680	1681 1690	1691 1700	1661 1700	Grand Total
Royal	18	36	40	25	48	167	41	76	13	19	149	316
Noble	56	57	81	47	42	283	45	66	26	1	138	421
Other Gentry ..	12	27	49	22	38	148	9	39	31	7	86	234
Total Gentry ...	86	120	170	94	128	598	95	181	70	27	373	971
Non-Gentry	1	0	1	2	2	6	0	5	0	0	5	11

together account for 75% of all owners. In comedy, on the other hand, 70% of the gentry are ordinary gentry, and less than 4% are royal. During the century, there are changes in the ratios of the different types of gentry, and these are in opposite senses in comedy and tragedy: in comedy there is a shift towards the bottom of the scale, in tragedy a shift towards the top. Thus in tragedy, the proportion of ordinary gentry falls slightly (25% in the first half-century to 23% in the second), while the proportion of royal personages rises greatly (28 % to 40%), gaining at the expense of the nobility. In comedy, the proportion of ordinary gentry rises from 59% to 78%, and the other two groups both fall (royal steeply, from nearly 7% to 2%). This is no doubt a result of the tendency for tragedy to move in ever more exalted spheres (the heroes and heroines of Restoration tragedy are usually of royal birth), while comedy tends increasingly to be naturalistic, reflecting the life of the gentry in contemporary London. The change in comedy may also reflect a real change in society, a tendency for the ordinary gentry to insist more strongly on their right to possess honour, and not to regard it mainly as a prerogative of the nobility; but of this it is difficult to be certain.[1])

Perhaps the most important thing in the tables, however, is the ratio of gentry to non-gentry: less than 2.7% of the examples are owned by non-gentle characters (4.3% in comedy and 1.1% in tragedy). The reason for the larger number in comedy is that the majority of these non-gentle cases are comic or satirical, and I am not in fact convinced that there is in my material a single serious case of R/RH/H applied to a non-gentle character with the approval of the dramatist, except possibly in the sense of "professional reputation". Since this is important for the question of honour as a specifically upper-class prerogative, it seems worth giving details of quite a few of the 51 non-gentle examples.

Quite a lot of the non-gentle examples can be classified as cases of pretentiousness: characters are implicitly claiming the status of gentry, to which they are not entitled. One example of this is Pistol (*Henry V* V.1.88, *Merry Wives* II.2.20, 28), who in fact claims to be "as good a gentleman as the emperor" (*Henry V* IV.1.39). Possibly the same is true of Volpone as mountebank (*Volpone* II.2.170), but this may alternatively be an example of professional reputation (reputation as a doctor) and not meant to sound pretentious. Another example is Cacafogo (*Rule a Wife* pp. 178, 199), a usurer's son, who seems intended as a pretender to gentry, a comic parvenu. Less certain is the landlady in *The Chances* (p. 210, three examples); she is perhaps

---

[1]) If this is so, it may reflect the fact that, during the century, the ordinary gentry increased in wealth and power compared with the nobility: see p. 124, note 1.

intended to sound pretentious, but it is possible that she is a gentlewoman, despite the fact that she lets lodgings. A clear case is provided, however, by the followers of Warbeck (*Perkin Warbeck* 1156): they are citizens (mercer, tailor, scrivener, etc.), but here they are obviously playing up to their parts as courtiers, followers of the would-be king. Obvious, too, is the case of Haircut the barber (*Lady of Pleasure* p. 35): he is passing himself off as somebody important at court, on the strength of his function as court barber. The comic parvenu appears again in Fulgoso (*Lady's Trial* 753), an "upstart gallant", who says he can dispense with honour if necessary. In the second half of the century, an example is provided by "Duke Trincalo" (*Tempest* pp. 166—7): the seaman is acting his part as self-appointed ruler of the island.

Such cases of pretentiousness shade off into sheer imposture, and some of my 51 examples might well have been considered as cases of imposture (and therefore not classified as non-gentry). For example, there is Jack Cade (*Henry VI.2* IV.8.63): since he is claiming to be heir to the throne, it seems likely that he is here acting his part. Jeremy, similarly, is acting the part of Face the captain (*Alchemist* I.2.71), and this too could be classed as an imposture. Another false captain is Pandolfo the tapster (*Imposture* p. 250), who is simply playing a practical joke.

Occasionally, honour is probably attributed to a character out of flattery, although the speaker is perfectly aware that the character is not entitled to it. Examples of this are probably seen in Minos the apothecary (*Poetaster* III.4.78) and in Hoard the usurer (*A Trick to Catch the Old One* IV.4.126); in both cases, it should be noticed, the character is being persuaded to part with money.

In a large group of cases the usage is obviously either jocular or ironical. Obviously jocular, for example, are the following attributions of honour: Mistress Purge, a citizen's wife and whore (*Family of Love* III.6.3); the porter's man (*Henry VIII* V.3.59); Geta the clown (*The Prophetess* p. 326) (later examples from the same character are after he has become an aedile, and is acting his new social part); Calandrino, "a merry fellow, servant to Giovanni" (*Great Duke of Florence* p. 214) (he is a comic figure, and it is here part of the joke that, since coming to court, he should claim to have honour to swear by); the barber (*Fancies* 2376) (or possibly professional reputation); Laura the waitingwoman (*Man's the Master* p. 102); a waiter (*Gentleman Dancing-Master*

p. 147) (the joke resides in the fact that a waiter should have the scruples of conscience appropriate only to a gentleman); and Alderman Smuggler (*Constant Couple* p. 161). Clear examples of the ironical attribution of honour where it is known not to be due are provided by Mrs Striker and Mrs Friske, citizens' wives and whores (*Humorists* p. 200), and by Bettris the waiting-woman, where there is also a pun on "maid of honour" (*Man's the Master* p. 25).

In the second half of the century, there are several attributions of honour to servants, who mimic their masters' speech and manners. Some of them are witty, others comically pretentious, but in neither case, obviously, is the claim to honour taken seriously by the audience. The witty ingenious servant is seen in Warner (*Sir Martin Mar-all* p. 55) and in Maskall (*Evening's Love* pp. 283, 338, 341). The comically pretentious variant is seen in Benito (*Assignation* pp. 398, 418, 455) and in Jacomo (*Libertine* pp. 26, 36, 85). Jodelet also belongs to the latter class, but here imposture too is involved: he gladly resigns from his rôle of gentleman, which involves so much dangerous fighting, and makes a bawdy pun on *honour* as he goes (*Man's the Master* p. 102). The claims of these servants to possess honour (which no doubt had their counterparts in real life) are obviously to be taken as either jocular or pretentious, either intentionally or unintentionally amusing, an aping of their masters the gentry.

In the Restoration period, too, there are examples of kept mistresses laying claim to honour; for example Tricksy (*Kind Keeper* p. 118) and Phillis (*Woman Captain* p. 74, first of the two examples). These may also be pretentious: whores, it seems from the plays, tended to give themselves the airs of fine ladies. It is possible, however, that these characters really are gentlewomen, especially as their keepers eventually agree to marry them.

Practically all my examples of non-gentle possessors of honour fall into one or more of these types. Indeed, only one of the 51 examples seems to be entirely serious and unironical: this is Jolenta, in *The Devil's Law Case* (I.1.227). Jolenta is the sister of Romelio, who explicitly calls himself a citizen; but she is engaged to be married to a nobleman, and the word *honour* is in fact applied to the pair of them simultaneously ("our honors"). Moreover, Romelio is not a simple citizen, but a rich merchant, and is often treated as though he were a gentleman: for example, it is arranged that he shall fight a judicial combat. It seems probable, therefore, that the dramatist thought of Jolenta as a gentlewoman. Indeed, the evidence for the exclusive right of the gentry to R/RH/H is so strong that it seems justifiable to reverse the argument, and to assert that people to whom honour (R/RH/H) is seriously attributed with the approval of the dramatist are to be considered as gentry. This criterion of gentry can be applied to the score of borderline cases that I omitted from the tables, and these may then provide evidence about the way the dramatists drew the frontier between gentle and non-gentle in different parts of the century. These borderline cases are mainly professional men: lawyers, surgeons, merchants, etc. In the first half of the century there are 16 examples, involving 12 different characters. Three examples, however, and possibly a fourth, can be discounted as not wholly serious: two concern La Writt, a lawyer (*The Little French Lawyer* pp. 395 and 449); La Writt behaves like a gentleman, fights duels, etc., but the whole joke is that a mere lawyer should set up as a gentleman and a fighting-man, and at the end of the play he is taught a lesson and resumes the customs of his own social station; a third concerns a usurer, Hornet (*The Constant Maid* p. 488), but is part of a practical joke, in which Hornet is made to believe that he has been knighted, and is being treated as a great man; the possible fourth example is in *The Platonic Lovers* (p. 24), and refers to scholars, especially to Buonateste, a physician and philosopher, who has refused money for his services; the speaker seems slightly amused that Buonateste should stand on his honour in this way, so perhaps the example is to be considered not entirely serious. There are a further three cases, involving three characters, where the honour involved is reputation for ability in one's profession; since this does not relate directly to the code of conduct, it may possibly have been used of professional men without implying that they were gentlemen; one of the examples is a physician, Alibius (*The Changeling* I.2.114); the second concerns a couple of surgeons (*A Very Woman* p. 445); and the third is Charles the wrestler (*A. Y. L. I.* I.1.132), who is presumably a professional, and whom one would not expect to be a gentleman. This leaves us with nine serious cases, involving six different characters; three of the characters are merchants, Antipholus (*Comedy of Errors* V.1.30) (who certainly behaves and talks like a gentleman), Antonio (*Merchant of Venice* III.2.294) (who is a friend of the young nobleman Bassanio, and who is referred to by Lorenzo as a gentleman, III.4.6), and Corvino (*Volpone* II.6.72, III.7.38 two examples) (who may reject the demands of honour, but obviously ought not to); one is a sea captain, Antonio (*12th Night* V.1.47), who is perhaps also a merchant; one is a citizen's son, Giovanni ('*Tis Pity* 2402), who always talks and behaves like a gentleman; and one is a physician, Eudemus (*Sejanus* I.1.325, 326). In these nine cases at least we should presume that the character is being regarded by the dramatist as a gentleman. In the second half of the century there are only six examples, involving five characters. One of these, involving a city knight, occurs in a highly farcical passage, and is probably not to be taken too seriously (*Sir Patient Fancy* p. 83). One refers to a lawyer, but is in effect a denial that lawyers have honour (*The Plain Dealer* p. 384); somewhat similar is the case of Hackwell Senior, the anabaptist colonel (*The Volunteers* p. 175), for he himself rejects the demands of honour, and so may not regard himself as a gentleman; however, Welford seems to treat him as one, so he is a doubtful case. Two of the examples refer to an Inns of Court man, Young Maggot (*True Widow* pp. 316, 350); he mixes in society and behaves like a gentleman, but is probably to be classed as a pretender to gentry, as his relations with his father show. The final example concerns a rich merchant, Antonio (*The False Count* p. 105), and is perfectly serious. In the second half of the century, therefore, we have only two examples (Antonio and Hackwell) where honour is unironically attributed to people of the trading and professional classes near the social boundary between gentry and non-gentry (and even one of these is a bit doubtful). In the first half-century, therefore, there are nine such examples out of 1222 (about 0.74%), while in the second half-century there are two examples out of 1099 (about 0.18%). This difference is possibly significant, and it looks as though dramatists became increasingly reluctant to attribute honour (and therefore gentry) to people who worked for their living, and in particular to merchants.

Moreover, in the earlier period there are explicit references to trade as a source of honour, but I have found no such references in the drama of the later period. In *Eastward Ho* occur the following lines, spoken by the "good apprentice" Goulding, and obviously to be approved of by the audience:

From trades, from artes, from valor honor springs,
These three are founts of gentry, yea of Kings.
(I.1.150—1)

Arts and arms were recognized sources of honour (R, MTP), but here trade is added, and is explicitly said to be a source of gentry. It is also worth comparing the apprentices in *Eastward Ho* with a gentleman-apprentice in a post-Restoration play, George Marteen in Behn's *Younger Brother*; Marteen is the hero of the play, and is held up for admiration, but his attitudes and his behaviour closely resemble those of Quicksilver, the "bad apprentice" of *Eastward Ho*, who is held up for condemnation; they both despise trade and the kind of work they have to do, pride themselves inordinately on their gentle blood, and take every opportunity to escape to the other end of the town (where both have caches of fine clothes) in order to swagger it as gentlemen; Goulding, the good apprentice of *Eastward Ho*, is also of gentle birth, but he has the bourgeois virtues, and works his way up in his trade by hard work and ability (and of course marries his master's daughter). Another example is found in *The Devil's Law Case*; Romelio, the rich merchant, urges Contarino not to lie idle:

> Vertue is ever sowing of her seedes:
> In the Trenches for the Souldier; in the wakefull study
> For the Scholler; in the furrowes of the sea
> For men of our Profession — of all which
> Arise and spring up Honor.
(I.1.73—7)

Here we have Arts, Arms, and Commerce as the sources of honour. Romelio calls himself a citizen, but he seems to be treated as a gentleman, and, as we have seen, his sister Jolenta marries a nobleman. The authors of these plays were not specially catering for middle-class taste;[1] if anything, they tended to write for the more scholarly part of the audience, which would be mainly gentle. If the citizen-plays of Heywood and Dekker had been included in the material, examples of this kind would probably have been even more numerous.

---

[1] Wright admittedly points to *Eastward Ho* as one of the best dramatic expressions of bourgeois ideals, but he himself goes on to emphasize the fact that it did not set out to be so, but was rather intended as an answer to the perverted ethics of *Westward Ho* (*op. cit.*, pp. 630—1). It was written, it should be noted, for the private theatre.

It looks as though we have here another symptom of the cleavage that grew up in the seventeenth century between court and city. Even in the sixteenth century there was dispute as to whether trade was a suitable occupation for a gentleman, and even medicine was not absolutely above suspicion: ideally, the gentleman should not put his talents out to hire.[1]) In the Restoration period, the doubt seems to have become almost a certainty, at least for the theatre-going classes; in my Restoration material, Antonio in *The False Count* is the only member of the commercial classes to whom honour (R/RH/H) is seriously attributed; the attitude the audience was expected to have to commerce is probably seen in George Marteen. But the qualification *for the theatre-going classes* must be clearly remembered: the age of Dryden was also the age of Milton, of Bunyan, of Locke, of Newton, of the Royal Society, and the attitudes of the theatre were never more than those of a small social group, powerful and influential though it was.

The same suspicion of commerce may be reflected in the relatively small number of knights who are depicted as possessing honour (R/RH/H); in the R group, for example, there are only 22 in the first half-century (out of 764 examples) and 24 in the second (out of 433 examples). This is not due to any absence of knights from the plays; quite a large number of plays are set in England, especially in the second half of the century, and knights are quite common among the characters, but there are many knights to whom honour is never attributed. This is perhaps due to a tendency for knighthood to be regarded almost as the mark of the parvenu. James I and Charles I are notorious for the way they conferred knighthoods on people to increase their revenues;[2]) and throughout the century it seems to have been common for men who made money, especially in business, to enhance their social prestige by becoming knights. A knight, therefore, was not necessarily felt to be a gentleman, as a passage from *Love in a Wood* illustrates:

> *Lydia.* But if you are for proving your wit, why do not you write a play?

---

[1]) See Kelso, *op. cit.*, pp. 42—69.
[2]) See G. Davies, *The Early Stuarts*, pp. 1, 81, 101.

Dapperwit. Because 'tis now no more reputation to write a play, than it is honour to be a knight. Your true wit despises the title of poet, as much as your true gentleman the title of knight; for as a man may be a knight and no gentleman, so a man may be a poet and no wit, let me perish!

(II.1, p. 40)

Dapperwit is asserting that knighthood is not an S, does not confer R or E; and perhaps also that it is not really an M, since its possessors lack D; and the reason for this is that many knights are not gentlemen. Not all knights are portrayed unsympathetically in the plays, of course, and many of them are obviously gentlemen, but it is rare for a knight to be the hero of a play, and knights are often presented as foolish or affected characters and as parvenus. Aphra Behn, an ardent royalist and Tory, is especially fond of depicting unsympathetic knights, and she makes frequent use of the term "city knight", which to her is an expression of contempt; her city knights (like Sir Cautious and Sir Feeble in *The Lucky Chance* and Sir Timothy in *The City Heiress*) are never shown as possessors of honour (R/RH/H), except in comic examples. On the other hand, the relatives of city knights are often represented as gentlemen and possessors of honour: in *The City Heiress*, for example, Wilding, the nephew of Sir Timothy ("an old seditious knight" of the City, i. e. a Whig) is a Tory and a man of honour. This emphasis on the non-honour-bearing city knight seems to be greater in the second half of the century, but there are similar cases in the first half: Sir John Frugal in *The City Madam*, for example, and Sir Moth Interest in *The Magnetic Lady*. Sir Giles Overreach is a similar type; Lord Lovell sneers at his citizen blood, and Sir Giles desires above all things to marry his daughter into the nobility (the kind of honour he is interested in is TP); Sir Giles, however, is not like Aphra Behn's Aunt Sallies: he has courage and ability, and is prepared to fight if necessary to force Lovell to marry his daughter — but not on account of his honour (R): indeed, he despises reputation, and says so.

Honour is sometimes attributed to groups or classes of persons instead of to individuals; one of the recurrent attributions of this kind is to soldiers and armies, and honour is sometimes referred to as being especially the province of the soldier. In the "seven ages of man" it will be remembered that it is the soldier who is

Ielous in honor, sodaine, and quicke in quarrell,
Seeking the bubble Reputation
Euen in the Canons mouth:

(*A. Y. L. I.*, II.7.151—3)

The soldier seeks military glory, and is also especially sensitive about duelling honour ("quicke in quarrell"), because the slur of cowardice is particularly distasteful to him. The association of the soldier with honour (R/RH/H) occurs all through the century, and may be thought to go against the contention that honour is the prerogative of the gentry. This is not necessarily so, however; if we consider the "seven ages of man" speech, we shall see that it really means "the seven ages of a gentleman": the child has a nurse, the lover writes poetry (obviously a man of education), and the middle-aged man is a justice; and there are many other passages where "the honour of a soldier" similarly means "the honour of a soldier and a gentleman". However, there are doubtful cases, and in particular there are cases where honour (usually military reputation) is possessed by a whole army; an example of this can be seen in *The Loyal Subject*, where Archas makes a farewell speech to his army, and refers to their honour (R) (I.3, p. 88). It is possible, therefore, that soldiers constitute an exception to the rule that honour (R/RH/H) is possessed exclusively by the gentry; it is equally possible, however, that the opposite explanation is true, namely that all soldiers were considered (or at any rate considered themselves) to be gentlemen, whatever their rank. Kelso says that, in the sixteenth century, one of the causes of "nobility dative" was service in the wars; ten years' service in some position of command was usually set as necessary for the assumption of gentility.[1]) In sixteenth-century Italy, according to Bryson, even common soldiers were held by some authorities to rank as gentry.[2]) It may easily be imagined that soldiers themselves accepted the easier of these qualifications, and the plays do rather suggest a tendency by soldiers to pretend to gentry: many of the bullies and swaggerers are soldiers or pretended soldiers, like Pistol. However, the tendency for these bullies to assume the title of captain (a habit referred to contemptuously by Doll Tearsheet, *Henry IV.2* II.4.138—49) suggests that their title to gentry might not be very secure unless they enhanced their status in this way.

[1]) *Op. cit.*, p. 29.
[2]) *Op. cit.*, p. 19.

In summary it can be said that there are no absolutely certain attributions of honour (R/RH/H) to non-gentle individuals, except jocularly, ironically, or in cases of imposture or pretentiousness (of which the audience is intended to disapprove). In the first half of the century, there are a handful of examples of "professional reputation", where the owner is possibly non-gentle. On the other hand, there are a score of cases where other types of R/RH/H (i. e. other than professional reputation) are attributed to members of the commercial and professional classes, and it seems likely that here the owners are to be regarded as gentle; attributions of this kind are much more frequent in the first half of the century than in the second, and this suggests that in the second half of the century the theatre-going public was more reluctant to recognize members of these classes as gentlemen. Honour is also quite often attributed to soldiers in general or to armies, and it is possible that this is a case where honour (at any rate in the sense of "military reputation") is attributable to non-gentle characters; on the other hand, it is possible that even common soldiers claimed the status of gentleman. As the tables show, the overwhelming majority of the individual possessors of R/RH/H are gentlemen, and a large proportion of them are noble or royal personages.

Honour (R) is not only possessed by the gentry, but is also reputation in the eyes of the gentry; characters often combine great concern about their R with an outspoken contempt for public opinion, for reputation in the eyes of the mob. In the following passage from Otway's *Don Carlos*, the hero is addressing his father, who has caused him to lose R by accusing him of adultery with his step-mother:

> When you forgot a Father's Love, and quite
> Depriv'd me of a Sons and Princes right:
> Branded my Honour, and pursu'd my Life,
> My Duty long with Nature was at strife:
> Not that I fear'd my Memory or Name
> Could suffer by the voice of common Fame;
> A thing I still esteem'd beneath my pride;
> For though condemn'd by all the world beside,
> Had you but thought me just, I could have dy'd.
> (IV.1.500—8)

Of course, Don Carlos is saying that his father's opinion of him is more important to him than anybody else's, but all the same he is combining a contempt of "common Fame" with a concern about his honour (R).

This kind of thing is said even about military reputation, where popular acclamation might be expected to play a large part; in the following passage from Dryden's *Spanish Friar*, Torrismond has won a great military victory, and is replying to Prince Bertram, who has congratulated him on the great popular acclamations that have met him on his return:

> You wrong me, if you think I'll sell one drop
> Within these veins for pageants; but, let honour
> Call for my blood, and sluice it into streams:
>
> (I.1, p. 423)

The pageants are the "popular applause" and "noisy praise / Of giddy crowds" to which Torrismond has referred with contempt a few lines earlier; they are no motive for military prowess, but honour (RH) is. The clearest examples of this attitude occur in the Restoration period, which is not surprising, but in fact it is found all through the century, and the point is made quite explicitly by Ashley: he is distinguishing between honour and glory:[1]

> ... for yt ys of glorie when any mans name ys magnified amongst many and ys much spoken of in euery bodyes mouth as renowned and very rare. Honour on the contrary being content with the ample approbacion of the better sort yea and peradventure with a few doth neither seeke after fame nor magnificence, nor affecteth great prayses.

By "the better sort" Ashley would doubtless explain that he meant "the virtuous", but the plays suggest that in practice the gentleman was above all concerned with his reputation in the eyes of the gentry. Characters who set the greatest store by honour (R) are often those who are most bitterly hostile to the common man; Coriolanus is an obvious example.

There is not much to be said about the characters of the possessors of honour, since it is attributed to people of all kinds. For the most part, the dramatists are uncritical of the code (R/RH/H), so the sympathetic characters are normally shown as accepting it and as attaching importance to it, and those who reject or evade its demands are either contemptible or villainous; but this does not mean that many unsympathetic characters, and even villainous characters, are not concerned

---

[1] *Op. cit.*, p. 36.

about honour. The villain, of course, may be more concerned about R than about H, like Jonson's Sejanus, but there are plenty of unsympathetic characters to whom H is attributed: it is possible to be a thoroughly undesirable type, yet still behave like a gentleman. I have not attempted any systematic analysis of the characters of the possessors of honour in the drama, but in my reading of the plays I have not been able to discover any marked change during the century in the types to which it is attributed.

C. Possessors of Honour, Rc/RcC/C Group

In my material, honour (Rc/RcC/C) is usually possessed only by women. There are a few cases where honour demands chastity in a man, and some of these (all in the early part of the period) are serious; but usually, while honour demands that a man shall marry a gentlewoman if he seduces her under promise of marriage, it does not demand complete continence of him; the male cases, therefore, nearly always come under R/RH/H. In the second half of the century, at any rate in comedy, the idea that a man should be chaste is considered positively comic, and the application of *honour* to male chastity (or reputation for it) occurs only in farcical situations. The cases of male chastity will be considered in more detail later.

Tables 13, 14, and 15 show the social rank of the possessors of Rc/RcC/C, for All Plays, Comedy, and Tragedy respectively. The category "lesser nobility" covers the ladies of knights and baronets, and the reason for showing them separately will be clear from the tables themselves.

TABLE 13. *Social Rank of Possessors of Rc/RcC/C: All Plays.*

Period from to	1591 1600	1601 1610	1611 1620	1621 1630	1631 1640	1591 1640	1661 1670	1671 1680	1681 1690	1691 1700	1661 1700	Grand Total
Royal	2	18	12	7	13	52	2	27	6	2	37	89
Noble	3	5	16	40	22	86	2	9	15	5	31	117
Lesser Nobility .	4	1	0	0	1	6	24	26	25	12	87	93
Other Gentry ..	1	39	52	19	39	150	27	97	46	9	179	329
Total Gentry ...	10	63	80	66	75	294	55	159	92	28	334	628
Non-Gentry	3	2	2	4	0	11	4	15	4	1	24	35

TABLE 14. *Social Rank of Possessors of Rc/RcC/C: Comedy.*

Period from to	1591 1600	1601 1610	1611 1620	1621 1630	1631 1640	1591 1640	1661 1670	1671 1680	1681 1690	1691 1700	1661 1700	Grand Total
Royal	1	1	1	1	6	10	1	1	0	0	2	12
Noble	3	3	8	6	11	31	0	7	14	2	23	54
Lesser Nobility .	0	1	0	0	1	2	24	26	25	12	87	89
Other Gentry ..	1	29	34	16	20	100	23	86	33	9	151	251
Total Gentry ...	5	34	43	23	38	143	48	120	72	23	263	406
Non-Gentry	3	2	2	1	0	8	4	12	4	1	21	29

TABLE 15. *Social Rank of Possessors of Rc/RcC/C: Tragedy.*

Period from to	1591 1600	1601 1610	1611 1620	1621 1630	1631 1640	1591 1640	1661 1670	1671 1680	1681 1690	1691 1700	1661 1700	Grand Total
Royal	1	17	11	6	7	42	1	26	6	2	35	77
Noble	0	2	8	34	11	55	2	2	1	3	8	63
Lesser Nobility .	4	0	0	0	0	4	0	0	0	0	0	4
Other Gentry ..	0	10	18	3	19	50	4	11	13	0	28	78
Total Gentry ...	5	29	37	43	37	151	7	39	20	5	71	222
Non-Gentry	0	0	0	3	0	3	0	3	0	0	3	6

The pattern of these tables is very similar to that for R/RH/H (cf. Tables 10—12). The overwhelming majority of the owners are gentry, and there is a large proportion of noble and royal characters, which is greater in tragedy than in comedy. If the two halves of the century are compared, there is a shift which is in opposite senses in comedy and tragedy: in comedy the proportion of ordinary gentry increases; in tragedy it remains about the same, but the proportion of royal characters increases from about 28% to about 49%, so that there is a shift towards the top of the social scale. This is exactly what was found for R/RH/H, but in the Rc/RcC/C tables the whole pattern is a little lower in the social scale: in comedy, about 84% of the gentry are ordinary gentry (including lesser nobility), and only about 3% royal, compared with about 75% and about 4% respectively in the R/RH/H group; in tragedy, about 63% of the gentry are royal or noble, compared with about 75% in the R/RH/H group; and the proportion of non-gentle owners is higher (6.7% comedy and 2.6% tragedy, compared with 4.3% and 1.1% in the R/RH/H group). The general pattern is obviously explicable in the same way as that for R/RH/H; the fact that it is a little lower in the social scale suggests that, in the minds of the dramatists, Rc/RcC/C is less firmly associated with rank than is R/RH/H.

Support to this view is given by a study of the non-gentle owners of Rc/RcC/C. These form only a small group, but, in contrast to the similar group in R/RH/H, they cannot all be explained away as pretentious or ironic or jocular; quite a few of them can, but there is a hard core of about twenty examples which are to be read seriously as attributions to non-gentry. A few examples will be given. Only three of the clearer examples occur in the first half of the century: in *Michaelmas Term* (II.2.32) there is a "country wench"; it hardly seems likely that this expression would be applied to a gentlewoman; in *The Captain* (p. 242) there is a waiting-woman; it is not a case of pretentiousness, because it is not the waiting-woman herself who uses the word, but her mistress, a "wanton widow", nor is it ironical; in *The Bondman* (p. 110) there is a slave-girl, Timandra, whom the speaker (a gentleman) believes to have been raped; Timandra is actually a gentlewoman in disguise, but the speaker does not know this, and his use of the word *honour* is a perfectly serious one. In the second half of the century I have found 19 examples, but four of these are perhaps to be considered pretentious or farcical. Some of the characters involved are the following: an old woman in *The Libertine* (p. 46), who is dragged in from the street for Don John to rape; it does not seem likely that the dramatist would describe a gentlewoman as an "old woman"; a supposed old woman (actually a man in disguise) (*The Virtuoso* pp. 148—9, 158), who is obviously not considered to be a gentlewoman; the situation is highly farcical, but the use of the word *honour* is perfectly serious and straightforward; Elvira, the wife of Gomez the usurer, who is obviously a citizen (*The Spanish Friar* p. 446); her husband, admittedly, has just addressed her as "gentlewoman", but this word sometimes seems to be used out of courtesy to citizen's wives, and perhaps need not imply that she is of gentle blood; Susan the housekeeper, resisting the advances of Smerk the chaplain (*The Lancashire Witches* p. 173); a servant's wife (*Amphitryon* pp. 50—51); and a chamber-maid, of whom the word is used by her mistress, Lady Fancyful (*The Provoked Wife* p.

123). The number of examples is not large, but there are some fairly certain cases, and it does seem that Rc/RcC/C could be seriously attributed to non-gentle women. Such examples, however, constitute a very small minority, and the vast majority of attributions are to gentlewomen.

There are also a number of borderline cases: in the first half of the century, the wives and relatives of merchants and professional men, like Adriana (*The Comedy of Errors*), Mrs Ford (*The Merry Wives*), Celia (*Volpone*), Jolenta (*The Devil's Law Case*), Amaranta (*The Spanish Curate*), Annabella (*'Tis Pity*), etc.; in the second half of the century, city heiresses and the wives and relatives of city knights, like Lady Flippant (*Love in a Wood*), Isabella (*Sir Patient Fancy*), Lady Galliard (*The City Heiress*), Lady Fulbank (*The Lucky Chance*), etc.; since honour (Rc/RcC/C) was occasionally attributed seriously to non-gentry, we cannot assert that these characters must belong to the gentry, though many of them may do so. There are some cases, too, where honour (Rc/RcC/C) is attributed to a woman, while honour (R/RH/H) is never attributed to her husband or male relatives: Adriana (*The Comedy of Errors*), for example, and Mrs Ford (*Merry Wives*) (and Mrs Ford is another of the citizens' wives who is referred to as "gentlewoman"); and, in the Restoration period, the wives of the Roundhead aristocracy (*The Roundheads*), and the wives and daughters of many city knights, like Lady Fulbank (*The Lucky Chance*).

The difference in the treatment of men and of women may in part be due to the fact that the daughters of rich citizens were regarded as eminently good matches for needy gentlemen. In an age of price-revolution, when the commercial classes were increasing in wealth, and when many of the landowning classes were finding it increasingly difficult to make ends meet (and were often losing their land to the "new men"),[1]) the hard-pressed gentleman often hoped to repair his finances by marrying a city heiress, and the rising citizen, for his part, was often quite eager to improve the status of his family by marrying

---

[1]) It seems likely that, in the first half of the century, the nobility and some of the older gentry declined in economic power, while many of the holders of medium-sized estates improved their position, as did many of the new landowning gentry (lawyers, merchants, ex-yeomen); but economic historians still seem to disagree on many points here: see the articles in the *Economic History Review* by Tawney, Stone, and Trevor-Roper, listed in my bibliography (Appendix D).

his daughters into the gentry, or better still the nobility.[1]) This is a theme that runs all through the drama of the period, and is perhaps especially prominent in the first half of the century: needy gallants pursue rich heiresses and widows, or even (like Lorenzo) elope with the daughters of moneylenders. This naturally produces a difference in attitude towards the fathers and the daughters: Margaret Overreach and Jessica are presented in quite a different light from Sir Giles and Shylock. This may help to explain why the dramatists sometimes use the word "gentlewoman" of citizens' wives and daughters (while the citizens are rarely called gentlemen), and attribute honour (Rc/RcC/C) to them. It is also possible, of course, that there was a tendency for gentlewomen to marry citizens, but this is not a theme that appears much in the drama; flaunting city-wives sometimes claim to come from gentle families, but often this is obviously meant to sound pretentious.

These marriages of convenience, then, may be one reason for the different treatment of men and women in the attribution of honour; but they can hardly be the whole reason, since they do not explain the attribution of honour (Rc/RcC/C) to waiting-women, a slave-girl, a country wench, etc. . Another reason may be this: chastity as a female ideal is not confined to the gentry, but is the normal ideal of the time for all women, and is demanded by religion; men's honour, on the contrary, often demands conduct different from that expected from other social classes (indeed, this is a good deal of the point of the code of honour); it may, therefore, have been easier for speakers to transfer the use of *honour* (Rc/RcC/C) to the non-gentry than to make a similar transfer of *honour* (R/RH/H); even so, the predominantly upper-class associations of the word were obviously strong enough to prevent any such transfer occurring on a large scale.

A related question is that of the lesser nobility, i. e. the ladies of knights and baronets (mainly in fact the former). As can be seen from the tables, the one really striking difference between the pattern of ownership for R/RH/H and that for Rc/RcC/C is the large group of lesser nobility that appears in the latter in the Restoration period

---

[1]) See Knights, *Drama and Society*, Chapters 2 and 3, esp. pp. 125—6. Some of the wealthier in fact married their daughters to peers: see R. H. Tawney, "The Rise of the Gentry, 1558—1640", in *Econ. Hist. Rev.* XI, p. 11; L. Stone, "The Anatomy of the Elizabethan Aristocracy", in *Econ. Hist. Rev.* XVIII Nos 1 & 2, pp. 25, 39.

(comedy only): in Restoration comedy there are no less than 87 owners of Rc/RcC/C from the lesser nobility, 26% of the gentry in question; elsewhere, the number from the lesser nobility is small, just as it is in the R/RH/H group. The prominence of knights' wives in Restoration comedy is probably to be seen as a result of one of its popular themes: the seduction by gallants of the wives of fools, and especially the wives of citizens. The knights are not always fools or parvenus, of course, but often they are one or the other, and sometimes both; and, as we have seen, they seldom have honour (R/RH/H) attributed to them. As in the case of marriages of convenience, the ladies are treated with more respect than their male relatives: the husband is a fool, possibly an upstart, but his lady of course despises him and admires the fine gentlemen who make love to her; as the actual or potential mistress of the fine gentleman, she is treated as a gentlewoman even if her husband is despised. On the other hand, a distinction is usually made between these knights' ladies (many of whom, after all, move in high society) and ordinary citizens' wives, who are also considered fair game for the gallant. The citizen's wife is also treated with seeming respect by her seducer or would-be seducer, but it is not often that honour is attributed to her; for example, in *The Old Bachelor*, Laetitia Fondlewife, whose husband is a banker and an alderman, is seduced by Bellmour; she speaks of her reputation, but never of her honour. On the other hand, honour is attributed to such characters as Lady Flippant (knight's widow and alderman's sister) in *Love in a Wood*, Lady Galliard (widow of a city knight) in *The City Heiress*, and Lady Fulbank (wife of a city knight) in *The Lucky Chance*. It seems, therefore, that, while Rc/RcC/C is sometimes seriously attributed to women of non-gentle origins, the likelihood of such attribution increases greatly with their social pretensions: the wife of the city knight is likely to claim it, the ordinary citizen's wife is not.

As in the case of R/RH/H, there is no obvious correlation between the possession of honour (Rc/RcC/C) and qualities of character. The sympathetic characters usually possess it and attach importance to it, but it is also possessed by unsympathetic characters, and there are some sympathetic characters who lack it. Whether a woman is tame or spirited, intelligent or stupid, natural or affected, good-natured or malicious, does not matter: she can possess honour (and equally well lack it). Even unchaste women are among its possessors, though naturally it is Rc that they possess, not C.

CHAPTER 5

Two Aspects of Reputation

A. Reputation, Positive and Negative

It has already been seen that the head-meaning R can sometimes be positive, meaning "glory", and sometimes negative, meaning "good name"; I shall denote the former by the symbol Rg, and the latter by the symbol Rn. Since, however, many examples contain no indication as to whether Rg or Rn is intended, and others contain both meanings, it is convenient to have a third symbol to denote these two types, and I combine them under the heading Ru (with the u mnemonic for "unclassified"). All examples of R and of RH are therefore classified as Rg, or as Rn, or as Ru; no example can appear in more than one of these classes.

Kelso points out the distinction between Rg and Rn; she paraphrases a sixteenth-century source on the subject:[1]

> There are two kinds of honor, he said, the natural, which is imperfect, and the acquired, which is perfect. Natural honor is a common opinion that a man has never failed in justice or valor, that he is good if he does not appear to the contrary. This is born in one, and is lost only by an infamous act; but it is imperfect because negative. A man is thereby honorable only because he has done nothing wrong. Acquired honor is a reward for well doing, and is perfect because it is positive and requires action. The duel is grounded upon the first sort.

Here "natural honour" corresponds to my Rn; "acquired honour" includes my Rg, but is perhaps wider, because it may include M. This passage goes back to an Italian source, but it corresponds well with

---

[1] *Op. cit.*, p. 98. Kelso is paraphrasing a passage from John Keepers, *The Courtiers Academie* (London 1598), which is a translation of Romei. The original passage in Romei is also referred to by Bryson (*op. cit.*, pp. 9—10), who however interprets it differently.

seventeenth-century usage in the drama. A gentleman normally has Rn, "born in him", but he can lose it by disgraceful behaviour, for example by breaking an oath, or by tamely submitting to insult or injury; Rg, on the other hand, is something that he usually acquires by his actions, for example by military exploits or by wise administration. As type examples of Rn and Rg we can take two passages cited earlier:

> Your oathes are past, and now subscribe your names:
> That his owne hand may strike his honour downe,
> That violates the smallest branch heerein:
> (*L.L.L.*, I.1.19—21)

> What neuer-dying Honor hath he got,
> Against renowned *Dowglas*?
> (*Henry IV.1*, III.2.106—7)

Breaking an oath will cause loss of good name; feats of arms bring military glory. The following two passages can serve as examples of Ru:

> Who then perswaded you to stay at home?
> There were two Honors lost: Yours, and your Sonnes.
> (*Henry IV.2*, II.3.15—16)

> If well-respected Honor bid me on,
> I hold as little counsaile with weake feare,
> As you, my Lord, or any Scot that this day liues.
> (*Henry IV.1*, IV.3.10—12)

In the first of these two examples, both Rn and Rg are present: Hotspur lost his military glory, and Northumberland lost his good name by breaking his word and behaving like a coward. The second example is equivocal: the R element can be either Rn or Rg (or both), and there is no means of deciding between them; Vernon may be spurred on to battle by the fear of the stigma of cowardice, or by the desire to achieve military glory. (This example is also equivocal in another way, since it is classified RH, but this is irrelevant for our present purposes: we are considering only the R element.)

Rn is most often spoken of when it is lost, or in danger of being lost, and Rg when it is won. This criterion, however, is not absolute: as can be seen from the third of the four above examples, Rg can also be lost. There are also some examples of Rg where it can hardly be said to have been gained: for example, the glory that arises from the possession of inherited high rank.

TWO ASPECTS OF REPUTATION 129

The classification of each separate example as Rn, Rg, or Ru is given in Chapters 7 and 8, where I reproduce the R and RH examples classified according to content. In Tables 16 to 18 below are given the numbers and percentages of Rn, Rg, and Ru in each decade, for All Plays, Comedies, and Tragedies respectively. R and RH are shown separately, and then combined.

It will be seen from the tables that Rn is more frequent than Rg: Rn accounts for over half the total, and Rg for a little more than a quarter. Rn outnumbers Rg much more heavily in comedy than in tragedy: the ratio of Rn to Rg is about 1½:1 in tragedy, but greater than 3:1 in comedy; this difference is highly significant. The difference between comedy and tragedy is not surprising: tragedy deals more with a world of ideal heroic achievement, where Rg is to be expected.

TABLE 16. *Numbers and Percentages of Rn, Rg, and Ru : All Plays.*

Period from to	1591 1600	1601 1610	1611 1620	1621 1630	1631 1640	1591 1640	1661 1670	1671 1680	1681 1690	1691 1700	1661 1700	Grand Total
R n (a)	38	49	83	84	103	357	66	146	48	23	283	640
(b)	36.9	42.6	43.5	47.2	58.2	46.7	68.0	67.3	65.7	50.0	65.4	53.4
g (a)	44	41	78	63	50	276	24	42	16	17	99	375
(b)	42.7	35.6	40.9	35.4	28.2	36.2	24.8	19.4	21.9	37.0	22.8	31.3
u (a)	21	25	30	31	24	131	7	29	9	6	51	182
(b)	20.4	21.7	15.7	17.4	13.6	17.1	7.2	13.4	12.3	13.0	11.8	15.2
RH n (a)	12	11	13	17	31	84	41	58	23	13	135	219
(b)	48.0	33.3	28.9	37.8	67.4	43.3	75.9	66.6	59.0	52.0	65.8	54.8
g (a)	0	4	11	7	5	27	5	5	4	1	15	42
(b)	0.0	12.1	24.4	15.6	10.9	13.9	9.3	5.8	10.3	4.0	7.3	10.5
u (a)	13	18	21	21	10	83	8	24	12	11	55	138
(b)	52.0	54.6	46.7	46.7	21.8	42.8	14.8	27.6	30.8	44.0	26.8	34.8
All n (a)	50	60	96	101	134	441	107	204	71	36	418	859
(b)	39.1	40.5	40.7	45.4	60.0	46.0	70.9	67.0	63.4	50.7	65.5	53.8
g (a)	44	45	89	70	55	303	29	47	20	18	114	417
(b)	34.4	30.4	37.7	31.4	24.7	31.6	19.2	15.5	17.9	25.4	17.9	26.2
u (a)	34	43	51	52	34	214	15	53	21	17	106	320
(b)	26.6	29.1	21.6	23.4	15.3	22.3	9.9	17.4	18.7	24.0	16.6	20.0

(a) Number of examples.
(b) Percentage of examples.

TABLE 17. *Numbers and Percentages of Rn, Rg, and Ru : Comedy.*

Period from to			1591 1600	1601 1610	1611 1620	1621 1630	1631 1640	1591 1640	1661 1670	1671 1680	1681 1690	1691 1700	1661 1700	Grand Total
R	n	(a)	15	18	33	48	46	160	46	91	31	16	184	344
		(b)	40.5	46.1	68.8	56.5	59.7	55.9	78.0	78.4	75.5	53.3	74.8	64.6
	g	(a)	12	11	10	23	21	77	11	13	8	10	42	119
		(b)	32.4	28.2	20.8	27.0	27.2	26.9	18.7	11.2	19.5	33.3	17.1	22.4
	u	(a)	10	10	5	14	10	49	2	12	2	4	20	69
		(b)	27.0	25.6	10.4	16.5	13.0	17.1	3.4	10.3	4.9	13.3	8.1	13.0
RH	n	(a)	6	4	9	11	13	43	15	26	9	6	56	99
		(b)	75.0	28.6	64.3	45.8	68.4	54.4	75.0	74.4	47.4	46.2	64.4	59.6
	g	(a)	0	2	3	2	1	8	2	2	3	1	8	16
		(b)	0.0	14.3	21.4	8.3	5.3	10.1	10.0	5.7	15.8	7.7	9.2	9.6
	u	(a)	2	8	2	11	5	28	3	7	7	6	23	51
		(b)	25.0	57.1	14.3	45.8	26.3	35.5	15.0	20.0	36.8	46.2	26.4	30.7
All	n	(a)	21	22	42	59	59	203	61	117	40	22	240	443
		(b)	46.6	41.5	67.7	54.1	61.5	55.6	77.3	77.5	66.7	51.2	72.1	63.5
	g	(a)	12	13	13	25	22	85	13	15	11	11	50	135
		(b)	26.6	24.5	21.0	23.0	22.9	23.3	16.5	9.9	18.3	25.6	15.0	19.4
	u	(a)	12	18	7	25	15	77	5	19	9	10	43	120
		(b)	26.6	34.0	11.3	23.0	15.6	21.1	6.3	12.6	15.0	23.2	12.9	17.2

(a) Number of examples.
(b) Percentage of examples.

The Rn/Rg ratio is consistently higher in RH than in R. This is very natural: if H demands certain conduct, then deviation from this conduct will cause loss of Rn, but performance of the conduct will not necessarily bring Rg; the achievement of Rg is a work of supererogation, something beyond the minimum demands of H. It is therefore normal for RH to be used of situations where H demands certain action for the avoidance of loss of Rn. In other words, Rn is more closely linked to the idea of honour as a code of conduct than is Rg, although the desire for Rg naturally also influences behaviour.

The most interesting thing in the tables, however, is the change with time, which is seen when the two half-centuries are compared (most of the fluctuations within the half-centuries are not significant).

Both in comedy and in tragedy, both in R and in RH, the percentage of Rn increases with time, while the percentage of Rg falls. Some of

TABLE 18. *Numbers and Percentages of Rn, Rg, and Ru : Tragedy.*

Period from to	1591 1600	1601 1610	1611 1620	1621 1630	1631 1640	1591 1640	1661 1670	1671 1680	1681 1690	1691 1700	1661 1700	Grand Total
R n (a)	23	31	50	36	57	197	20	55	17	7	99	296
(b)	34.8	40.8	35.0	38.7	57.0	41.2	52.6	54.5	53.1	43.7	53.0	44.5
g (a)	32	30	68	40	29	199	13	29	8	7	57	256
(b)	48.5	39.5	47.5	43.0	29.0	41.6	34.2	28.7	25.0	43.7	30.5	38.5
u (a)	11	15	25	17	14	82	5	17	7	2	31	113
(b)	16.7	19.7	17.5	18.3	14.0	17.2	13.2	16.8	21.9	12.5	16.6	17.0
RH n (a)	6	7	4	6	18	41	26	32	14	7	79	120
(b)	35.3	36.9	12.9	28.6	66.7	35.6	76.4	61.6	70.0	58.3	67.0	51.5
g (a)	0	2	8	5	4	19	3	3	1	0	7	26
(b)	0.0	10.5	25.8	23.8	14.8	16.5	8.8	5.8	5.0	0.0	5.9	11.2
u (a)	11	10	19	10	5	55	5	17	5	5	32	87
(b)	64.7	52.6	61.3	47.6	18.5	47.8	14.7	32.7	25.0	41.7	27.1	37.4
All n (a)	29	38	54	42	75	238	46	87	31	14	178	416
(b)	35.0	40.0	31.0	36.8	59.0	40.1	63.9	56.8	59.6	50.0	58.4	46.3
g (a)	32	32	76	45	33	218	16	32	9	7	64	282
(b)	38.5	33.7	43.6	39.5	26.0	36.8	22.2	20.9	17.3	25.0	21.0	31.4
u (a)	22	25	44	27	19	137	10	34	12	7	63	200
(b)	26.5	26.3	25.3	23.7	15.0	23.1	13.9	22.2	23.1	25.0	20.6	22.3

(a) Number of examples.
(b) Percentage of examples.

the changes are considerable, and nearly all are significant.[1]) There are no great differences between comedy and tragedy, except that in tragedy the largest change occurs in RH, while in comedy it occurs in R.

The increase in the Rn/Rg ratio during the century shows that the attitude to R became more defensive and more negative: honour became less a thing to be won by positive achievement, and more a thing to be protected and preserved. Since the change takes place in tragedy as well as in comedy, it seems that the idealized self-portrait changed as well as the actual practice. The change may be connected with the rise of H, and the tendency for the gentry to elevate honour

---

[1]) The only exceptions are in RH comedy, where neither the increase in Rn nor the decrease in Rg is significant. In view, however, of the similar (and significant) trend in the rest of the material, it is probable that these changes too are real.

into a code of conduct different from that of the rest of the community, for, as we have seen, the idea of honour as a code of behaviour calls Rn into play more readily than Rg. In addition, however, the increase in Rn may reflect changes in the code itself, an increase in prohibitions and a decrease in positive incentives to action (especially heroic action); the Restoration period was notoriously unheroic, and its fashionable London society much concerned with etiquette and forms. Harbage suggests that the rise of "Puritan and democratic opposition to those in high places" helped to crystallize the social coterie of London society: in their increasing isolation, the "fashionable idlers" were forced into self-discovery and into abrasive social intercourse with one another, and this led to the evolving of "an artificial code of conduct".[1] To this I would add the positive desire of the "idlers" to be different from those that they considered non-gentry, both in the externals of conduct and in morals, and their increased emphasis on honour as the determinant of their behaviour. On this view, the rise of H and the increase in the Rn/Rg ratio are both part of the same process. As will be seen later (Chapters 6—10), there are other changes which support this view of the social causes of the development of H and Rn: the conduct prescribed becomes less heroic and more conventional.

In the Rc and RcC groups, the u type is very small and the g type almost non-existent: Rc is nearly always Rcn. I have found four possible examples of Rcg in the first half-century (out of 187 examples of Rc and RcC) and one possible example in the second half-century (out of 263), but none of these is absolutely certain. This is not surprising, of course: chastity was normally expected of a woman, and (except in unusual circumstances) its preservation was not considered to call for heroic effort; chastity was not a work of supererogation, but (for women) the most important single requirement; so n is normal and g exceptional. Since the frequency of Rc and RcC increases in the second half of the century, there is (in absolute terms) an increase in the frequency of the n element, parallel to the increase of n in R and RH.

B. Mere Reputation

In his treatise on honour, Robert Ashley frequently insists on the close relationship between honour and virtue; he defines honour as "a certeine testemonie of vertue shining of yt self geven of some man

---

[1] *Cavalier Drama*, pp. 79—80. But cf. note 1, p. 103 above.

by the iudgement of good men",[1]) and this is a point that he often returns to. He seems to be referring mainly to R and M, and especially perhaps the former; he is asserting, then, that R must always be accompanied by the good qualities to which it refers. In my material, this is in fact usually the case: a man with military R normally has courage and fighting qualities, and a woman with Rc is usually chaste. But this is not always so: R and Rc are sometimes possessed or claimed by people who lack the relevant qualities. Sometimes this is a matter of pretence or deceit; for example, in *Richard II* Aumerle is accused of having arranged the murder of Gloucester, and makes the following reply:

> What answer shall I make to this base man?
> Shall I so much dishonor my faire Starres,
> On equall termes to giue him chasticement?
> Either I must, or haue mine honor soyl'd
> With th' Attaindor of his sland'rous Lippes.
> (IV.1.20—24)

The audience seems to be intended to consider Aumerle guilty, so he is laying claim to R to which he is not entitled. There is a similar case, this time with Rc, in *King John*; Lady Faulconbridge comes in pursuit of her son Robert, who is trying to dispossess his elder brother of his land by proclaiming that he is illegitimate:

> Where is that slaue thy brother? where is he?
> That holds in chase mine honour vp and downe.
> (I.1.222—3)

A few lines later, the Bastard asks her who his real father is, and she replies in indignation:

> Hast thou conspired with thy brother too,
> That for thine owne gaine shouldst defend mine honor?
> (I.1.241—2)

Both these examples are to be classified as Rc. Later, Lady Faulconbridge admits that the accusation of unchastity is true, and that the Bastard is her son by Richard I, so it is plain that she has been laying claim to Rc without in fact possessing C. Examples of this kind are not particularly common; in R and RH, I have found 17 clear examples in my material, 11 in comedy and 6 in tragedy; in Rc and

---
[1]) *Op. cit.*, p. 34.

RcC I have found 34, 29 in comedy and 5 in tragedy. They are more frequent in the second half of the century than the first, especially in the Rc/RcC group, where 27 of the 34 examples are in the second half.

There is, however, a more interesting type. This is the case where the relevant qualities are lacking, but no deception is intended. R or Rc is claimed or attributed, although the speaker and the hearers are aware that the requisite qualities or attributes are lacking. The absence of the quality in question then in effect becomes part of the meaning of the word *honour* in the sentence in question. An example with Rc can be given from *The Winter's Tale*; Leontes, believing that Hermione has committed adultery with Polixenes, is persuading Camillo to murder the latter; Camillo stipulates as a condition that Leontes shall take no action against Hermione, and Leontes agrees:

> Thou do'st aduise me,
> Euen so as I mine owne course haue set downe:
> Ile giue no blemish to her Honor, none.
> (I.2.338—40)

Leontes means "I will not cause her to lose Rc (although we know that she lacks C)". The fact that Hermione is really chaste is irrelevant: the point is that the speaker believes her to be unchaste, and believes his hearer to share this view. An example with R can be given from *Volpone*; Lady Would-bee is about to be produced as a witness to testify that Celia had played the harlot with Sir Politick Would-bee in a gondola; Mosca introduces her to the court:

> Here is the lady her selfe, that saw 'hem too,
> Without; who, then, had in the open streets
> Pursu'd them, but for sauing her knights honour.
> (IV.5.150—2)

The honour is Sir Politick's R for moral behaviour (not going with courtesans), and it was saved by not attracting attention to his behaviour; now, however, in court, attention *is* being attracted to it, and it is still Sir Politick's honour, although it is agreed that he did go with a courtesan. (The fact that the whole story is untrue is irrelevant: the court is supposed to believe it true, and indeed does so.) Another example is from *The Maid's Tragedy*, one that has already been discussed:

Nor let the King
Know I conceive he wrongs me, then mine honour
Will thrust me into action, that my flesh
Could bear with patience;

(II.1, p. 23)

This is classified RH, and the R element is R for sensitivity to injury; it is clear, however, that Amintor is not really sensitive about injury, but only about his reputation for sensitivity to injury. As long as it is believed that he is ignorant of the injury, he is willing to leave it unrevenged; only if he is known to be aware of it will he feel forced to take revenge. He says this quite explicitly, and it seems reasonable to class this as an example of R without the relevant qualities. In all three of the examples given, there is an idea of deceit or concealment at some stage of the process; the distinguishing feature is, however, that there is no deceit or concealment between the speaker and his hearers, so that the absence of the relevant quality is part of the meaning intended. I shall denote this type by appending a small o after the symbol for the head-meaning: Ro and Rco. (The o, standing for zero, is mnemonic for the absence of a quality.) For the earlier type, in which the speaker attempts to deceive his hearers about the absence of the relevant quality (or is himself deceived), I shall add brackets round the o: R(o) and Rc(o).

It is easier to detect Rco than Ro; unchastity, at any rate in the purely physical sense, is often more clearly established by the dramatist than, for example, lack of courage or of magnanimity; a woman who lays claim to Rc when she is actually an adulteress is presumably aware of the discrepancy between claim and reality, but a man can more easily deceive himself about his lack of fighting qualities, truthfulness, generosity, etc. This is perhaps one reason why Ro is less frequent than Rco. Tables 19 and 20 give the numbers and percentages for Ro and Rco respectively; as the numbers are small, no breakdown is given into decades, but only into half-centuries; for the same reason, the figures for R and RH are combined, and so are those for Rc and RcC.

In both tables, frequency falls in tragedy and increases in comedy. The increase in comedy is significant in both cases, but the decrease in tragedy is not. Even if the figures for Ro and for Rco are combined, the change in tragedy remains too small to be statistically significant,

TABLE 19. *Numbers and Percentages of Ro.*

		1591 to 1640	1661 to 1700	Total
Comedy	(a)	5	21	26
	(b)	1.37	6.27	3.71
Tragedy	(a)	12	3	15
	(b)	2.02	0.99	1.67

(a) Number of examples.
(b) Percentage.

TABLE 20. *Numbers and Percentages of Rco.*

		1591 to 1640	1661 to 1700	Total
Comedy	(a)	11	80	91
	(b)	12.2	35.6	28.9
Tragedy	(a)	18	5	23
	(b)	18.6	13.2	17.0

(a) Number of examples.
(b) Percentage.

so no importance can be attached to the apparent fall. The increase in frequency in comedy shows an increasing tendency to attribute R in situations where R is known to be undeserved; it is a remarkable fact that, in Restoration comedy, more than one-third of the attributions of Rc and RcC are of this type. The implication seems to be that greater importance came to be attached to appearances, and less importance to actual character and conduct, which fits well with the known tendency of Restoration high society to place great emphasis on forms and etiquette without setting a high moral standard. The fact that the change occurs in comedy suggests that it is a reflection of a real change in usage in society.

CHAPTER 6

Virtue and Convention: (I) General

When people discuss honour (R/RH/H) as a code of conduct, they often suggest that this code is in some sense conventional. For example, the definition of *honour* (2a) in the *N. E. D.* (corresponding to my H) concludes as follows: "a fine sense of and strict allegiance to what is due or right (also, to what is due according to some conventional or fashionable standard of conduct)". This implies that there is some absolute standard of conduct ("what is due or right") which is not conventional, contrasted with other standards which are merely "conventional or fashionable". This assumption obviously will not command universal assent, but the philosophical problems raised are really irrelevant for my purposes: it is sufficient to observe that in seventeenth-century England most people in fact believed that there was an absolute moral code, and that in some respects the code of honour differed from this moral code (and was to this extent "conventional or fashionable"). Even if it could be shown that the generally accepted moral code of seventeenth-century society was not believed to be absolute, we should still be left with a situation where there were two different codes of conduct, the general moral code and the gentleman's code of honour. The interesting question is whether these two codes differed to any great extent, and whether the difference changed during the century. In Chapters 7 to 9, when I display my material for R, RH, and H, I shall adopt certain broad classifications aimed at answering this question.

The universally accepted moral code in seventeenth-century England was a Christian one. "A vast and august body of beliefs — the Christian religion — had survived with scarcely impaired authority into this philosophic century, together with all its associated imagery, its world-picture, its scale of values, its way of life."[1]) There was of course a change of intellectual climate during the century, with the great advances of rationalism and of science, but the task of the new rationalizing theologians was to state the old beliefs in terms acceptable to a rationalist age. "It is significant that in the seventeenth century most of the religious rationalising is carried on conservatively; there is no appearance, and usually no intention, of destructive criticism. The assumption always is that the core of religious truth is sound, if only it can be freed from the traditional accretions."[2]) In the Restoration period, admittedly, there was a certain amount of upper-class atheism, often based on Hobbes;[3]) but in the broad masses of the people the traditional Christian beliefs and standards of conduct continued to be firmly rooted, throughout the seventeenth century and much later. Right at the end of the century, Bunyan's *Pilgrim's Progress* (a work beneath the consideration of the polite society of the time) sold about 100,000 copies in less than fifteen years; and *Pilgrim's Progress* is traditional, popular, and representative.[4])

At the same time, it is clear that seventeenth-century English Christians could differ violently from one another in their beliefs, as the civil wars demonstrate; but even Christians who fought one another about their beliefs had a great deal in common, more than they have in common with a modern non-Christian; they might disagree about predestination and free will, about salvation by faith and salvation by works, about the positioning of the communion-table and the wearing of vestments, but they agreed in believing in the Christian scheme of Creation, Fall, Redemption, and Judgment; moreover, they agreed on many basic points of human conduct, such as the undesirability of theft, adultery, and murder, and the desirability of meekness, mercy, and charity. It is such basic points of human conduct that I shall take as the moral norm for the seventeenth century; the Ten Commandments and the Beatitudes provide the basis, though they have to be supplemented by such generally-accepted ideas of

---

[1]) Willey, *The Seventeenth Century Background*, pp. 119—20. See also Bush, *op. cit.*, pp. 294 sqq.; Clark, *op. cit.*, pp. 317—24; A. R. Humphreys, *The Augustan World*, pp. 138—67.

[2]) *Ibid.*, p. 133.

[3]) See Beljame, *op. cit.*, pp. 6—8.

[4]) See Leavis, *The Common Pursuit*, pp. 206—8; Talon, *John Bunyan, l'homme et l'oeuvre*, pp. 37—53, 101—2, 362.

the period as the religious duty of obeying one's parents and one's civil governors. This generalized seventeenth-century Christian standard of conduct will be referred to as "Christian virtue".

The demands of honour (R/RH/H) sometimes coincided with the demands of Christian virtue, but sometimes did not; when honour demanded truthfulness, its demands coincided with those of Christian virtue, but when it demanded the taking of revenge its demands were absolutely contradictory to those of Christian virtue. I shall denote these differing types of honour by suffixing the letters v and k respectively to the symbol for the head-meaning: Rv, Rk. (The letters are mnemonic for "virtue" and "convention".) The v/k classification can apply equally well to R, to RH, and to H; Rv is reputation for qualities or behaviour that are also demanded by Christian virtue, Hv these qualities or this behaviour themselves. The classification of an example of *honour* in the v category does not imply that in this context *honour* means "Christian virtue"; it happens that the conduct demanded is the same, but the motive and the sanction are different. The Christian obeys the Christian code because it is the will of God; the gentleman follows the code of honour because it is the accepted thing for people of his class to do, and failure to follow it will cause him to fall in the opinion of the other members of the class.

In some contexts "honour" is contrasted with "vertue", without an exact content being specified for either; I do not take this as sufficient reason for classifying the example of *honour* as k. For one thing, the contrast may be one of motive, not of conduct, and for another, "vertue" does not necessarily mean "Christian virtue"; in the seventeenth century, "vertue" often means simply "desirable quality", "desirable qualities".

In general I have found in my material the same kinds of content for R, for RH, and for H (though not always in the same proportions). There are a few exceptions: for example, there is no quality of H exactly corresponding to the R which arises from the possession of high rank; but normally the conduct demanded by H is the same as that which preserves (or gains) R. I therefore lump all three head-meanings together in the lists that follow. These are lists of the commoner contents of R/RH/H that I have found in the plays, i. e. the qualities or conduct that are demanded by or for honour (R/RH/H). I give separate lists for k and for v, to show the general principles of classification on which I have worked. The lists are not intended to be exhaustive.

Typical k Contents

1. Sensitivity to injury and insult. Honour demands that a gentleman shall revenge wrongs and insults to himself or his family. This often means challenging and fighting the wronger, though sometimes circumstances dictate secret revenge, e. g. by murder. If the injury consists in the seduction of a female relative, honour can often also be satisfied by marriage; in Restoration drama, there are even examples of a man insisting on the seducer marrying his wronged sister, and then challenging him afterwards.

2. Not tolerating a rival in love. Especially in the Restoration period, the very fact of being a rival is sometimes considered sufficient grounds for a challenge, and the dearest friends will fight one another when they find that they love the same woman.

3. Observing the rules of duelling. A gentleman must not refuse a challenge from an equal (though noblemen are sometimes shown as refusing one from an inferior); he must, on request, bear a challenge for a friend, and act as his second (which in the second half of the century involves fighting the rival's second); he must keep duelling appointments, and be punctual at them; he must observe the conventions of fair fight (equality of weapons, fair division of ground and sun, etc.).

4. Not being outwitted, jilted, or in other ways made to lose face. There are examples where there is no ground for a challenge (being jilted by a woman is a clear case), but where the man is worsted in some way; in this case he loses R.

5. Insisting on one's rights. Honour is not meek. The gentleman must insist on every tittle that he considers due to him, e. g. in matters of precedence. A woman says in *Wit without Money*:

> In you men, 'tis held a coolness, if you lose your right, affronts and loss of honour: streets, and walls, and upper ends of tables, had they tongues could tell what blood has followed, and what feud about your ranks.
>
> (III.1, p. 171)

As this suggests, the points disputed are sometimes extremely petty.

6. High rank. The holding of high rank or office in itself brings R, and H can include ambition for such rank. The R is increased by a large number of dependants and followers, and by due ceremonial.

7. Ostentation. Closely related to Point 6 is the demand of honour that a man should live up to his position (or even above it). This is what Kelso calls *liberality*, or (in a great lord) *magnificence*, and she brings out clearly its self-centredness and its fundamental difference from Christian alms-giving.[1])

8. Not having one's authority flouted. A father loses R if a child disobeys him, a king if his subjects do. Among equals, it is a point of honour not to be dictated to, or even appear to be (see for example *Troilus and Cressida*, IV.4.135—6). A king loses honour if he is obliged to accept humiliating peace-terms at the end of a war.

9. Making good marriages. R is gained by making socially advantageous marriages for oneself or one's relatives, and is lost by marrying below one's station.

10. Not performing menial tasks. A gentleman must avoid doing any kind of work considered inappropriate to his rank.

11. Reflected R. A gentleman can lose R through the behaviour of others, especially his relatives, although he himself is in no way to blame. A man loses R if his wife or any of his female relatives is unchaste, even though his own conduct has been irreproachable. He gains a certain amount of R from the good qualities and achievements of his relatives, even if he does not share in them. I classify these cases under k.

12. Not withdrawing from a proposed marriage. This is a type that I sometimes classify as k, and sometimes as v, according to the circumstances and the attitude of the dramatist. Sometimes the engagement is represented as a solemn contract, equivalent to marriage itself, and in this case I classify as v. In other cases it is taken much more lightly: sometimes it is not even clear whether there is a formal engagement (this is the case, for example, with the marriage arranged between Alonzo and Hippolyta in Behn's *The Dutch Lover*); sometimes there is certainly a formal engagement, but withdrawal from it (while causing loss of honour) is not represented as something really shocking and sinful — it is simply not the done thing; an example of this kind is the engagement between Sparkish and Alithea in *The Country Wife*; these cases I classify as k.

13. Recognizing the claims of friendship. A gentleman must stand by his friends, simply because they are his friends. Frequently, the behaviour required by the claims of friendship is such that the example

---
[1]) *Op. cit.*, pp. 88—91.

is obviously k (lying, fighting duels, etc.). Sometimes, on the other hand, the behaviour is precisely what would be demanded by v, but I nevertheless class the example as k if it is implied that, but for the claims of friendship, the behaviour would be different. For example, honour demands that one shall not seduce the wife of a friend, but it is often made clear that it is quite in order to seduce other men's wives (and the honourable man is shown busy doing so); I class such examples as k, because the demands of honour are not simply "not seducing", but "not seducing a friend's wife although seducing the wives of other men". This making of exceptions in the favour of one's friends is not, I feel, in the Christian spirit. It is not always easy to be certain whether the motive of friendship is operative, since a man embarking on a course of action at the dictates of honour does not always make it clear whether or not friendship is a dominant motive; if in doubt, I assume that it is not.

14. *Sexual virility.* In Restoration comedy, a man of honour has to be a good wencher. Honour also demands that he shall faithfully keep adulterous assignations, and sometimes that he shall be constant to his adulterous mistress (though it is more often the mistress who takes this view than the man himself).

15. *Protecting a woman's reputation.* In the second half of the century, a gentleman must scrupulously protect the reputation of a woman with whom he has committed (or may be thought to have committed) adultery, even if it involves injustice to other people. In *The Country Wife* (V.4) Horner protects the reputation of Mrs Pinchwife, even though this involves slandering Alithea.

16. *Not being under an obligation.* To be under an obligation to anybody (and especially to an enemy) is often felt to involve loss of R, and a gentleman will try to repay the obligation and so be free of it. Honour forbids fighting with a man to whom you are under an obligation, and there are several examples where a man scrupulously repays an obligation to a rival and then challenges him (as Acacis does Montezuma in *The Indian Queen*, IV.2, p. 264).

17. *Being polite and courteous, especially to ladies.* This is occasionally represented as being required by honour.

18. *Observing the conventions of civilized warfare.* Honour forbids a prisoner of war to escape or to attempt to escape. It also forbids the starting of a war without formal declaration of war, and demands a

distinction between combatants and non-combatants. As in the case of Point 16, it is the implications that make me classify this as k: when honour forbids a soldier to kill non-combatants, it implies that it is in order for him to kill other people; war is a licensed killing, where honour lays down the permissible categories of victims.

19. Not suffering an ignominious death. When a gentleman is executed, he loses R if the manner of execution is inappropriate to his rank. In general it is felt less degrading to be beheaded than to be hanged. Execution, however, causes some loss of R however it is carried out, and a gentleman would prefer to die fighting.

20. Committing suicide. Sometimes a situation is reached where a character feels that the only course of action consistent with honour is to commit suicide. Since, for a Christian, suicide is sinful, such cases are classified as k.

Typical v Contents

1. Telling the truth. In theory, a gentleman does not lie, and to accuse him of doing so is a deadly insult. The close connection between honour and truthfulness is seen in the frequent use of the phrase "on my honour" to certify the truth of an assertion.

2. Keeping promises and oaths. Oath-breaking and promise-breaking are forbidden by honour. Usually I classify this as v, but there are exceptions: the keeping of an unlawful or irreligious oath (which is demanded by honour) is forbidden by religion, and I classify such examples as k. The point is made by Cardinal Pandulph in *King John* (III. 1.263—97), when he explains to Philip of France that religion forbids him to keep an irreligious oath. Similarly, the honour involved in keeping a promise is classified as k if the promise is, say, to fight a duel or to commit adultery.

3. Not withdrawing from a marriage contract. Honour forbids withdrawal from an engagement; if this is represented as a solemn contract, almost equivalent to marriage, the example is classified as v. A clear case can be seen in *Henry VI.1*, V.5.25—9, where withdrawal from a betrothal is explicitly stigmatized as sin.

4. Obedience to civil governors. Honour forbids treason and rebellion. I classify this as v, since Christianity traditionally insisted on the impiety of rebellion against a lawful ruler. Admittedly this view must have lost some of its force in the middle of the seventeenth century,

when puritan revolutionaries executed Charles I; but it nevertheless seems probable that, at most times during the century, the majority of Christians continued to view rebellion as impious.[1]) In any case, a good deal obviously hinges on the definition of a "lawful ruler"; in this respect, the dramatists usually make it quite clear what we are intended to think; occasionally, rebellion is shown as praiseworthy and even as religious (e. g. Richmond's rebellion in *Richard III*).

5. Filial piety. Honour demands obedience to parents. In the seventeenth century this was still considered a religious duty.[2])

6. Not committing murder.

7. Honesty. A gentleman should not steal or cheat, or indulge in sharp financial practices. He should pay his debts.

8. Not conniving at or encouraging unchastity. It is contrary to honour for a gentleman to act as a bawd or procurer, or to connive at the prostitution of female relatives or dependants. This is different from reflected R (Point 11 of k), in which a man loses honour through no fault of his own; in the present type, he knowingly permits or even actively promotes unchastity, and so I classify the examples as v.

9. Sexual continence. Seduction, adultery, and rape are often held to be contrary to honour, especially by women. But cf. Point 14 of k.

10. Not being envious. Not very common.

11. Not being ungrateful, especially to benefactors.

12. Piety. Occasionally, in the first half of the century, it is shown as contrary to honour to be irreligious or hostile to the church.

13. Justice. Not indulging in or conniving at bribery and corruption, not perverting justice.

14. Occasionally, the gentler Christian virtues are represented as demanded by honour or as bringing honour: mercy and forgiveness, peacemaking, selflessness, humility. But these are rare.

Many of the demands of honour in these two lists are incompatible, sometimes absolutely contradictory. The lists, however, cover a period of a whole century, and both comedy and tragedy by various authors; the contradictions are less violent within a given play, and also within a given decade. Even so, quite contradictory demands of honour can be found in the same decade, and even in the same play; there is no

---

[1]) See for example that popular mid-seventeenth-century tract, *The Whole Duty of Man*, pp. 187—9.

[2]) *Ibid.*, pp. 193—8.

clear-cut and agreed code of honour in seventeenth-century England such as seems to have existed in Spain.[1])

In the lists of typical contents for k and v there is one important omission: military honour. This is a fairly common type. Rg can be gained by military prowess, Rn can be lost by cowardice in battle; H can impel a man to fight, in order to gain Rg or avoid loss of Rn, H can also denote the actual fighting qualities of character (courage, a sense of military duty, high morale, etc.) and allegiance to a specifically military code of conduct. When I began classifying my material as k or v, I assumed that military honour ought to be classed as k: the pursuit of military glory did not seem to fit well with the sixth commandment or with the spirit of the Beatitudes. I soon realized, however, that this is not at all the attitude adopted by the dramatists, for whom military prowess is not only consistent with Christian virtue but can even be demanded by it: fighting for one's sovereign and one's country is represented as a pious duty.[2]) The critical attitude to war implicit in *Henry IV.1* and *Troilus and Cressida* is unusual in the drama, and is especially rare after the age of Shakespeare; there is a passage in Davenant's *The Wits* (I.1, pp. 121—2) which recognizes that warfare is contrary to the spirit of Christianity, but this is cynical in tone. It is often recognized that it is morally wrong to fight a war in an unjust cause, but the responsibility for deciding whether or not a war is just is usually left to the sovereign, as in the famous discussion between Henry V and the soldiers (*Henry V*, IV.1); the soldier's duty is to obey his sovereign and to fight for him. A distinction is therefore made between war and duelling: Christian moralists usually admit the former as permissible, the latter not; the supporters of duelling indeed sometimes try to justify it by the analogy of war, but this does not seem to be accepted by Christian thinkers.[3]) The moralist's point of view is eloquently put by Jonson in *The New Inn*, in Lovel's oration on the nature of true valour; one of his most important points is that true valour is exercised only for the public good, not in a private cause.

---

[1]) See E. M. Wilson, "Family Honour", pp. 19—20.

[2]) Sir George Clark has pointed out that in seventeenth-century Europe war was an *institution*, i. e. was accepted as a normal and necessary part of society. He made the point in detail in the Wiles Lectures on the History of Civilization, given in the Queen's University, Belfast, in October 1956.

[3]) See F. T. Bowers, *Elizabethan Revenge Tragedy*, pp. 12—34.

Since military honour forms a very distinctive group, and since arguments could be advanced for including it either in the k group or in the v group, I have assigned it to a separate group of its own, which I shall denote by adding the symbol m to the letter for the head-meaning: Rm, etc.. Rm usually denotes military reputation won (or lost) in battle. There are a few places, however, where Rm is won or lost in private fight, duel or brawl; this is different from the Rk which impels a man to fight a duel with another: it is the actual military glory which is won by being victorious in the duel (or the military reputation lost by being defeated in it); I shall denote it when necessary by the symbol Rkm, but I shall treat it as a special case of m, not as a special case of k, and in my statistics I shall include it in the figures for m; there are very few examples of km.

Examples of R, RH, and H can therefore be classified as k, as v, or as m (including km). I never place an example in more than one of these categories; if its reference is so wide that no single one of the three can be considered dominant, I leave it unclassified. There are also examples left unclassified because the content is unspecified, or because it does not fall into any of the three categories: for example, a physician's R for skill in his profession is not a moral matter, and the k/v classification is irrelevant; but this type is not very common. It is convenient to have a symbol for the examples which are left unclassified with respect to k, v, and m; since I have already taken the symbol u for another purpose (with g and n), I shall here adopt the symbol x: Rx, etc. All examples of R, RH, and H must therefore fall into one (and only one) of the four categories k, v, m, and x.

There are sometimes problems in applying the k/m/v/x classification when the word *honour* is used figuratively. We can consider the following example from *Rule a Wife*; in the course of a slanging-match, Estifania tells Perez (a soldier) that she has been looking for him in brothels and such places:

> I sought ye where no safe thing would have ventur'd,
> Amongst diseases, base and vile, vile Women,
> For I remembered your old Roman axiom,
> The more the danger, still the more the Honour.
>   (IV.1, p. 209)

I class this as m, not as k. Estifania is not seriously suggesting that libertinism brings honour, and is really implying the opposite; she is in effect saying sarcastically, "As a soldier, you know that the greatest Rgm is won from the greatest danger, and I suppose you are trying to apply this principle to your sex-life". The sex/war comparison is not uncommon. Another type that recurs, expecially in the Restoration period, is the comparison of a love-assignation with a duelling assignation. For example, a character in *Love in a Wood* says, of a woman who is believed to have written to a man making an assignation:

> I think, since she has the courage to challenge him, she'll have the honour of being first in the field.
> (IV.5, p. 93)

He obviously means, "Since she is so anxious to have this meeting with him, she will be there first"; he does not at all mean that arriving first for a love-assignation will bring her honour; honour is brought in by the duelling half of the comparison (it is quite common in a duel for the side who arrive first to say that they have the honour of the field) and belongs only to it. I therefore group the example with those concerned with duelling etiquette, not with those concerned with love assignations (both k). There is no space to discuss each such example, but I have of course tried to judge each case on its merits.

The next three chapters will be devoted to displaying the classified material, one chapter being given to R, one to RH, and one to H. In each chapter, the material will be given by decades; in each decade, the examples will be given for k, m, v, and x in turn, and the division into comedy and tragedy shown. For R and RH, the classification into n, g, or u will also be shown. In cases with multiple head-meanings, the full head-meaning will be given in brackets at the end of the example. It must be remembered that the content assigned to each example is only intended as a brief label, and is often unable to do justice to the complexity of the situation involved.

Those who are not interested in the material itself, but only in my findings, would be well advised to skip the next three chapters and pass straight on to Chapter 10.

CHAPTER 7

Virtue and Convention:
(II) The R Material

A. 1591—1600

In this decade there are 103 examples of R, of which 37 are in comedy and 66 in tragedy. In 10 of the examples, R is not the sole head-meaning; the combined head-meanings found are RM (one), RT (two), RP (one), RMT (one), RTP (three), RE (one), and REM (one).[1]) Of the 103 examples, 13 are countables and 47 uncountables, while the remaining 43 are equivocal from this point of view. The examples are the following.

(a) The k Group

Sensitivity to affront, revenging injury, etc.:

Comedy: Rn: Ielous in honor, sodaine, and quicke in quarrell (*A. Y. L. I.*, II.7.151).

Tragedy: Rn: If guilty dread hath left thee so much strength,/ As to take vp mine Honors pawne, then stoope (*Richard II*, I.1.73—4). Mine Honor is my life (*Ibid.*, I.1.182). Take Honor from me, and my life is done (*Ibid.*, I.1.183). Then (deere my Liege) mine Honor let me trie (*Ibid.*, I.1.184). Ere my toong,/ Shall wound mine honor with such feeble wrong (*Ibid.*, I.1.190—1). there is my honors pawne (*Ibid.*, IV.1.55, Q text only). there is mine Honors pawne (*Ibid.*, IV.1.70). Old I do waxe, and from my wearie limbes honour is Cudgeld (*Henry V*, V.1.87—8).

Insisting on one's rights, not being meek:

Tragedy: Rn: But thou preferr'st thy Life, before thine Honor (*Henry VI.3*, I.1.246).

High rank:

Tragedy: Rg: But all the Honor *Salisbury* hath wonne (*Henry VI.2*, III.2.275) (RM). While he enioyes the Honor, and his ease (*Henry VI.3*,

---

[1]) In this chapter and the next two, no account will be taken of O as a joint head-meaning, since the status of O is different from that of the other head-meanings; if an example of O is also classified as R, then there are not two head-meanings, but only one, namely R.

IV.6.52) (RT). An outward Honor, for an inward Toyle (*Richard III*, I.4.79) (RT).

Ostentation:

Tragedy: Rg: As much as would maintaine, to the Kings honor,/ Full fifteene Earles, and fifteene hundred Knights (*Henry V*, I.1.12—13).

Making socially good marriages:

Tragedy: Rg: For matching more for wanton Lust, then Honor (*Henry VI.3*, III.3.210) (RTP). for thy Honor giue consent,/ Thy daughter shall be wedded to my King (*Henry VI.1*, V.3.136—7).

Not promoting marriage of dependant to an unchaste woman:

Comedy: Rn: hee hath wronged his Honor (*Much Ado*, II.2.22). in a loue of your brothers honor who hath made this match (*Ibid.*, II.2.34—6).

Not performing menial tasks:

Comedy: Rn: you'll not beare a Letter for mee you roague? you stand vpon your honor (*Merry Wives*, II.2.19—20). vnder the shelter of your honor (*Ibid.*, II.2.28—9) (R(o)?).

Reflected (relatives' disloyalty to ruler):

Tragedy: Rn: And with these Boyes mine Honour thou hast wounded (*Titus Andron.*, I.1.365). Mine honor liues, when his dishonor dies (*Richard II*, V.3.69).

Recognizing the claims of friendship:

Tragedy: Rn: Takes on the point of Honor, to support/ So dissolute a crew (*Richard II*, V.3.11—12).

Gained by travel:

Comedy: Rg: He after Honour hunts, I after Loue (*Two Gentlemen*, I.1.63).

Tragedy: Rg: Go, say I sent thee foorth to purchase honour (*Richard II*, I.3.282) (Q text only).

(b) *The m Group*

Comedy: Rg: A Sonne, who is the Theame of Honors tongue (*Henry IV.1*, I.1.81). So Honor crosse it from the North to South (*Ibid.*, I.3.196). To plucke bright Honor from the pale-fac'd Moone (*Ibid.*, I.3.202). And plucke vp drowned Honor by the Lockes (*Ibid.*, I.3.205). What neuer-dying Honor hath he got (*Ibid.*, III.2.106). this same Child of Honor and Renowne (*Ibid.*, III.2.139). What honor dost thou seeke vpon my head (*Ibid.*, V.3.2—3). Sir *Walter Blunt*, there's Honour for you (*Ibid.*, V.3.32—3). I like not such grinning honour (*Ibid.*, V.3.61—2). if not, honour comes vnlook'd for, and ther's an end (*Ibid.*, V.3.63—4).

Comedy: Ru: I tell thee *Ned,* thou hast lost much honor *(Henry IV.1,* II.4.21) (RE). Honor prickes me on *(Ibid.,* V.1.129—30). how if Honour pricke me off *(Ibid.,* V.1.130—31). Can Honour set too a legge? *(Ibid.,* V.1.131—2). Honour hath no skill in Surgerie, then? *(Ibid.,* V.1.133—4). What is Honour? *(Ibid.,* V.1.134). What is that word Honour? *(Ibid.,* V.1.134—5). Honour is a meere Scutcheon *(Ibid.,* V.1.140).

Tragedy: Rn: heauens and honor be witnesse *(Henry VI.2,* IV.8.63). O, for honor of our Land,/ Let vs not hang like roping Isyckles *(Henry V,* III.5.22—3). But that our Honours must not *(Ibid.,* IV.2.32).

Tragedy: Rg: That dims the Honor of this Warlike Isle: *(Henry VI.2,* I.1.125). To emblaze the Honor that thy Master got *(Ibid.,* IV.10.75). 'Tis the more honour, because more dangerous *(Henry VI.3,* IV.3.15). I like it better then a dangerous honor *(Ibid.,* IV.3.17). Courage my Masters: Honor now, or neuer: *(Ibid.,* IV.3.24). Let not slouth dimme your Honors, new-begot; *(Henry VI.1,* I.1.79). This is a double Honor, *Burgonie: (Ibid.,* III.2.116). Hath sullied all his glosse of former Honor *(Ibid.,* IV.4.6). laden with Honours Spoyles *(Titus Andr.,* I.1.36). With Honour and with Fortune is return'd *(Ibid.,* I.1.67). And Triumphs ouer chaunce in honours bed *(Ibid.,* I.1.178). Mine Honours Ensignes humbled at my feete *(Ibid.,* I.1.252). Because they died in honours lofty bed *(Ibid.,* III.1.11). the Honor-giuing-hand/ Of *Cordelion (John,* I.1.53—4) (RMT). Honors thought/ Reignes solely in the breast of euery man *(Henry V,* II. Prol. 3—4). The fewer men, the greater share of honour *(Ibid.,* IV.3.22). if it be a sinne to couet Honor *(Ibid.,* IV.3.28). I would not loose so great an Honor *(Ibid.,* IV.3.31). And draw their honors reeking vp to Heauen *(Ibid.,* IV.3.101). his honour-owing-wounds *(Ibid.,* IV.6.9). And no man else hath Honor by his death *(Julius Caesar,* V.5.57).

Tragedy: Ru: Now for the honour of the forlorne French *(Henry VI.1,* I.2.19). Woman, do what thou canst to saue our honors *(Ibid.,* I.2.147). Else farwell *Talbot,* France, and Englands honor *(Ibid.,* IV.3.23). Liues, Honours, Lands, and all, hurrie to losse *(Ibid.,* IV.3.53). You his false hopes, the trust of Englands honor *(Ibid.,* IV.4.20). Flight cannot stayne the Honor you haue wonne, /But mine it will, that no Exploit haue done *(Ibid.,* IV.5.26—7).

(c) The v Group

Truthfulness:

Tragedy: Rn: Thereon I pawne my Credit, and mine Honor *(Henry VI.3,* III.3.116) (R(o)).

Keeping oaths and promises:

Comedy: Rn: Here is her oath for loue, her honors paune *(Two Gentlemen,* I.3.47). That his owne hand may strike his honour downe *(L. L. L.,* I.1.20).

Tragedy: Rn: For which your Honor and your Faith is pawn'd *(Richard III,* IV.2.89).

Keeping a marriage-contract:

Tragedy: Rn: And not deface your Honor with reproach (*Henry VI.1*, V.5.29). Tendring our sisters honour and our owne (*Titus Andr.*, I.1.476).

Loyalty to ruler:

Comedy: Rn: redeeme/ Your banish'd Honors (*Henry IV.1*, I.3.180—1). Comedy: Ru: dresse the ougly forme/ Of base, and bloodie Insurrection,/ With your faire Honors (*Henry IV.2*, IV.1.39—41) (RTP).
Tragedy: Rn: to repaire my Honor lost for him,/ I heere renounce him (*Henry VI.3*, III.3.193—4). Is in opinion and in honour wrong'd (*Titus Andr.*, I.1.416).
Tragedy: Ru: And he shall spend mine Honour, with his Shame (*Richard II*, V.3.67).

Not committing treason and murder:

Comedy: Rn: What thing, in Honor, had my Father lost (*Henry IV.2*, IV.1.113).

Not murdering:

Tragedy: Rn: or haue mine honor soyl'd/ With th'Attaindor of his sland'rous Lippes (*Richard II*, IV.1.23—4) (R(o)). We will not lyne his thin-bestained cloake/ With our pure Honors (*John*, IV.3.24—5) (RTP).

Honesty:

Comedy: Rn: it is as much as I can doe to keepe the termes of my hononor (*sic*) precise (*Merry Wives*, II.2.21—2).

Abjuring the world:

Comedy: Rg: That honour which shall bate his sythes keene edge (*L. L. L.*, I.1.6).

(d) *The x Group*

Comedy: Rn: passed sentence may not be recal'd/ But to our honours great disparagement (*Comedy of Errors*, I.1.147—8). the best ward of mine honour, is rewarding my dependants (*L. L. L.*, III.1.129—30) (Q text). Alas (sweet Wife) my Honor is at pawne (*Henry IV.2*, II.3.7). To hold your Honor more precise and nice (*Ibid.*, II.3.40). I would bee loth to foyle him, as I must for my owne honour (*A. Y. L. I.*, I.1.131—2).
Comedy: Ru: There were two Honors lost: Yours, and your Sonnes (*Henry IV.2*, II.3.16).
Tragedy: Rg: Thy George prophan'd, hath lost his Lordly Honor (*Richard III*, IV.4.370). In peace and Honour rest you heere my Sonnes (two ex., *Titus Andr.*, I.1.150, I.1.156). In peace and Honour, liue Lord *Titus* long (*Ibid.*, I.1.157).
Tragedy: Ru: Shame on himselfe, for my Desert is Honor (*Henry VI.3*, III.3.192) (REM). Nor Age, nor Honour, shall shape priuiledge (*Titus*

Andr., IV.4.57) (RP). 'tis a throane where Honour may be Crown'd (*Romeo*, III.2.93). you beare a many superfluously, and 'twere more honor some were away (*Henry V*, III.7.75—6).

It will be seen that in several of the x group there is quite a well-defined content. However, either this is not classifiable in terms of v/m/k (like *A. Y. L. I.* I.1.131—2), or it spreads over more than one category (like *Henry IV.2*, II.3.16), or the classification is disputable; for example, in the first example given (from *Comedy of Errors*), the Duke may mean that he will lose face simply from the fact of changing a decision (which would be k), or he may mean that he will lose his reputation for being just (which would be v). In some of the examples from *Henry IV.2*, II.3, the R is that involved in keeping a promise, but it is difficult to decide whether in the circumstances it is virtuous to keep the promise; the promise is to aid a rebellion, but the conspirators may well argue that they are in fact supporting the rightful king, since Mortimer's claim to the throne is better than Henry's; on the other hand, they have sworn allegiance to Henry; on the whole it seems best to classify as x.

(e) *Summary, R 1591—1600*

Table 21 gives a summary of the k/m/v/x classification of R for the decade 1591—1600. It will be seen that, in total, the m group is the largest, with 46.5% of the examples. The k group accounts for 24%, the v group for 15.5%, and the x group for 13.5%. There are no significant differences between comedy and tragedy. There are 38 examples classified as n (37%), and 44 as g (42.5%); as could be expected, the g group is strongly represented in m, and the n group in k. There are no examples of km in this section.

B. 1601—1610

In this decade there are 115 examples of R, 39 in comedy and 76 in tragedy. In 15 of the examples, R is not the sole head meaning; the combined head meanings found are RE (eight), RM (two), RP (one), RMT (one), RTP (one), RETP (one), and RV (one). Of the 115 examples, 11 are countables and 44 uncountables, the remaining 60 being equivocal. The examples are as follows.

THE R MATERIAL 153

TABLE 21. *Numbers of k, m, v and x: R material, 1591—1600.*

		k	m	v	x	Total
Comedy	n	5	0	5	5	15
	g	1	10	1	0	12
	u	0	8	1	1	10
	Total	6	18	7	6	37
Tragedy	n	12	3	8	0	23
	g	7	21	0	4	32
	u	0	6	1	4	11
	Total	19	30	9	8	66
All Plays	n	17	3	13	5	38
	g	8	31	1	4	34
	u	0	14	2	5	21
	Total	25	48	16	14	103

(a) *The k Group*

Sensitivity to affront, revenging injury, etc.:

Tragedy: Rn: But greatly to find quarrel in a straw/ When honour's at the stake (*Hamlet*, IV.4.55—6) (Q2 text). But in my termes of Honor/ I stand aloofe (*Ibid.*, V.2.245—6). honour, losse of time, trauaile, expence (*Troilus*, II.2.4). That hold their Honours in a wary distance (*Othello*, II.3.54). Who hast not in thy browes an eye-discerning/ Thine Honor (*Lear*, IV.2.52—3). Thy Sister is a thing to me so much/ Above mine honour (*Maid's Tragedy*, V.1, p. 69).

Accepting challenges, observing rules of duelling, etc.:

Comedy: Rn: the Gentleman will for his honors sake haue one bowt with you (*12th Night*, III.4.307—9). you had held your life contemptible, in regard of your honor (*Epicoene*, IV.5.59—60).

Tragedy: Rn: That I may kill him, and not stain mine honour (*Maid's Tragedy*, I.1, p. 7) (honour forbids fighting a man if he is old and helpless). you would be loth to lose/ Honour that is not easily gain'd again (*Ibid.*, V.1, p. 68).

Insisting on one's rights etc.:

Tragedy: Rn: So farre aske pardon, as befits mine Honour/ To stoope in such a case (*Antony*, II.2.101—2) (RP). if I loose mine Honour,/ I loose my selfe (*Ibid.*, III.4.22—3).

Rebelling rather than submit to injustice from rulers:

Tragedy: Rn: The cause is publique, and the honour, name,/ The immortalitie of euery soule/ That is not bastard, or a slaue in *Rome,/* Therein concern'd (*Sejanus,* IV.1.149—52).

High rank, office, wealth, etc.:

Tragedy: Rn: you can loose no honor,/ By trusting ought to me (*Sejanus,* I.1.326—7). Which to preserue mine honour, I'le performe (*Pericles,* II. 2.16).

Tragedy: Rg: but honour for those honours/ That are without him (first of the two examples) (*Troilus,* III.3.81—82) (RE; Q text). Those deeds breathe honor, that do sucke in gaine (*Sejanus,* I.1.332). Let the high Office and the Honor go (*Coriolanus,* II.3.121) (RMT). of him, I gather'd Honour (*Cymbeline,* III.1.71) (RM).

Tragedy: Ru: By doing euery thing safe toward your Loue/ And Honor (*Macbeth,* I.4.26—7) (RE).

Ostentation:

Comedy: Ru: But it is for his honour; and therefore I take no name of it (*Epicoene,* III.2.92—3).

Having authority maintained:

Tragedy: Ru: the dignitie,/ And honor of the state (*Sejanus,* III.1.213—4).

Precedence:

Tragedy: Rn: Who bates mine Honor, shall not know my Coyne (*Timon,* III.3.26).

Favourable peace-terms:

Tragedy: Rg: We haue made peace/ With no lesse Honor to the *Antiates/* Then shame to th' Romaines (*Coriolanus,* V.6.78—80).

Reflected (from Rc/C):

Comedy: Rn: by the honour of my family, which her lust hath profaned (*Blurt,* V.1.19—20). whose age and honour/ Both suffer vnder this complaint we bring (*All's Well,* V.3.160—1).

Tragedy: Rn: Why thinks my friend I will forget his honour (*Maid's Tragedy,* III.1, p. 41). Whose honour thou hast murdered (*Ibid.,* IV.1, p. 46). have a care/ My honour falls no farther (*Ibid.,* IV.1, p. 51).

Tragedy: Ru: Either to bring our banisht honours home,/ Or create new ones (*Maid's Tragedy,* V.1, p. 65).

Reflected (from lover's military qualities):

Comedy: Rg: Now for Violetta's honour! (*Blurt,* I.1.131).

Comedy: Ru: play at barriers with scourge-sticks, for the honour of my punk (*Family of Love,* III.6.2—3) (perhaps a pun on C).

Reflected (from relative's virtue):

Tragedy: Rn: it would make a great gap in your owne Honor (*Lear*, I.2.86—87).

Being jealous:

Comedy: Rn: Honour? tut, a breath (*Volpone*, III.7.38) (R(o)).

Successfully completing anything once started:

Comedy: Rn: 'Tis for your honours, gentlemen (*Trick to Catch*, III.1.248).

Tragedy: Rn: a quarrell/ Which hath our seuerall Honours all engag'd (*Troilus*, II.2.123—4).

(b) *The m Group*

Comedy: Rn: the fortune of the field/ Is death with honour, or with shame to yield (*Blurt*, I.1.157—8). He weares his honor in a boxe vnseene (*All's Well*, II.3.282).

Comedy: Rg: Cride fame and honor on him (*12th Night*, V.1.57). a pox a' that honour that must have nothing but barber-surgeons to wait upon't (*Blurt*, I.1.17—18). Wars dustie honours I pursue not young? (*Poetaster*, I.1.46). And give to Hymen th' honour of the field (*Family of Love*, III.2.117). Not to wooe honour, but to wed it, when/ The brauest questant shrinkes (*All's Well*, II.1.15—16). Till honour be bought vp, and no sword worne (*Ibid.*, II.1.32).

Comedy: Ru: honour was never dyed in grain till it was dipt in the colours of the field (*Blurt*, I.1.15—16). this instrument of honour (*All's Well*, III.6.65—66). come of, Knight, with a counterbuff, for the honor of knighthood (*Eastward Ho*, II.1.93—4).

Tragedy: Rn: It wounds thine Honor that I speake it now (*Antony*, I.4.69).

Tragedy: Rg: That holds his Honor higher then his ease (*Troilus*, I.3.266). both our Honour, and our Shame in this,/ Are dogg'd with two strange Followers (*Ibid.*, I.3.364—5). She is a theame of honour and renowne (*Ibid.*, II.2.199). perseuerance, deere my Lord,/ Keepes honor bright (*Ibid.*, III.3.150—1). For honour traueis in a straight so narrow (*Ibid.*, III.3.154). I, and perhaps receiue much honor by him (*Ibid.*, III.3.226). Cozen, all honor to thee (*Ibid.*, IV.5.138) (RE). A thought of added honor, torne from Hector (*Ibid.*, IV.5.145). Fall Greekes, faile Fame, Honor or go, or stay (*Ibid.*, V.1.42). Where rather Ile expect victorious life,/ Then death, and Honor (*Antony*, IV.2.43—4). Then Honour be but a Goale to my Will (*Pericles*, II.1.165). I came vnto your Court for Honours cause (*Ibid.*, II.5.61). I should freelier reioyce in that absence wherein he wonne Honor (*Coriolanus*, I.3.3—4). considering how Honour would become such a person (*Ibid.*, I.3.10—11). He had rather venture all his Limbes for Honor (*Ibid.*, II.2.81). Ha's clock'd thee to the Warres: and safelie home/ Loden with Honor (*Ibid.*, V.3.163—4). that onely seemes to seeke out danger/ I' th' name of Fame, and Honor (*Cymbeline*, III.3.50—1).

Tragedy: Ru: That can from *Hector* bring his Honor off (*Troilus*, I.3.334). But why should Honor out-liue Honesty? (*Othello*, V.2.245). Or bathe my dying Honor in the blood/ Shall make it liue again (*Antony*, IV.2.6—7). To day, how many would haue giuen their Honours/ To haue sau'd their Carkasses? (*Cymbeline*, V.3.67—8).

(c) *The v Group*

Keeping promises:

Tragedy: Rn: Pawne me to this your Honour, she is his (*Timon*, I.1.151). Mine Honour on my promise (*Ibid.*, I.1.152).

Not committing treason and murder:

Comedy: Rn: 'Tis forged against mine honour and my life (*Phoenix*, V.1.82) (R(o)).

Not murdering:

Comedy: Rn: You kill your honours more in this revenge (*Blurt*, V.3.34).

Paying debts:

Tragedy: Rn: the detention of long since due debts/ Against my Honor (*Timon*, II.2.42—3).

Not conniving at unchastity:

Comedy: Rn: Before your honour? (*Volpone*, III.7.38).
Comedy: Ru: And six or seuen winters more respect/ Then a perpetuall Honor (*M. for M.*, III.1.73—4).

Sexual continence:

Comedy: Rn: this dire massacre, on your honour (*Volpone*, IV.2.25). had in the open streets/ Pursu'd them, but for sauing her knights honour (*Ibid.*, IV.5.151—2) (Ro).
Tragedy: Rn: by his fall, my honour must keepe hie (*Pericles*, I.1.149) (Ro).

Not permitting immodest language:

Comedy: Rn: Preserue the honour of the court (*Volpone*, IV.5.120). To scandalize your honours, or my sexes (*Ibid.*, IV.6.9) (RY).

Not being ungrateful:

Tragedy: Rn: This Slaue vnto his Honor,/ Has my Lords meate in him (*Timon*, III.1.59—60) (Ro).

THE R MATERIAL 157

Not being corrupt and lecherous:
Comedy: Rn: Or else thou art suborn'd against his honor (*M. for M.*, V.1.106).

Resisting and exposing vice and corruption:
Comedy: Rg: Grace of the Duke, reuenges to your heart,/ And general Honor (*M. for M.*, IV.3.136—7) (RE).

Modesty, clemency:
Tragedy: Rg: shall acquire no Honour/ Demuring vpon me (*Antony*, IV.15.28—9).

(d) The x Group

Comedy: Rn: My Honor's at the stake (*All's Well*, II.3.151). They were stil prest to engage their Honour (*Eastward Ho*, V.1.39—40).
Comedy: Rg: in both which honours the noble Hippolito had most excellent possession (*Blurt*, I.1.43—5). From trades, from artes, from valor honor springs (*Eastward Ho*, I.1.150) (RTP). the flowrie plaines of honour, and reputation (*Volpone*, II.2.169—70) (R(o)).
Comedy: Ru: And these breed honour (*All's Well*, II.3.135). His sword can neuer winne the honor that he looses (*Ibid.*, III.2.95—6). My house, mine honor, yea my life be thine (*Ibid.*, IV.2.52). fruits of comfort and of honour (*Roaring Girl*, V.2.96).
Tragedy: Rn: I pawn'd/ Mine Honor for his truth (*Coriolanus*, V.6.19—20). I'le right your honours (*Philaster*, III.1, p. 113) (Qq read *honour*). I dare lay mine Honour (*Cymbeline*, I.1.174). And pawne mine Honor for their safety (*Ibid.*, I.6.193). So they must,/ Or doe your Honour iniury (*Ibid.*, II.4.79—80). How he may bear himself, and save his honour (*Maid's Tragedy*, II.1, p. 20).
Tragedy: Rg: And not a man for being simply man,/ Hath any honour (*Troilus*, III.3.80—81) (RE). that I shold Purchase the day before for a little part, and vndo a great deale of Honour (*Timon*, III.2.51—2). Honor, health, and compassion to the Senate (*Ibid.*, III.5.5) (RE). The condemn'd Pompey,/ Rich in his Fathers Honor (*Antony*, I.3.49—50). Then to be thirsty after tottering honour (*Pericles*, III.2.40). to our Noble Consull/ Wish we all Ioy, and Honor (*Coriolanus*, II.2.153—4) (RE). To *Coriolanus* come all ioy and Honor (*Ibid.*, II.2.155) (RE).
Tragedy: Ru: bring him to his wonted way againe,/ To both your Honors (*Hamlet*, III.1.41—2). And of great BRVTVS honour mindfull be (*Sejanus*, III.1.459). The best of Happines, Honor, and Fortunes/ Keepe with you (*Timon*, I.2.236—7) (RM). Ile pawne my Victories, all my Honour to you (*Ibid.*, III.5.81—2). The Senators shall beare contempt Hereditary,/ The Begger Natiue Honor (*Ibid.*, IV.3.10—11) (RETP). Of *Caesar* seeke your Honour, with your safety (*Antony*, IV.15.46). by our Greatnesse, and the grace of it/ (Which is our Honour) (*Cymbeline*, V.5.132—3). It is more honour for you that I die (*Maid's Tragedy*, V.1.67).

(e) Summary, R 1601—1610

Table 22 gives a summary of the k/m/v/x classification of R for the decade 1601—1610. It will be seen that, in total, k and m are about equally prominent (31% and 29% respectively), while v is rather less than half (about 14%); x accounts for about 26%. There are no examples of km in this decade. The difference between comedy and tragedy with respect to v is significant, but the differences for k and for m are not. There are 49 examples classified as n (about 42.5%), and 41 as g (about 35.5%). The m group is more strongly represented in g, and the k and v groups in n.

TABLE 22. *Numbers of k, m, v, and x: R material, 1601—10.*

		k	m	v	x	Total
Comedy	n	6	2	8	2	18
	g	1	6	1	3	11
	u	2	3	1	4	10
	Total	9	11	10	9	39
Tragedy	n	19	1	5	6	31
	g	5	17	1	7	30
	u	3	4	0	8	15
	Total	27	22	6	21	76
All Plays	n	25	3	13	8	49
	g	6	23	2	10	41
	u	5	7	1	12	25
	Total	36	33	16	30	115

C. 1611—1620

In this decade there are 191 examples of R, 48 in comedy and 143 in tragedy. In 23 of the examples, R is not the sole head meaning; the combined head meanings found are RM (three), RP (three), RTP (eight), RMTP (five), REM (one), RETP (one), RC (one), and RRcC (one). Of the 191 examples, 21 are countables, 73 uncountables, and 97 equivocal. The examples are as follows.

(a) *The k Group*

Sensitivity to affront, revenging injury, etc.:

Comedy: Rn: I'd lost my honour else (*Fair Quarrel*, III.1.133). There you touch my honour (*Little Fr. Lawyer*, I.1, p. 376). that ever cursed I,/ Should give my honour up (*Ibid.*, III.1, p. 404). These shall forget their honour, I my wrongs (*Ibid.*, III.1, p. 407). to repair/ His honour by the sword (*Custom of the Country*, II.1, p. 319). Yet dare not wear a sword to guard your Honour (*Ibid.*, II.1, p. 327).

Comedy: Ru: poor life, which in respect/ Of life in honour is but death and darkness (*Fair Quarrel*, III.1.32—3).

Tragedy: Rn: To see alike mine Honor, as their Profits (*Winter's Tale*, I.2.308). the cause/ I hang upon, which in few, is my honour (*King and No King*, IV.1, p. 204) (Ro). You cannot hang too much Sir, for your honour (*Ibid.*). yet you had lost no honour (*Ibid.*, IV.1, p. 205). has askt me Mercy, and my honour's safe (*Ibid.*, V.1, p. 216) (Ro). his honour is come off clean and sufficient (*Ibid.*, V.1, p. 220) (Ro). Captain we must request your hand now to our honours (*Ibid.*, V.1, p. 221) (Ro). what is honour/ We all so strangely are bewitch'd withal? (*Valentinian*, III.3, p. 49). Can honour 'twixt the incensed Prince and Envy,/ Bear up the lives of worthy men? (*Ibid.*). Can honour pull the wings of fearful Cowards (*Ibid.*). A friend is more than all the world, than honour (*Ibid.*). And honour on thy head, his blood is reckon'd (*Ibid.*, IV.2, p. 59). Nor what that cursed name of honour was (*Ibid.*, IV.4, p. 72). We have suffer'd beyond all repair of honour (*Loyal Subject*, V.4, p. 161).

Not backing out of a duel, accepting challenges:

Comedy: Rn: You command/ What with mine honour I cannot obey (*Little Fr. Lawyer*, I.1, p. 389). and yet name your honours? (*Ibid.*, I.1, p. 390). to this honour/ A firm and worthy friend (*Ibid.*, II.1, p. 391). To leave my friend engag'd, mine honour tainted? (*Ibid.*, II.1, p. 397). the Gentleman preserv'd your honour (*Ibid.*, II.1, p. 399). no pretious time to lose, no friends,/ No honour, nor no life (*Ibid.*, II.1, p. 402). so well he loves his honour/ Beyond his life (*Ibid.*, III.1, p. 406).

Not being made to lose face:

Comedy: Rn: We have our honours home, and they their pains (*Little Fr. Lawyer*, III.1, p. 423).

Tragedy: Rn: you durst engage both life, and honor (*Catiline*, IV.1.692). To quench mine Honor (*Henry VIII*, V.2.16). Peace, if it may be/ Without the too much tainture of our honour (*Humorous Lieutenant*, III.6, p. 329) (not submitting to humiliating peace-terms).

Insisting on one's rights:

Comedy: Rn: 'tis held a coolness, if you lose your right, affronts and loss of honour (*Wit Without Money*, III.1, p. 171).

High rank, wealth, due ceremony, etc.:

Comedy: Rn: yet for mine honours sake (*Wit Without Money*, V.1, p. 204).
Comedy: Rg: what honour can ye add to me (*Custom of the Country*, V.1, p.381) (RTP).
Tragedy: Rn: No face of favour, if you love your honour (*Loyal Subject*, II.1, p. 97).
Tragedy: Rg: To whom as great a Charge, as little Honor/ He meant to lay vpon (*Henry VIII*, I.1.77—8) (RM). a heart, that wishes towards you/ Honor, and plenteous safety (*Ibid.*, I.1.103—4) (RTP). You tender more your persons Honor (*Ibid.*, II.4.115) (RTP). the great Childe of Honor, Cardinal *Wolsey* (*Ibid.*, IV.2.6) (RTP). Though from an humble Stocke, vndoubtedly/ Was fashion'd to much Honor (*Ibid.*, IV.2.49—50) (RMTP). an ambassador sent from a king/ Has honour by th'employment (*Witch*, IV.2.18—19). I intend, high heaven knows, but your honour (*Loyal Subject*, II.1, p. 97). they cannot/ Or rise to wealth or honour (*Bloody Brother*, I.1, p. 247) (RTP). now shall my honour,/ My power and vertue walk alone (*Ibid.*, V.2, p. 312) (RTP).
Tragedy. Ru: so may you depart/ Your Country, with more honour (*Duchess of Malfi*, III.2.355—6). He forced the Empress with him for more honour (*Valentinian*, V.4, p. 83). No friends Sir, to your honour (*Bloody Brother*, II.1, p. 259).

Having distinguished guests, mixing with the great, etc.:

Tragedy: Rg: I haue receiu'd much Honour by your presence (*Henry VIII*, V.4.71). what honour thou dost gain by me,/ I cannot lose it (*Laws of Candy*, III.1, p. 271) (RM).

Making socially good marriages:

Tragedy: Rn: That makes himselfe (but for our Honor therein)/ Vnworthy thee (*Winter's Tale*, IV.3.440—1). as you love your honour (*Mad Lover*, IV.1, p. 53). Take heed, for honours sake take heed (*Ibid.*, IV.1, p. 54).
Tragedy: Ru: I will marry for your honour (*Duchess of Malfi*, III.1.53).

Reflected (from Rc/C):

Comedy: Rn: That that is something more than ours, our honours (*Captain*, III.4, p. 277). Besides your Fathers Honour (*Custom of the Country*, I.1, p. 305).
Tragedy: Rn: Thou hast stain'd the spotlesse honour of my house (*White Devil*, IV.2.110). Foolish men, /That ere will trust their honour in a Barke (*Duchess of Malfi*, II.5.46—7). An evil that so much concerns your honour (*Humorous Lieutenant*, V.5, p. 368).

Seducing a woman:

Tragedy: Rg: I'le deal with you then,/ For here's the honour to be won (*Loyal Subject*, IV.3, p. 142) (perhaps also figurative Rgm, and a pun on C and on the woman's name).

Committing murder in service of king:
Tragedy: Rg: The honour of the service (*False One*, II.1, p. 316).
Suicide:
Tragedy: Rn: If she were any thing to me but honour (*Valentinian*, III.1, p. 41).
Tragedy: Ru: To keep your memories, and honours living (*Valentinian*, IV.4, p. 71).
Miscellaneous:
Comedy: Rn: And howsoever they forget their honour (*Little Fr. Lawyer*, I.1, p. 383) (not brawling in the street, but duelling respectably in private). a Judge/ Can judge best what belongs to wounded honour (*Ibid.*, III.1, p. 411) (sensitivity to insult/ professional reputation). why should I mix mine honour/ With a fellow, that has ne're a lace in's shirt? (*Ibid.*, IV.1, p. 427) (duelling honour/social rank).
Tragedy: Rg: My next brave battel/ I dedicate to your bright honour (*Mad Lover*, V.1, p. 74) (having a great warrior as your servant).

(b) The m Group

Comedy: Rn: then compound too without the loss of honour (*Wit Without Money*, I.1, p. 154) (RRcC).
Comedy: Rg: Forgive me, Honour, I'll make use of thee (*Captain*, II.1, p. 252). To get or wealth, or honour (*Little Fr. Lawyer*, I.1, p. 381). An old, and tatter'd colours, to the enemy,/ Is of more honour (*Ibid.*, IV.1, p. 427).
Comedy: Ru: For the honour of our Country (*Little Fr. Lawyer*, I.1, p. 374).
Tragedy: Rn: from your place, and honour of a Souldier,/ I here seclude you (*Valentinian*, II.3, p. 24) (RTP). A way to fetch these off, and save their honours (*Humorous Lieutenant*, III.6, p. 329). stings my honour,/ And leaves me dead in fame (*Laws of Candy*, II.1, p. 258).
Tragedy: Rg: Kept from the honor of it, by disease (*Catiline*, V.1.3). if our destinie enuie our vertue/ The honor of the day (*Ibid.*, V.1.415—6). Wherein the danger almost paiz'd the honor (*Ibid.*, V.1.633). their honours, time outdaring (*Valentinian*, I.3, p. 11). To see the warlike Eagles mew their honours/ In obscure Towns (*Ibid.*, I.3, p. 15). And even began to prey upon our honours (*Ibid.*, IV.4, p. 69). Report and honour/ Drew her to doe you favours (*Mad Lover*, I.1, p. 7). For so much the more danger, the more honour (*Ibid.*, I.1, p. 10). Farewel to him, and all our honours (*Ibid.*, IV.1, p. 55). 'tis necessity,/ Or we must lose our honours (*Ibid.*). And know thine envy to mine honour (*Ibid.*, V.1, p. 63). *Keep your Ranks close, and now your honours win* (*Ibid.*). look on his Honour Sister,/ That bears no stamp of time (*Ibid.*, V.1, p. 70). Then flew this Bird of honour bravely (*Loyal Subject*, I.3, p. 84). A little time will bring thee to his honour (*Ibid.*, I.3, p. 87) (Ro). When the great rest of all your honour's

up (*Ibid.*, I.3, p. 88). Come home the Son of Honour (*Ibid.*, I.5, p. 95). What labour would these men neglect, what danger/ Where honour is (*Ibid.*, II.1, p. 102). That nurs'd your honour up, held fast your vertue (*Ibid.*, III.3, p. 123). If you your self will spare him so much honour (*Humorous Lieutenant*, I.1, p. 289). Not covetous of blood, and death, but honour (*Ibid.*, I.1, p. 290). Nor too ambitious to get honour instantly (*Ibid.*, I.1, p. 291). To bury in an hour his age of honour (*Ibid.*, II.2, p. 298). Fortune has hours of loss, and hours of honour (*Ibid.*). And here must he be pricking out for honour (*Ibid.*, II.2, p. 299). And kill one another foolishly for honour (*Ibid.*, III.3, p. 317). Honour, the spur of all illustrious natures (*Ibid.*, III.6, p. 330). And thine be this days honour, great *Seleucus* (*Ibid.*, III.6, p. 331). The interest which the inheritance of your vertue/ And mine own thrifty fate can claim in honour (*Laws of Candy*, I.2, p. 241). to take/ The life of my yet infant-honour from me (*Ibid.*). to renown/ Your honours through the world (*Ibid.*, I.2, p. 246). to gain/ The crown of honour from him (*Ibid.*). in honours cause (*Ibid.*). the Law compell'd him for his honour (*Ibid.*, II.1, p. 256). The richest jewel of my life, my honour (*Ibid.*, II.1, p. 257). Let not thirst/ Of Honour, make you quite forget (*Ibid.*, III.1, p. 269). gave him the full prospect/ Of honour, and preferment (*Ibid.*, V.1, p. 289). kick'd against mine honour, scorned all/ My services (*Ibid.*). your peevish thirst of honour (*Ibid.*, V.1, p. 295). as far as honour/ Is from shame and repentance (*Bloody Brother*, V.1, p. 303). That high plum'd honour built up for her own (*False One*, II.1, p. 315). Where Kings were fair competitours for honour (*Ibid.*, II.1, p. 316). what honour?/ Nay everlasting glory had *Rome* purchas'd (*Ibid.*, III.4, p. 342). Beauty and honour are the marks they shoot at (*Ibid.*, IV.2, p. 349). Scarrs, and those maims of honour/ Are memorable crutches (*Ibid.*, IV.3, p. 353).

Tragedy: Ru: I was faine to draw mine Honour in, and let'em win the Worke (*Henry VIII*, V.3.59—60). the other deprives him of honour (*Duchess of Malfi*, I.1.104). honour,/ That truly is a Saint to none but Souldiers (*Valentinian*, I.2, p. 5) (RC). to quit mine honour,/ And on thee single (*Mad Lover*, V.1, p. 63). the Drums beat;/ I dare not slack your honour (*Humorous Lieutenant*, I.1, p. 295). And lost my People, left mine Honour murder'd (*Ibid.*, II.4, p. 305). My maiden Honour, never to be ransom'd (*Ibid.*). a man/ That has outliv'd his honour (*Laws of Candy*, II.1, p. 258). She is sent to dispossess you of your honour (*False One*, II.3, p. 326). burying of his honour there? (*Ibid.*, IV.2, p. 351).

Under m are also to be classified the following examples of km:

Comedy: Rn: men, from whom no honour can be lost (*Little Fr. Lawyer*, I.1, p. 384).

Comedy: Rg: What honour can you both win on me single? (*Little Fr. Lawyer*, II.1, p. 391). For the matter of honour, 'tis at your own disposure (*Ibid.*, II.1, p. 397). And his the honour (*Ibid.*, III.1, p. 405). There were no honour in't (*Ibid.*, IV.1, p. 429).

Comedy: Ru: He has fought thrice, and come off still with honour (*Custom of the Country*, II.1, p. 318).

Tragedy: Rg: now they think to get honour on me (*King and No King*, III.1, p. 187).

(c) *The v Group*

Telling the truth:

Comedy: Rn: A reprobate out of the state of honour (*Captain*, I.2, p. 237).

Keeping promises:

Tragedy: Rn: I must have you promise/ Upon your honors (*Duchess of Malfi*, V.4.10—11). Let our honors bind this trifle (*Ibid.*, V.4.13). to laugh me out of mine honour! (*Ibid.*, V.5.35).

Obedience to civil governors, not being treasonable:

Tragedy: Rn: Life, Honour, Name and all/ That made me happy (*Henry VIII*, II.1.116—7) (RTP). have perform'd no more than what/ I ought, for honours safety (*Laws of Candy*, IV.1, p. 282).

Tragedy: Rg: What an honor/ Hath shee atchieued to her selfe! (*Catiline*, III.1.344—5).

Tragedy: Ru: keep/ Thy honour living, though thy body sleep (*Bloody Brother*, V.1, p. 306).

Not murdering:

Comedy: Rn: Hold, Reverend Sir, for honour of your Age (*Captain*, IV.4, p. 299).

Not conniving at unchastity:

Tragedy: Rn: we must hazard honors/ A little (*Catiline*, I.1.170—1).

Not gained by raping:

Tragedy: Rg: what had you purchas'd by it?/ What Honour won? (*Humorous Lieutenant*, IV.5, p. 351).

Not being ungrateful:

Tragedy: Rn: this is too foul play/ Boy to thy good, thine honour (*Loyal Subject*, IV.5, p. 148).

Miscellaneous:

Tragedy: Rn: a Noble Lie,/ 'Cause it must shield our honors (*Duchess of Malfi*, III.2.217—18) (for not carrying on an illicit love-affair?). And you be more indulgent to your passion,/ Then to your honor (*Catiline*, V.1.457 —8) (for putting law and reason above passion). Out of our easinesse and childish pitty/ To one mans Honour (*Henry VIII*, V.2.60—1) (Ro) (not being a heretic). all respects of honour in your selves/ Be in your fury choakt (*Bloody Brother*, I.1, p. 254) (not being wrathful and covetous).

Tragedy: Rg: The fairest Stars in the bright Sphere of honour (*Bloody Brother*, I.1, p. 257) (for virtue which leads to Heaven).

(d) *The x Group*

Comedy: Rn: for the honour of our Booth (*Bartholomew Fair*, II.5.57). Know your own honour then (*Wit Without Money*, III.1, p. 169) (RP). eaters of others honours (*Ibid.*, III.1, p. 173). without baseness,/ Without the stain of honour? (*Monsieur Thomas*, III.1, p. 125). it concernes, the first be a perfect *Businesse*,/ For his owne honour! (*Devil is an Ass*, III.3. 113—4). Mine? my honour, sir? (*Fair Quarrel*, II.1.72). my honour bearing part on't (*Ibid.* II.1.85). *tis a businesse/That concernes both our honors* (*Devil's Law-Case*, I.1.226—7).

Comedy: Rg: The honour of this deed will be your own (*Little Fr. Lawyer*, III.1, p. 421). of all which/ Arise and spring up Honor (*Devil's Law-Case*, I.1.76—7).

Comedy: Ru: *Honor, riches, marriage, blessing* (*Tempest*, IV.1.105) (RETP). Than usefull to his honour I preserve it (*Custom of the Country*, IV.1, p. 358).

Tragedy: Rn: The sacred Honor of himselfe, his Queenes (*Winter's Tale*, II.3.84). care not, whose honor you wound (*Catiline*, II.1.272). We would spare their honor (*Catiline*, V.1.555) (RP). you that stand so much upon your honour (*White Devil*, I.2.301). Not vnconsidered leaue your Honour (*Henry VIII*, I.2.15). Whose Honor Heauen shield from soile (*Ibid.*, I.2. 26). 'Twill be much,/ Both for your Honour better, and your Cause (*Ibid.*, III.1.94—5) (Ro). To keepe mine Honor, from Corruption (*Ibid.*, IV.2.71). Gentlemen like, and jealous of our honours (*Mad Lover*, I.1, p. 10). for it much concernes mine honour (*Ibid.*, II.1, p. 27). Consumes all honour, credit, faith (*Loyal Subject*, IV.3, p. 143).

Tragedy: Rg: So I grow stronger, you more Honour gaine (*Henry VIII*, V.2.216) (RM). His Honour, and the greatnesse of his Name (*Ibid.*, V.4.50). But when the vertue's known, the honour's doubled (*Valentinian*, I.2, p. 5). Honour wait on *Caesar* (*Ibid.*, V.4, p. 84) (REM). And *Romulus*, thou Father of our honour (*Ibid.*, V.8, p. 89).

Tragedy: Ru: And, to her honor, so did knit (*Catiline*, II.1.399). the Cardinall/ Does buy and sell his Honour as he pleases (*Henry VIII*, I.1. 191—2). *Honour that is ever living* (*Valentinian*, V.8, p. 89) (RMTP). *Honour that is ever giving* (*Ibid.*) (RMTP). *Honour that sees all and knows* (*Ibid.*) (RMTP). *Honour that rewards the best* (*Ibid.*) (RMTP). Yet for your good, and honour (*Mad Lover*, V.1, p. 72). I'de not partake/ Ought, but what should concern your honour (*Laws of Candy*, III.1, p. 267). hast rob'd this Kingdom/ Of honour and of safety (*Ibid.*, V.1, p. 295) (RP).

(e) *Summary, R 1611—1620*

Table 23 gives a summary of the k/m/v/x classification of R for the decade 1611—1620. In total, k and m are still about equally prominent

(35% and 37% respectively), but v has sunk to about a quarter of either of them (9%); the x group accounts for about 19%. There are 7 examples of km in this decade, one in tragedy and the remainder in comedy; over half the examples of m in comedy are km (6 out of 11). The difference between comedy and tragedy is significant for k and for m; k is more frequent in comedy than in tragedy (48% against 31%), but m is less frequent (23% against 41%). The difference between comedy and tragedy for v is not significant. As in the previous decade, the numbers of n and g are about equal (about 43.5% n, and about 41% g), and k is strongest in n, while m is strongest in g.

TABLE 23. *Numbers of k, m, v, and x: R material, 1611—20.*

		k	m	v	x	Total
Comedy	n	21	2	2	8	33
	g	1	7	0	2	10
	u	1	2	0	2	5
	Total	23	11	2	12	48
Tragedy	n	25	3	11	11	50
	g	14	46	3	5	68
	u	5	10	1	9	25
	Total	44	59	15	25	143
All Plays	n	46	5	13	19	83
	g	15	53	3	7	78
	u	6	12	1	11	30
	Total	67	70	17	37	191

D. 1621—1630

In this decade there are 178 examples of R, 85 in comedy and 93 in tragedy. In 17 of the examples, R is not the sole head-meaning; the combined head-meanings found are RM (6), RTP (9), RE (one), and RPD (one). Of the 178 examples, 13 are countables, 69 uncountables, and 96 equivocal. The examples are as follows.

(a) The k Group

Sensitivity to affront, revenging injury, etc.:

Comedy: Rn: His anger slow, but certain for his honour (*Wild Goose Chase*, I.1, p. 328). To the repairing of mine honour, and hurt here (*Beggars Bush*, II.3, p. 234). Thou hast wrong'd mine honor (*Rule a Wife*, I.1, p. 178). no, 'tis Honour (*Chances*, I.2, p. 179). Honour, my noble friends (*Ibid.*). that Idol, Honour (*Ibid.*). 'tis no matter, whether you, or honour,/ Or both (*Ibid.*). is not his honour/ Open'd to his hand (*Ibid.*, I.8, p. 185). my honour (unto which compar'd she's nothing) (*Elder Brother*, V.1, p. 51). the reputation of a man, the honour (*Ibid.*, V.1, p. 52). to find ye thus tender of your honour (*Ibid.*). this cause that concerns the honour of our Family (*Ibid.*, V.1, p. 56).

Comedy: Ru: And only now for honours sake defies ye (*Pilgrim*, IV.2, p. 206).

Tragedy: Rn: the airy words of Honour,/ And false stamp'd reputation (*Lover's Progress*, V.1, p. 141). bee rul'd as you respect <your> honour (*'Tis Pity*, 1885—6). In point of honour/ Discretion knowes no bounds (*Broken Heart*, 1748—9).

Tragedy: Rg: To cozen thee of honour (*Broken Heart*, 2242).

Keeping duelling appointments, observing rules of duelling:

Comedy: Rn: Their Honours are engag'd (*Chances*, III.1, p. 211). Pawning our honours then to meet again (*Ibid.*, IV.3, p. 231). oh mine honor, Sir (*Cure for a Cuckold*, I.2.136). if I survive/ The ruine of that Honor (*Ibid.*, I.2.167—8). But you stand by my honor when 'tis falling (*Ibid.*, III.1.59). I cannot with my honour wound thee (*Witty Fair One*, V.2, p. 352).

Not being jilted:

Tragedy: Rn: To make me reparation in mine honour (*Bondman*, V.3, p. 118).

For high rank, wealth, due ceremony, etc.:

Comedy: Ru: and with more honour,/ Than exercise ten thousand Fools (*Rule a Wife*, III.1, p. 199). We keep a handsom port, for the Kings honour (*Ibid.*, IV.1, p. 215).

Tragedy: Rg: Omit no Ceremony/ That may be for his honour (*Prophetess*, II.3, p. 343). To woo this purblind honour (*Ibid.*, III.1, p. 346) (RTP). Some sad malignant Angel to mine honour (*Ibid.*, III.1, p. 350) (RTP). Honour, and Empire, absolute command (*Ibid.*, V.1, p. 377) (RTP). The maker of great minds, and nurse of honour (*Ibid.*, V.2, p. 379) (RTP). for his further honour, Sanazarro (*Great Duke of Florence*, I.2, p. 202).

Tragedy: Ru: You must forget their names; your honour bids ye (*Prophetess*, III.2, p. 352) (RTP).

Entertaining the great:

Comedy: Rg: to whose honor comes/ The Duke in person (*Fair Maid of the Inn*, V.3.27—8).

Having illustrious dependants:

Tragedy: Rg: will add honour/ To the great bestower (*Great Duke of Flor.*, I.1, p. 200).

Not being too easily accessible to petitioners:

Comedy: Rn: And honour. Here'll be visitants (*Staple of News*, II.1.57).

Ostentation, hospitality:

Comedy: Ru: which shall spend itself/ For my lady's honour (*New Way*, I.3, p. 352).

Not having authority flouted:

Comedy: Rn: kills her husbands honour (*Elder Brother*, III.1, p. 22).
Tragedy: Rn: thou suffer'st/ In honour for thy friends (*Prophetess*, IV.2, p. 367).

Making socially good marriages:

Comedy: Rn: I cannot find/ How it can taint my honour (*New Way*, V.1, p. 372). Honor! (*Fair Maid of the Inn*, IV.1.167).
Comedy: Rg: A work of fame. Of honor. Celebration (*Staple of News*, I.6.86).

Having a good suitor:

Comedy: Rg: to lose the honour,/ And reputation, she hath had (*New Inn*, II.6.151—2) (RM).

Reflected (from Rc/C):

Comedy: Rn: I stand upon the ground of mine own Honour (*Rule a Wife*, III.1, p. 205). And at one instant kill both Name and Honour (*Ibid.*, III.1, p. 206). H'as taken a brave way to save his honour (*Ibid.*, IV.1, p. 215). One that would clip his credit out of his honour (*Ibid.*, V.1, p. 230). The honour of my house crack'd (*Chances*, I.2, p. 178). blasted for ever/ In name and honour (*Ibid.*, I.2, pp. 178—9).

Tragedy: Rn: To whom my son ows his, with life, his honour (*Lover's Progress*, V.1, p. 140). to hold your honour/ Shipwrack'd in such a Daughter (*Ibid.*, V.1, p. 145). And would you force a high-way through mine honour (*Wife for a Month*, IV.1, p. 46) (probably also L). your losse of Honour ('*Tis Pity*, 2255—6). In one vnseemely thought against your honour (*Broken Heart*, 1299).

Reflected (from good or bad qualities of relatives):

Comedy: Rn: my till now untainted blood and honour (*Spanish Gipsy*, III.3.87). That are so ill preservers of mens honors (*Fair Maid of the Inn*, V.1.25).

Sexual virility, success in love:

Comedy: Rg: Now for thine honour Pinac (*The Wild-Goose-Chase*, II.1, p. 331).

Tragedy: Rn: And trench upon that honour that he brags of (*Wife for a Month*, II.1, p. 20).

Victory in the war of the sexes:

Comedy: Rn: Give up without your honours saved (*Wild-Goose-Chase*, V.3, p. 383).

Comedy: Rg: And who shall have honour then (*Wild-Goose-Chase*, V.2, p. 381).

Not being under an obligation:

Tragedy: Ru: what can take/ More from our honour (*Prophetess*, V.2, p. 378).

Politeness to ladies:

Comedy: Rn: when with terms, not taking from his honour,/ He does solicit me (*New Way*, IV.3, p. 370).

Miscellaneous:

Comedy: Rn: a Rape done to Honour (*Elder Brother*, V.2, p. 57) (lost by abduction of daughter). If it may stand with the honour of the Court (*New Inn*, IV.4.25) (dignity).

Tragedy: Rn: any wrong that malic'd/ The honour of our house (*Broken Heart*, 1434—5) (lost by unspecified injury).

Tragedy: Rg: *which is the scorn of love, and rust of honour* (*Lover's Progress*, II.1, p. 93) (lost with coming of old age). Nor fortune pointed out a path to Honour,/ Straighter and nobler (*Wife for a Month*, I.1, p. 15) (choosing marriage and death rather than no marriage).

Tragedy: Ru: Rivals and honours make men stand at distance (*Lover's Progress*, II.1, p. 91) (unspecified, but clearly k). I'll kiss him for the honour of my country (*Bondman*, I.3, p. 93) (primarily for producing ladies who are good lovers). Such honour comes by accident, not nature (*Broken Heart*, 1073) (for acts conventionally thought to bring honour, arising from passion).

(b) *The m Group*

Comedy: Rg: Your Gallants, they get Honour (*Spanish Curate*, II.1, p. 76). to run mad for Honour (*Rule a Wife*, I.1, p. 174). The more the danger, still the more the Honour (*Ibid.*, IV.1, p. 209). we bring home/ Honor and profit (*Cure for a Cuckold*, III.3. 114—15). there we sought/Honour, and wealth through dangers (*Fair Maid of the Inn*, I.1.142—3). With the honor/ To give the daring enemy an affront (*Ibid.*, I.2.27—8).

Comedy: Ru: Which place we have heard/ He did discharge with honour (*Beggars Bush*, I.1, p. 209). Not daring, or for honour, or revenge/ Again to tempt his fortune (*Ibid.*, I.1, p. 210).

Tragedy: Rn: redeem our mortgaged honours (*Maid of Honour*, I.1, p. 228). I will redeem my friends,/ And with my friends mine honour (*Prophetess*, IV.2, p. 366). How! your slaves?/ O stain of honour (*Bondman*, I.3, p. 96).

Tragedy: Rg: Honour, be thou my ever-living mistress (*Maid of Honour*, I.2, p. 230). the Port/ Of glorious Honour (*Prophetess*, IV.2, p. 367). You shall not have the honour of my death (*Ibid.*, IV.5, p. 373). Make up for honour,/ The *Persians* shrink (*Ibid.*). Alike we sought our dangers and our honours (*Lover's Progress*, II.1, p. 90). As you are a profess'd souldier, court your honour (*Ibid.*, IV.1, p. 133). Honour and glorious triumph made the garland (*Bondman*, I.3, p. 96). Honour won in war (*Ibid.*, I.3, p. 97). Be bribed to part with the least piece of honour (*Ibid.*). mine eye, fix'd/ Upon the hill of honour (*Ibid.*, II.1, p. 99). You have outstripp'd me in the race of honour (*Ibid.*, III.4, p. 107). my new-got honour/ Assisted by the general applause (*Ibid.*). But I can lay no claim to the least honour (*Ibid.*). sent me forth/ To trade for honour (*Ibid.*). with the dear expense of sweat and blood/ Have purchased honour (*Ibid.*, IV.2, p. 108). The honours I can call my own, thought scandals (*Ibid.*, V.3, p. 117) (RM). I' the pride of all his honours, birth, and fortunes (*Ibid.*) (RM). all their boasted honours,/ Purchased with blood and wrong (*Renegado*, IV.3, p. 140) (RM). He in this Firmament of honour, stands/ Like a Starre (*Broken Heart*, 260—1).

Tragedy: Ru: we can nor live/ Nor die with honour (*Maid of Honour*, II.4, p. 235). forsake mine honour,/ Labour and sweat (*Prophetess*, I.3, p. 330). When liberty and honour fill one scale (*Bondman*, I.3, p. 96). one that haue got/ Mine honour with expence of blood ('*Tis Pity*, 159—60).

Under m are also to be classified the following examples of km:

Comedy: Rg: Besides there is no honour won on Reprobates (*Wild-Goose-Chase*, III.1, p. 346).

Comedy: Ru: I brought him on and off, with honour, lady (*A New Way*, I.3, p. 354).

(c) *The v Group*

Truthfulness:

Tragedy: Rn: My honour's pawn'd for it (*Great Duke of Flor.*, V.2, p. 220).

Not being a hypocrite:

Comedy: Rn: for sacred virtue's honour (*Game at Chess*, V.2.25).

Keeping promises:

Tragedy: Rn: here I pawn my honour,/ Which is the best security (*Great Duke of Flor.*, III.1, p. 209).

Honesty (not accepting money known to be dishonestly obtained):

Comedy: Rn: so tender/ Of what concerns you, in all points of honour (*New Way*, IV.1, p. 367) (Ro).

Not conniving at unchastity:

Comedy: Rn: Mine honour (*Chances*, III.1, p. 210). And 'twere not for mine honour (*Ibid.*). Come, your honour,/ Your house, and you too (*Ibid.*).

Tragedy: Rn: The remedy and cure of all my honour (*Wife for a Month*, IV.1, p. 40). Poore Honour! thou art stab'd, and bleed'st to death (*Broken Heart*, 598).

Sexual continence:

Comedy: Rn: Though the acknowledgment must wound mine honour (*Spanish Curate*, III.3, p. 103). Was not this brought about well for our honours (*Game at Chess*, II.2.241) (Ro).

Tragedy: Rn: Because he would dispatch his honour too (*Prophetess*, I.1, p. 322).

Obedience and loyalty to husband:

Comedy: Rn: And your sick will aims at the care of honour (*Rule a Wife*, V.1, p. 224) (perhaps also Rc).

Comedy: Rg: you shall gain much honor by it (*Anything for a Quiet Life*, V.1.203—4).

Piety, devotion to church:

Tragedy: Ru: To pull down Churches with pretension/ To build 'em fairer, may be done with honour,/ And all this time believe no gods (*Wife for a Month*, I.1, p. 9) (RE) (Ro).

Saving the innocent, protecting virtue:

Comedy: Rg: And we embrace as partner of that honour (*Game at Chess*, III.1.165).

Tragedy: Rn: I fear'd/ Death more than loss of Honour (*Lover's Progress*, V.1, p. 141).

Miscellaneous:

Comedy: Rn: 'twill stand with your honour to doe something/ For this wronged woman (*Spanish Curate*, III.3, p. 104) (recompensing those you have wronged).

Comedy: Rg: Will make much for my honour (*Wild-Goose-Chase*, I.1, p. 319) (reclaiming a libertine).

Tragedy: Rn: The Kingdoms honour suffers in this cruelty (*Wife for a Month*, II.1, p. 17) (lost by cruelty).

Tragedy: Rg: When it comes crown'd with honour (*Wife for a Month*, II.1, p. 19) (dying virtuously; perhaps also Rc). But reall Honour/ Is the reward of vertue (*Broken Heart*, 1075—6) (for virtue, justice, and valour in a just cause).

Tragedy: Ru: Honour consists not in a bare opinion (*Broken Heart*, 1070) (not clearly specified, but obviously v).

(d) *The x Group*

Comedy: Rn: thou sham'st the *Spanish* Honour (*Pilgrim*, II.2, p. 172). you've drawn blood, life-blood, yea, blood of honour (*Game at Chess*, III.1. 60). basely to have bent mine honour (*Chances*, III.4, p. 222). Reseruing, still, the honour of my Lady (*New Inn*, I.6.75). stood out/ So long, without conditions, for mine honor (*Ibid.*, IV.4.304—5).

Comedy: Rg: For the Kings sake/ And honour these (*Pilgrim*, V.6, p. 225). To the King, honour, and all Joy (*Ibid.*). an end/ Fit for thy creature, and worthy of thine honour (*Beggars Bush*, III.2, p. 242). Where slept mine honour all the time before (*Game at Chess*, Ind. 16). honour grows on him,/ And wealth pil'd up for him (*Ibid.*, III.2.63—4) (RTP). Full increase of honour wait ever on your Lordship (*Elder Brother*, I.2, p. 11) (RM). wisdom loaded with the weight of honour (*Ibid.*, V.1, p. 50) (RM). Let after-times report, and to your honour (*New Way*, IV.1, p. 366).

Comedy: Ru: of ever speaking/ But to her honour (*Wild-Goose-Chase*, IV.2, p. 369). Take the bare name of honour (*Pilgrim*, II.2, p. 180). Is not their honour ours (*Ibid.*, IV.2, p. 207). And leave your youth, your honour and your state (*Rule a Wife*, V.1, p. 231) (RTP). that honour you would build up, you destroy (*Elder Brother*, V.2, p. 56) (RPD). It is for your honour (*Witty Fair One*, II.2, p. 301). honour/ By virtuous ways achieved, and bravely purchased (*New Way*, IV.1, p. 368) (RTP).

Tragedy: Rn: with his honour,/ His liberty lost (*Maid of Honour*, V.2, p. 249). Redeem your mortgaged honour (*Ibid.*, V.2, p. 251). From the tooth of a mad Beast, and the tongue of a Slanderer/ Preserve thine honour (*Prophetess*, I.3, p. 326). For the honour of the Empire, and of *Rome* (*Ibid.*, V.2, p. 380). If you esteem your honour more than tribute (*Ibid.*, V.2, p. 381). My honour being engag'd to make that good (*Lover's Progress*, V.1, p. 144). my honour's at the stake too (*Ibid.*, V.1, p. 145). The less your honour (*Bondman*, I.3, p. 95). Lady, take me, and I'le maintain thine honour (*Wife for a Month*, V.1, p. 65). without prejudice to either's honours (*Great Duke of Flor.*, II.1, p. 205). A secret of no less importance than/ My honour (*Ibid.*, III.1, p. 209). but I'll pawn my honour,/ That (*Ibid.*, IV.1, p. 214). more carefull of thine honour,/ Thy health (*Broken Heart*, 181—2). more then what suited/ With iustice of mine honour (*Ibid.*, 1067—8).

Tragedy: Rg: Thou only sun in honour's sphere (*Maid of Honour*, III.3, p. 240). for the honour of my sex, to fall so (*Ibid.*). Seek you in *Rome* for honour (*Prophetess*, IV.6, p. 376). Wish rest to me, I honour unto you

(*Ibid.*, IV.6, p. 377). 'Twould add an honour to your worthy pains (*Changeling*, I.2.114). And will be still remembered to your honour (*Bondman*, I.3, p. 94). Victorious *Thomyris* ne'r won more honour (*Wife for a Month*, IV.1, p.53). No prince disguised, no man of mark, nor honour (*Renegado*, III.3, p. 134) (RTP). Honour/ Attend thy counsels euer (*Broken Heart*, 2284—5).

Tragedy: Ru: No indeed am I not; and 'tis for mine honour too (*Prophetess*, I.3, p. 326). The Master of his Fortune, and his Honour (*Ibid.*, IV.4, p. 370). Honour, you hack i' pieces with your swords (*Lover's Progress*, II.1, p. 98). I'le come off with honour (*Ibid.*, V.1, p. 144). Think of your honour (*Renegado*, IV.2, p. 140). But know then *Orgilus* what honour is (*Broken Heart*, 1069).

(e) *Summary, R 1621—1630*

Table 24 gives a summary of the k/m/v/x classification of R for the decade 1621—1630. In total, k is now by far the most prominent group, and has almost twice as many examples as m (39% against 20%); v is still smaller than m, with 13%, and x accounts for the remaining 28%. There are two examples of km in this decade, both in comedy. As in the previous decade, k is more frequent in comedy than in tragedy (50.5% against 29%), while m is more frequent in tragedy than in comedy (28% against 12%); these differences are significant. For v,

TABLE 24. *Numbers of k, m, v, and x: R material, 1621—30.*

		k	m	v	x	Total
Comedy	n	34	0	9	5	48
	g	5	7	3	8	23
	u	4	3	0	7	14
	Total	43	10	12	20	85
Tragedy	n	12	3	7	14	36
	g	10	19	2	9	40
	u	5	4	2	6	17
	Total	27	26	11	29	93
All Plays	n	46	3	16	19	84
	g	15	26	5	17	63
	u	9	7	2	13	31
	Total	70	36	23	49	178

there is no significant difference between comedy and tragedy. In contrast to the previous decade, n is now considerably more frequent than g (47% against 35%); this difference, however, is due entirely to comedy. As before, k, and perhaps also v, are most strongly represented in n, while m is most strongly represented in g.

E. 1631—1640

In this decade there are 177 examples of R, 77 in comedy and 100 in tragedy. In 18 of the examples, R is not the sole head-meaning; the combined head-meanings found are RE (one), REM (one), RMT (one), RMP (one), RP (three), RTP (seven), RD (one), RPD (one), and RRc (two). Of the 177 examples, 7 are countables, 59 uncountables, and 111 equivocal. The examples are as follows.

(a) The k Group

Sensitivity to affront, revenging injury, etc.:

Comedy: Rn: a world of honour,/ And publicke reputation to defend (*Magnetic Lady*, III.6.155—6). The least that you can do,/ In the terms of honour (*Guardian*, II.3, p. 416). your studied care/ In what concerns my honour (*Ibid.*). my wounded reputation/ And honour suffer (*Ibid.*, III.3, p. 422). can you answer/ The debt you owe your honour (*Ibid.*). my honour too/ Neglected for this purchase (*Ibid.*, IV.2, p. 429). For reparation of my wounded honour (*Ibid.*, V.4, p. 436). Take care your honour lies upon't (*News from Plymouth*, IV.1, p. 164). budge not from him/ An inch, your grounds are honor (*Lady's Trial*, 773—4). to best advantage of your fame / And honour (*Royal Master*, I.1, p. 112).

Comedy: Ru: to cut some few throats fairly/ For honour's sake (*Distresses*, V.1, p. 358).

Tragedy: Rn: To cure their honour with some strange revenge (*Very Woman*, I.1, p. 441). tender conscience/ Makes me forget mine honour (*Ibid.*, IV.2, p. 456). in honour/ Wronged him so, I'll right it on myself (*Ibid.*, IV.2, p. 457). There's honour, justice, and full satisfaction (*Ibid.*). Fair hope left for me, to repair mine honour (*Ibid.*, V.6, p. 465). The reputation of men's fame and honours (*Ibid.*). My honour in the general report/ Tainted and soil'd (*Ibid.*). For the recovery of a wounded honour (*Ibid.*). That have, and dare bid high again for honour (*Politician*, III.1, p. 129). How much my honour suffers (*Imposture*, I.2, p. 194). then my honour is concerned (*Ibid.*, V.1, p. 250). and pity you/ Should lose so much your honour (*Ibid.*, V.1, p. 251). provides with art to save his honour,/ But trusts his soul to chance (*Ibid.*, V.4, p. 259). to revenge my honour, stain'd and trampled on (*Cardinal*, IV.3, p. 329).

Keeping duelling appointments, observing rules of duelling:

Comedy: Rn: any Gentleman, who loves his honour (*Fancies*, 2515). satisfy/ My anger to my honour's loss (*Distresses*, II.1, p. 298).

Tragedy: Rn: I will not lose so much of my own honour,/ To kill him basely (*Cardinal*, IV.2, p. 324).

Not being jilted, outwitted, rebuffed, etc.:

Comedy: Rn: a/ Disguise to save my honour (*Hyde Park*, III.2, p. 503). Honour <, by> being my servant (*Ibid.*, IV.3, p. 512). I must not see/ Her lost to honour (*Royal Master*, IV.1, p. 154). how much it doth concern/ The honour of a cavalier (*Distresses*, IV.1, p. 327).

Tragedy: Rn: your resentment/ Of the affront in the point of honour (*Emperor of the East*, IV.1, p. 300). at such/ Expense of honour to go off unsatisfied (*Imposture*, II.3, p. 208).

High rank, power, wealth, etc.:

Comedy: Rn: Purchas'd beneath my honour (*Lady of Pleasure*, I.1, p. 9) (RTP).

Comedy: Rg: Honour of blood (*Lady of Pleasure*, II.1, p. 25) (RPD). carries/ Honour and profit (*Ibid.*, II.2, p. 35). Advance it/ To honour and regard (*Constant Maid*, III.2, p. 488) (RTP). To be a witness of your honour, sir (*Ibid.*).

Tragedy: Rn: O suffer not, for your own honour's sake (*Emperor of the East*, III.4, p. 299). fall no further/ Or in my oath, or honour (*Ibid.*, III.4, p. 300).

Tragedy: Rg: Honour on him that is your conqueror (*Love and Honour*, I.1, p. 104) (RD). should prefer her honour/ And peace of mind (*Bashful Lover*, V.3, p. 492) (RTP). 'Tis for such/ Access of honour (*Cardinal*, I.2, p. 284) (RMP).

Ostentation, keeping up one's position:

Comedy: Rn: it doth concern your love and honour (*Lady of Pleasure*, I.1, p. 7). with safety of/ Your birth and honour (*Ibid.*, I.1, p. 8).

Comedy: Rg: for my lord's honour (*Guardian*, IV.2, p. 428). Strike up for the honour of the Bride (*Fancies*, 871).

Comedy: Ru: to sell my honour,/ By living poor and sparingly (*Lady of Pleasure*, I.1, p. 10). spend it/ For my lady's honour (*Ibid.*, II.1, p. 29).

Tragedy: Rg: what's done for your honour must not be/ Curb'd (*Emperor of the East*, III.2, p. 297). Since 'twas done for your honour (*Ibid.*, III.4, p. 299).

Not having authority flouted:

Tragedy: Rn: is already/ The killing of your honour (*Politician*, IV.1, p. 140).

Making socially good marriages:

Tragedy: Rn: the rape done on mine honor (*Perkin Warbeck*, 1353). should/ Be so unkind to his own blood and honour (*Politician*, III.3, p. 136).
Tragedy: Rg: What honor, what felicitie can followe (*Perkin Warbeck*, 1909). Columbo's love is yet more sacred/ To honour and yourself (*Cardinal*, II.3, p. 300).
Tragedy: Ru: Some way to snatch his honour from this flame (*Cardinal*, II.3, p. 303).

Number of dependants or suitors:

Tragedy: Rg: The meanest altar raised up to mine honour (*Bashful Lover*, I.1, p. 470).

Reflected (from Rc/C):

Comedy: Rn: He that hath sav'd my h<on>oure, though by chance (*Magnetic Lady*, V.10.140). their fame/ Bleeds in my wounded honour (*Royal Master*, IV.1, p. 156). be that rare friend,/ And save our honours (*Ibid.*, IV.1, p. 167) (RRc). wounding all our honours (*Ibid.*, V.1, p. 182) (RRc).
Tragedy: Rn: the honour of his family/ Depends upon the purity of his bed (*Emperor of the East*, V.2, p. 308) (RP). the cruelty of my wounded honour (*Ibid.*). To the ruin of his honour (*Ibid.*, V.3, p. 310). I wrong'd the honour of the emperor's bed (*Ibid.*). Respect the honour of your house (*Unfortunate Lovers*, I.1, p. 26).

Reflected (from good or bad qualities of relatives):

Tragedy: Rn: let not my fame,/ And honour, be concern'd (*Politician*, III.1, p. 125) (lost by husband's unfaithfulness). and care of your much-loved honour (*Imposture*, III.2, p. 215) (son's lack of military qualities).

Not withdrawing from proposed marriage, and related contents:

Comedy: Rn: 'Tis my duty/ To clear his honour in't (*Royal Master*, II.2, p. 131). it were/ More for her honour, she would mock no prince (*Ibid.*, IV. 1, p. 153). But to set right her honour (*Ibid.*, IV.1, p. 154). (These three are "Not insulting a prince by proposing a marriage-alliance with no intention of carrying it out".) in his very first attempt of love,/ Would blast my honour (*Ibid.*, V.1, p. 174). Not only wound myself to death of honour (*Ibid.*). (These two are "Not accepting a suitor who has thereby to throw over another woman".) will this change/ Be for my honour, or my fame (*Constant Maid*, I.1, p. 458).

Sexual virility, wenching:

Comedy: Ru: For their countries' honour, after a long vacation (*City Madam*, III.1, p. 389). Dispatch her first for your honour (*Guardian*, II.3, p. 417).

Not suffering an ignominious death:

Tragedy: Rn: for his honour,/ He'll choose another death (*Traitor*, I.1, p. 102).

Miscellaneous:

Comedy: Rn: Your lordship will not so much stain your honour (*Lady of Pleasure*, III.1, p. 43) (discriminating in favour of women of rank, not bringing them to justice). scandall/ (Out of a libertie of ease and fulnesse)/ Against our honour (*Fancies*, 2152—4) (having a decorously conducted household). do, for their honours, so contrive it (*Royal Master*, III.3, p. 144) (having bad handwriting as a mark of gentry). To place my own revenge above her honour (*Ibid.*, IV.1, p. 163) (recognizing special claims of guests).

Comedy: Ru: It being for the city's honour (*City Madam*, IV.4, p. 400) (decent observance of social distinctions, esp. in dress). I have honour / And never fight for't (*News from Pymouth*, II.2, p. 132) (RP) (sensitivity to affront and socially good marriage).

Tragedy: Rn: Requires in poynt of honor (pray mistake not) (*Perkin Warbeck*, 1116) (contributing to celebration of lord's marriage). It would be/ More for my honour (*Imposture*, II.1, p. 200) (not being won too easily as wife).

Tragedy: Rg: Have robbed us of the honour (*Emperor of the East*, II.1, p. 293) (initiating emperor into the art of love). Honour? Is that the word (*Love and Honour*, I. 1, p. 104) (not clearly specified, but plainly k).

Tragedy: Ru: a grave, in which the prince of Tarent/ Buried his honour (*Very Woman*, I.1, p. 441) (lost by being defeated in love by an obscure rival).

(b) *The m Group*

Comedy: Rg: Charge home, and come off with honour (*Guardian*, III.5, p. 423). Nothing but honour could seduce thee (*Wits*, I.1, p. 121) Honour! which is the hope of the youthful (*Ibid.*). Not a brass thimble to me; but honour (*Ibid.*, I.1, p. 122). how to use a sword/ To honour's best advantage (*Lady of Pleasure*, IV.3, p. 77). Get honour!/ And bring home a rich prize (*News from Plymouth*, V.1, p.198). till when honour's my mistress (*Ibid.*, V.1, p. 199). For gaining, what? a bloudy nose of honour (*Lady's Trial*, 107).

Tragedy: Rn: my wounded honour calls/ For reparation (*Bashful Lover*, II.3, p. 474). We had died with honour/ By the enemy's sword (*Politician*, III.3, p. 137).

Tragedy: Rg: proceede/ To high attempts of honor (*Perkin Warbeck*, 781—2). Their fainting honour hovering o'er our crests (*Love and Honour*, I.1, p. 106). To ravish from thy crest the honour that/ I lent thee (*Ibid.*, III.1, p. 145). May stop me in my full career to honour (*Bashful Lover*, I.1, p. 471). borne up/ To the supreme sphere of honour (*Ibid.*, II.4, p. 475). how to march to honour/ Through death (*Politician*, I.1, p. 102). We did there fight for honour (*Ibid.*, IV.2, p. 142). he that conquers may/ Get honour, and deep wounds (*Imposture*, I.1, p. 188). By your great blaze, saw his next way to honour (*Ibid.*, III.2, p. 216). act/ Or precept, that could light your son to honour (*Ibid.*, III.2, p. 217). War, and grim-/ Faced Honour are his mistresses (*Cardinal*, I.2, p. 282). Engag'd to war, in his hot thirst of honour (*Ibid.*, I.2, p. 288).

Tragedy: Ru: I will not save his life/ To rob him of his honour (*Bashful Lover*, II.3, p. 474). Better to fall... than survive thine honour (*Ibid.*, II.6, p. 476). reference to you,/ And to your honour (*Ibid.*, V.3, p. 492). To repair this/ With honour, gentlemen (*Cardinal*, II.1, p. 289). But with a brave thought of their country's honour (*Ibid.*, II.1, p. 290). when <a> cause,/ With honour, calls to action (*Ibid.*, II.1, p. 291).

Under m are also to be classified the following ten examples of km:

Comedy: Rn: whose life and honour, I/ Of late (*Distresses*, II.1, p. 308). My honour and/ My life I will engage (*Ibid.*, III.1, p. 326).

Comedy: Rg: the honour/ Of having had the better (*News from Plymouth*, II.1, p. 129). the joy he takes/ In the unlucky honour of this day (*Distresses*, V.1, p. 356).

Tragedy: Rn: against/ His own life and his honour (*Very Woman*, V.6, p. 465). Honour, revenge, the maid too,/ Lie at the stake (*Bashful Lover*, III.3, p. 481). to repair my honour/ On a high mysterious power (*Fair Favourite*, V.1, p. 274). When my honour's lost, so vainly shift me off (*Ibid.*). My honour's lost, and now I want a cause (*Ibid.*, V.1, p. 275).

Tragedy: Rg: I/ Shall lose much honour in his fall (*Cardinal*, IV.3, p. 330).

(c) The v Group

Truthfulness, not practising deceit and imposture:

Tragedy: Rn: my honour will bleed for it (*Imposture*, II.1, p. 201). to save herself,/ Our honours, and the kingdom (*Ibid.*) (Ro). To rob herself, both of her life and honour (*Ibid.*, V.5, p. 266).

Keeping promises:

Comedy: Rn: Upon the engagement of your honour (*Hyde Park*, III.1, p. 493). I have bound myself in honour/ Not to betray (*Royal Master*, III.1, p. 135).

Tragedy: Rn: My honor is engag'd for payment (*Fair Favourite*, II.1, p. 223).

Loyalty to rulers, not committing treason:

Tragedy: Rn: Or my infected honor white againe (*Perkin Warbeck*, 548).
Tragedy: Ru: Advance your profit much, your honour more (*Unfortunate Lovers*, IV.1, p. 61).

Filial piety, and loyalty to ruler:

Tragedy: Rn: so great/ A stain upon his hopeful, his green honour (*Politician*, V.2, p. 175).

Not murdering:

Tragedy: Rn: In death to rob me of my fame, my honour (*Bashful Lover*, II.7, p. 478).

Not duelling:

Tragedy: Rn: Hold, hold, gentlemen!/ For your own honours (*Imposture*, IV.3, p. 235).

Not conniving at unchastity:

Tragedy: Rn: An act so fatal unto honour (*Traitor*, II.1, p. 112).

Sexual continence:

Tragedy: Rn: hoodwink'd to mine honour (*Bashful Lover*, IV.2, p. 486).

Not abducting:

Tragedy: Ru: A gentleman, that have more right to honour (*Imposture*, III.3, p. 224) (RE).

Not being corruptible:

Tragedy: Rn: My honour's touch'd in't (*Very Woman*, II.2, p. 446).

Works of charity:

Comedy: Rg: ambitious/ Of glittering honour, and an after-name (*Guardian*, V.4, p. 434). for the honour of our *Familie* (*Fancies*, 2206).

(d) *The x Group*

Comedy: Rn: My mistress' love and honour is engaged (*Hyde Park*, I.1, p. 465). A mistress love and honour! this is pretty (*Ibid.*). Entreat you, for my honour, do not penance them (*Lady of Pleasure*, III.2, p. 61). Yea honour, as it were (*Lady's Trial*, 753). My honour is engaged, then, to convince you (*Royal Master*, II.2, p. 132) (R(o)) (not lying, or not being incorrectly informed). But so your jealousy may wound her honour (*Ibid.*, III.1, p.135). He will have more care of his honour (*Ibid.*, V.1, p. 172). His honour suffers much if he be found (*Distresses*, II.1, p. 310). For th' honour of your reason (*Ibid.*, IV.1, p. 328).

Comedy: Rg: Who covets honour,/ Covets it infinitely (*Magnetic Lady*, II.6.52—3) (RTP). hath deserv'd/ All honour and opinion (*Lady of Pleasure*, III.2, p. 57) (REM). I wish/ His honour had been greater (*Distresses*, V.1, p. 352).

Comedy: Ru: Where is the honour of my science now (*Platonic Lovers*, IV.1, p. 62). as I hope to shave cleane and get honour by't (*Fancies*, 2376). Honour a bubble is, that is soon broke (*Royal Master*, IV.1, p. 166) (RMT).

Tragedy: Rn: *this seducer* of my honor (*Perkin Warbeck*, 1619). submit/ Unto my bonds, and keep my honour free (*Fair Favourite*, II.1, p. 223). physician is so nice/ I' th'honour of his science (*Ibid.*, IV.1, p. 259). to think the/ Conquer'd lose their honour (*Ibid.*, V.1, p. 275). and damn thy honour to/ All ages (*Imposture*, IV.5, p. 245). And form the aptest way for all our honour (*Ibid.*, V.2, p. 254). there's no other way,/ With safety of my honour, to revisit her (*Cardinal*, II.1, p. 293).

Tragedy: Rg: Deserve this, with the honour that will follow (*Very Woman*, II.2, p. 445). Will raise you into name, preferment, honour (*Bashful Lover*, I.1, p. 471) (RTP). The ascent/ To the height of honour is by arts or arms (*Ibid.*, I.2, p. 472) (RP). May have alone the honour to die nobly (*Ibid.*, II.6, p. 476). prepare yourself/ For honour in your age (*Ibid.*, V.1, p. 489) (RTP). The noble sons of Pompey kept their honour (*Fair Favourite*, V.1, p. 275).

Tragedy: Ru: Your vigilance for my safety as my honour (*Emperor of the East*, II.1, p. 293). all man's honour/ Depends not on the most uncertain favour (*Very Woman*, I.1, p. 441). Not wealth,/ Wisdom nor honour (*Unfortunate Lovers*, I.1, p. 28) (RTP). You have lost/ More honour in those minutes (*Politician*, III.1, p. 120).

(e) Summary, R 1631—1640

Table 25 give a summary of the k/m/v/x classification of R for the decade 1631—1640. In total, the predominance of k has now become even more marked than in the previous decade, and it has almost 2½ times as many examples as m (51% against 21.4%); v is still a good deal smaller than m, with 9.6%, and x accounts for the remaining 18%. There are ten examples of km, four in comedy and six in tragedy. Once again, k is more frequent in comedy than in tragedy (60% against 40%), and this difference is just significant. Both m and v are more frequent in tragedy than in comedy (26% m and 13% v against 16% and 5% respectively), and these differences are possibly significant. The frequency of n has now increased to almost twice that of g, and the difference is almost as great in tragedy as in comedy. As before, k and v are most strongly represented in n, while m is most strongly represented in g.

F. 1661—1670

In this decade there are 97 examples of R, 59 in comedy and 38 in tragedy. In four of the examples, R is not the sole head-meaning; the combined head-meanings found are RC (one), RRcC (one), and RK (two). Of the 97 examples, 3 are countables, 38 uncountables, and 56 equivocal. The examples are as follows.

180   HONOUR IN THE ENGLISH DRAMA

TABLE 25. *Numbers of k, m, v, and x: R material, 1631—40.*

		k	m	v	x	Total
Comedy	n	33	2	2	9	46
	g	6	10	2	3	21
	u	7	0	0	3	10
	Total	46	12	4	15	77
Tragedy	n	32	7	11	7	57
	g	10	13	0	6	29
	u	2	6	2	4	14
	Total	44	26	13	17	100
All Plays	n	65	9	13	16	103
	g	16	23	2	9	50
	u	9	6	2	7	24
	Total	90	38	17	32	177

(a) *The k Group*

Sensitivity to affront, revenging injury, etc.:

Comedy: Rn: But this wou'd not secure your Honour (*Comical Revenge*, III.5.10). it is not for my honour to be friends (*Evening's Love*, III.1, p. 314). 'tis not for my honour, to be assisting to you (*Ibid.*, V.1, pp. 350—1). Hold, Sir, think upon your Honour (*Sullen Lovers*, III.1, p. 51). Master Huffes honour is disturb'd (*Ibid.*, III.1, p. 55). some-/thing that concerns your Honour (*She Would*, IV.1.78—9). for the securing his Person and his Honour (*Ibid.*, V.1.37) (Ro). his Life and Honour shall be both secure (*Ibid.*, V.1.78) (Ro). In care of her I must neglect my honour (*Man's the Master*, I.1, p. 19). a perfect judge of combats of honour (*Ibid.*, II.1, p. 29). a servant, sir,/ Should own an int'rest in his master's honour (*Ibid.*, III.1, p. 59). make promises of honour to one of thy low condition (*Ibid.*, III.1, p. 60). wicked entertainments of honour (*Ibid.*, III.2, p. 63). he shall repair my honour (*Ibid.*, IV.1, p. 71). Pray call him back to save his honour (*Ibid.*, IV.1, p. 83). but for the honour of yours, he does that (*Ibid.*, IV.1, p. 85). I shall come off with Honour (*Humorists*, III.1, p. 217) (Ro). you do not understand these nice points of honour (*Ibid.*) (RK). I shall save honour, and you will get it (*Ibid.*, IV.1, p. 228) (Rnk moves on to Rgkm) (Ro).

Tragedy: Rn: Does to my honour more injurious prove (*Tyrannic Love*, IV.1, p. 431). Who sells thee and his Honour for a Tear (*Forced Marriage*, II.7, p. 325). And I so strangely jealous of your Honour (*Ibid.*, III.1, p. 327).

Tragedy: Ru: What honour is't to let him murder you (*Forced Marriage*, IV.6, p. 351).

Keeping duelling appointments, observing rules of duelling, etc.:

Comedy: Rn: I hold it not for our honour to stand idle (*Evening's Love*, IV.3, p. 341). and leave me agen for your Honour forsooth (*Sullen Lovers*, IV.1, p. 60). It were loss of honour to avoid him (*Man's the Master*, II.1, p. 31). this engagement of my honour (*Ibid.*, IV.1, p. 75). that, without loss of my honour, I might kill thee (*Ibid.*, IV.1, p. 81).

Tragedy: Rn: Kill not my honour to preserve my life (*Indian Emperor*, V.1, p. 395).

Ostentation, keeping up appearances:

Comedy: Rn: to the censure of both our Honours (*She Would*, III.3.420).

Comedy: Ru: I can huswife it better for your honour (*Wild Gallant*, III.1, p. 75.

Not negotiating under duress:

Comedy: Rn: I cannot, with my honour, treat without your submission (*Tempest*, III.3, p. 166). stand likewise on their honours (*Ibid.*, III.3, p. 167).

Tragedy: Rn: Those means, you might have then with honour used (*Indian Emperor*, IV.2, p. 375).

Reflected (from Rc/C):

Comedy: Rn: Don John's my master, and his honour's mine (*Man's the Master*, III.1, p. 57).

Reflected (lost by relative marrying enemy):

Tragedy: Rn: Talk not to me of love, when honour suffers (*Rival Ladies*, IV.3, p. 199). At once my honour and his love I'll save (*Ibid.*).

Not breaking off a proposed marriage:

Comedy: Rn: The honour of our House now lies at stake (*Comical Revenge*, I.4.38). to maintain/ Our Honour, and prevent this threatning stain (*Ibid.*, III.6.1—2). and my Honour rate/ Below the value of a poor Estate (*Ibid.*, IV.4.24—5). (N. B. These three examples are quite clearly k, not v.)

Sexual virility, wenching, keeping adulterous assignations:

Comedy: Rn: he may yet redeem his Honour (*She Would*, II.2.12).

Tragedy: Rn: I'll stand up for the honour of my vocation (*Secret Love*, IV.1, p. 474).

Not being swayed by love:

Comedy: Rn: Which is the Path that doth to Honour lead (*Comical Revenge*, IV.5.29). Too rigidly my Honour I pursue (*Ibid.*, V.3.32).

Prisoner of war not escaping:

Tragedy: Rn: If such injustice should my honour stain (*Indian Queen*, I.1, p. 233).

Tragedy: Rg: And, losing liberty, hast honour won (*Ibid.*, I.1, p. 234).

Miscellaneous:

Comedy: Rn: the keeping of ones word is a thing below the honour of a Gentleman (*She Would*, II.2.209—10). there are Punctilio's of Honour among Whores (*Humorists*, I.1, p. 200) (RK) (e. g. being kept by one man, not shared by several).

Comedy: Rg: You would have the honour of the business (*Law against Lovers*, III.1, p. 152) (armed rescue of convicted prisoner). be not too covetous of honour (*Evening's Love*, V.1, p. 353) (being a good liar). leave you all the honour of it (*Ibid.*, V.1, p. 354) (the same).

Tragedy: Rg: 'twould be more honour to me, if that Lord were a wiser man (*Royal Shepherdess*, V.1, p. 161) (being executed in distinguished company).

(b) *The m Group*

Comedy: Rg: I wish you some danger,/ That you may get the more honour (*Law against Lovers*, V.1, p. 193). some honour I have gotten in/ The face of enemies (*Ibid.*, V.1, p. 196). in honour's game,/ Where many throw (*Ibid.*, V.1, p. 199). I'll stay, and keep the honour of the field (*Evening's Love*, IV.3, p. 343). I'le pluck bright Honour from the pale-fac'd Moon (*Sullen Lovers*, V.1, p. 79).

Tragedy: Rn: we have lost/ Freedom, wealth, honour (*Indian Emperor*, IV.3, p. 381). The honour of our Country lies at stake (*Royal Shepherdess*, I.1, p. 104).

Tragedy: Rg: First dye his honour in a purple flood (*Indian Emperor*, II.2, p. 347). Kill her, and see what honour will be won (*Ibid.*). I go to meet/ New honour, but to lay it at your feet (*Ibid.*, II.2, p. 348). I sought not honour on so base a train (*Ibid.*, II.4, p. 350). A death, with honour, for my country's good (*Ibid.*, IV.2, p. 375). He blasts my early honour in the bud (*Tyrannic Love*, I.1, p. 390). Honour! The Fools Paradise (*Royal Shepherdess*, I.1, p. 104). that Trifle/ *Honour;* the breath of a few Giddy People (*Ibid.*). Concerns us more than broken Pates for honour (*Ibid.*). I cannot possibly find what honour there is in having Oylet-holes made in a man's body (*Ibid.*, II.1, p. 119). Honour's the only idol of his eyes (*Conquest of Granada.1*, I.1, p. 45).

Tragedy: Ru: I want strength to die with honour (*Rival Ladies*, V.3, p. 212). Honour, be gone! what art thou but a breath (*Indian Emperor*, II.2, p. 348). And didst not thou a death with honour choose (*Tyrannic Love*, I.1, p. 394).

Under m are also to be classified the following three examples of km:

Comedy: Rn: but I hope I lost no Honour (*Humorists*, IV.1, p. 233) (R(o)).

Comedy: Rg: wherein there's Honour to be gain'd (*Comical Revenge*, IV.1.15—16). I'll rest contented with honour gotten in the dark (*Man's the Master*, V.1, p. 102) (RC).

(c) The v Group

Truthfulness:

Comedy: Rn: do you think I'll stain my honour to swallow a lie for you (*Evening's Love*, II.1, p. 283) (or perhaps k?).

Keeping promises:

Comedy: Rn: to engage my Honour I would return again (*She Would*, II.2.33—4).

Tragedy: Rn: To save my honour I my love must lose (*Rival Ladies*, IV.3, p. 199). Yet you must spare me for your honour's sake (*Indian Emperor*, III.2, p. 362). And with thy person leave thy honour free (*Ibid.*, III.3, p. 364). I'll engage my honour to lay down my arms (*Secret Love* V.1, p. 500).

Not conniving at unchastity:

Comedy: Ru: six or seven short winters more respect/ Than a perpetual honour (*Law against Lovers*, III.1, p. 159).

(d) The x Group

Comedy: Rn: all your honour and your virtue too (*Law against Lovers*, III.1, p. 161). the honour of my wit is engaged in it (*Sir Martin Mar-all*, IV.1, p. 55). Nay, and you talk of honour (*Evening's Love*, V.1, p. 351). Sir, it concernes your Honour (*Sullen Lovers*, II.1, p. 34). you can never come off with Honour (*Ibid.*, III.1, p. 50) (perhaps k?). a business that concerned both his Honour and Fortune (*She Would*, IV.1. 42—3). My Honour! you ought in Duty to do it (*Ibid.*, IV.1.80).

Comedy: Rg: How little honour then you had obtain'd (*Law against Lovers*, IV.1, p. 189) (RRcC).

Tragedy: Rn: The honour of the flame (*Rival Ladies*, IV.1, p. 190). To save my honour I my blood will pay (*Indian Emperor*, II.2, p. 347). Honour, once lost, is never to be found (*Ibid.*). Engage your honour that she shall be mine (*Ibid.*, IV.3, p. 382). Both for my love, and for my honour too (*Secret Love*, IV.2, p. 487).

Tragedy: Ru: In painted honour you would seem to shine (*Indian Queen*, I.1, p. 233).

(e) *Summary, R 1661—1670*

Table 26 gives a summary of the k/m/v/x classification of R for the decade 1661—1670. In total, k is still by far the largest group (with nearly 54%), and is over twice as large as m (25%); v is very small (just over 7%), and x accounts for the remaining 14%. There are three examples of km, all in comedy. For the first time, the pattern in comedy is markedly different from that in tragedy, k being largest in comedy and m in tragedy. In comedy, k is higher than ever before, with 68%, and m is still low, at 13.5%. In tragedy, on the other hand, m is the largest group, with 42%, against 31.5% k. The differences between comedy and tragedy with respect to k and m are significant. The difference between comedy and tragedy for v is not significant, on the other hand. The frequency of n is now two and a half times greater than that of g, the difference being much greater in comedy than in tragedy. Once again, k and v are strongest in n, while m is strongest in g.

TABLE 26. *Numbers of k, m, v, and x: R material, 1661—70.*

		k	m	v	x	Total
Comedy	n	36	1	2	7	46
	g	3	7	0	1	11
	u	1	0	1	0	2
	Total	40	8	3	8	59
Tragedy	n	9	2	4	5	20
	g	2	11	0	0	13
	u	1	3	0	1	5
	Total	12	16	4	6	38
All Plays	n	45	3	6	12	66
	g	5	18	0	1	24
	u	2	3	1	1	7
	Total	52	24	7	14	97

G. 1671—1680

In this decade there are 217 examples of R, 116 in comedy and 101 in tragedy. In four of the examples, R is not the sole head-meaning;

the combined head-meanings found are RTP (two), RMTP (one), and RK (one). Of the 217 examples, 2 are countables, 57 uncountables, and 158 equivocal. The examples are as follows.

(a) *The k Group*

Sensitivity to injury, revenging affront, etc.:

Comedy: Rn: And punish him, or with my Honour die (*Amorous Prince*, I.2, p. 131). thy Honour's safe,/ Since yet none knows that Cloris was thy Sister (*Ibid.*, V.3, p. 206) (Ro). trust a coward with your honour (*Gent. Danc. Master*, II.1, p. 155). The wounds of honour must have blood and wounds (*Ibid.*, II.2, p. 166). rob'st me of my Name,/ And wouldst my Honour too (*Dutch Lover*, IV.3, p. 304). Nay, then, my honour's concerned (*Country Wife*, II.1, p. 274). Is it for your honour, or mine, to suffer (*Ibid.*, III.2, p. 294). But 'tis your honour too I am concerned for (*Ibid.*, III.2, p. 295). will you be more concerned for his honour than he is (*Ibid.*). Let his honour alone, for my sake and his (*Ibid.*). Your care of his honour argues his neglect of it (*Ibid.*). let his honour go which way it will (*Ibid.*). with your jealousy and fears, and virtue and honour (*Ibid.*). play with any man's honour but mine (*Ibid.*, IV.3, p. 330). That you would do for your own honour (*Plain Dealer*, I.1, p. 385). to doe my own Honour Justice (*Friendship in Fashion*, IV.1.241). nor Sir, is my Honour (*Ibid.*, IV.1.255). Well, honour is (*Kind Keeper*, IV.1, p. 90). honour, and I must go (*Ibid.*). Does it concern my Honour? Madam, I'll cut their throats (*True Widow*, III.1, p. 325).

Tragedy: Rn: I could not now desist, in point of honour (*Amboyna*, IV.3, p. 68). of so little value prize/ The honour of your blood (*Alcibiades*, III.1. 230). at once mine, and your own honour save (*Ibid.*, V.1.59). But, Sir, my Honour is concern'd with yours (*Abdelazer*, I.2, p. 21). And in bright Arms demand my Honour back (*Ibid.*, II.1, p. 26). All for a little worthless Honour lost (*Ibid.*). whose Honour, and whose Life,/ Lies at your Mercy (*Ibid.*, II.1, p. 27). E'er for its safety I forego mine Honour (*Ibid.*, IV.1, p. 61). That brave Revenge was due to injur'd Honour (*Orphan*, V.1.104).

Not tolerating a rival in love:

Comedy: Rn: I have a trick to save your Honour, Sir (*Dutch Lover*, IV.1, p. 292) (Ro).

Observing duelling code, accepting challenges, etc.:

Comedy: Rn: to commit a Gentleman-like murder for his Honour (*Epsom Wells*, V.1, p. 169). with all my Soul — but your Honour, Sir — (*Town Fop*, II.3, p. 28). My Honour! 'tis but Custom that makes it honourable to fight Duels (*Ibid.*).

Comedy: Rg: she'll have the honour of being first in the field (*Love in a Wood*, IV.5, p. 93). Ours is the honour of the field, madam (*Assignation*, IV.5, p. 447). (Both figurative, duelling/love assignations.)

Comedy: Ru: I shall get much honour, I take it (*Epsom Wells*, II.1, p. 130).

Tragedy: Rn: that I might kill thee/ Without a stain to honour (*All for Love*, I.1, p. 357). let them be punctual to the point of honour (*Troilus*, IV.2, p. 371).

Not fighting a man to whom under an obligation:

Comedy: Rn: That I may fight with him, and keep my Honour safe (*Rover.1*, IV.1, p. 63).

Not being outwitted, rebuffed, jilted, etc.:

Comedy: Rg: To show such a fear to your rival, were for his honour (*Gent. Danc. Master*, I.1, p. 137).

Comedy: Ru: That were not for my honour (*Gent. Danc. Master*, I.1, p. 137).

Tragedy: Rn: Nay, with my honour too my life must bleed (*Alcibiades*, V.1.70). I was fit Guardian of my Houses Honour (*Orphan*, V.1.97).

Insisting on one's rights:

Comedy: Rn: My honour, and my subjects, I betray (*Marriage à la Mode*, IV.5, p. 340).

High rank, etc.:

Tragedy: Rn: Thus 'tis you think to heal up smarting Honour (*Caius Marius*, V.1.30). For the late slight his Honour suffer'd there (*Orphan*, I.1.19).

Tragedy: Ru: I am depriv'd of Empire, and of Honour (*Abdelazer*, V.3, p. 92) (RTP).

Not taking one's lovers from the lower classes:

Comedy: Rn: for a noble person to neglect her own honour (*Country Wife*, II.1, p. 277).

Ostentation, maintaining one's position:

Comedy: Ru: for my Master's honour, Robin (*Man of Mode*, I.1.309—10). and do honour to her profession (*Ibid.*, I.1.510—11). to drink for the Honour of his country (*Friendship in Fashion*, IV.1.17).

Tragedy: Ru: Cursed is that king, whose honour's in their hands (*Conquest of Granada.2*, I.2, p. 130).

Not having authority flouted:

Comedy: Rn: Robbed of my honour, my daughter, and (*Gent. Danc. Master*, V.1, p. 239). my revenge too! O my dear honour! (*Ibid.*).

Tragedy: Rn: I can hear/ With honour your demands (*Spanish Friar*, V.2, p. 508).

Not submitting to humiliating peace-terms:

Tragedy: Rn: Who has preserved my life, my love, my honour (*All for Love*, III.1, p. 385). I love your honour,/ Because 'tis mine (*Ibid.*, III.1, p. 388).

Tragedy: Ru: Weigh you the worth and honour of a king (*Troilus*, II.1, p. 303). on which our Trojan honour/ And common reputation will depend (*Ibid.*, II.1, p. 304).

Reflected (from female relatives' Rc/C):

Comedy: Rn: Pish! a mere jealousy of honour (*Marriage à la Mode*, V.1, p. 355). I have regard unto thy Honour, Friend (*Amorous Prince*, I.4, p. 138). as thou art my Friend, and lov'st my Honour (*Ibid.*, I.4, p. 139). With thee my Wife and Honour too are safe (*Ibid.*) (Ro). Has now betray'd thy Honour with her own (*Ibid.*, II.3, p. 155). the care you have of the Honour of his House (*Ibid.*, IV.4, p. 188). have no designs upon your House or Honour (*Ibid.*, IV.4, p. 190). the unreasonable burden of the Honour/ Of our House (*Ibid.*, V.1, p. 195). a Spanish care of the honour of my family (*Gent. Danc. Master*, II.1, p. 154). in his Spanish strictness and punctilios of honour (*Ibid.*, III.1, p. 176) (RK). the shame and stain of his honour and family (*Ibid.*). jest with my honour, *voto!* (*Ibid.*, V.1, p. 230). On which the Honour of my House depends (*Dutch Lover*, II.2, p. 247). Pray, Sir, forgive them, your Honour being safe (*Ibid.*, V.1, p. 321). the honour of your family will sooner suffer in your wife (*Country Wife*, II.1, p. 266). His honour is least safe (too late I find) (*Ibid.*, V.4, p. 360). My Honour! and my Reputation, now (*Town Fop*, III.2, p. 50). Nor cou'd my Honour with thy Fame decline (*Ibid.*). take heed of the Honour of our House (*Rover.1*, III.1, p. 44). trust the honour of my Family in your hands (*Friendship in Fashion*, III.1.24) (R(o)). reason to be concern'd for the Honour of my Family (*Ibid.*, IV.1.245—6) (R(o)). A pox of the Honour of your Family (*Ibid.*, IV.1.252—3). the Honour of a Gentleman and your Friend (*Ibid.*, IV.1.263). my Daughter, my Honour — my Daughter, my Reputation (*Sir Patient Fancy*, IV.4, p. 83). one I dare trust my Honour with (*Ibid.*, V.1, p.90) (Ro). be just and kind for thy own Honour's sake (*Ibid.*). to save the Honour of your Family (*Woman Captain*, IV.1, p. 58). If you'd preserve your Honours, or your Lives (*Ibid.*, V.1, p. 85). as he tenders his own honour (*Soldier's Fortune*, I.1. 519—20). against her Chastity, and my Honour (*Ibid.*, II.1.187). an incorrigible Enemy of your honour (*Ibid.*, III.1.256—7). that enemy of my Honour, and Theif of my good Name (*Ibid.*, IV.1.218).

Comedy: Ru: were it for my honour to marry a woman whose virtue I suspected (*Country Wife*, III.2, p. 295).

Tragedy: Rn: My love, my honour, ruined and betrayed (*Conquest of Granada.2*, IV.3, p. 199). Your love and honour! mine are ruined worse

(*Ibid.*). What can your love, or what your honour, be (*Ibid.*). Not now for love, but for my honour's sake (*Ibid.*, V.1, p. 201). and preserve my honour into the bargain (*Amboyna*, II.1, p. 35). 'tis honour in the world (*Ibid.*, IV.1, p. 58) (Ro). so is your honour safe, and so is hers (*Ibid.*, IV.3, p. 68) (Ro). I sav'd the Honour of the Family by it (*Libertine*, I.1, p. 27). Foul ravisher of all my Honour, hence (*Don Carlos*, III.1.296). Yet for my honour, and my rest she dies (*Ibid.*, IV.1.665). She by whose lust my honour was betray'd (*Ibid.*, V.1.248). a nobler Sacrifice to make/ To my declining Honour (*Abdelazer*, III.1, p. 43). That's not enough, his Honour must be touch'd (*Ibid.*, III.2, p. 46). the Sacrifice I make/ To my lost Honour (*Ibid.*, III.2, p. 48). In something that concerns my Peace and Honour (*Orphan*, II.1.150). Tell me but what thou know'st concerns my Honour (*Ibid.*, III.1.231).

Reflected (from relative's lack of virtue):

Tragedy: Rn: See here my Honour and thy Duties stains (*Don Carlos*, IV.1.475) (also flouting of authority).

Not breaking off a proposed marriage:

Comedy: Rn: Nay, if my honour — (*Country Wife*, II.1, p.274). since my honour is engaged so far to him (*Ibid.*, III.2, p. 304).

Recognizing obligations of friendship:

Comedy: Rn: as well for his own Honour as mine (*Friendship in Fashion*, II.1.61) (Ro).

Sexual virility, wenching, requiting illicit love:

Comedy: Ru: 'Tis much for the honour of the gentlemen of this age (*Love in a Wood*, IV.2, p. 82).

Tragedy: Rn: 'Twill to your honour be but ill apply'd (*Alcibiades*, IV.1. 101).

Tragedy: Ru: And love her, for the honour of my race (*Aureng-Zebe*, IV.1, p. 269).

Not continuing to love a woman who is false to you:

Comedy: Rn: It concerns more than my life, — my honour (*Plain Dealer*, III.1, p. 429). your honour was dearer to you than your life (*Ibid.*, III.1, p. 430). Think of your honour, sir: love! — (*Ibid.*, IV.1, p. 456).

Not marrying into family of an enemy:

Comedy: Rn: At least to save your fortune and your honour (*Spanish Friar*, IV.2, p. 492). I think, you love your honour more (*Ibid.*, IV.2, p. 493).

Tragedy: Rn: or canst prize/ Thy Father's Honour (*Caius Marius*, I.1. 309—10).

THE R MATERIAL 189

Burning a nunnery:
Tragedy: Rg: you shall stay, and get Honour, *Jacomo* (*Libertine*, V.1, p. 85). Pox of Honour (*Ibid.*).

Miscellaneous:
Comedy: Rn: Why, now I can consent with honour (*Kind Keeper*, V.1, p. 118) (not accepting marriage on humiliating terms). Honour is concern'd in it (*True Widow*, IV.1, p. 345) (for arranging satisfactory financial terms for a girl that you procure as a gentleman's mistress). I would not have my Honour touch'd (*Ibid.*) (the same).
Tragedy: Rn: Disgrace the native honour of our isle (*Amboyna*, IV.3, p. 73) (for producing strong silent men with stiff upper lips).
Tragedy: Ru: whose greatest Honour lies in preserving their Beards (*Libertine*, III.1, p. 60) (preserving one's beard and not being cuckolded).

(b) The m Group

Comedy: Rn: for the safeguard of my honour (*Spanish Friar*, I.2, p. 428). while I can retreat with honour (*Ibid.*, III.2, p. 460) (both figurative).
Comedy: Rg: Next to the gods, brave friends, be yours the honour (*Marriage à la M.*, V.1, p. 360). your brisk dealers in honour (*Plain Dealer*, I.1, p. 378). I have heard of a thing called grinning honour (*Ibid.*, V.2, p. 487). and kills men for Honour, who never anger'd him (*Woman Captain*, III.1, p. 49). War Friend, and shining Honour has bin our Province (*Soldier's Fortune*, IV.1.277—8) (R(o)).
Tragedy: Rg: Be mine the honour, but the profit yours (*Conquest of Granada.2*, I.1, p. 125). Then while the paths of honour we pursue (*Ibid.*, II.1, p. 144). Almanzor vowed he would for honour fight (*Ibid.*, III.1, p. 161). And foes, who fought for honour, then are friends (*Ibid.*, III.3, p. 168). Where honour's th'only Mistress of the brave (*Alcibiades*, III.1.365). But 'tis a rugged honour got in Arms (*Ibid.*, III.1.366). Honour I sought, the generous mind's reward (*Aureng-Zebe*, I.1, p. 214). I long for work where Honour's to be got (*Don Carlos*, IV.1.193). To show thee, honour was my only motive (*Oedipus*, I.1, p. 152). My Honour, proud presumptuous Boy (*Caius Marius*, III.1.392). And promise Honour in the day of Battel (*Ibid.*, IV.1.403). She is a subject of renown and honour (*Troilus*, II.1, p. 304). But when I see him arming for his honour (*Ibid.*, II.1, p. 307). But when you fight for honour and for me (*Ibid.*, II.1, p. 308). Who holds his honour higher than his ease (*Ibid.*). For both our honour and our shame in this (*Ibid.*, II.3, p. 315). How he struts in expectation of honour (*Ibid.*, III.1, p. 326). Yes, and perhaps shall gain much honour by him (*Ibid.*, IV.2, p. 353). Thine be the honour, Ajax (*Ibid.*, IV.2, p. 356). Let honour go or stay (*Ibid.*, IV.2, p. 360). Why, it portends me honour and renown (*Ibid.*, V.1, p. 373). Such honour as the brave gain after death (*Ibid.*). Whence he with honour is expected back (*Orphan*, I.1.62).

Tragedy: Ru: O stain to honour!/ O lasting shame (*All for Love*, II.1, p. 372). You give what's nothing, when you give your honour (*Oedipus*, III.1, p. 179). Could'st thou, when Honour call'd thee, whine for Love (*Caius Marius*, I.1.370). Who could from Hector bring his honour off (*Troilus*, II.3, p. 315).

Under m are also to be classified the following two examples of km:

Comedy: Rn: With Honour, Sir, I protest (*Town Fop*, III.3, p. 52).

Tragedy: Rg: a man can get no honour by fighting with such Poletroons (*Libertine*, I.1, p. 36).

(c) *The v Group*

Keeping promises:

Comedy: Rn: unless you engage your honour I shall pay it you again (*Love in a Wood*, III.2, p. 60). I will not engage my honour for such a trifle (*Ibid.*). as poor a pawn to take up money on as honour (*Ibid.*, III.4, p. 77) (Ro).

Tragedy: My honour stands engaged to meet Achilles (*Troilus*, V.1, p. 373). If I should lose my honour for a dream (*Ibid.*).

Not rebelling against ruler:

Tragedy: Rn: His honour, sir, will suffer in the cause (*Aureng-Zebe*, I.1, p. 208) (R(o)).

Not committing murder and treason:

Tragedy: Rn: To hazard life and honour for your sake (*Alcibiades*, V.1.80).

Not committing rape and murder:

Tragedy: Rn: He sells his honour at too cheap a rate (*Alcibiades*, IV.1.284).

Not being a "villain":

Tragedy: Rn: That has been very busie with my Honour (*Orphan*, V.1.90).

Not being a libertine:

Tragedy: Rn: I shall lose my Honour by you, Sir (*Libertine*, I.1, p. 26).

Sexual continence:

Comedy: Rn: But you will promise then to have the care of my honour? pray, good madam, have de care of my honour, pray have de care of my honour. Will you have care of my honour? pray have de care of my honour, and do not tell if you can help it (*Gent. Dancing Master*, I.2, p. 152) (five examples, all Ro).

Tragedy: Rn: Branded my Honour, and pursu'd my Life (*Don Carlos*, IV.1.502).

Reclaiming a libertine:

Comedy: Rg: the more honour you'll have in reclaiming us (*Epsom Wells*, II.1, p. 134).

(d) The x Group

Comedy: Rn: I've stipulated, upon mine honour, that you shall come (*Assignation*, II.2, p. 398). asseverations, that make against my honour (*Ibid.*, III.1, p. 418). the time to repair the lost honour of thy wit (*Ibid.*, V.2, p. 455). I am resolv'd to redeem the honour of our Sex (*Epsom Wells*, I.1, p. 113). no blemish to his honour neither (*Friendship in Fashion*, II.1.542). I had rather lose my Honour, and starve (*True Widow*, V.1, p. 350). something that concerns our Honour (*Woman Captain*, V.1, p. 74). And what can shock my honour in a queen (*Spanish Friar*, IV.2, p. 493).

Comedy: Rg: they go away with the honour of it (*Love in a Wood*, I.1, p. 17) (Ro). 'tis won, miss, with the more honour and pleasure (*Gent. Danc. Master*, II.1, p. 169). Honour is the Child of Virtue (*Dutch Lover*, I.1, p. 228) (RMTP). women, no more than honour, are compassed by bragging (*Country Wife*, I.1, p. 250).

Comedy: Ru: he cannot but esteem me, 'tis for his honour (*Love in a Wood*, I.2, p. 22). that swears and lyes for the honour of his Horse (*Epsom Wells*, III.1, p. 143). That I think is for your honour (*Country Wife*, III.2, p. 295). If your honour or good name be injured (*Plain Dealer*, I.1, p. 394). but never of starving honour (*Ibid.*, V.2, p. 487).

Tragedy: Rn: Show me yours or your honours enemy (*Alcibiades*, IV.1.72). Your honour, Rascal (*Libertine*, I.1, p. 26). My honour so had had this just defence (*Don Carlos*, III.1.190). can any Sin/ I could commit, undo my Honour more/ Than his late Insolence (*Abdelazer*, III.1, pp. 41—2). our Lives he may dispose,/ As he has done our Honours (*Ibid.*, III.1, p. 42). more tender of,/ Than my own Life or Honour (*Ibid.*). I know what's due to Honour, and Revenge (*Ibid.*, IV.6, p. 67). Uncrowned, a captive, nothing left but honour (*Oedipus*, III.1, p. 178). to preserve/ Your Houses Honour (*Orphan*, IV.1.332).

Tragedy: Rg: home returned with honour and great wealth (*Amboyna*, I.1, p. 17). How sickly joyes, honour and greatness grant (*Alcibiades*, II.1.58) (RTP). He'l have the honour of it, in your cause (*Don Carlos*, III.1.216).

Tragedy: Ru: Lose not the honour you have early won (*Aureng-Zebe*, I.1, p. 218). Honour is nothing but a vapour to you (*Libertine*, V.1, p. 84). what's the intrinsick value of honour when a man is under ground (*Ibid.*). Opprest my Friends, and robb'd me of my Honour (*Caius Marius*, I.1.92). he'd sacrifice/ His Country's Honour (*Ibid.*, I.1.188—9). But meerly of his choice my Honour's friend (*Ibid.*, I.1.368). to my Soul thou'rt dear,/ As honour to my name (*Orphan*, IV.1, pp. 196—7).

(e) Summary, R 1671—1680

Table 27 gives a summary of the k/m/v/x classification of R for the decade 1671—1680. In total, k maintains its overwhelmingly predominant position, with 59% of the examples; it is now three and a half times as great as m, which has about 16.5%; v is still very small, with less than 8%, and x accounts for about 16.5%. There are two examples of km, one in comedy and one in tragedy. It is worth noticing that five of the examples of v, which occur together in the *The Gentleman Dancing Master*, I.2, might very well be left out of account, since they are so obviously meant to be ridiculous: the audience is supposed to think it enormously comic that a man should fear loss of honour through going to a brothel; if these five examples are omitted, the percentage of v drops to under six. It is also worth observing that, of the 36 examples of m, no less than 12 occur in *Troilus and Cressida*, which is an adaptation of Shakespeare; however, this does not necessarily mean that the large number of m examples in the play is due to the influence of Shakespeare, for 4 of the 12 examples are entirely new ones, introduced by Dryden himself and without parallels in Shakespeare's play.

Once again, the predominance of k is much stronger in comedy than in tragedy; in comedy, k reaches a new peak, with over 70% of the examples, while in tragedy it accounts for 45.5%. Again, too, the opposite is the case with m, which is much more strongly represented in tragedy; in comedy, indeed, m is now even smaller than v, with less than 7%, while in tragedy it is nearly 28%. The differences between comedy and tragedy are highly significant both for k and for m. There is no difference between comedy and tragedy for v, which is just under 8% for both; even if the five examples of v in *The Gentleman Dancing Master* are omitted, the difference between comedy and tragedy is still nowhere near significant.

The predominance of n over g is greater than ever; it is now three and a half times as frequent as g (seven times as frequent in comedy, and nearly twice as frequent in tragedy). Most of the examples of k and of v are n, while most of the m examples are g.

H. 1681—1690

In this decade there are 73 examples of R, 41 in comedy and 32 in tragedy. In one of the examples, R is not the sole head meaning; this

TABLE 27. *Numbers of k, m, v, and x: R material, 1671—80.*

		k	m	v	x	Total
Comedy	n	72	3	8	8	91
	g	3	5	1	4	13
	u	7	0	0	5	12
	Total	82	8	9	17	116
Tragedy	n	38	0	8	9	55
	g	2	24	0	3	29
	u	6	4	0	7	17
	Total	46	28	8	19	101
All Plays	n	110	3	16	17	146
	g	5	29	1	7	42
	u	13	4	0	12	29
	Total	128	36	17	36	217

example is classified RTP. Of the 73 examples, 2 are countables, 19 uncountables, and 52 equivocal. The examples are as follows.

(a) *The k Group*

Sensitivity to insult, revenging injury, etc.:

Comedy: Rn: 'Tis for my Honour, my Honour (*Lancashire Witches*, III.1, p. 140) (two examples). But when my Honour's injur'd (*Atheist*, III.1.251—2). ventur'd our Lives for one another's Honour (*Bury Fair*, IV.1, p. 348). his Nature's vindicative in Honour's Cause (*Ibid.*, V.1, p. 359). With necessary vindication of our Honour (*Scowrers*, V.1, p. 139).

Tragedy: Rn: My injured honour, and my ravished love (*Don Sebastian*, I.1, p. 332). Give me my love, my honour; give them back (*Ibid.*, IV.3, p. 438).

Not tolerating a rival in love:

Comedy: Rn: my honour, my honour, I must kill him (*Lancashire Witches*, V.1, p. 186) (two examples). For my Honour (*Atheist*, IV.1.649).

Accepting challenges, keeping duelling appointments:

Comedy: Rn: what a deal of Love and Honour have I upon my Hands (*Atheist*, III.1.318—19). we must be there, for our Honours sake (*Bury Fair*, IV.1, p. 345).

Not being rebuffed, outwitted, jilted, etc.:

Comedy: Rn: rather for my own honour have conceal'd it (*Squire of Alsatia*, III.1, p. 248). for her Honour's mine (*Younger Brother*, V.1, p. 384). Are you concern'd for the honour of my Aunt (*Scowrers*, IV.1, p. 125).

Tragedy: Ru: All my long avarice of honour lost (*Don Sebastian*, IV.3, p. 438). Has honour's fountain then sucked back the stream (*Ibid.*).

High rank and office:

Comedy: Rg: 'tis Honour, but no Salary (*Roundheads*, III.1, p. 382) (RTP).

Not having authority flouted:

Comedy: Rn: Murderers of my honour (*Lancashire Witches*, V.1, p. 186).

Tragedy: Rn: The Honour of my House (*Venice Preserved*, I.1.12). our Fortunes, our Honours, and our Lives are at stake (*Widow Ranter*, I.2, p. 236). who will trust his Honour with Sycophants so base (*Ibid.*, II.4, p. 263).

Not performing menial tasks, not being humble:

Tragedy: Ru: learnt in Christian Schools to lay/ My Honour down (*Constantine*, I.1, p. 10).

Making socially good marriages:

Comedy: Rg: what e're I do shall be to her Honour (*Scowrers*, V.1, p. 147).

Reflected (from female relatives' Rc/C):

Comedy: Rn: Hold, my Honour's concerned (*False Count*, V.1, p. 173). The Injury she brings upon thy Honour (*Atheist*, III.1.397). On what a tott'ring Point his Honour stands (*Ibid.*, IV.1.678). base designs upon the Honour of my Family (*Ibid.*, V.1.500—1). vindicate the honour of your Family (*Squire of Alsatia*, III.1, p. 237). what concerns your Honour, and my Love (*Ibid.*, V.1, p. 276). This foul indignity done to my honour (*Amphitryon*, III.1, p. 64). woe to those/ Who thus betrayed my honour (*Ibid.*). I fear my honour, too (*Ibid.*, IV.1, p. 79). to wound the Honour of my Family (*Amorous Bigot*, II.1, p. 40). I cannot think on her, my Honour (*Ibid.*). Having wounded my honour in so sensible a part (*Ibid.*, III.1, p. 48). prostitute the honour of our family (*Ibid.*, III.1, p. 50).

Tragedy: Rn: Vertuous and noble, faithfull to your honour (*Venice Preserved*, V.1.40). But to rebate your jealousy of honour (*Duke of Guise*, III.1, p. 59).

Not submitting to humiliating peace-terms:

Tragedy: Ru: but little Honour would be left me (*Widow Ranter*, II.1, p. 249).

Not loving man who has killed your husband in battle:

Tragedy: Rn: thou'st sav'd my Honour, and hast given me Death (*Widow Ranter*, V.3, p. 300).

Not being executed in an ungentlemanly way:

Tragedy: Rn: Is't fit a Souldier, who has liv'd with Honour (*Venice Preserved*, V.1.445).

Social rank and not being a coward:

Comedy: Rn: I will not hear his Honour lessen'd so (*Bury Fair*, V.1, p. 361).

(*b*) *The m Group*

Comedy: Rg: Honour and Renown attend the Brave (*Younger Brother*, I.1, p. 328). for Money and a little Honour (*Amorous Bigot*, I.1, pp. 22—3). a man of shining honour, by his Deeds in Arms (*Ibid.*, V.1, pp. 65—6).

Tragedy: Rn: Since you've regain'd your Honour so gloriously (*Widow Ranter*, V.2, p. 298).

Tragedy: Rg: those that bring you Conquests home and Honours (*Venice Preserved*, IV.1.229). 'tis Honour calls you to increase your Fame (*Widow Ranter*, II.1, p. 247). We have atchiev'd Honour enough already (*Ibid.*, V.1, p. 294) (R(o)).

As m are also to be classified the following three examples of km:

Comedy: Rg: and he as much Honour, by being beaten (*Atheist*, II.1. 257—8). if I reap the Honour of the Field (*Bury Fair*, IV.1, p. 344). Now Ralph here's Honour to be gotten (*Scowrers*, IV.1, p. 135).

(*c*) *The v Group*

Loyalty to rulers, not committing treason:

Tragedy: Rn: to redeem your honour,/ Unfold the truth (*Venice Preserved*, IV.1.139—40).

Tragedy: Rg: To eternal Honour (*Venice Preserved*, IV.1.4).

Not knowingly committing incest:

Tragedy: Rn: His only way to rectify mistakes,/ And to redeem her honour, is to die (*Don Sebastian*, V.1, p. 461).

(*d*) *The x Group*

Comedy: Rn: I'll trust my Life, my Honour (*False Count*, I.1, p. 105). I'll protect ye, on my honor be it (*Scowrers*, V.1, p. 144).

Comedy: Ru: has the honour of it (*Atheist*, IV.1.21—2) (Ro). and do demand the Combat for her Honour (*Bury Fair*, V.1, p. 361).

Tragedy: Rn: with these thy Life, thy Honour,/ Thy Love, all's stak't (*Venice Preserved*, III.2.194—5). Were I to choose a Guardian of my Honour (*Ibid.*, III.2.289). I have engaged my honour (*Duke of Guise*, I.3, p. 36). Honour's a sacred thing in all but kings (*Ibid.*, V.1, p. 107). So should my honour, like a rising swan (*Don Sebastian*, V.1, p. 453).

Tragedy: Rg: Eternal Honour or perpetual Infamy (*Venice Preserved*, III.2.348). Shall be adorn'd with Statues to thy honour (*Ibid.*, IV.1.11). To his own Disgrace, and your immortal Honour (*Constantine*, IV.1, p. 52). What honour is there in a woman's death (*Don Sebastian*, II.1, p. 359).

Tragedy: Ru: The State of *Venice*, honour, or its safety (*Venice Preserved*, IV.1.109). peace,/ Honour and safety (*Ibid.*, V.1.294—5). I would not ask your Honour (*Widow Ranter*, II.1, p. 249).

(e) *Summary, R 1681—1690*

Table 28 gives a summary of the k/m/v/x classification of R for the decade 1681—1690. In total, k is still the largest group, with 60% of the examples; the m group is only a quarter the size of k, with 14%, and v has shrunk to hardly more than 4%. There are three examples of km, all in comedy. The predominance of k is more marked in comedy than in tragedy (75.5% against 41%), and this is significant; for m, the difference between comedy and tragedy is not significant. The n group is three times as large as the g group, and the difference is more marked in comedy than in tragedy (about four to one compared with about two to one). Most of the examples of k are n, while most of m are g.

TABLE 28. *Numbers of k, m, v, and x: R material, 1681—90.*

		k	m	v	x	Total
Comedy	n	29	0	0	2	31
	g	2	6	0	0	8
	u	0	0	0	2	2
	Total	31	6	0	4	41
Tragedy	n	9	1	2	5	17
	g	0	3	1	4	8
	u	4	0	0	3	7
	Total	13	4	3	12	32
All Plays	n	38	1	2	7	48
	g	2	9	1	4	16
	u	4	0	0	5	9
	Total	44	10	3	16	73

I. 1691—1700

In this decade there are 46 examples of R, 30 in comedy and 16 in tragedy. In two of the examples, R is not the sole head meaning; these two examples are classified RRc. Of the 46 examples, 2 are countables, 19 uncountables, and 25 equivocal. The examples are as follows.

(a) *The k Group*

Sensitivity to insult, revenging affront, etc.:
Comedy: Rn: 'Tis enough my Honours satisfied (*Volunteers*, IV.1, p. 202). But how will Honour be had again (*Ibid.*). He touch'd my Honour to the Quick (*Ibid.*, IV.1, p. 206). I must revenge the affront done to my honour (*Old Bachelor*, V.2, p. 79).

Not tolerating a rival in love:
Comedy: Rn: Sir, my honour's concerned (*Constant Couple*, IV.1, p. 190). Nay, if your honour be concerned (*Ibid.*).

Accepting a challenge:
Comedy: Rn: There's Honour in the Case; 'tis a Challenge (*Provoked Wife*, IV.2, p. 156) (figurative).

Not submitting to humiliating peace-terms:
Tragedy: Rn: Thy life, thy liberty, thy honour safe (*King Arthur*, V.1, p. 192).

Reflected (from female relatives' Rc/C):
Comedy: Rn: have I impaired the honour of your house (*Old Bachelor*, V.5, p. 87). But I will protect my honour (*Double Dealer*, II.1, p. 124). Your honour! you have none (*Ibid.*). consider your own and my honour (*Ibid.*, III.1, p. 134) (RRc). I am tender of your honour (*Way of the World*, II.1, p. 338). to save the honour of my house (*Ibid.*, V.2, p. 397) (Ro).

Reflected (from good qualities of relative):
Comedy: Rg: 'Tis to your honour (*Volunteers*, I.2, p. 175).

Miscellaneous:
Tragedy: Rn: If one must die, to set your honour free (*Love Triumphant*, IV.1, p. 444) (not marrying man you don't love as long as man you do love is still alive). heat of boiling youth,/ And ill-weighed honour (*Ibid.*, V.1, p. 470) (lost by having one's own prisoner harshly treated by sovereign, contrary to own wishes).

(b) *The m Group*

Comedy: Rg: gotten much Honour in the Reduction of *Ireland* (*Volunteers*, Dram. Pers., p. 162). gotten much Honour in the late Wars (*Ibid.*).

Chewing the Cud upon honour (*Ibid.*, I.1, p. 169). has won immortal honour (*Ibid.*, I.2, p. 175). How should Gentlemen get honour Boy, ha (*Ibid.*, II.1, p. 184). Courtship to another Mistress: Honour (*Ibid.*, III.1, p. 196). Honour is the Out-work to Love (*Ibid.*). all Wealth, Power, and Honour (*Ibid.*). contented with my venturing for Honour (*Ibid.*, V.1, p. 214).

Tragedy: Rg: Honour, who leads them to that steepy height (*King Arthur*, V.1, p. 198). The fewer partners in the share of honour (*Cleomenes*, V.2, p. 349). Come up with death or honour (*Ibid.*, V.2, p. 352). Whose share of honour in that glorious day (*Love Triumphant*, I.1, p. 387). laid asleep in the damned bed of honour (*Ibid.*, I.1, p. 393). Farewell the honours of the dusty field (*Ibid.*, IV.1, p. 448).

(c) *The v Group*

Keeping promises:

Tragedy: Rn: My wishes are the honour of my king (*Cleomenes*, III.1, p. 307).

Filial piety:

Tragedy: Rn: I love you much, but love my honour more (*Love Triumphant*, IV.1, p. 444). But could I, with my honour, safe have stayed (*Ibid.*, V.1, p. 468).

Honesty:

Comedy: Rn: forfeit his honour in dealings of business (*Constant Couple*, II.4, p. 163). My honour in dealings of business (*Ibid.*).

Sexual continence:

Comedy: Rn: to secure both our honours (*Constant Couple*, II.4, p. 161) (RRc) (Ro).

(d) *The x Group*

Comedy: Ru: the motto upon my Sword is Love and Honour, because Gentlemen fight for nothing else (*Volunteers*, III.1, p. 199). Unmask, for the honour of *France* (*Provoked Wife*, V.5, p. 181). My honour can be nowhere more concerned than here (*Constant Couple*, V.3, p. 227). 'tis for the honour of England, that all Europe should know we have blockheads of all ages (*Way of the World*, I.2, p. 325).

Tragedy: Rn: hazard/ Your life and honour in this bold appeal (*Cleomenes*, IV.1, p. 320).

Tragedy: Rg: *Honour prizing,/ Death despising* (*King Arthur*, I.2, p. 150).

Tragedy: Ru: *And hoigh for the honour of old England* (*King Arthur*, V.1, p. 196) (two examples).

(e) Summary, R 1691—1700

Table 29 gives a summary of the k/m/v/x classification of R for the decade 1691—1700. It will be seen that, in total, k is still the largest group, with 37%, but its preponderance is much reduced compared with the previous decade; m, on the other hand, has increased in frequency, and is not much smaller than k, with 32.5%; v is still small, but larger than in the previous decade, with 13%; x accounts for the remaining 17.5%. However, it should be observed that, of the 15 examples of m, no less than 9 occur in one play, Shadwell's *The Volunteers*: this is very much a post-revolution Whig play, full of ardent propaganda for William III's wars in Ireland, and is perhaps not wholly typical of the theatre of the time; this does not mean that it should be completely neglected: it may in fact be a sign of new currents in the theatre; but, as it contains a relatively large number of examples, it probably unbalances the figures for the decade as a whole. *The Volunteers* contains 14 examples of R (9 m, 4 k, and 1 x), and if these are omitted from the table the percentage of m is reduced considerably; the figures then become k 41%, m 19%, v 19%, and x 22%. Even these figures, however, show changes compared with the previous decade, and the increase in v is significant and the decrease in k possibly significant;

TABLE 29. *Numbers of k, m, v, and x: R material, 1691—1700.*

		k	m	v	x	Total
Comedy	n	13	0	3	0	16
	g	1	9	0	0	10
	u	0	0	0	4	4
	Total	14	9	3	4	30
Tragedy	n	3	0	3	1	7
	g	0	6	0	1	7
	u	0	0	0	2	2
	Total	3	6	3	4	16
All Plays	n	16	0	6	1	23
	g	1	15	0	1	17
	u	0	0	0	6	6
	Total	17	15	6	8	46

the change in m, however is not significant (while with *The Volunteers* included it is just significant). If the supplementary material is added (see Appendix E), and *The Volunteers* is omitted, there is actually a decline in m for the decade, both in comedy and in total; the rise in v remains, however.

To return to Table 29, tragedy once again shows a greater proportion of v and of m than comedy, and comedy shows a greater proportion of k. The n group is larger than the g group in comedy, but not so markedly as in the previous decade, obviously because of the large number of examples of m, which are all g. In tragedy, g and n are equal. There are no examples of km.

On the whole, although the material is small for this decade, there are some signs of a reversal of the general trends that have hitherto prevailed through the century. As far as m is concerned, this reversal can be dismissed as purely temporary, and caused by one play alone, but the rise of v, though small, may well be real.

J. Summary, R 1591—1700

The findings will be discussed in Chapter 10, but some of the obvious changes in R during the century can be noted here. In general, there is a clear tendency for the proportion of k to increase during the century, and for m and v to decline; in other words, there is less emphasis on the things that overlap with the demands of Christian virtue, and less emphasis on military reputation. The increase in k is correlated with the increase in n (cf. Chapter 5, A). Inside the k group, reputation arising from high rank or position becomes less frequent, while two other types become more frequent: first, the kind of reputation connected with duelling (sensitivity to affront, observing the rules of duelling, etc.); and second, the kind of reputation that is lost by the unchastity of a female relative (which of course may also be a motive for duelling). These changes all tend to be more marked in comedy than in tragedy. There is also a significant decline in the proportion of examples with joint head-meanings; this may be due in part to the decline in frequency of reputation arising from high rank, since this type often forms joint head-meanings with members of the MTP group; it may also be due in part to the tendency in the Restoration period for writers to aim at simplicity and clarity in style, rather than at the complex effects of the Jacobean dramatists.

CHAPTER 8

Virtue and Convention: (III) The RH Material

A. 1591—1600

In this decade there are 25 examples of RH, of which 8 are in comedy and 17 in tragedy. In two of the examples, RH is not the sole head-meaning; these two are classified RHP. Of the 25 examples, one is a countable, 15 are uncountables, and 9 are equivocal. The examples are the following.

(a) The k Group

Not accepting humiliating peace-terms:
Tragedy: Rn: such offers of our peace,/ As we with honor and respect may take (*John*, V.7.84—5).

Reflected (from Rc/C):
Comedy: Rn: if you loue her, then to morrow wed her: But it would better fit your honour to change your minde (*Much Ado*, III.2.104—6).

(b) The m Group

Comedy: Ru: If well-respected Honor bid me on (*Henry IV.1*, IV.3.10).
Tragedy: Ru: Vp Princes, and with spirit of Honor edged,/ More sharper then your Swords, high to the field (*Henry V*, III.5.38—9).

(c) The v Group

Truthfulness:
Tragedy: Ru: Beleeue me for mine Honor, and haue respect to mine Honor, that you may beleeue (*Julius Caesar*, III.2.14—16) (two examples).

Keeping oaths:
Comedy: Rn: without breach of Honour may/ Make tender of (*L. L. L.*, II.1.170—1).

Not committing treason and witchcraft:
Tragedy: Rn: if shee haue forgot/ Honour and Vertue (*Henry VI.2*, II.1.188—9).

Not cheating and equivocating:

Comedy: Rn: leauing the feare of heauen on the left hand, and hiding mine honor in my necessity, am faine to shufflle (*Merry Wives*, II.2.23—5).

Not being ungrateful:

Comedy: Rn: My honor would not let ingratitude/ So much besmeare it (*Merchant of Venice*, V.1.218—19).

Sanctity, piety, obedience to church:

Tragedy: Rn: That which vpholdeth him, that thee vpholds,/ His Honor, Oh thine Honor, *Lewis* thine Honor (*John*, III.1.315—16) (three examples) (supporting a righteous cause at the command of the church).

Tragedy: Ru: If Honor may be shrowded in a Herse (*Richard III*, I.2.2) (RHP).

Not taking bribes:

Tragedy: Ru: And sell the mighty space of our large Honors/ For so much trash (*Julius Caesar*, IV.3.25—6).

(d) The x Group

Comedy: Rn: if it stand as you your selfe still do,/ Within the eye of honour (*Merchant of Venice*, I.1.136—7). then with safety of a pure blush, thou maist in honor come off againe (*A. Y. L. I.*, I.2.27—8).

Comedy: Ru: Thou art the King of Honor (*Henry IV.1*, IV.1.10).

Tragedy: Rn: That died in Honour and *Lauinia's* cause (*Tit. And.*, I.1.377).

Tragedy: Ru: I doubt not, but with Honor to redresse (*Henry VI.1*, II.5.126). Thou Ragge of Honor, thou detested — (*Richard III*, I.3.234). Now by the stocke and Honour of my kin (*Romeo*, I.5.60) (RHP). Set Honor in one eye, and Death i'th other (*Julius Caesar*, I.2.86). I loue/ The name of Honor, more then I feare death (*Ibid.*, I.2.88—9). Well, Honor is the subiect of my Story (*Ibid.*, I.2.92).

(e) Summary, RH 1591—1600

Table 30 gives a summary of the k/m/v/x classification of RH for the decade 1591—1600. In total, v is the largest group (something that was not found in any decade for R), and the difference between v and k or between v and m is significant. As could be expected when the number of examples is so small, there are no significant differences between comedy and tragedy. There are no examples of g (cf. p. 130 above), nor of km.

TABLE 30. *Numbers of k, m, v, and x: RH material, 1591—1600.*

		k	m	v	x	Total
Comedy	n	1	0	3	2	6
	g	0	0	0	0	0
	u	0	1	0	1	2
	Total	1	1	3	3	8
Tragedy	n	1	0	4	1	6
	g	0	0	0	0	0
	u	0	1	4	6	11
	Total	1	1	8	7	17
All Plays	n	2	0	7	3	12
	g	0	0	0	0	0
	u	0	2	4	7	13
	Total	2	2	11	10	25

B. 1601—1610

In this decade there are 33 examples of RH, 14 in comedy and 19 in tragedy. In three of the examples, RH is not the sole head-meaning; the joint head-meanings found are RHC (one), RHTP (one), and RHK (one). Of the 33 examples, none are countables, 17 are uncountables, and 16 are equivocal. The examples are the following.

(a) *The k group*

Sensitivity to insult, revenging injury, etc.:

Tragedy: Rn: then mine honour/ Will thrust me into action (*Maid's Tragedy*, II.1, p. 23) (Ro). The thing that we call Honour, bears us all/ Headlong unto sin (*Ibid.*, IV.1, p. 60).

Tragedy: Ru: Till by some elder Masters of knowne Honor,/ I haue a voyce, and president of peace (*Hamlet*, V.2.247—8).

Ostentation, magnificence:

Comedy: Ru: Pay, pay; 'tis honour, MINOS (*Poetaster*, III.4.78).

Not accepting humiliating peace-terms:

Tragedy: Ru: Weigh you the worth and honour of a King (*Troilus*, II.2.26).

Reflected (from Rc/C):

Comedy: Rn: In the point of honour,/ The cases are all one (*Volpone*, II.6.72—3) (RHK).

Tragedy: Rn: I am full as resolute/ As fame and honour can inforce me be (*Maid's Tragedy*, III.1, p. 40). as far/ As honour gives me leave, be thy *Amintor* (*Ibid.*, IV.1, p. 51).

(b) *The m Group*

Comedy: Rg: I did bestow him, as the prize of mine honour, upon my love (*Blurt*, V.1.3—4). a noble scarre, is a good liu'rie of honor (*All's Well*, IV.5.100—101).

Comedy: Ru: as well as poor musty soldiers do by their honour (*Blurt*, II.2.233—4) (Ro).

Tragedy: Rg: But in mine emulous honor let him dye (*Troilus*, IV.1.29).

Tragedy: Ru: Mine honour keepes the weather of my fate (*Troilus*, V.3.26). the deere man/ Holds honor farre more precious, deere, then life (*Ibid.*, V.3.27—8). Your Honor calles you hence (*Antony*, I.3.97). Experience, Man-hood, Honor, ne're before,/ Did violate so it selfe (*Ibid.*, III.10.23—4).

(c) *The v Group*

Not committing treason and murder:

Tragedy: Rn: I have begun a slaughter on my honour (*Maid's Tragedy*, V.1, p. 61).

Not conniving at unchastity:

Comedy: Rn: Would barke your honor from that trunke you beare (*Measure for Measure*, III.1.69).

Not betraying a trust:

Tragedy: Rn: In any act, that may preserue mine honour (*Sejanus*, I.1.325).

Miscellaneous:

Comedy: Ru: Whose aged honor cites a vertuous youth (*All's Well*, I.3.211). to whose honour/ And modest fame I am a servant vow'd (*Roaring Girl*, V.2.186—7) (RHC).

Tragedy: Ru: Your idle, vertuous *definitions*/ Keepe honor poore (*Sejanus*, I.1.330—1).

(All three probably v, though content not clearly specified.)

(d) *The x Group*

Comedy: Rn: How with mine honor may I giue him that (*12th Night*, III.4.214). Now, I dare heare you with mine honour (*Alchemist*, I.2.71).

Comedy: Ru: I'd have you come off with honour (*Trick to Catch*, IV.4. 126). Thou art vertue, fame,/ Honour (*Volpone*, I.1.25—6) (RHTP) (Ro). Do we love Heaven and honour (*Philaster*, I.1, p. 84). I shall then out-live/ Vertue and honour (*Ibid.*, V.1, p. 132).

Tragedy: Rn: condemne vs/ As poysonous of your Honour (*Coriolanus*, V.3.134—5).

Tragedy: Rg: that selfe-hand/ Which writ his Honor in the Acts it did (*Antony*, V.1.21—2).

Tragedy: Ru: What an alteration of Honor has desp'rate want made (*Timon*, IV.3.464—5). Our Fealty & *Tenantius* right, with Honor to maintaine (*Cymbeline*, V.4.73—4). Life, Honour, joyes Eternal, all Delights (*Maid's Tragedy*, II.1, p. 19).

(e) *Summary, RH 1601—1610*

Table 31 gives a summary of the k/m/v/x classification of RH for the decade 1601—1610. There are no significant differences in frequency between k, m, and v, and no significant differences between comedy and tragedy. The n group is larger than the g group, but (as also in the previous decade) the u group is the largest. There are no examples of km.

TABLE 31. *Numbers of k, m, v, and x: RH material, 1601—10.*

		k	m	v	x	Total
Comedy	n	1	0	1	2	4
	g	0	2	0	0	2
	u	1	1	2	4	8
	Total	2	3	3	6	14
Tragedy	n	4	0	2	1	7
	g	0	1	0	1	2
	u	2	4	1	3	10
	Total	6	5	3	5	19
All Plays	n	5	0	3	3	11
	g	0	3	0	1	4
	u	3	5	3	7	18
	Total	8	8	6	11	33

C. 1611—1620

In this decade there are 45 examples of RH, 14 in comedy and 31 in tragedy. In four of the examples, RH is not the sole head-meaning; the joint head-meanings found are RHP (one), RHC (one), RHTP (one), and RHK (one). Of the 45 examples, 2 are countables, 24 uncountables, and 19 equivocal. The examples are the following.

(a) *The k Group*

Sensitivity to insult, revenging affront, etc.:

Comedy: Rn: By manhood's reverend honour, but we must (*Fair Quarrel*, II.1.248). My honour does compel me to entreat you (*Little Fr. Lawyer*, I.1, p. 386). Honour the first place holds, the second Love (*Ibid.*, I.1, p. 387).

Tragedy: Rn: are things weary of their lives, and know not honour (*King and No King*, IV.1, p. 206) (RHK). Or fetch ye off, where honour had ingag'd ye (*Valentinian*, III.3, p. 51).

Keeping duelling appointments, observing duelling code, etc.:

Comedy: Rn: And rage will force me do what will grieve honour (*Fair Quarrel*, III.1.123) (not killing a man who refuses to fight). That poor and base renouncing of your honour (*Little French Lawyer*, II.1, p. 400). To hide his head then, when his honour call'd him (*Ibid.*).

Not recanting under threat:

Comedy: Rn: nor can I with mine honour/ Recant my words (*Little French Lawyer*, I.1, p. 385).

Loyalty to fellow-criminals:

Tragedy: Ru: all the thoughts of honor, and reuenge (*Catiline*, III.1.500).

(b) *The m Group*

Comedy: Rg: whose honours/ We heave our hands at (*Captain*, I.2, pp. 237—8).

Tragedy: Rg: disgraces, and contempt of Honour/ Reign now (*Loyal Subject*, I.3, p. 85). my own honour,/ Cure of my Country murder me (*Ibid.*, IV.5, p. 151). come I am honours Martyr (*Ibid.*). Extreamly envious of your youth, and honour (*Humorous Lieutenant*, I.2, p. 293).

Tragedy: Ru: Then takes the edge of Honour (*Valentinian*, I.3, p. 14). Thine honour bids thee, Souldier (*Mad Lover*, II.1, p. 22). a greater power than love commanded,/ Commands my life, mine honour (*Humorous Lieutenant*, I.2, p. 295). Honour and Arms, no emulation left me (*Ibid.*, II.4, p. 306). When honour pricks ye on (*Ibid.*, III.3, p. 316). Swallow'd thy youth, made shipwrack of thine honour (*Ibid.*, IV.2, p. 338). For shame reflect upon your self, your honour (*False One*, II.3, p. 327). let thine honour,/ The soul of a commander, give ear (*Ibid.*, II.3, p. 329).

Under m are also to be classified the two following examples of km:

Comedy: Rg: fight for any cause,/ And carry it with honour (*Little Fr. Lawyer*, II.1, p. 395). I say, honour (*Ibid.*, IV.1, p. 424).

(c) *The v Group*

Loyalty to ruler, not being a rebel:

Tragedy: Ru: A person both of bloud and honor (*Catiline*, III.1.329) (RHP).

Not conniving at unchastity:

Tragedy: Rn: a buriall plot,/ For both your Honours (*White Devil*, I.2. 267—8).

Miscellaneous:

Tragedy: Ru: To taint that honour euery good Tongue blesses (*Henry VIII*, III.1.55) (and perhaps RcC). To make our actions worthy of your Honour (*Loyal Subject*, III.2, p. 117). (Neither of these two very specific, but fairly clearly v.)

(d) *The x Group*

Comedy: Rn: where my honour, or my friend is questioned,/ I have a Sword (*Little French Lawyer*, I.1, p. 376). Honour, and a fair grave (*Custom of the Country*, I.1, p. 316).

Comedy: Ru: You Sir know/ I got it, and with honour (*Little Fr. Lawyer*, I.1, p. 380). that staff of honour, my age lean'd on (*Custom of the Country*, V.1, p. 381).

Tragedy: Rn: dare not in his private honour suffer/ So great a blemish (*False One*, II.3, p. 328).

Tragedy: Rg: from the sacred Ashes of her Honour (*Henry VIII*, V.4.45) (RHC). Get up into your honour,/ The top branch of your bravery (*Mad Lover*, III.1, p. 37). Vertue and blooming honour bleed to death here (*Ibid.*, III.1, p. 41). Turn'd honour into earth, and faithful service (*Ibid.*, III.1, p. 42).

Tragedy: Ru: You haue as little Honestie, as Honor (*Henry VIII*, III.2. 271). Where lives vertue,/ Honour, discretion, wisdom (*Valentinian*, I.3, p. 10) (RHTP). the Father of the Empires honour (*Ibid.*, II.4, p. 34). Bound by the chains of honesty and honour (*Loyal Subject*, III.3, p. 124). take the enemie to honour,/ The knave to worth (*Ibid.*, V.6, p. 168). That honour aim'd by all at for a pattern (*Humorous Lieutenant*, V.5, p. 368). Bribes justice, cut-throats honour (*Laws of Candy*, IV.1, p. 283).

TABLE 32. *Numbers of k, m, v, and x: RH material, 1611—20.*

		k	m	v	x	Total
Comedy	n	7	0	0	2	9
	g	0	3	0	0	3
	u	0	0	0	2	2
	Total	7	3	0	4	14
Tragedy	n	2	0	1	1	4
	g	0	4	0	4	8
	u	1	8	3	7	19
	Total	3	12	4	12	31
All Plays	n	9	0	1	3	13
	g	0	7	0	4	11
	u	1	8	3	9	21
	Total	10	15	4	16	45

(e) *Summary, RH 1611—1620*

Table 32 gives a summary of the k/m/v/x classification of RH for the decade 1611—1620. The largest group is now m, and v has become the smallest; k is more frequent in comedy than in tragedy, and this difference is significant; otherwise there are no significant differences between comedy and tragedy. There are two examples of km, both in comedy. In total, n and g are about equally frequent, but the u group is still larger than either. Most of the examples of k are also n.

D. 1621—1630

In this decade there are 45 examples of RH, 24 in comedy and 21 in tragedy. In four of the examples, RH is not the sole head-meaning: the joint head-meanings found are RHP (two) and RHTP (two). Of the 45 examples, none are countables, 31 are uncountables, and 14 are equivocal. The examples are the following.

(a) *The k Group*

Sensitivity to affront, revenging injury, etc.:

Comedy: Rn: Honour's a thing too subtil for his wisdom (*Rule a Wife*, II.1, p. 183). Honour is nothing with you (*Elder Brother*, V.1, p. 49).

Comedy: Ru: H'as no capacity what honor is?/ For that's the Souldiers god (*Rule a Wife*, II.1, p. 183).

Tragedy: Ru: *Reuenge is mine; Honour doth loue Command* ('*Tis Pity*, 2402).

Keeping a duelling appointment:

Comedy: Rn: my Reputation/ (The life and soul of Honor) (*Cure for a Cuckold*, I.2.161—2) (RHP).

Insisting on one's rights:

Comedy: Rn: but no more than honour can give way to (*Elder Brother*, V.1, p. 53).

Not breaking off a proposed marriage:

Tragedy: Rn: than you may/ Come oft with honour (*Bondman*, V.1, p. 113).

Miscellaneous:

Comedy: Rn: Troth, Roderigo, anything in the way of honour (*Spanish Gipsy*, I.1.33) (not raping a girl if she is of noble family).

Tragedy: Rg: Stuck all with stars of honour shining clearly (*Wife for a Month*, IV.1, p. 57) (preferring death and consummation of marriage to no consummation).

(b) *The m Group*

Comedy: Rg: There, I would follow you as a guide to honour (*Spanish Curate*, I.1, p. 63). Suffer abundantly? 'tis the Crown of Honour (*Rule a Wife*, I.1, p. 174) (with a pun on venereal disease).

Tragedy: Rg: Cannot the beams/ Of honour thaw your icy fears (*Maid of Honour*, I.1, p. 227). the least spark of honour that took life/ From your sweet breath (*Bondman*, II.1, p. 98). I saw the child of honour, for he was young (*Wife for a Month*, V.1, p. 68).

Tragedy: Ru: and prefer/ Your ease before your honour (*Maid of Honour*, I.1, p. 227).

(c) *The v Group*

Keeping a vow:

Comedy: Rn: I would not crack my vow, start from my honour (*Chances*, I.10, p. 189).

Keeping a treaty:

Tragedy: Rn: And so far in my honour I was tied (*Maid of Honour*, I.1, p. 227).

Doing duty to brother:

Tragedy: Rn: should so far/ Forsake his honour (*Maid of Honour*, III.3, p. 240).

Not being revengeful, not committing crimes for revenge:

Comedy: Rn: You cannot be so unrighteous,/ To your own honour (*Fair Maid of the Inn*, II.1.146—7). for honours sake stay your foule purpose (*Ibid.*, II.1.163).
Tragedy: Rn: He then failes/ In honour, who for lucre of Reuenge (*Broken Heart*, 1078—9).
Tragedy: Ru: honour must be grounded/ On knowledge, not opinion (*Broken Heart*, 1083—4). Of what becomes the grace of reall Honour (*Ibid.*, 1088).

Not conniving at unchastity:

Comedy: Rn: Though you could dispense/ With your own honour (*New Way*, III.2, p. 362).
Tragedy: Rn: I'll not taint/ My honour for the dukedom (*Great Duke of Florence*, II.2, p. 206).
Tragedy: Ru: Was this the expectation of my Youth,/ My growth of Honour (*Wife for a Month*, IV.1, p. 47).

Sexual continence, not being a libertine:

Comedy: Rn: cannot be friend/ To his own honour (*Chances*, III.4, p. 218). I will grow old in the study of my honour (*Witty Fair One*, V.3, p. 358).

Miscellaneous:

Comedy: Ru: poore thinne membranes/ Of honour (*Staple of News*, III.2. 245—6) (equated with "virtue and honesty"). the scope/ Is alwayes honour, and the publique good (*New Inn*, IV.4.45—6) (context excludes k, but might be m).
Tragedy: Rn: as far/ As justice and mine honour can give way (*Bondman*, V.3, p. 116) (integrity as ruler).

(d) *The x Group*

Comedy: Ru: If honour lye in eating, he is right honourable (*Rule a Wife*, II.1, p. 183). As ever you lov'd honour (*Chances*, I.7, p. 184). degraded him/ From the honor he was born (*Cure for a Cuckold*, IV.2.194—5) (RHP). No scruple lessen'd in the full weight of honour (*New Way*, I.2, p. 352). *all the principles tending to honour/ Are taught* (*Ibid.*). I will not be more true to mine own honour (*Ibid.*, III.1, p. 360). No sense of any vertue, honour,/ Gentrie or merit (*Staple of News*, II.4.59—60) (RHTP). And rancks him in the file of prayse and honour (*Fair Maid of the Inn*, III.2. 146).

Tragedy: Rg: Some sparks of fire, which, fann'd with honour's breath,/ might rise into a flame (*Maid of Honour*, III.3, p. 240).

Tragedy: Ru: Ambition, that eats into/ With venom'd teeth, true thankfulness, and honour (*Prophetess*, V.1, p. 377). My birth, my honour, and what's dearest to me (*Bondman*, V.3, p. 116) (RHTP). But when we love with honour to our ends (*Wife for a Month*, II.1, p. 19). Honour, and everlasting love his mourners (*Ibid.*, IV.1, p. 51). The noble heir of nature, and of honour (*Ibid.*, V.1, p. 60).

(e) *Summary, RH 1621—1630*

Table 33 gives a summary of the k/m/v/x classification of RH for the decade 1621—1630. The largest group is v, both in comedy and in tragedy, and the smallest group is m. There is no example of km. There are no significant differences between comedy and tragedy. The n group is larger than the g group, but u is still larger than either of them.

TABLE 33. *Numbers of k, m, v, and x: RH material, 1621—30.*

		k	m	v	x	Total
Comedy	n	5	0	6	0	11
	g	0	2	0	0	2
	u	1	0	2	8	11
	Total	6	2	8	8	24
Tragedy	n	1	0	5	0	6
	g	1	3	0	1	5
	u	1	1	3	5	10
	Total	3	4	8	6	21
All Plays	n	6	0	11	0	17
	g	1	5	0	1	7
	u	2	1	5	13	21
	Total	9	6	16	14	45

E. 1631—1640

In this decade there are 46 examples of RH, 19 in comedy and 27 in tragedy. In two of the examples, RH is not the sole head-meaning; these two are classified RHMT and RHK respectively. Of the 46 examples, one is a countable, 26 are uncountables, and 19 are equivocal. The examples are the following.

(a) *The k Group*

Sensitivity to affront, revenging injury, etc.:

Comedy: Rn: Provok'd to battle by our honour (*News from Plymouth*, III.1, p. 154). my honour binds me/ To teach you better manners (*Ibid.*, V.1, pp. 195—6). Mine honour is my tutour,/ Already try'd (*Lady's Trial*, 2021—2).

Tragedy: Rn: These terms of honour have but little grace (*Imposture*, V.4, p. 259).

Not evading challenges, observing duelling-code, etc.:

Comedy: Rn: stand/ On point of honour, not t'have any odds (*Magnetic Lady*, III.4.87—8) (RHK). No reconcilement can be made with honour,/ Till one or both have bled for it (*News from Plymouth*, III.1, p. 151). my honour may expect/ To be excus'd (*Distresses*, I.1, p. 292).

Tragedy: Rn: that I might kill thee/ Without a blush to honour (*Imposture*, III.3, p. 224).

Not submitting to humiliating peace-terms:

Tragedy: Rn: on such terms/ As honour would give way to (*Bashful Lover*, I.2, p. 473).

Making socially suitable marriages:

Comedy: Rn: can I with mine honour/ Mix my blood with his (*City Madam*, I.3, p. 383).

Tragedy: Rn: We have too much forgot ourself, and honour (*Politician*, III.1, p. 124).

Reflected (from Rc/C):

Tragedy: Rn: If Altophil do breed his honour with/ Strict discipline (*Unfortunate Lovers*, I.1, p. 21).

Not breaking off a proposed marriage:

Comedy: Rn: And that you could quit all your ties with honour (*Royal Master*, V.1, p. 175) (not breaking off a marriage unless the other party agrees).

Tragedy: Rn: let him answer/ And justify his honour (*Traitor*, IV.1, p. 154).

Miscellaneous:

Comedy: Ru: Mine honour claimes/ The last foot in the field (*Lady's Trial*, 2041—2) (precedence; being the less cowardly of two rivals).

Tragedy: Rn: 'twere a sin honour could not forgive (*Imposture*, I.1, p. 184) (doubting the courage or integrity of an ally). Obedience, honour, common gratitude (*Ibid.*, I.1, p. 185) (not refusing to marry the man who has saved your country in war).

(b) *The m Group*

Comedy: Rn: lay no scandall/ Upon my martiall honour (*Lady's Trial*, 1912—13).

Tragedy: Rg: in future deeds/ Of honour, and of loyal faith (*Love and Honour*, V.1, p. 182). her more potent eye/ Buries alive mine honour (*Bashful Lover*, IV.1, p. 484). where so much honour/ Secures his praise (*Cardinal*, I.1, p. 278).

Tragedy: Ru: Forgetful of yourselves, allegiance, honour (*Bashful Lover*, II.7, p. 477). One man that does not ask to bleed with honour (*Cardinal*, II.1, p. 291). bring more effeminacy than man,/ Or honour, to your bed (*Ibid.*, II.3, p. 301).

(c) *The v Group*

Not being guilty of adultery and treason:

Tragedy: Rn: Above his honour (*Emperor of the East*, IV.5, p. 304).

Not conniving at unchastity:

Tragedy: Rn: So most degenerate, and lost to honour (*Politician*, I.1, p. 97).

Sexual continence:

Comedy: Rn: On that which you propounded, sir, your honour (*Hyde Park*, III.1, p. 493). 'Twere better not to have been born to honours,/ Than forfeit them so poorly (*Ibid.*, V.1, p. 529) (RHMT).

Tragedy: Rn: to guard/ My honour, now beseiged by lust (*Bashful Lover*, IV.1, p. 484). O! think upon your honour, sir (*Unfortunate Lovers*, IV.1, p. 64). since thou could'st forget/ Thy honour of a prince (*Imposture*, III.3, p. 220).

Justice:

Tragedy: Rn: have you lost/ All feeling of humanity, as honour (*Emperor of the East*, V.1, p. 307).

Miscellaneous:

Comedy: Rn: rebells/ To all that's honest, that's to truth and honour (*Fancies*, 1720—1) (esp. not being meretricious).

Comedy: Ru: Would prostitute al honour to the luxurie of ease (*Fancies*, 385) (not clearly specified, but opposed to "full tide of blood" and "luxurie of ease").

Tragedy: Rn: It would become the justice of my cause/ And honour (*Politician*, III.1, p. 119) (not being guilty of flattery, insolence, pride, and "liberty"). Which you may cure with honour (*Imposture*, II.1, p. 201) (not conniving at imposture, not marrying off a nun). He dares not/ Blemish his honour so (*Ibid.*, II.3, p. 210) (not abducting a woman from a nunnery).

(d) The x Group

Comedy: Rn: Name and honour./ What are they (*Fancies*, 463—4).

Comedy: Rg: His deeds of honour are so high (*Distresses*, V.1, p. 361).

Comedy: Ru: I must beseech you stay, for honour (*Lady of Pleasure*, IV.3, p. 80). As I love honour, and an honest name (*Fancies*, 748). Honor and duty/ Stand my compurgators (*Lady's Trial*, 1531—2).

Tragedy: Rn: Thy honour Oramont is forfeited/ Already in thy jealousy (*Fair Favourite*, II.1, p. 223).

Tragedy: Rg: whose name is great/ I' the register of honour (*Imposture*, I.2, p. 192).

Tragedy: Ru: Add to your honour by assisting us (*Distresses*, IV.1, p. 337). Grow up in honour (*Imposture*, III.2, p. 216).

(e) Summary, RH 1631—1640

Table 34 gives a summary of the k/m/v/x classification of RH for the decade 1631—1640. In total, k is the largest group and m the smallest. There are no examples of km. There are no significant differences between comedy and tragedy. The n group is now considerably larger than either g or u.

TABLE 34. *Numbers of k, m, v, and x: RH material, 1631—40.*

		k	m	v	x	Total
Comedy	n	8	1	3	1	13
	g	0	0	0	1	1
	u	1	0	1	3	5
	Total	9	1	4	5	19
Tragedy	n	8	0	9	1	18
	g	0	3	0	1	4
	u	0	3	0	2	5
	Total	8	6	9	4	27
All Plays	n	16	1	12	2	31
	g	0	3	0	2	5
	u	1	3	1	5	10
	Total	17	7	13	9	46

F. 1661—1670

In this decade there are 54 examples of RH, 20 in comedy and 34 in tragedy. In three of the examples, RH is not the sole head-meaning; these three are classified RHTP (two) and RHK (one). Of the 54 examples, one is a countable, 34 are uncountables, and 19 are equivocal. The examples are the following.

(a) The k Group

Sensitivity to injury, revenging affront, etc.:

Comedy: Rn: The war which honour makes in streets (*Man's the Master*, IV.1, p. 85). My honour will less yield, that you, sir, should deprive (*Ibid.*, V.1, p. 98). My honour now makes me forsake your cause (*Ibid.*, V.1, p. 99). Such satisfaction as your honour does require (*Ibid.*, V.1, p. 100).

Tragedy: Rn: 'Tis now too late:/ I am by honour hindered (*Rival Ladies*, I.2, p. 156). The honour of a prince would then deny (*Indian Queen*, V.1, p. 269).

Not evading challenges, observing the duelling code, etc.:

Comedy: Rn: had he prov'd untrue/ To Honour, he had then (*Comical Revenge*, IV.5.36—7). with safety/ Of the unblemished honour, which you taught me (*Tempest*, II.2, p. 139). it was my honour oblig'd me to go along (*Sullen Lovers*, IV.1, p. 58). men of honour have allow'd it (*Man's the Master*, IV.1, p. 78) (RHTP). My honour will not suffer me to share (*Ibid.*, V.1, p. 98).

Tragedy: Rn: could it with honour be,/ I'd seek thy friendship (*Indian Emperor*, V.1, p. 394). Abusive Coward, hast thou no sense of honour (*Forced Marriage*, III.2, p. 332). Sense of honour! ha, ha, ha, poor *Cleontius* (*Ibid.*).

Not fighting a man to whom under an obligation:

Tragedy: Rn: Pretending breach of honour if you fight (*Rival Ladies*, II.1, p. 171) (RHK).

Insisting on one's rights:

Tragedy: Rn: Honour is what myself, and friends, I owe (*Conquest of Granada. 1*, IV.1, p. 80) (also demands of friendship).

Living up to one's station:

Comedy: Rn: formerly had been Persons of great worth and honour (*She Would*, I.1.20—1) (living up to one's station here involves using professional pimps, not procuring for oneself).

Sexual virility, wenching, etc.:

Comedy: Rn: will boggle at nothing that becomes a man of Honour (*She Would*, I.1.163—4) (especially wenching and drinking) (RHTP).

Observing the conventions of civilized warfare:

Tragedy: Rn: I, as a prisoner, am by honour tied (*Indian Queen*, I.1, p. 232) (prisoner-of-war not escaping). It was an act my honour bound me to (*Indian Emperor*, I.2, p. 339) (not attacking without formal declaration of war; or possibly could be not having authority flouted). I could not do it on my honour's score (*Ibid*.) (the same).

Not marrying into an enemy family:

Tragedy: Rn: Be friends with Manuel, I am thine; till when/ My honour's (*Rival Ladies*, I.2, p. 158).

Committing suicide:

Tragedy: Rn: Honour requires your death (*Indian Emperor*, V.2, p. 407).

Miscellaneous:

Comedy: Rn: When Honour first made you your Love decline (*Comical Revenge*, V.3.48) (not seeming partial to the man you love).
Tragedy: Rn: Rivals with honour may together die (*Indian Queen*, II.3, p. 246) (honour not infringed by rivals co-operating, if it is for the rescue of their mistress). honour must give, not take (*Indian Emperor*, IV.2, p. 375) (probably "not being under an obligation"). Those gifts I cannot with my honour take (*Ibid*., V.2, p. 410) (not accepting office under the conquerer of your country).
Tragedy: Ru: But if vain honour can confirm the soul (*Tyrannic Love*, IV.1, p. 438) (not clearly specified, but explicitly contrasted with religion).

(b) *The m Group*

Comedy: Rg: all such ancient and discreet records of love and honour (*Man's the Master*, II.1, p. 27). the Spur to Honour and all Glorious Actions (*Humorists*, I.1, p. 196).
Tragedy: Rg: Now, rival, let us run where honour calls (*Indian Emperor*, III.4, p. 366). In fields they dare not fight, where honour calls (*Tyrannic Love*, I.1, p. 386).

There is also one example of km:

Comedy: Ru: You'l meet with Honour blown, not in the bud (*Comical Revenge*, IV.1.9).

(c) *The v Group*

Keeping one's word, paying one's debts:

Tragedy: Rn: call themselves men of Honour to borrow Money with; ... they wou'd have both their Honours and Estates pass for Security (*Royal Shepherdess*, IV.1, p. 142) (two examples; possibly Ro?).

Loyalty to ruler, not breaking trust:
Comedy: Rn: My office does engage my honour to/ Make good the sentence (*Law against Lovers*, V.1, p. 197).
Tragedy: Rn: Your honour is obliged to keep your trust (*Indian Queen*, I.1, p. 232).

Observing due limits of behaviour for a married woman:
Tragedy: Rn: 'tis all I can, with honour, give (*Tyrannic Love*, III.1, p. 417).

Refusing to countenance divorce:
Tragedy: Rn: She has but done what honour did require (*Tyrannic Love*, III.1, p. 419).

(d) *The x Group*

Comedy: Rn: My Honour! Why, who dares call it in question (*Sullen Lovers*, II.1, p. 34). Are you one of those Fopps that talk of honour (*Ibid.*, IV.1, p. 58).
Comedy: Ru: Do you love Generosity and Honour (*Sullen Lovers*, II.1, p. 34). if ever I had to do with Love and Honour more (*Humorists*, IV.1, p. 237).
Tragedy: Rn: Love yielded much, till honour asked for all (*Rival Ladies*, III.1, p. 176). we are alike to honour just (*Indian Queen*, I.1, p. 235). a nobler way,/ Than for my love my honour to betray (*Ibid.*, III.1, p. 250). Honour could not give this, or can give more (*Indian Emperor*, II.2, p. 347. let honour, faith, and virtue fly (*Tyrannic Love*, IV.1, p. 440). Your quiet, honour, and our friendship too (*Conquest of Granada. 1*, III.1, p. 60).
Tragedy: Rg: I must myself thy honour's rival make (*Indian Queen*, I.1, p. 234).
Tragedy: Ru: What is this honour which does love control (*Indian Emperor*, II.2, p. 347). Honour, that's a word for some (*Royal Shepherdess*, IV.1.142). Pride, Honour, Glory, and Ambition strive (*Forced Marriage*, IV.5, p. 349). I'm in earnest;/ As I love Honour (*Ibid.*, V.5, p. 377).

(e) *Summary, RH 1661—1670*

Table 35 gives a summary of the k/m/v/x classification of RH for the decade 1661—1670. By far the largest group, in total, is now k, with over 50% of the examples; both m and v are now small, with about 10%. There is one example of km, in comedy. The differences between comedy and tragedy are not significant. The n group, with 75% of the examples, is now overwhelmingly predominant over both g and u. The k and v groups are strongly represented in n, while the few examples of m are mostly in g.

TABLE 35. *Numbers of k, m, v, and x: RH material, 1661—70.*

		k	m	v	x	Total
Comedy	n	12	0	1	2	15
	g	0	2	0	0	2
	u	0	1	0	2	3
	Total	12	3	1	4	20
Tragedy	n	15	0	5	6	26
	g	0	2	0	1	3
	u	1	0	0	4	5
	Total	16	2	5	11	34
All Plays	n	27	0	6	8	41
	g	0	4	0	1	5
	u	1	1	0	6	8
	Total	28	5	6	15	54

G. 1671—1680

In this decade there are 87 examples of RH, 35 in comedy and 52 in tragedy. In six of the examples, RH is not the sole head-meaning; the joint head-meanings found are RHP (two), RHTP (three), and RHK (one). Of the 87 examples, none are countables, 54 are uncountables, and 33 are equivocal. The examples are the following.

(a) *The k Group*

Sensitivity to affront, revenging injury, etc.:

Comedy: Rn: Not thy own Honour, nor thy Love to *Laura* (*Amorous Prince*, III.3, p. 170). My Honour, and my Love, are there ingag'd (*Ibid.*, V.3, p. 201). Hilts and blades, men of honour beaten (*Epsom Wells*, I.1, p. 114) (R(o)). That will not satisfy my Honour (*Dutch Lover*, II.7, p. 261). my honour will suffer no jesting (*Country Wife*, IV.3, p. 329). Have you no sense of honour in you (*Kind Keeper*, IV.1, p. 90). Now, in the name of honour, sir, I beg you (*Spanish Friar*, IV.2, p. 496). O that I could, with honour, love her more (*Ibid.*, V.1, p. 497).

Tragedy: Rn: Shall he thus affront men of our quality and honour (*Libertine*, IV.1, p. 71).

Tragedy: Ru: Revenge is honour, the securest way (*Troilus*, V.2, p. 383).

Not tolerating a rival:

Comedy: Rn: He! he has no honour (*Country Wife*, III.2, p. 295). when Love or Honour bids me draw (*True Widow*, IV.1, p. 341).

Tragedy: Rn: Since we are rivals, honour does command/ We should not die but by each other's hand (*Conquest of Granada.2*, IV.2, p. 181).

Accepting challenges:

Comedy: Rn: I would renounce my Honour for my Love (*Epsom Wells*, V.1, p. 170).

Insisting on one's rights:

Comedy: Ru: What honour bids you do, nature bids me prevent (*Marriage à la Mode*, IV.5, p. 340).

Not forgiving a disloyal mistress:

Tragedy: Rn: But honour stops my ears (*All for Love*, IV.1, p. 416).

Reflected (from Rc/C):

Comedy: Rn: Did Gentlemen and Men of Honour marry Whores in the last Age (*Virtuoso*, V.1, p. 179) (RHP).

Recognizing the claims of friendship:

Comedy: Rn: I will my Honour to my Love prefer (*Amorous Prince*, I.4, p. 142).

Tragedy: Rn: Yet what's my duty if my honour bleed (*Alcibiades*, IV.1.272). I in revealing honour should offend (*Ibid.*, IV.1.350).

Sexual virility:

Comedy: Rn: a Substantiall Dish, a man of Heat and Honour (*Friendship in Fashion*, V.1.598—9) (also fiery spirit, sensitivity to affront).

Not being under an obligation:

Tragedy: Rn: Was ever such a strife of sullen honour (*All for Love*, III.1, p. 388).

Prisoner-of-war not escaping:

Tragedy: Rn: But you desert your honour in your flight (*Conquest of Granada.2*, II.1, p. 137). My honour's glad of a pretence of stay (*Ibid.*).

Constancy in adultery:

Tragedy: Rn: Faith, honour, virtue, all good things forbid (*All for Love*, II.1, p. 376).

Suicide:

Tragedy: Ru: And I'm the lag of honour (*All for Love*, V.1, p. 430).

Miscellaneous:

Comedy: Ru: my friend, a person of honour (*Spanish Friar*, IV.1, p. 473) (RHP) (obviously k, though not clearly specified).

Tragedy: Rn: Yet, though you give my honour just offence (*Conquest of Granada*.2, III.3, p. 169) (not changing sides out of consideration for personal safety). In all events preserve your honour free (*Ibid.*) (the same). But, now you go, I may with honour own (*Ibid.*, V.2, p. 212) (not admitting illicit love for a man unless he is going away).

Tragedy: Rg: You've given my honour such an ample field (*Conquest of Granada. 2*, II.3, p. 154) (obeying mistress without reward).

Tragedy: Ru: But honour has decreed she must not go (*Conquest of Granada. 2*, III.2, p. 167) (men to suffer rather than women). Both worthy of your Honour and your Blood (*Don Carlos*, IV.1.152) (high spirit, willingness to rebel).

(b) *The m Group*

Comedy: Rn: a man may with Honour retire (*Friendship in Fashion*, V.1.240—1) (fig.).

Comedy: Rg: Rivals in Honour, as we're now in Love (*Amorous Prince*, V.2, p. 200). we women love honour inordinately (*Plain Dealer*, II.1, p. 414) (with pun on TP).

Comedy: Ru: let honour/ Call for my blood (*Spanish Friar*, I.1, p. 423).

Tragedy: Rn: As much as honour will permit, I'll shun (*Conquest of Granada. 2*, II.1, p. 143). I may/ With honour quit the fort (*Amboyna*, IV.3, p. 66) (fig. for k, suicide). I love/ Beyond life, conquest, empire, all, but honour (*All for Love*, I.1, p. 359). True, he's hard prest, by interest and by honour (*Ibid.*, II.1, p. 363). A lady's favours may be worn with honour (*Ibid.*, II.1, p. 368).

Tragedy: Rg: Let's then o' th' Wings of Love and honour fly (*Alcibiades*, I.1.176).

Tragedy: Ru: Up, up, for honour's sake; twelve legions wait you (*All for Love*, I.1, p. 355). in honour's name, I ask you,/ For manhood's sake (*Ibid.*, II.1, p. 368). In balance with your fortune, honour, fame (*Ibid.*, II.1, p. 376). my Honour and my Country's Cause/ Call'd me (*Caius Marius*, V.1.77—8). in honour's name,/ What do you mean (*Troilus*, V.1, pp. 374—5).

(c) *The v Group*

Keeping promises, vows, etc.:

Comedy: Rn: My Life, my Fortune, and my Honour too (*Town Fop*, V.4, p. 93).

Tragedy: Rn: In your defence my honour bids me stay (*Conquest of Granada. 2*, V.2, p. 212). my Father's Honour will not suffer him to dispense with his promise (*Libertine*, III.1, p. 64).

Keeping one's word, paying debts:

Comedy: Rn: Honour, a Pox on his Honour (*Epsom Wells*, I.1, p. 110) (two examples, both Ro).

Loyalty to ruler:

Tragedy: Rn: That party I, with honour, cannot take (*Conquest of Granada. 2*, II.1, p. 143).

Filial piety:

Tragedy: Rn: The points of honour poets may produce (*Aureng-Zebe*, II.1, p. 237) (RHK).

Tragedy: Ru: Honour, which only does the name advance (*Aureng-Zebe*, II.1, p. 237).

Not marrying a woman without her parents' consent:

Comedy: Rn: Think what a prince, with honour, may receive (*Marriage à la Mode*, IV.5, p. 338).

Not conniving at unchastity:

Comedy: Rn: my Honour is dearer to me than all the World (*True Widow*, III.1, p. 320).

Not making love to a married woman:

Comedy: Rn: But now I may with honour own my Passion (*Amorous Prince*, V.3, p. 209).

(d) *The x Group*

Comedy: Rn: He's a Man of Honour, and of Wealth (*Virtuoso*, III.1, p. 143) (RHP). the wise *Italian* thinks himself a Man of Honour (*Town Fop*, II.3, p. 28). I shall consult my Love and Honour, Sir (*Rover. 1*, V.1, p. 91). And had no sense of honour, country, king (*Spanish Friar*, IV.2, p. 487). No honour bids me fight against myself (*Ibid.*, IV.2, p. 494).

Comedy: Ru: can no more be asunder than love and honour (*Love in a Wood*, III.2, p. 61). those old Enemies Love and Honour will never agree (*Epsom Wells*, V.1, p. 174). As well as you do truth or honour (*Plain Dealer*, I.1, p. 385). makes Wit and Honour sneak (*Rover. 1*, III.1, p. 46) (RHTP).

Tragedy: Rn: But honour now forbids me to do more (*Conquest of Granada. 2*, III.1, p. 162). Were you obliged in honour by a trust (*Ibid.*, III.3, p. 169). To accept, with honour, what I wish (*Ibid.*, III.3, p. 171). You wrong his honour by this mean distrust (*Alcibiades*, I.1.22). Unblemish't Honour, and a spotless Love (*Ibid.*, I.1.136). Unworthy of my honour or your Crown (*Ibid.*, IV.1.422). For me my honour I'l maintain (*Ibid.*, V.1. 122). My virtue, prudence, honour, interest, all (*Aureng-Zebe*, II.1, p. 220). thou hast no sense of Vertue or Honour left (*Libertine*, II.1, p. 45). Vertue and Honour! There's nothing good or ill (*Ibid.*). Traduc'd my Honour (*Orphan*, III.1.21).

Tragedy: Rg: They best of honour judge (*Alcibiades*, IV.1.25).
Tragedy: Ru: I beg you, by the honour of your nation (*Amboyna*, IV.3, p. 69). Who on Earth to their honour are just (*Alcibiades*, II.1.232). Such may be swayed by honour or by love (*Aureng-Zebe*, III.1, p. 252). Senceless what Honour or Ambition means (*Don Carlos*, IV.1.29) (RHTP). Love and Honour I have always made/ The Business (*Abdelazer*, IV.6, p. 68). Rise, and command my Life, my Soul, my Honour (*Ibid.*, V.2, p. 91). O false love, false honour (*Oedipus*, III.1, p. 178).

(*e*) *Summary, RH 1671—1680*

Table 36 gives a summary of the k/m/v/x classification of RH for the decade 1671—1680. With 38%, k is still the largest group, though not quite so overwhelmingly as in the previous decade; v is still quite small, with 12.5%, and m is rather larger, with 17%. It should be noted, however, that, of the 15 examples of m, no less than 6 are from *All for Love*; this play is not an adaptation of *Antony and Cleopatra*, but it is on the same theme, and it is not impossible that (as with *Troilus and Cressida*) the effect on Dryden of handling a Shakespeare theme is to encourage him to use m forms; this, however, can only be considered as a very tentative suggestion. There are no examples of km. The differences between comedy and tragedy are not significant. The n

TABLE 36. *Numbers of k, m, v, and x: RH material, 1671—80.*

		k	m	v	x	Total
Comedy	n	14	1	6	5	26
	g	0	2	0	0	2
	u	2	1	0	4	7
	Total	16	4	6	9	35
Tragedy	n	12	5	4	11	32
	g	1	1	0	1	3
	u	4	5	1	7	17
	Total	17	11	5	19	52
All Plays	n	26	6	10	16	58
	g	1	3	0	1	5
	u	6	6	1	11	24
	Total	33	15	11	28	87

group is still very much larger than the g group, both in comedy and in tragedy, but the u group is a fair size. Most of the examples of v and of k are in the n group.

H. 1681—1690

In this decade there are 39 examples of RH, 21 in comedy and 18 in tragedy. In 9 of the examples, RH is not the sole head-meaning; these nine are classified RHTP (two) and RHK (seven). Of the 39 examples, none are countables, 29 are uncountables, and 10 are equivocal. The examples are the following.

(a) The k Group

Sensitivity to insult, revenging affront, etc.:

Tragedy: Rn: Retire my Life, and doubt not of my Honour (*Venice Preserved*, III.2.200). Which I can ask with honour (*Don Sebastian*, IV.3, p. 433). And, Honour, be thou judge (*Ibid.*, IV.3, p. 434).

Keeping duelling-appointments:

Comedy: Rn: Time fleets quick away, and Honour calls (*Bury Fair*, IV.1, p. 344).

Reflected (from Rc/C):

Comedy: Ru: there's nothing but Honour meant to you (*Squire of Alsatia*, V. 1, p. 273).

Recognizing the claims of friendship:

Comedy: Rn: the punctilio's of Honour are sacred to me (*Squire of Alsatia*, III.1, p. 246) (RHK). a fine Subject for a Love and Honour Poet (*Bury Fair*, IV.1, p.353). and take it for a point of Honour (*Scowrers*, V.1, p. 143) (RHK).

Protecting a woman's Rc:

Comedy: Rn: will clear my honour for revealing this (*Amorous Bigot*, V.1, p. 72).

Dying without showing concern:

Tragedy: Rn: I bear the Sentence as becomes my Honour (*Constantine*, II.1, p. 32) (RHTP).

Loyalty to fellow-criminals:

Tragedy: Rn: And meet to morrow where your honour calls you (*Venice Preserved*, III.2.461). And gave up honour to be sure of ruine (*Ibid.*, IV.1. 256).

Miscellaneous:

Comedy: Rn: a man of Honour, and of excellent disposition (*Squire of Alsatia*, Dram. P., p. 206) (not specified, but libertinism permitted). This is a nice point of Honour I have hit (*Bury Fair*, V.1, p. 361) (RHK) (challenging anybody who affirms that your mistress is not without an equal).

Comedy: Ru: I love Magnanimity and Honour (*Squire of Alsatia*, I.1, p. 212) (not clearly specified, but abduction and street-fighting not barred).

Tragedy: Rn: Forgot his Manhood, Vertue, truth, and Honour (*Venice Preserved*, IV.1.17) (ties of friendship, loyalty to fellow-criminals, keeping an oath to rebel).

Tragedy: Ru: Would it not seem more worthy your past Honour (*Constantine*, II.1, p. 22) (RHTP) (not clearly specified, but assassination not barred).

(b) The m Group

Comedy: Rg: He shall go where Honour calls him (*Amorous Bigot*, IV.1, p. 54). Honour calls and he must go (*Ibid.*). Does Honour call so soon (*Ibid.*).

Comedy: Ru: when he is called by honour (*Amphitryon*, II.1, p. 34).

(c) The v Group

Keeping one's word, not being treacherous:

Tragedy: Rn: the punctilio of Honour is such a thing (*Widow Ranter*, I.1, p. 238) (RHK).

Loyalty to ruler:

Tragedy: Rn: an act/ Your honour, though unasked by me, requires (*Duke of Guise*, IV.3, p. 86).

Not committing incest:

Tragedy: Rn: Live, if thou canst with Honour (*Constantine*, III.2, p. 47).

Tragedy: Ru: rather to sustain an infamous Life,/ Than die with Honour (*Constantine*, IV.2, p. 63).

(d) The x Group

Comedy: Rn: any thing Reason or Honour will allow (*Scowrers*, IV.1, p. 121). do you make this so nice a point of Honour (*Ibid.*, V.1, p. 143) (RHK).

Comedy: Ru: by the Honour of a Soldier consider on some way (*Atheist*, II.1.155). Heroic Numbers upon Love and Honour (*Bury Fair*, II.1, p. 313). in Romances, and Love and Honour Plays (*Ibid.*, III.1, p. 339). Is this your sence of Honour (*Scowrers*, V.1, p. 139).

Tragedy: Rn: was that like a cavalier of honour (*Don Sebastian*, III.2, p. 399). self-preservation is a point above honour (*Ibid.*). I'll do whate'er my honour will permit (*Duke of Guise*, IV.3, p. 86). I've not offended Honour nor Religion (*Widow Ranter*, II.4, p. 261).

Tragedy: Rg: For I am fit for Honour's toughest task (*Venice Preserved*, II.1.148).

Tragedy: Ru: Honour befriend us both (*Don Sebastian*, IV.3, p. 434). Honour, a Pox on't; what is that (*Widow Ranter*, I.2, p. 238) (RHK). Honour that keeps such a bustle in the World (*Ibid.*) (RHK).

(*e*) *Summary, RH 1681—1690*

Table 37 gives a summary of the k/m/v/x classification of RH for the decade 1681—1690. The figures are too small for much to be said, but it will be seen that k is still the largest group; n is much more frequent than g, and u is intermediate; there are no examples of km.

I. 1691—1700

In this decade there are 25 examples of RH, 13 in comedy and 12 in tragedy. In three of the examples, RH is not the sole head-meaning; these three are classified RHP, RHK, and RHRcC respectively. Of the 25 examples, none are countables, 18 are uncountables, and 7 are equivocal. The examples are the following.

TABLE 37. *Numbers of k, m, v, and x: RH material, 1681—90*

		k	m	v	x	Total
Comedy	n	7	0	0	2	9
	g	0	3	0	0	3
	u	2	1	0	4	7
	Total	9	4	0	6	19
Tragedy	n	7	0	3	4	14
	g	0	0	0	1	1
	u	1	0	1	3	5
	Total	8	0	4	8	20
All Plays	n	14	0	3	6	23
	g	0	3	0	1	4
	u	3	1	1	7	12
	Total	17	4	4	14	39

(a) *The k Group*

Sensitivity to injury, revenging insult, etc.:

Comedy: Rn: does not care to be put upon, being a man of honour (*Old Bachelor*, III.3, p. 44). won't be put upon, sir, being a man of honour (*Ibid.*).

Not tolerating a rival:

Comedy: Rn: Since honour may oblige them to play the fool (*Constant Couple*, II.3, p. 158).

Accepting challenges, observing the duelling code, etc.:

Comedy: Ru: Honour is your province, captain (*Old Bachelor*, V.2, p. 79) (RHK).

Tragedy: Rn: The man, who dares not when his honour calls (*Cleomenes*, V.2, p. 345).

Not being made a property:

Tragedy: Rn: make a shoeing-horn of a man of honour (*Love Triumphant*, II.2, p. 411).

Recognizing claims of friendship:

Tragedy: Rn: But first my honour must be justified (*Cleomenes*, V.2, p. 345) (conflicting with claims of filial piety).

Miscellaneous:

Tragedy: Rn: Your debt of honour you have cleared this day (*Love Triumphant*, IV.1, p. 442) (rebelling rather than permit forced marriage of mistress to a rival).

(b) *The m Group*

Comedy: Rg: honour calls, and I must go (*Volunteers*, III.1, p. 191).

Comedy: Ru: O monstrous! what are conscience and honour (*Love for Love*, III.4, p. 259) (RHRcC). 'twas once the life of honour, but now its hearse (*Constant Couple*, I.2, p. 143).

Tragedy: Ru: But honour calls (*King Arthur*, IV.1, p. 183). is honour in such haste (*Ibid.*). But when your service, and my honour called (*Love Triumphant*, I.1, p. 384).

(c) *The v Group*

Nil.

(d) *The x Group*

Comedy: Rn: this Friend of mine, who is a man of honour (*Volunteers*, I.1, p. 168) (RHP). were I not engag'd in honour this Campaigne (*Ibid.*,

II.1, p. 179). that turns the flowing Tide of Honour (*Provoked Wife*, III.1, p. 144).

Comedy: Ru: he has as much Vertue and Honour (*Volunteers*, I.2, p. 174). Vertue and Honour will bring him but to hell (*Ibid.*, I.2, p. 175). He vertue and honour (*Ibid.*).

Tragedy: Rn: For honour never summons without reason (*Cleomenes*, V.2, p. 345). Not vindicate my honour (*Love Triumphant*, I.1, p. 386). My honour is my own (*Ibid.*).

Tragedy: Ru: My virtue, fame, and honour are my own (*Cleomenes*, III.3, p. 318). Esteem your honour, and embrace your love (*Love Triumphant*, IV.1, p. 442).

(e) *Summary, RH 1691—1700*

Table 38 gives a summary of the k/m/v/x classification of RH for the decade 1691—1700. The figures are so small that very little can be said about them; the total absence of v is worth noticing, however, and so is the continued predominance of n over g. There are no examples of km.

TABLE 38. *Numbers of k, m, v, and x: RH material, 1691—1700.*

		k	m	v	x	Total
Comedy	n	3	0	0	3	6
	g	0	1	0	0	1
	u	1	2	0	3	6
	Total	4	3	0	6	13
Tragedy	n	4	0	0	3	7
	g	0	0	0	0	0
	u	0	3	0	2	5
	Total	4	3	0	5	12
All Plays	n	7	0	0	6	13
	g	0	1	0	0	1
	u	1	5	0	5	11
	Total	8	6	0	11	25

J. Summary, RH 1591—1700

The number of examples of RH is relatively small, but nevertheless it is possible to see trends similar to those in R. Thus, the proportion of k becomes greater during the century, while v, and to a lesser extent m, declines. In both halves of the period, however, the proportion of v is considerably greater than in R. Inside the k group, there is a clear tendency for the number of examples concerned with duelling to increase (sensitivity to affront, etc.). The ratio of n to g increases, but it is to be noticed that the percentage of u is much greater in RH than in R, in both halves of the century; the combination ux is particularly common. This is not really surprising; many examples of RH are so classified because of the absence of clear determinants in the context that would enable one to select either R or H alone as the head-meaning; this same absence of contextual determinants quite naturally also makes it more difficult to decide between n and g, and between k, v, and m, and in consequence there is a tendency for RH, u, and x to occur together. The n/g ratio also tends to be higher in RH than in R; the reason for this has been suggested on page 130 above. There is no significant change in the number of examples with joint head-meanings; if the examples of RHK are left out of account, there is still no significant change. The findings will be discussed in more detail in Chapter 10.

CHAPTER 9

Virtue and Convention:
(IV) The H Material

A. 1591—1600

In this decade there are 21 examples of H, of which 8 are in comedy and 13 in tragedy. In two of the examples, H is not the sole head-meaning; these two are classified HP and HTP respectively. Of the 21 examples, none are countables, 15 are uncountables, and 6 are equivocal. The examples are the following.

(a) *The k Group*

Insisting on one's rights:

Tragedy: In whose cold blood no sparke of Honor bides (*Henry VI.3*, I.1.184).

Miscellaneous:

Comedy: in whom/ The ancient Romane honour more appeares (*Merchant of Venice*, III.2.293—4) (unspecified, but presumably k).

Tragedy: Thy life hath had some smatch of Honor in it (*Julius Caesar*, V.5.46) (unspecified, but such as will make him help a man to commit suicide).

(b) *The m Group*

Nil.

(c) *The v Group*

Truthfulness:

Tragedy: his Honor is as true/ In this Appeale, as thou art all vniust (*Richard II*, IV.1.44—5).

Not slandering:

Comedy: Two of them haue the verie bent of honor (*Much Ado*, IV.1.186).

Loyalty to rulers:

Tragedy: in thy face I see/ The Map of Honor, Truth, and Loyaltie (*Henry VI.2*, III.1.202—3). those thoughts/ Which honor and allegeance cannot thinke (*Richard II*, II.1.207—8). she is bound in honor still to do/ What you in wisedom still vouchsafe to say (*John*, II.1.522—3).

Not conniving at incest:

Tragedy: That God, the Law, my Honor, and her Loue,/ Can make seeme pleasing (*Richard III*, IV.4.342—3).

Sexual continence:

Comedy: Vpon whose faith and honor, I repose (*Two Gentlemen*, IV.3.26).

Not committing bigamy:

Tragedy: Could to no issue of true honour bring (*Romeo*, IV.1.65).

Justice, integrity:

Comedy: Sweet Princes: what I did, I did in Honor (*Henry IV.2*, V.2.35).

(d) *The x Group*

Comedy: Ile proue mine honor, and mine honestie (*Comedy of Errors*, V.1.30). So honor peereth in the meanest habit (*Taming of the Shrew*, IV.3.172). How much low peasantry would then be gleaned/ From the true seede of honour (*Merchant of Venice*, II.8.45—6, Q text) (HTP). And how much honor/ Pickt from the chaffe and ruine of the times (*Ibid.*, II.8.46—7, F text).

Tragedy: If he may be repeal'd, to trie his Honor (*Richard II*, IV.1.85). Thou Mappe of Honor, thou King *Richards* Tombe (*Ibid.*, V.1.12). High sparkes of Honor in thee haue I seene (*Ibid.*, V.6.29). Any exploit worthy the name of Honor (*Julius Caesar*, II.1.317). Such as he is, full of regard, and Honour (*Ibid.*, IV.2.12).

(e) *Summary, H 1591—1600*

Table 39 gives a summary of the k/m/v/x classification of H for the decade 1591—1600. The figures are too small for much to be said about them; it may be noted, however, that v is considerably more frequent than k or m.

TABLE 39. *Numbers of k, m, v, and x: H material 1591—1600.*

	k	m	v	x	Total
Comedy	1	0	3	4	8
Tragedy	2	0	6	5	13
All Plays	3	0	9	9	21

B. 1601—1610

In this decade there are 64 examples of H, 18 in comedy and 46 in tragedy. In four of the examples, H is not the sole head-meaning; these four are classified HTP (two), HP (one), and HS (one). Of the 64 examples, 3 are countables, 38 uncountables, and 23 equivocal. The examples are the following.

(a) The k Group

Sensitivity to injury, revenging affront, etc.:

Comedy: his honour/ Clocke to it selfe, knew the true minute when/ Exception bid him speake (*All's Well*, I.2.39—41).

Tragedy: That might your nature honour, and exception/ Roughly awake (*Hamlet*, V.2.230—1). It was our honour drew us to this act,/ Not gain (*Maid's Tragedy*, V.1, p. 66).

Observing the rules of duelling:

Tragedy: honour cannot take/ Revenge on you (*Philaster*, V.1, p. 143) (not fighting a woman).

Not taking orders from another:

Tragedy: but that you say, be't so;/ Ile speake it in my spirit and honor, no (*Troilus*, IV.4.135—6).

Making socially good marriages, pride in rank:

Comedy: The honor sir that flames in youre faire eyes (*All's Well*, II.3.81—2) (HP). Lay a more noble thought vpon mine honour (*Ibid.*, V.3.178).

Killing unchaste female relative:

Tragedy: For nought I did in hate, but all in Honour (*Othello*, V.2.296). it will be cal'd/ Honour in thee to spill thy Sisters blood (*Maid's Tragedy*, III.1, p. 41). Stay, I must ask mine honour first (*Ibid.*, IV.1, p. 47).

Deceiving and dissimulating in interests of friends or political party:

Tragedy: it shall hold Companionship in Peace/ With Honour, as in Warre (*Coriolanus*, III.2.49—50). I would dissemble with my Nature, where/ My Fortunes and my Friends at stake, requir'd/ I should do so in Honor (*Ibid.*, III.2.62—4).

(b) The m Group

Comedy: There's honour in the theft (*All's Well*, II.1.34). Whence honor but of danger winnes a scarre (*Ibid.*, III.2.123). O for the loue of laughter hinder not the honor of his designe (*Ibid.*, III.6.41—2).

Tragedy: Manhood and Honor/ Should haue hard hearts (*Troilus*, II.2.47—8) (Q reads *hare hearts*). So well thy words become thee, as thy wounds,/

They smack of Honor both (*Macbeth*, I.2.44—5). That sleepe and feeding may prorogue his Honour,/ Euen till a Lethied dulnesse (*Antony*, II.1.26—7). Your presence glads our dayes, honour we loue (*Pericles*, II.3.21). Mine Emulation/ Hath not that Honor in't it had (*Coriolanus*, I.10.12—13). Honor and Policy, like vnseuer'd Friends,/ I' th' Warre do grow together (*Coriolanus*, III.2.42—3). If it be Honor in your Warres, to seeme/ The same you are not (*Ibid.*, III.2.46—7).

There is also one example of km:

Tragedy: Nor did he soyle the fact with Cowardice,/ (And Honour in him, which buyes out his fault) (*Timon*, III.5.16—17) (probably to be read "An Honour").

(c) *The v Group*

Truthfulness:

Tragedy: reconcil'd my thoughts/ To thy good Truth, and Honor (*Macbeth*, IV.3.116—17). let it looke/ Like perfect Honor (*Antony*, I.3.79—80). I had thought thy mind/ Had been of honour (*Philaster*, III.1, p. 105). who is as farre/ From thy report, as thou from Honor (*Cymbeline*, I.6.144—5).

Keeping an oath:

Tragedy: The Honour is Sacred which he talks on now (*Antony*, II.2.89).

Loyalty to rulers:

Comedy: Breaking the bonds of honour and of duty (*Blurt*, V.3.14).
Tragedy: To plainnesse honour's bound (*Lear*, I.1.147) (putting sovereign's true interests above your own). I will maintaine/ My truth and honor firmely (*Ibid.*, V.3.101—2). Try honours cause; forbeare your suffrages (*Pericles*, II.4.41). This Sword shall prooue, hee's Honours enemie (*Ibid.*, II.5.64). whose false Oathes preuayl'd/ Before my perfect Honor (*Cymbeline*, III.3.66—7).

Not murdering:

Tragedy: 'Tis not my profit that does lead mine Honour:/ Mine Honour it (*Antony*, II.7.78—9) (two examples).

Not conniving at unchastity:

Comedy: Yet hath he in him such a minde of Honor (*Measure for Measure*, II.4.179). She (hauing the truth of honour in her) (*Ibid.*, III.1.162—3).

Sexual continence:

Comedy: I could not answer in that course of Honour (*All's Well*, V.3.98). Till your deeds gaine them fairer: proue your honor,/ Then in my thought it lies (*Ibid.*, V.3.181—2). Ha? Little honor, to be much beleeu'd (*Measure for Measure*, II.4.149).

Tragedy: The Shees of Italy should not betray/ Mine Interest, and his Honour (*Cymbeline*, I.3.29—30).

Not listening to unchaste proposals:

Tragedy: I must withdraw in honour (*Philaster*, I.1, p. 90).

Not repudiating wife:

Tragedy: there can be no euasion/ To blench from this, and to stand firme by honour (*Troilus*, II.2.67—8).

Not being ungrateful:

Tragedy: There was verie little Honour shew'd in't (*Timon*, III.2.20).

Mercy and forgiveness:

Comedy: 'Tis honour to forgive those you could kill (*Phoenix*, IV.1.206).

Miscellaneous:

Comedy: Thus when all hearts are tun'd to honour's strings (*Phoenix*, V.1.347) (penitence of all evil-doers in the play).
Tragedy: With boote, and such addition as your Honours/ Haue more then merited (*Lear*, V.3.303—4) (loyalty, self-sacrifice, etc.). your honour and your goodnes,/ Teach me too't (*Pericles*, III.3.26) (truthfulness, keeping promise, gratitude, etc.). That bears more honour in her breast than you (*Philaster*, II.1, p. 91) (benevolence, trustfulness, relieving miseries, etc.). 'Tis strange to me, thou shouldst haue worth and honour (*Maid's Tragedy*, III.1, p. 28) (not being "base", "false", and "treacherous").

(*d*) *The x Group*

Comedy: Honour's a good brooch to weare in a mans hat (*Poetaster*, I.2.161—2). that is honours scorne (*All's Well*, II.3.135). Which challenges it selfe as honours borne (*Ibid.*, II.3.136) (HTP). Daughter of honor (*Alchemist*, IV.1.116) (HTP).

Tragedy: His taints and Honours, wag'd equal with him (*Antony*, V.1. 30—1) (HS). For who hates honour, hates the Gods aboue (*Pericles*, II.3. 22). Recall not what we giue, and therein may/ Vse honour with you (*Ibid.*, III.1.25—6) (many modern edd. read *Vie* for Q *Vse*). I/ Will answer in mine Honor (*Coriolanus*, III.2.143—4). thou hast set thy mercy, & thy Honor/ At difference in thee (*Ibid.*, V.3.200—1) (loyalty to interests of enemy city which serving). He hath a kinde of Honor sets him off (*Cymbeline*, I.6.169). Royalty vnlearn'd, Honor vntaught (*Ibid.*, IV.2.178). Honour? where is't (*Maid's Tragedy*, III.1, p. 43). sought this safety/ More out of fear than honour (*Ibid.*, V.1, p. 65).

(*e*) *Summary, H 1601—1610*

Table 40 gives a summary of the k/m/v/x classification of H for the decade 1601—1610. It will be seen that the v group is by far the largest,

TABLE 40. *Numbers of k, m, v, and x: H material 1601—10.*

	k	m	v	x	Total
Comedy	3	3	8	4	18
Tragedy	9	8	20	9	46
All Plays	12	11	28	13	64

both in comedy and in tragedy, and accounts for about 44% of all the examples; k, m, and x are about equally frequent, with some 18% each. There is one example of km, in tragedy. There are no differences between comedy and tragedy.

C. 1611—1620

In this decade there are 74 examples of H, 21 in comedy and 53 in tragedy. In five of the examples, H is not the sole head-meaning; these five are classified HMTP (one), HP (one), HE (one), and HK (two). Of the 74 examples, five are countables, 50 uncountables, and 19 equivocal. The examples are the following.

(a) *The k Group*

Sensitivity to affront, willingness to revenge insult, etc.:
Comedy: Let but our honours teach us (*Little Fr. Lawyer*, V.1, p. 449).
Tragedy: I ask no more in honour (*King and No King*, V.1, p. 219) (satisfied by apology).

Keeping duelling appointments, observing rules of duelling:
Comedy: You know what honour is (*Little Fr. Lawyer*, II.1, p. 392) (HK). Are these the rules of honour (*Ibid.*, IV.1, p. 428) (HK).

Magnificence, hyper-courtesy:
Tragedy: With valour first he struck me, then with honour (*Humorous Lieutenant*, II.4, p. 308).

Miscellaneous:
Comedy: For now I may upbraid you, and with honour (*Little French Lawyer*, I.1, p. 379) (being rude to a woman after she has thrown you over, but not before).
Tragedy: the man must do it,/ The man in honour bound (*Mad Lover*, III.1, p. 36) (cutting out brother's heart so that brother shall keep a promise). a Patience/ That will with honour suffer me (*False One*, IV.2, p.

348) (expressing anger without being rude or losing dignity). He is all honour,/ Nor do I now repent me of my favours (*Ibid.*, V.4, p. 370) (not clearly specified, but plainly not v).

(*b*) *The m Group*

Comedy: When all was frozen in me but mine Honour (*Captain*, II.1, p. 251).

Tragedy: Thou child of honour and ambitious thoughts (*Loyal Subject*, I.3, p. 83). The goal and mark of high ambitious honour (*False One*, II.1, p. 317). Rude valors, so I let 'em pass; rude honours (*Ibid.*, III.2, p. 336).

There are also the three following examples of km:

Comedy: And out with honour's flaming lights within thee (*Fair Quarrel*, II.1.205). I am not for the fellowship of honour (*Ibid.*, II.1.215). Thou art all honour,/ Thy resolution would steel a Coward (*Little French Lawyer*, I.1, p. 387).

(*c*) *The v Group*

Loyalty to rulers:

Tragedy: the honor of the cause (*Catiline*, IV.1.782). Things to strike Honour sad (*Henry VIII*, I.2.128). And proue it too, against mine Honour, aught (*Ibid.*, II.4.38). the Honor of it/ Does pay the Act of it (*Ibid.*, III.2. 181—2). let flye/ Our killing angers, and forsake our honours (*Valentinian*, I.3, p. 11). Who justly knows 'tis not to try our honours (*Ibid.*, I.3, p. 12). Never my Souldier more, nor Friend to Honour (*Loyal Subject*, IV.6, p. 154). Thou excellent old man, thou top of honour (*Ibid.*, IV.6, p. 155).

Not murdering:

Tragedy: he (most humane,/ And fill'd with Honor) (*Winter's Tale*, III.2. 164—5). No richer then his Honor (*Ibid.*, III.2.169). Thou would'st haue poyson'd good *Camillo's* Honor (*Ibid.*, III.2.187). Full of himself, honour, and honesty (*Bloody Brother*, II.3, p. 269). He was a *Roman*, and the top of Honour (*False One*, II.1, p. 321).

Sexual continence:

Comedy: shall neuer melt/ Mine honor into lust (*Tempest*, IV.1.27—8). breaking all the Rules of honesty,/ Of honour and of truth (*Little Fr. Lawyer*, III.1, p. 419). Where all the pleas of honour are but laught at (*Custom of the Country*, I.1, p. 308). But 'tis not in your honour, to perform it (*Ibid.*, I.1, p. 310). Tell her, for my life thou hast lost thine honour (*Ibid.*, IV.1, p. 359).

Tragedy: my desires/ Run not before mine honor (*Winter's Tale*, IV.3. 33—4). And therefore nothing can be meant but honour (*Loyal Subject*, I.2, p. 83). A Scene of greater honour you ne're acted (*Ibid.*, IV.3, p. 143).

Not being ungrateful:

Tragedy: if thou ever yet heard'st tell of honour,/ I'le make thee blush (*False One*, II.1, p. 315).

Miscellaneous:

Comedy: whose honor cannot/ Be measur'd, or confin'd (*Tempest*, V.1. 121—2) (loyalty, humanity, etc.). His sword edg'd with defence of right and honour (*Little Fr. Lawyer*, III.1, p. 405) (not clearly specified, but what is defended is "honest" and "right"). know what does/ Belong to honour (*Ibid.*, IV.1, p. 433) (upholding law, rescuing even your personal enemies from brigands). The baits they laid for us, were our own honours (*Ibid.*, IV.1, p. 438) (the same).

Tragedy: I lou'd him, as in Honor he requir'd (*Winter's Tale*, III.2.63) (innocent love). Commit me, for committing honor (*Ibid.*, II.3.49) (speaking truth, defending the innocent). the needle toucht with honour (*Loyal Subject*, III.2, p. 118) (not clearly specified "virtues" and "goodness"). Like a good Master tack about for Honour (*Ibid.*) (the same). *Honor* thy name is, and I hope thy Nature (*Ibid.*, III.4, p. 127) (the same).

(d) *The x Group*

Comedy: If there be honour in the minds of men (*Scornful Lady*, III.1, p. 261). By the justice/ I owe to honour, I came off untouch'd (*Fair Quarrel*, IV.3.27—8). Then honour is not dead in all parts, coz (*Ibid.*, V.1.412). is there no honour in you (*Little Fr. Lawyer*, III.1, p. 421).

Tragedy: all the parts of man,/ Which Honor do's acknowledge (*Winter's Tale*, I.2.399—400). I will tell you,/ Since I am charg'd in Honor (*Ibid.*, I.2.405—6). to locke vp honesty & honour from/ Th'accesse of gentle visitors (*Ibid.*, II.2.10—11) (HP). your honor, and your goodnesse is so euident (*Ibid.*, II.2.43). Whose honor, and whose honestie till now,/ Endur'd all Weathers (*Ibid.*, V.1.193—4). our whole blouds are one stone;/ And honor cannot thaw vs (*Catiline*, I.1.214—15). in honesty/ And honour thou art bound to meet her vertues (*King and No King*, IV.1, p. 198). Beauty and Honour in her are so mingled (*Henry VIII*, II.3.76). From her shall read the perfect way of Honour (*Ibid.*, V.4.37). nor any thing without the addition, *Honor*,/ Sway your high blood (*Duchess of Malfi*, I.1.323—4). There are a many wayes that conduct to seeming/ Honor (*Ibid.*, V.2.337—8) (HMTP). truth, honour,/ Are keepers of that blessed Place (*Valentinian*, III.1, p. 42). And, for I see your honour cannot lessen (*Ibid.*, IV.4, p. 68). And the true *Roman* honour, faith and valour (*Ibid.*, IV.4, p. 72). As I have honour in me, you shall have it (*Mad Lover*, I.1, p. 16). that Love, Sir,/ Which is the price of honour (*Ibid.*, II.1, p. 22). The Honour and the Valour of the Owner (*Ibid.*, III.1, p. 35). Use me with honour, I shall love thee dearly (*Ibid.*, V.1, p. 65) (HE). If his hot humour raign, and not his honour (*Loyal Subject*, I.1, p. 78). your own honour,/ The bounty of that mind, and your allegiance (*Ibid.*, I.5, p. 94).

And in the Eye of Honour truly triumph (*Ibid.*). Your first Vow honour made, your last but anger (*Ibid.*, I.5, p. 95). why should his wisdom,/ His age, and honour (*False One*, III.2, p. 332).

(e) Summary, H 1611—1620

Table 41 gives a summary of the k/m/v/x classification of H for the decade 1611—1620. The v group is still the largest, with 42% of the examples; k and m are still small, round about the 10% mark, while the x group accounts for about 36.5%. There are three examples of km, all in comedy. In general, the differences between comedy and tragedy are not significant, though the greater proportion of x examples in tragedy is just significant.

TABLE 41. *Numbers of k, m, v, and x: H material 1611—20.*

	k	m	v	x	Total
Comedy	4	4	9	4	21
Tragedy	5	3	22	23	53
All Plays	9	7	31	27	74

D. 1621—1630

In this decade there are 42 examples of H, 20 in comedy and 22 in tragedy. In four of the examples, H is not the sole head-meaning; these four are classified HK. Of the 42 examples, none are countables, 34 are uncountables, and 8 are equivocal. The examples are the following.

(a) The k Group

Sensitivity to injury, revenging affront, etc.:

Comedy: They must be chosen so, things of no honour (*Rule a Wife*, II.1, p. 182). If he have honour, I am undone (*Ibid.*).

Accepting challenges, oberving rules of duelling, etc.:

Comedy: That man to man, if he have honour in him (*Chances*, II.3, p. 206).

Tragedy: Though I bleed hard, my honour finds no Issue (*Lover's Progress*, II.1, p. 97) (dying rather than yield, in duel).

(b) The m Group

Tragedy: you in honour cannot/ Use the extremity of war (*Maid of Honour*, II.3, p. 234) (or perhaps k — conventions of civilized warfare). That so much honour, so much honesty/ Should be in one man (*Lover's Progress*, I.1, p. 89). mine honour/ Cannot consent to (*Bondman*, II.1, p. 99).

There is also one example of km:

Comedy: If the name of Honour were for ever to be lost (*Elder Brother*, IV.3, p. 43).

(c) The v Group

Foregoing revenge, not murdering:

Comedy: Submissive at his knees that knows not honour (*Pilgrim*, II.2, p. 172). Ye us'd me with much honour (*Ibid.*, IV.2, p. 205). yet time, and honour/ Shall find and bring forth that (*Ibid.*). Such mines of Spanish honour in his bosom (*Spanish Gipsy*, III.2.7).

Tragedy: mine honour is in question (*Changeling*, IV.2.1). what true honour in *Calista* suffers (*Lover's Progress*, IV.1, p. 137).

Sexual continence:

Comedy: love you with honour, I shall love so ever (*Elder Brother*, III.5, p. 32). and tempered with the quality of honour (*Ibid.*, IV.3, p. 40). I prefer a sentence/ Of cruelty before my honor (*Fair Maid of the Inn*, IV.1. 165—6) (not committing incest).

Tragedy: O Tyrant, Custom! and O Coward, Honour (*Lover's Progress*, III.1, p. 106). What have I said? what blasphemy to honour (*Ibid.*, III.1, p. 107).

Loyalty to husband:

Tragedy: O honour,/ Thou hard Law to our lives (*Lover's Progress*, I.1, p. 81) (HK). O mine honour;/ A Tyrant, yet to be obey'd (*Ibid.*, I.1, p. 82) (HK). Love with honour (*Ibid.*, III.1, p. 107). Honour? what's that? 'tis but a specious title (*Ibid.*).

Peacemaking, preventing duel:

Comedy: for honours sake/ Go with him, and allay him (*Chances*, III.1, p. 212).

Miscellaneous:

Comedy: Humanity and honour bids me help ye (*Chances*, I.7, p. 184) (helping those in distress). Euery house became/ An Academy of honour (*New Inn*, I.3.56—7) ("vertue" and "goodness").

Tragedy: Where cruelty reigns,/ There dwells nor love, nor honour (*Bondman*, V.1, p. 114) (not being cruel). Your age and honour will become a Nunnery (*Wife for a Month*, I.1, p. 8) (qualities suitable for a nun). Which shows all honour is departed from us (*Ibid.*, II.1, p. 24) (not being covetous).

(d) *The x Group*

Comedy: Thou painted honour, thou base man made backward (*Pilgrim*, II.2, p. 178). Honour and virtue guide him in his station (*Game at Chess*, IV.4.77). this fair structure/ Of comely honour (*Ibid.*, V.3.166—7). I'le meet you in the same line of Honour (*Elder Brother*, I.2, p. 6). He can giue *Armes*, and *markes*, he cannot *honour* (*Staple of News*, IV.4.156). wh<i>ther is honour fled/ *Cesario* (*Fair Maid of the Inn*, II.1.219—20).

Tragedy: fair maid, composed of worth and honour (*Maid of Honour*, V.2, p. 249). Honour guard the innocent (*Lover's Progress*, III.1, p. 109). will determine/ In points of honour (*Ibid.*, V.1, p. 143) (HK). what we in honour/ Should have taught others (*Bondman*, I.3, p. 96). So dear that honour that she nurs'd me up in (*Wife for a Month*, I.1, p. 7). with a look of honour/ Mingled with noble chastity (*Ibid.*, II.1, p. 18). Learn'd Arms and Honour, to become a Rascal (*Ibid.*, IV.1, p. 47) (HK).

(e) *Summary, H 1621—1630*

Table 42 gives a summary of the k/m/v/x classification of H for the decade 1621—1630. The pattern is very much as in the previous decade; v is still the largest group, with 50% of all examples, and k and m are both small, with 9.5%; x accounts for the remaining 31%. There is one example of km, in comedy. There are no significant differences between comedy and tragedy.

E. 1631—1640

In this decade there are 63 examples of H, 28 in comedy and 35 in tragedy. In five of the examples, H is not the sole head-meaning; the joint head-meanings found are HP (three), HTP (one), and HY (one). Of the 63 examples, none are countables, 39 are uncountables, and 24 are equivocal. The examples are the following.

TABLE 42. *Numbers of k, m, v, and x: H material 1621—30.*

	k	m	v	x	Total
Comedy	3	1	10	6	20
Tragedy	1	3	11	7	22
All Plays	4	4	21	13	42

(a) *The k Group*

Sensitivity to insult, revenging affront, etc.:

Comedy: his jealous honour waits/ For all occasions (*Distresses*, I.1, p. 290). the same/ Obedience keeps my honour in such awe (*Ibid.*, II.1, p. 308).

Tragedy: and may/ The soul of angry honour guide it (*Cardinal*, IV.2, p. 323).

Not tolerating a rival:

Comedy: Thy jealous honour is/ Most viciously and cruelly inclin'd (*Distresses*, V.1, p. 352).

Carrying challenges, observing the duelling code:

Comedy: I'am bound in honour,/ And by the Law of armes (*Magnetic Lady*, II.6.133—4). is bound in honour to imbrace/ The bearing of a Challenge (*Ibid.*, III.6.32—3).

Insisting on one's rights, and giving their rights to others:

Tragedy: honour, that clasps/ All-perfect justice in her arms (*Very Woman*, IV.2, p. 457).

Making socially good marriages:

Comedy: Allow her but the honour she was born with (*Royal Master*, III.1, p. 134) (HP).

Concern about reflected R (from Rc/C):

Tragedy: that I/ With my honour may conceal it (*Emperor of the East*, IV.5, p. 306).

Not breaking off a proposed marriage:

Comedy: any thought beneath your birth and honour (*Royal Master*, V.1, p. 175) (HP).

Recognizing the claims of friendship:

Comedy: If you have noble honour in you (*Distresses*, III.1, p. 313).
Tragedy: the least scruple of thy faith and honour (*Traitor*, I.1, p. 101).

Observing laws of civilized warfare:

Tragedy: Rudely to violate the Law of honor (*Perkin Warbeck*, 2329).

Miscellaneous:

Comedy: book-gallants, have oft their genty tricks/ Of nice honour (*Platonic Lovers*, II.1, pp. 23—4) (not accepting money for services). The Cavaleiro treates on termes of honor (*Lady's Trial*, 815) (terms constituting adequate satisfaction for an affront).

Tragedy: how far/ In honour are you bound to run (*Very Woman*, IV.2, p. 457) (correct behaviour prescribed for a lover). satisfaction in so high/

And unexampled way of honour (*Imposture*, II.1, p. 199) (recompensing seduced woman by marrying her off by an imposture-trick).

(*b*) *The m Group*

Tragedy: bred thee from thy childhood to a sense/ Of honour (*Love and Honour*, III.1, p. 146). thou hast no honour in thee,/ Not enough noble blood (*Cardinal*, II.1, p. 290).

(*c*) *The v Group*

Loyalty to ruler:

Comedy: Where should honour/ Shine with his pure and native lustre (*Royal Master*, V.2, p. 181).

Tragedy: to that name and honour/ I'll trust a prince's life (*Politician*, III.3, p. 138).

Not condoning murder:

Tragedy: 'tis the crown/ Of virtue to proceed in its own track,/ Not deviate from honour (*Cardinal*, IV.2, p. 326).

Refusing a challenge, and proving that it is ungrounded:

Comedy: honour/ Schooles me to fitter grounds (*Fancies*, 2296—7).

Not conniving at unchastity:

Tragedy: How my honour blushes/ To hear thee (*Traitor*, V.1, p. 172).

Sexual continence:

Comedy: I do believe your honour (*Hyde Park*, III.1, p. 492) (HY). I were too much wicked to suspect your honour (*Ibid.*, IV.1, p. 507).

Tragedy: hath eat into your soul/ Of honour (*Imposture*, III.3, p. 223).

Making amends to a woman by marriage:

Comedy: his honour, and his fame,/ May equal any man's (*Distresses*, IV.1, p. 332).

Tragedy: Which in your honour you are bound to cure (*Bashful Lover*, IV.2, p. 486).

Peacemaking, reconciliation:

Comedy: A motion of such honour (*Lady's Trial*, 2074).

Miscellaneous:

Comedy: by rewards,/ Crownes worthy actions, and invites to honour (*Lady's Trial*, 2135—6) (not clearly specified, but probably v). Honour and worthy actions, best beseeme/ Their lips who practice both (*Ibid.*, 2137—8) (the same).

Tragedy: Honour, to dare to live, and satisfy (*Very Woman*, IV.2, p. 457) (making amends for wrongs, justice, truthfulness, etc.). oh! this honour bears/ The right stamp (*Ibid.*) (the same). Of honour, honesty, religion (*Imposture*, II.1, p. 196) (not conniving at imposture and deceit, not conniving at marriage of a nun).

(d) *The x Group*

Comedy: Perfection of honour dwells in him (*Hyde Park*, II.3, p. 481). In whom was hid so much perfection/ Of honour (*Ibid.*, III.1, p. 495). speak of me as honour guides you (*Lady of Pleasure*, IV.3, p. 81). Steer all your resolutions by honour (*Royal Master*, III.1, p. 135). Where is now the honour/ You talk of (*Ibid.*, III.1, p. 138). to make/ Thy faith and honour shine (*Ibid.*, IV.1, p. 170). There is a spring of honour here (*Ibid.*, V.1, p. 185). I could not think/ My honour well dispos'd (*Distresses*, I.1, p. 285). his looks declare that he/ Hath honour in him (*Ibid.*, III.1, p. 324). She whom my virtue and my honour lov'd (*Ibid.*). such characters/ Of honour ne'er had real being (*Ibid.*, IV.1, p. 331).

Tragedy: I may engage my more/ Than equal honour (*Traitor*, I.2, p. 108) (HTP). I dare repose/ Upon Sciarrha's honour (*Ibid.*, II.1, p. 115). With honour, and religion, thus invite it (*Ibid.*, II.2, p. 127). but in affliction justifies/ His heart and honour (*Ibid.*, IV.2, p. 167). In which true honour is both learn'd and practised (*Emperor of the East*, I.1, p. 286). And have done nothing but what you in honour (*Ibid.*, III.4, p. 300). Honour is/ Virtue's allow'd ascent (*Very Woman*, IV.2, p. 457). Now speak, old soldier,/ The height of HONOUR (*Ibid.*). the honour of/ My birth and soul shall warrant it (*Love and Honour*, II.1, p. 123) (HP). So full of honour, temperance, and all virtues (*Bashful Lover*, V.3, p. 491). honour/ Doth dwell within, and cannot live abroad (*Fair Favourite*, II.1, p. 230). hold/ Your virtue and your honour in a high regard (*Ibid.*, V.1, p. 273). Seeing his youth improv'd with so much honour (*Imposture*, IV.1, p. 228). I do believe him all compos'd of honour (*Ibid.*). you did appear so full/ Of honour, virtue (*Ibid.*, IV.5, p. 243). Virtue and honour, I allow you names (*Ibid.*, V.2, p. 253). Where is honour,/ And gratitude of kings (*Cardinal*, III.2, p. 314).

(e) *Summary, H 1631—1640*

Table 43 gives a summary of the k/m/v/x classification of H for the decade 1631—1640. For the first time, the v group is not predominant; v and k are about equally numerous, with just over a quarter of the examples each; m is insignificant, with only some 3%; the x group is unusually large, with 44% of the examples. There are no examples of km. There are no significant differences between comedy and tragedy.

THE H MATERIAL. 243

TABLE 43. *Numbers of k, m, v, and x: H material, 1631—40.*

	k	m	v	x	Total
Comedy	9	0	8	11	28
Tragedy	8	2	8	17	35
All Plays	17	2	16	28	63

F. 1661—1670

In this decade there are 126 examples of H, 84 in comedy and 42 in tragedy. In ten of the examples, H is not the sole head-meaning; the joint head-meanings found are HP (two) and HK (eight). Of the 126 examples, none are countables, 100 are uncountables, and 26 are equivocal. The examples are the following.

(a) The k Group

Sensitivity to affront, revenging insult and injury, etc.:

Comedy: 'Tis Honour and not Envy brings you here (*Conical Revenge*, IV.4.40). d'ye think I have no sense of honour (*Sir Martin Mar-all*, IV.1, p. 66). 'Slife kick a man of honour as I am (*Sullen Lovers*, III.1, p. 55). I'le teach him to use a man of honour thus (*Ibid.*). honour has leave of conscience to be bloody in revenge (*Man's the Master*, V.1, p. 95). that courage against which your honour does contest (*Ibid.*, V.1, p. 96). According to the Laws of honour I make no question (*Humorists*, III.1, p. 217) (HK).

Tragedy: Justice and Honour on my Sword shall sit (*Forced Marriage*, II.1, p. 306).

Not tolerating a rival:

Comedy: My Honour is as forward as my Love (*Comical Revenge*, IV.1.3). Honour with Honour fights for Victory (*Ibid.*, IV.5.7) (two examples).

Tragedy: But friendship bars what honour prompts me to (*Indian Queen*, IV.2, p. 264).

Accepting challenges, observing rules of duelling, etc.:

Comedy: Because my Honour disobey'd her Will (*Comical Revenge*, V.1. 119). I cannot in honour suffer that (*Sullen Lovers*, III.1, p. 53). I am bound in honour to defend 'em (*Ibid.*). I cou'd not in honour refuse (*Ibid.*, IV.1, p. 58). I have not so little honour as to leave thee (*Ibid.*, IV.1, p. 59). have so little honour as to quit thee (*Ibid.*, IV.1, p. 60). honour taught me that patience (*Man's the Master*, V.1, p. 92). I see you are a man of honour (*Ibid.*). not by a single hand of honour but by confederacy (*Ibid.*,

V.1, p. 97). by a trick of honour, be made a second (*Ibid.*, V.1, p. 98) (HK). I ought in honour to fight (*Humorists*, IV.1, p. 228).

Tragedy: Unlucky honour, that control'st my will (*Indian Emperor*, III.3, p. 364).

Fighting to revenge mistress, at her command:

Tragedy: as ready to be damn'd/ In honour as any Lover (*Forced Marriage*, III.2, p. 334).

Not fighting a man to whom under an obligation:

Comedy: My Honour is dis-satisfied (*Comical Revenge*, IV.4.51). My scrup'lous Honour must obey my Flame (*Ibid.*, IV.4.70).

Not marrying man who killed your husband in a duel:

Tragedy: For she in Honour cannot him prefer (*Forced Marriage*, II.1, p. 306).

Ostentation, extravagant magnanimity:

Tragedy: Honour is but an itch in youthful blood (*Indian Queen*, III.1, p. 250).

Recognizing the claims of friendship:

Comedy: I should have thought myself obliged in honour (*Evening's Love*, V.1, p. 345).

Protecting a woman's reputation:

Comedy: the laws of Honour prescrib'd in such nice cases (*She Would*, II.1.17—18) (HK). I know your Honour, dear Sir (*Ibid.*, III.1.222). we believe you men of Honour (*Ibid.*, IV.2.234). This has almost redeem'd my opinion of his Honour (*Ibid.*, V.1.432—3).

Keeping adulterous assignations, constancy to adulterous mistress:

Comedy: he has more honour then to attempt any thing (*She Would*, I.2.3—4). he is a Person of much Worth and Honour (*Ibid.*, I.2.37—8). to believe him a man of Honour (*Ibid.*, V.1.13—14).

Not being under an obligation:

Tragedy: That which my honour owed thee I have paid (*Indian Queen*, IV.2, p. 264). As honour was, so love must be obeyed (*Ibid.*) (HK). Thou hast performed what honour bid thee do (*Ibid.*) (HK).

Politeness:

Comedy: He in the School of Honour has been bred (*Comical Revenge*, II.2.38). have you no sense of Honour nor modesty left (*She Would*, V.1.112—13).

Observing the conventions of civilized warfare:

Tragedy: only he, who has such honour shown (*Indian Emperor*, I.2, p. 339).

Suicide:

Comedy: Honour has plaid an after-game (*Comical Revenge*, IV.4.119). there's great Love and Honour to be shewn (*Sullen Lovers*, III.1, p. 52). not so fit to express Love and Honour with (*Ibid.*).

Miscellaneous:

Comedy: I am a man of honour (*Wild Gallant*, III.2, p. 82) (keeping one's word to commit adultery). Must in the beaten paths of Honour tread (*Comical Revenge*, II.2.124) (woman not revealing her virtuous love for a man). That I have Honour too, as well as Love (*Ibid.*, IV.5.23) (not marrying man you love if he fights a duel with his rival). I did what I in honour ought to do (*Ibid.*, V.3.52) (the same). To him with honour I my Heart resign (*Ibid.*, V.5.22) (marrying the one of your two suitors that you do not love, if he is wounded in a duel with the one that you do love). Such Honour and such Love as you have shown (*Ibid.*, V.5.23) (the same). if it be a purchase that may with honour be divided (*She Would*, I.1.39) (only sharing certain types of women with a friend — it probably depends whether or not she's a gentlewoman). you must not in Honour flye off now (*Ibid.*, IV.2.262—3) (keeping a love-assignation, fig. from duelling). Honour is a fool in the field when it wants stratagem (*Man's the Master*, V.1, p. 93) (unspecified, but related to duelling). in my youth did love to see the exercise of honour (*Ibid.*, V.1, p. 95) (qualities shown in duelling) (or possibly war? — m). a person of much generosity and honour (*Humorists*, I.1, p. 194) (suffering for the sake of women, viz. from venereal disease).

Tragedy: It was my honour made my duty err (*Indian Queen*, III.1, p. 247) (gratitude to friend and benefactor overriding filial piety and duty to country). Your honour rivalled by my piety (*Ibid.*, IV.2, p. 267) (not clearly specified, but probably k). If honour would not, shame would lead the way (*Ibid.*) (voluntarily sharing execution of mistress). I'll not strain honour to a point too high (*Indian Emperor*, III.3, p. 363) (keeping promise to a rival, but fighting him afterwards).

(*b*) *The m Group*

Tragedy: Honour burns in me not so fiercely bright (*Conquest of Granada. 1*, III.1, p. 71).

(*c*) *The v Group*

Truthfulness:

Comedy: do you take me for a man of honour (*Evening's Love*, IV.3, p. 338). for honour does oblige me to 't (*Man's the Master*, V.1, p. 99). and honour now does join with truth (*Ibid.*).

Keeping promises:

Comedy: I owe myself to one by blood, and to the other by honor (*Man's the Master*, III.1, p. 45).

Tragedy: Fantastic honour, thou hast framed a toil (*Indian Emperor*, IV.2, p. 379). To this, since honour ties me, I agree (*Conquest of Granada. 1*, V.2, p. 110).

Loyalty to ruler:

Tragedy: But in this strait, to honour I'll be true (*Indian Emperor*, IV.2, p. 377). he swallowed down/ His forfeit honour (*Ibid.*, IV.2, p. 379). True, I strain/ A point of honour (*Secret Love*, IV.1, p. 479) (HK). A flight, no honour ever reached before (*Tyrannic Love*, V.1, p. 459). My honour is not wholly put to flight (*Conquest of Granada. 1*, II.1, p. 56). I hope you only would my honour try (*Ibid.*).

Filial piety:

Tragedy: And on our Honour lays too great a weight (*Forced Marriage*, I.3, p. 303).

Not murdering:

Tragedy: Honour sits on me like some heavy armour (*Rival Ladies*, III.1, p. 182). It is enough that I your honour see (*Indian Emperor*, III.4, p. 369).

Not stealing:

Comedy: a man of honour is not capable of an unworthy action (*Evening's Love*, IV.2, p. 336).

Sexual continence:

Comedy: Ha! little honour to be much believ'd (*Law against Lovers*, III.1, p. 149). You are too unjust if you suspect my honour (*Sullen Lovers*, II.1, p. 29) (intending marriage). Do you still distrust my Honour (*Ibid.*, II.1, p. 30) (faithfulness to wife). we will accept of the Challenge, and believe you men of Honour (*She Would*, V.1.538—9) (intending marriage). Injure me not to suspect my honour (*Humorists*, II.1, p. 211). I have so absolute a confidence in your honour (*Ibid.*, IV.1, p. 234) (intending marriage). I can sooner distrust my self than your honour (*Ibid.*, V.1, p. 249) (faithfulness to wife).

Tragedy: But those from dictates of his Honour took (*Forced Marriage*, I.3, p. 302).

Not being envious:

Tragedy: my birth, my courage, and my honour (*Secret Love*, I.3, p. 432) (HP).

Not being ungrateful:

Tragedy: What prudence will not venture, honour must (*Indian Queen*, III.1, p. 250).

Incorruptibility:

Comedy: Fare you well, maid of honour (*Man's the Master*, II.1, p. 25) (ironical, and with pun on usual sense of "maid of honour").

Preventing duels:

Comedy: what I in honour ought to do (*Sullen Lovers*, IV.1, p. 63).
Tragedy: Whoe'er you are, if you have honour, part them (*Rival Ladies*, I.3, p. 160).

Selflessness:

Comedy: I did no more then Honour press'd me to (*Comical Revenge*, V.5.7). You so excel in Honour and in Love (*Ibid.*, V.5.9).
Tragedy: Wonder of honour (*Rival Ladies*, V.3, p. 219).

Miscellaneous:

Comedy: Those men want Honour who stake that at play (*Comical Revenge*, III.7.46) (not gambling with money not your own). be sure you tread in honour's paths (*Tempest*, III.5, p. 175) (not clearly specified, but probably v). how can I, in honor, refuse to assist her (*Man's the Master*, III.1, p. 45) (helping to right a wronged woman).

Tragedy: this one act of honour (*Secret Love*, V.1, p. 500) (letting justice and humanity triumph over passion). So great a Villain, and talk of Honour (*Royal Shepherdess*, V.1, p. 159) (not being a villain).

(d) The x Group

Comedy: Madam, you believe me to have some honour (*Law against Lovers*, III.1, p. 150). Honour, would that without religion do (*Ibid.*, V.1, p. 207). Which honour and your duty both approve (*Comical Revenge*, II.2.51). 'Tis some extream of Honour, or of Love (*Ibid.*, II.2.56). All that have sence of Honour or of Love (*Ibid.*, III.7.2). Y'ave done what men of Honour ought to do (*Ibid.*, IV.4.47). here Honour did with Courage vie (*Ibid.*, IV.4.83). Honour her self does bleed (*Ibid.*, IV.4.97). That will not Honour but Injustice be (*Ibid.*, V.1.88). Honour with Justice always does agree (*Ibid.*, V.1.89) (not necessarily v, since the supporters of duelling sometimes uphold duelling as a form of justice). call a man of honour fool (*Sir Martin Mar-all*, V.1, p. 78). thou art a Man of Honour (*Sullen Lovers*, II.1, p. 35) (keeping a secret). a Person of Worth and Honour (*She Would*, III.1.258—9). A Gentleman of wit and honour (*Humorists*, Dram. Pers., p. 191). thou art a man of honour, and I will not fight with thee (*Ibid.*, IV.1, p. 228). I hope you have so much honour, to impute my easiness (*Ibid.*, IV.1, p. 234). I see *Raymund* is a man of honour (*Ibid.*, IV.1, p. 239). he is a good natur'd Person and a Child of Honour (*Ibid.*, V.1, p. 240).

Tragedy: Which kindles honour into noble acts (*Rival Ladies*, I.1, p. 148). How poorly have you pleaded honour's laws (*Indian Queen*, I.1, p. 233)

TABLE 44. *Numbers of k, m, v, and x: H material, 1661—70.*

	k	m	v	x	Total
Comedy	47	0	19	18	84
Tragedy	14	1	18	9	42
All Plays	61	1	37	27	126

(HK). Your Spanish honour does the world excel (*Indian Emperor*, II.4, p. 352). His noble heart, to honour ever true (*Ibid.*, IV.2, p. 376). As I am a man of honour (*Secret Love*, V.1, p. 493) (HP). Dying for love's, fulfilling honour's laws (*Tyrannic Love*, IV.1, p. 431) (HK). O honour, how can'st thou invent a way (*Ibid.*, IV.1, p. 440). Honour and faith let argument debate (*Ibid.*). He does my honour want of duty call (*Conquest of Granada. I*, V.1, p. 102).

(e) Summary, H 1661—1670

Table 44 gives a summary of the k/m/v/x classification of H for the decade 1661—1670. For the first time, the k group is clearly predominant in total, with about 48% of all examples; the v group is still quite large, with 29%, but the m group is completely insignificant, with only one example out of the 126 (about 0.8%); the x group accounts for about 21%; there are no examples of km. However, there are now considerable differences between comedy and tragedy; the predominance of k is very strongly marked in comedy, where it accounts for 56% of the examples, against 23% for v; in tragedy, on the other hand, the v group, with 43%, is actually the largest, for k is here only 33%; these differences are just significant. The percentage of x is exactly the same in comedy and in tragedy, and m is too small for any comparison to be made.

G. 1671—1680

In this decade there are 176 examples of H, 111 in comedy and 65 in tragedy. In twelve of the examples, H is not the sole head-meaning; the joint head-meanings found are HK (seven), HP (three), HMT (one), and RcH (one). Of the 176 examples, one is a countable, 130 are uncountables, and 45 are equivocal. The examples are the following.

(a) The k Group

Sensitivity to insult, revenging affront, etc.:

Comedy: Should satisfy her Honour and Revenge (*Amorous Prince*, V.3, p. 209). I'll have another turn of honour in revenge (*Gent. Danc. Master*, V.1, pp. 235—6). If you have honour in you bear it not (*Epsom Wells*, IV.1, p. 158). why should I expect such honour from you (*Ibid.*, IV.1, p. 159). tyrannick Honour/ Presents the Credit of my House (*Dutch Lover*, II.1, p. 243). till I know how to satisfy my Honour (*Ibid.*, V.1, p. 310). And if thou think'st our Honour satisfy'd (*Ibid.*, V.1, p. 321). this man of tame honour (*Plain Dealer*, II.1, p. 413). a man of so much honour and experience (*Ibid.*, II.1, pp. 417—8). cannot deny a Man of Honour your assistance (*True Widow*, II.1, p. 316). Lovers take it as ill to be parted, as Men of Honour (*Ibid.*, V.1, p. 352).

Tragedy: you cannot, in honour, accept an invitation (*Amboyna*, III.2, p. 44). Who only Honours dictates did pursue (*Don Carlos*, V.1.405) (HK). A Victim to an injur'd Mother's Honour (*Abdelazer*, IV.4, p. 62).

Not tolerating a rival:

Comedy: Would you have a man of honour (*Gent. Danc. Master*, I.1, p. 137).

Accepting challenges, keeping duelling appointments, observing the rules of duelling, etc.:

Comedy: As a man of honour ought, sister, when he is challenged (*Assignation*, III.1, p. 406) (fig.). I warrant you they are men of honour (*Epsom Wells*, II.1, p. 126). they are men of Honour, and will answer a Challenge (*Ibid.*, II.1, p. 133). We did not doubt your Honour (*Ibid.*, II.1, p. 136). he has too much honour not to meet him singly (*Ibid.*, V.1, p. 173). you had not honour enough to answer me (*Virtuoso*, II.1, p. 120) (fig.). You are men of Honour, and may be trusted with your swords (*True Widow*, III.1, p. 327).

Tragedy: If you have honour, — since you nature want (*Conquest of Granada. 2*, II.1, p. 139). This debt of honour, which I owe, to pay (*Ibid.*, IV.2, p. 181). I am a Spaniard, sir; that implies honour (*Amboyna*, II.1, p. 32). I trust thy honour (*Troilus*, IV.2, p. 369).

In battle, revenging fallen friend or falling oneself:

Tragedy: as honour justly will command (*Alcibiades*, I.1.184). Such gallant courage and such honour wear (*Ibid.*, I.1.189).

Not preventing private revenge:

Tragedy: No man of honour will protect those (*Libertine*, IV.1, p. 71).

Not being meek or cowardly:

Comedy: I find you are a brisk man of honour (*Gent. Danc. Master*, V.1, p. 240). firm stiff Spanish honour (*Ibid.*). When a Man of Honour can turn Coward (*True Widow*, III.1, p. 319).

Knowing exactly what due to oneself and to others:

Tragedy: More delicate than honour's nicest sense (*Aureng-Zebe*, V.1, p. 297).

Not breaking off a proposed marriage:

Comedy: Love and Honour were at odds within me (*Dutch Lover*, I.3, p. 241). She that is Honour's Choice I never saw (*Ibid.*, I.3, p. 242). hold my self no longer ingag'd in Honour to *Hippolyta* (*Ibid.*, II.3, p. 251) (the man considers himself no longer bound in honour to marry the woman, since her relatives refuse to see him: this shows clearly that it is k). against your word and rigid honour (*Country Wife*, IV.1, p. 308).

Recognizing the claims of friendship:

Comedy: A man of honour (*Gent. Danc. Master*, I.2, p. 147). it's impossible to be a man of honour in these Cases (*Epsom Wells*, I.1, p. 109). you are oblig'd in honour (*Friendship in Fashion*, II.1.464). Say you so, Sir? oblig'd in honour (*Ibid.*, II.1.466). I'll treat you like a man of Honour (*Woman Captain*, III.1, p. 52).

Tragedy: A very civil person, a man of Honour (*Libertine*, II.1, p. 46).

Sexual virility, being a good wencher:

Comedy: you shall find that I am a man of honour (*Marriage à la Mode*, III.2, p. 314). Excellent honour, to leave a Lady (*Epsom Wells*, V.1, p. 174). that's spoken again like a man of honour (*Country Wife*, II.1, p. 282). all men of honour desire to come to the test (*Ibid.*). I have so strong a faith in your honour (*Ibid.*). If I do not show my self a Man of Honour (*Virtuoso*, III.1, p. 137). You are a Man of Honour (*Ibid.*, III.1, p. 143).

Constancy in adultery:

Comedy: Yes, I thank you, you are a man of Honour (*Epsom Wells*, III.1, p. 141). I do not doubt your honour (*Ibid.*, V.1, pp. 172—3).

Keeping assignations:

Comedy: you shall always find me a man of Honour (*Epsom Wells*, III.1, p. 141). am not I a woman of honour (*Country Wife*, IV.3, p. 320). I'll not be behindhand with you in honour (*Ibid.*).

Being a rake:

Comedy: That a woman of honour should have the word match (*Love in a Wood*, II.1, p. 34). Christina is so much a person of honour (*Ibid.*, IV.5, p. 92) (telling truth, but also not being ashamed of it, being rakish). Christina is a person of honour (*Ibid.*, IV.5, p. 98) (the same). Well said, my Boy! A Man of Honour (*Town Fop*, IV.3, p. 64) (not having petty sins, but going to the devil in a big way).

Betraying a friend in the interests of wenching:

Comedy: I cannot in honour but betray him (*Love in a Wood*, I.2, p. 24).

Being jealous, not introducing another man to one's mistress:
Comedy: But do not censure my honour (*Love in a Wood*, III.1, p. 58).

Protecting a woman's reputation:
Comedy: whose faith and honour she may be secure of (*Love in a Wood*, IV.3, p. 88). you need not distrust his honour or his faith (*Ibid.*, IV.5, p. 96). A Gentleman ought in Honour to lye for his Mistress (*Epsom Wells*, III.1, p. 143). have they no sense of honour (*Ibid.*, IV.1, p. 154). guessing you to be Men of Honour (*Dutch Lover*, I.1, p. 229). so generous, so truly a man of honour (*Country Wife*, II.1, p. 282). so much a man of honour, that I must save my mistress (*Country Wife*, V.4, p. 354). some kind Amour, something of Love and Honour (*Sir Patient Fancy*, IV.1, p. 66) (RcH). I see Lodwick's a Man of Honour (*Ibid.*, IV.2, p. 80).
Tragedy: My honour first her danger must remove (*Conquest of Granada. 2*, V.1, p. 202) (fighting as champion for mistress, although believing her guilty, i. e. unchaste).

Good manners:
Comedy: to have so little honour and good breeding (*Gent. Danc. Master*, I.2, p. 150). the severer rules, and stricter methods of honour (*Virtuoso*, I.1, p. 109) (HK). there is no Honour, no Civility in the world (*Friendship in Fashion*, III.1, p. 185).

Observing conventions of civilized warfare:
Tragedy: You kill'd, 'cause he more honour had then you (*Alcibiades*, IV.1.440) (then moves to v, treason and murder).

Suicide:
Tragedy: Self-homicide, which was, in heathens, honour (*Amboyna*, IV.3, p. 65) (or S?).

Miscellaneous:
Comedy: those of so much worth and honour and love (*Love in a Wood*, V.2, p. 105) (spending money on one's mistresses rather than on one's wife and children). by your own Spanish rules of honour (*Gent. Danc. Master*, V.1, p. 231) (HK) (helping a man whom you have brought into danger, although he is your rival). And put on the Spanish honour with the habit (*Ibid.*, V.1, p. 235) (the same). ye have as little Honour as yon Bullies have (*Epsom Wells*, II.1, p. 136) (keeping love/duelling appointments). it is a silly Honour that will hinder a man the satisfying of his love (*Ibid.*, V.1, p. 165) (real-life honour asserted to be consistent with unscrupulousness). behave my self like a man of honour (*Ibid.*, V.1, p. 175) (paying for your whores). I am a man of honour, sir (*Country Wife*, III.2, p. 298) (knowing what liberties other men can be permitted with your wife). I hope you are so much a man of honour (*Plain Dealer*, IV.2, p. 477) (not insisting on knowing a woman's secrets). I cannot in Honour but forgive

her (*Town Fop*, V.1, p. 73) (forgiving kept mistress for inconstancy if she pitches an ingenious and plausible story). I am a friar of honour (*Spanish Friar*, III.1, p. 452) (faithfully performing commission, viz. to forward a love-intrigue with a married woman).

Tragedy: can't in honour less/ Then crown your Love (*Alcibiades*, I.1. 155—6) (accepting faithful second-string lover if first is found to be inconstant). am obliged in honour not to act as a Magistrate (*Libertine*, IV.1, p. 72) (duty as host, overriding duty as magistrate).

(*b*) *The m Group*

Comedy: the first are the effects of our pleasure, and the last of our honour (*Epsom Wells*, I.1, p. 108).

Tragedy: It kindles all the soul with honour's fire (*Conquest of Granada. 2*, I.1, p. 128). My forward Honour was Ambition call'd (*Don Carlos*, I.1.108). What sparks of honour/ Fly from this child (*Troilus*, II.1, p. 305).

(*c*) *The v Group*

Truthfulness, not slandering:

Comedy: I always took you for a man of honour (*Country Wife*, V.4, p. 354).

Tragedy: what a Contest/ Of Love and Honour swells (*Abdelazer*, V.1, p. 74).

Keeping promises, etc.:

Comedy: I'l sooner trust the honour of a Country Horse-Courser (*Epsom Wells*, I.1, p. 110). I cannot help making my honour yield to my love (*Ibid.*, I.1, p. 116). if you are men of Honour, you'll keep your words (*Ibid.*). So Gentlemen, you are men of honour (*Ibid.*, V.1, p. 175).

Tragedy: to think/ There could be faith or honour in the Dutch (*Amboyna*, IV.3, p. 73).

Loyalty to rulers:

Tragedy: My Honour and Religion bids me serve him (*Abdelazer*, IV.6, p. 67). those Principles/ My Honour ever taught me to obey (*Ibid.*).

Not committing murder and treason:

Tragedy: And Chronicle my honour in their blood (*Alcibiades*, IV.1.456).

Loyalty to ruler, and filial piety:

Tragedy: I'm taught, by honour's precepts, to obey (*Aureng-Zebe*, II.1, p. 235) (HK). But, since my honour you so far suspect (*Ibid.*, III.1, p. 247). The just rewards of love and honour wear (*Ibid.*, V.1, p. 302).

Filial piety:

Tragedy: in honour will reveal it to the Father (*Libertine*, IV.1, p. 70).

Not committing rape and murder:

Tragedy: and seem to be men of Honour (*Libertine*, IV.1, p. 70).

Not being a cheat and swindler:
Comedy: my Lady is a Person of Honour (*True Widow*, V.1, p. 355).

Not committing rape and robbery:
Tragedy: Honour, you Villain (*Libertine*, III.1, p. 66).

Not conniving at unchastity or incest:
Comedy: his nice Honour/ Will ne'er permit that I should court (*Dutch Lover*, I.2, p. 231). Come, no dissembling honour (*Plain Dealer*, III.1, p. 430). Is my Charity thus rewarded? my Honour question'd (*True Widow*, III.1, p. 320).

Sexual continence:
Comedy: you have no more honour in love than needs must (*Epsom Wells*, V.1, p. 165). if you be not sure of your Honor (*Virtuoso*, III.1, p. 136).
Tragedy: Your honour cannot to ill thoughts give way (*Conquest of Granada. 2*, II.3, p. 153). When honour's present, and when love's away (*Ibid.*, IV.3, p. 192). The duty of poor honour were too hard (*Ibid.*).

Not abandoning woman seduced under promise of marriage:
Tragedy: Has he no Conscience, Faith, or Honour left (*Libertine*, I.1, p. 29).

Loyalty to husband:
Comedy: were I not in honour engag'd unto Sir *Nicholas* (*Virtuoso*, III.1, p. 135). Honour has the greatest Ascendent (*Ibid.*). But honour's a great matter (*Ibid.*).

Not being ungrateful:
Tragedy: And honour tells me Gratitude is due (*Alcibiades*, II.1.24).

Miscellaneous:
Comedy: is not like a person of honour (*Plain Dealer*, I.1, p. 376) (not backbiting).
Tragedy: My honour bids me succour the oppressed (*Conquest of Granada. 2*, II.1, p. 138). In that I did what honour urg'd me to (*Alcibiades*, II.1.23) (relieving sufferings). And, with true honour, ballasted my pride (*Aureng-Zebe*, V.1, p. 282) (not pursuing "unjust dominion"). Men of Honour! They are Devils (*Libertine*, II.1, p. 45) (not being a callous libertine).

(d) *The x Group*

Comedy: Which honour will not give you leave to grant (*Marriage à la Mode*, IV.3, p. 327). I trust your honour (*Ibid.*, IV.3, p. 328). Oh, where is all your Honour and your Virtue (*Amorous Prince*, III.1, p. 162). who pretends to so much Honour/ And Gravity (*Ibid.*, V.3, p. 201). so much

Love and Honour upon the Stage (*Epsom Wells*, I.1, p. 116). have you so little honour to believe the words (*Ibid.*, IV.1, p. 155). a man of such perfect honour (*Country Wife*, II.1, p. 270). But what a devil is this honour (*Ibid.*, IV.1, p. 308). Come, pray talk you no more of honour (*Ibid.*). counterfeit honour will not be current with me: I weigh the man, not his title (*Plain Dealer*, I.1, p. 381) (HMT). having no honour but his interest (*Ibid.*, I.1, p. 384) (HK). men of such honour and virtue (*Ibid.*, II.1, p. 405). you are a man of so much honour (*Ibid.*, II.1, p. 417). the brave, the reasonable, and man of honour (*Ibid.*, IV.1, p. 458). honour in a man they fear too much to love (*Ibid.*). I hope you are a person of honour (*Virtuoso*, III.1, p. 137). Now shew your self a man of Honour (*Ibid.*, V.1, p. 172). Without sense of Love, of Honour, or of Gratitude (*Man of Mode*, II.2. 155—6). against the rules of decency and honour (*Ibid.*, V.2.173—4) (HK). Have you no Sense of Honour, nor of Horrors (*Town Fop*, II.4, p. 36). there is no fidelity, no honour in Mankind (*Friendship in Fashion*, III.1. 638—9). honesty to his wit, and honour to his courage (*True Widow*, III.1, p. 327). I cannot in Honour pass you for my Souldiers (*Woman Captain*, IV.1, p. 68). Law, justice, honour, bid farewell to earth (*Spanish Friar*, IV.2, p. 491).

Tragedy: I'll cherish honour, then, and life despise (*Conquest of Granada*.2, I.2, p. 136). The effect of honour in the Spanish queen (*Ibid.*, II.1, p. 137). Things worthy the *Athenian* honour done (*Alcibiades*, I.1.212). Which prompted 'em that honour to abuse (*Ibid.*, I.1.216). By worth and honour Empires greatest grow (*Ibid.*, I.1.220). The honour and the justice of your cause (*Ibid.*, I.1.242). In honour's as renown'd as in his name (*Ibid.*, III.1. 174). Curse on his honour, 'twill my hopes destroy (*Ibid.*, III.1.263). judge that honour have (*Ibid.*, IV.1.25) (HP). His honour, and his Gallantry to you (*Ibid.*, IV.1.333). He could, why may not I your honour trust (*Ibid.*, V.1.47). Morat, perhaps, has honour in his breast (*Aureng-Zebe*, II.1, p. 237). Your strictness, honour, and your duty shake (*Don Carlos*, I.1.86). To see such honour and such hopes opprest (*Ibid.*, IV.1.136). Though it be fierce, has Gratitude and Honour (*Abdelazer*, V.2, p. 85). knows no honour/ Divided from his interest (*All for Love*, III.1, p. 385). Most worthy Patrons of her ancient Honour (*Caius Marius*, I.1.13) (HP). Courage, Nobility, and innate Honour (*Ibid.*, I.1.161) (HP). For when he dies, farewell all Honour (*Orphan*, I.1.32). Where is there Faith, or Honour to be found (*Ibid.*, I.1.271). My Mothers Vertues and my Fathers Honour (*Ibid.*, I.1. 339). Where Honour ought to have the fairest play (*Ibid.*, II.1.58). That liv'd up to the Standard of his Honour (*Ibid.*, II.1.207) (HK). Iv'e two, and both I hope have honour (*Ibid.*, IV.1.309). Thy Father's Honour's not above *Monimia's* (*Ibid.*, V.1.114).

(e) *Summary, H 1671—1680*

Table 45 gives a summary of the k/m/v/x classification of H for the decade 1671—1680. The pattern is very much the same as in the previous

THE H MATERIAL 255

TABLE 45. *Numbers of k, m, v, and x: H material, 1671—80.*

	k	m	v	x	Total
Comedy	71	1	15	24	111
Tragedy	17	3	20	25	65
All Plays	88	4	35	49	176

decade: the k group is the largest, with 50%, the v group is a fair size, with 20%, and the m group is very small, with less than 2.5%; the x group has about 28%; there are no examples of km. There are clear differences between comedy and tragedy: the predominance of k is strongly marked in comedy, where it has 64% of the examples, against 13.5 for v; in tragedy, on the other hand, v is larger than k, with 31% against 26%. The difference between comedy and tragedy is significant for v, and highly significant for k; it is not significant for m, and is just significant for x, which is stronger in tragedy than in comedy.

H. 1681—1690

In this decade there are 104 examples of H, 75 in comedy and 29 in tragedy. In six of the examples, H is not the sole head-meaning; these six are classified HK. Of the 104 examples, one is a countable, 83 are uncountables, and 20 are equivocal. The examples are the following.

(a) *The k Group*

Sensitivity to affront, revenging injury, etc.:

Comedy: I know what my honour would prompt me to (*Squire of Alsatia*, III.1, p. 246). My Honour is tender (*Ibid.*, V.1, p. 268). which becometh a man of Honour to do (*Bury Fair*, IV.1, p. 354). a Person of such Breeding, Quality, and Honour (*Ibid.*, V.1, p. 360). Honour! hang him, Scoundrel (*Ibid.*).

Keeping duelling-appointments, observing rules of duelling, etc.:

Comedy: These are your Men of Honour now (*Atheist*, IV.1.1). I have a greater share of Honour (*Bury Fair*, IV.1, p. 351). all this is done in the forms of honour (*Amphitryon*, V.1, p. 97) (HK).

Tragedy: Make much of honour, 'tis a soldier's conscience (*Duke of Guise*, V.1, p. 110).

Revenging affront to mistress:

Comedy: I find you are a Man of Honour (*Amorous Bigot*, II.1, p. 40).

Making a socially good marriage:

Comedy: I know you have so much honour (*Squire of Alsatia*, III.1, p. 238).

Recognizing the claims of friendship:

Comedy: My Honour will not let me strike thy Brother (*Squire of Alsatia*, III.1, p. 246). I understand Honour and Breeding (*Ibid.*) (HK). transgress the rules of Honour (*Ibid.*) (HK). 'Tis no matter; I know Honour (*Ibid.*) (HK). You still possess the same Honour which you ever had (*Bury Fair*, IV.1, p. 350). He is a man of Honour (*Scowrers*, V.1, p. 143). men of Honour assist one another (*Ibid.*).

Sexual virility:

Comedy: carry my self like a man of honour (*Amorous Bigot*, V.1, p. 68).

Constancy in adultery:

Comedy: and controuls all my Honour (*Younger Brother*, V.3, p. 389). the same man of honour I thought you (*Scowrers*, III.1, p. 120). Oh dear, dear *Wildfire*, thou art a Man of Honour (*Ibid.*, V.1, p. 141).

Keeping adulterous assignations:

Comedy: a Person of much Honour (*Lancashire Witches*, IV.1, p. 167). I will perform like a man of honour (*Amphitryon*, III.1, p. 66).

Protecting a woman's reputation:

Comedy: As you have Honour, go and cherish mine (*City Heiress*, IV.2, p. 272) (moves to Rco). as you are a Man of Honour, I must tell you (*Squire of Alsatia*, V.1, p. 277). You are a man of honour, and have promised me (*Amorous Bigot*, V.1, p. 72). Yet sure he's a man of Honour (*Scowrers*, III.1, p. 114). a Man of shining honour (*Ibid.*, V.1, p. 142).

Loyalty to fellow-criminals:

Tragedy: Spiritless, void of honour (*Venice Preserved*, IV.1.347).

Observing the conventions of civilized warfare:

Tragedy: against all the Laws of Honour and of Justice (*Widow Ranter*, V.1, p. 295) (HK).

Miscellaneous:

Comedy: a Royalist, a Man of Honour (*Roundheads*, Dram. Pers., p. 343) (adultery not barred). According to the strictest Rules of Honour (*City Heiress*, IV.1, p. 264) (HK) (beauty should be reward of love, not of wealth, and marriage irrelevant). Oh, trust me, Sir, I am a Maid of Honour (*Ibid.*, V.4, p. 290) (not telling tales). I am bound in Honour to protect it (*Bury Fair*, V.1, p. 357) (protecting man because his danger is due to his love for you). do you think I have no honour in me (*Amorous Bigot*,

IV.1, p. 57) (keeping one's word to commit murder). You are a man of honour (*Ibid.*, IV.1, p. 62) (keeping a secret, assisting an elopement).
Tragedy: Captain, you should be a Gentleman of honour (*Venice Preserved*, V.1.459) (understanding that a gentleman will wish to die decorously). you cannot, in honour, but protect her (*Don Sebastian*, IV.3, p. 429) (protecting a woman whose danger is due to her love for you). full of this silly thing call'd Honour (*Widow Ranter*, I.2, p. 238) (accepting word of a gentleman, not making preparations against possible treachery). spite of my Soul, spite of my boasted Honour (*Ibid.*, V.3, p. 300) (not loving man who killed your husband in battle).

(b) The m Group

Tragedy: The task of honour and the way to greatness (*Venice Preserved*, IV.1.240).

(c) The v Group

Truthfulness:

Comedy: you are a man of honour (*Amorous Bigot*, III.1, p. 49) (could also be interpreted k — not evading challenges).

Keeping promises:

Comedy: he is engaged in honour to your Father (*Lancashire Witches*, I.1, p. 112) (also not breaking off a proposed marriage). take a man of honour at his word (*Ibid.*, IV.1, p. 163). a Man whom Interest sways, not Honour (*Lucky Chance*, IV.1, p. 253) (also not breaking off a proposed marriage). he is thus far a Man of Honour (*Bury Fair*, II.1, p. 321).

Loyalty to rulers:

Tragedy: T'attempt his heart, and bring it back to honour (*Venice Preserved*, V.1.86). 'Tis hatched beneath, a plot upon mine honour (*Duke of Guise*, III.1, p. 57). but that my Honour's yet above my Anger (*Widow Ranter*, II.4, p. 262). Honour tells me 'tis an impious Zeal (*Ibid.*, IV.1, p. 281).

Not conniving at unchastity:

Comedy: you've lost your Honour with your wits (*False Count*, V.1, p. 165). What pimp for thee? and a man of Honour (*Scowrers*, V.1, p. 143).

Sexual continence:

Comedy: I'le trust your honour (*Lancashire Witches*, IV.1, p. 164). They were for Honour all (*City Heiress*, I.1, p. 214). do you not take me for a man of honour (*Amorous Bigot*, II.1, p. 36). known all over *Europe* to be a man of honour (*Ibid.*). Not take me for a man of honour (*Ibid.*). Not swear when my honour and constancy are in question (*Ibid.*, II.1, p. 37). Tragedy: Have I so little honour (*Duke of Guise*, IV.3, p. 87) (not raping).

Miscellaneous:

Comedy: But I have too much Honour in my Passion (*City Heiress*, V.5, p. 292) (not letting a woman ruin herself by being seduced by another man). *She cannot from the Paths of Honour rove* (*Lucky Chance*, III.2, p. 230) (following the dictates of Religion and Love).

(d) The x Group

Comedy: They are Women of Honour, and will keep their Words (*Lancashire Witches*, IV.1, p. 167). I am bound in Honour and Conscience (*Roundheads*, III.1, p. 381). for he has too much Honor (*False Count*, II.1, p. 119). if he have any thing in him, Sir, of Honour (*Ibid.*, III.2, p. 143). I conjure ye both, by all your Honour (*City Heiress*, I.1, p. 217). Deal like a Man of Honour by me (*Atheist*, II.1.182—3). Whither is Honour, Truth and Friendship fled (*Lucky Chance*, I.1, p. 193). And has such worth and honour (*Squire of Alsatia*, I.1, p. 221). I trusted to his Honour and his Oaths (*Ibid.*, IV.1, p. 260). I will trust thy Honour (*Ibid.*, V.1, p. 272). My Lord, you are a Man of Honour (*Bury Fair*, III.1, p. 339). so true a Friend, so much a Man of Honour (*Ibid.*, IV.1, p. 346). my mistake of Honour (*Ibid.*, IV.1, p. 347). You are a Man of strictest Honour (*Ibid.*). my Honour may be question'd (*Ibid.*, IV.1, p. 350). a man of Worth and Honour (*Ibid.*, IV.1, p. 353). and like a Man of Honour (*Ibid.*, V.1, p. 355). I scorn a lie, and am a man of honour in everything but just fighting (*Amphitryon*, III.1, p. 55). a well-bred Gentleman, and a man of Honour (*Amorous Bigot*, Dram. Pers., p. 15). You are a man of honour (*Ibid.*, V.1, p. 74). I see you are a man of Honour (*Scowrers*, II.1, p. 105). Ay but you are a man of honour (*Ibid.*, III.1, p. 119). He is a Man of Honour (*Ibid.*, IV.1, p. 125). who we know to be a man of Honour (*Ibid.*, IV.1, p. 130). confident he is a man of Honour (*Ibid.*, V.1, p. 142). We trust your Honour (*Ibid.*, V.1, p. 144).

Tragedy: To you, Sirs, and your Honours, I bequeath her (*Venice Preserved*, II.1.393). To you, Sirs, and to your Honour, I bequeath her (*Ibid.*, III.2.103). Here, my Honour's Brother (*Ibid.*, II.1.420). Breed him in vertue and the paths of Honour (*Ibid.*, V.1.337). Honour you've little, honesty you've less (*Duke of Guise*, IV.3, p. 87). nothing but Honour/ Provokes me in the Point (*Constantine*, II.1, p. 35). You've too much honour for a renegade (*Don Sebastian*, II.1, p. 356). The worth and honour of my soul unknown (*Ibid.*, III.1, p. 391). Where interest shared not more than half with honour (*Ibid.*, V.1, p. 454). Base, grovelling soul, who know'st not honour's worth (*Ibid.*). my mother's honour has been read/ By me, and by the world, in all her acts (*Ibid.*, V.1, p. 457). neither Friendship nor Honour enough to support me (*Widow Ranter*, I.1, p. 227). pretends to a little Honour, Loyalty, and Courage (*Ibid.*, I.2, p. 239). Honour returns, and Love all bleeding's fled (*Ibid.*, IV.2, p. 284). your upbraiding of my Honour (*Ibid.*, V.1, p. 295). these Gentlemen of Sense and Honour (*Ibid.*, V.5, p. 308).

TABLE 46. *Numbers of k, m, v, and x: H material, 1681—90.*

	k	m	v	x	Total
Comedy	34	0	15	26	75
Tragedy	7	1	5	16	29
All Plays	41	1	20	42	104

(e) *Summary, H 1681—1690*

Table 46 gives a summary of the k/m/v/x classification of H for the decade 1681—1690. The pattern is not much dissimilar to that in the previous two decades; in total, k is much larger than either v or m; k has 39% of the examples, and v 19%, while m is still insignificant, with only one example out of the 104; the x group is unusually large, with 40%; there are no examples of km. The dominance of k is more marked in comedy (45%) than in tragedy (24%), and this difference is just significant; in tragedy, however, k is now larger than v, in contrast to the previous two decades; in fact v is less frequent in tragedy (17%) than in comedy (20%), but this is due to the exceptionally large number of examples of x in tragedy (55%): if the x examples are left out of account, the percentage of v is considerably greater in tragedy than in comedy.

I. 1691—1700

In this decade there are 55 examples of H, 51 in comedy and 4 in tragedy. In four of the examples, H is not the sole head-meaning; these four examples are classified HK. Of the 55 examples, none are countables, 39 are uncountables, and 16 are equivocal. The examples are the following.

(a) *The k Group*

Sensitivity to affront, revenging injury, etc.:

Comedy: He is a Fellow of Honour (*Volunteers*, III.1, p. 194). but I suppose you know my Honour is so nice (*Ibid.*, III.1, p. 197).

Carrying a challenge, observing the rules of duelling, etc.:

Comedy: I have more Honour, than to fight (*Volunteers*, III.1, p. 199). You are a Judge of Honour (*Ibid.*, IV.1, p. 212) (IIK). If it be about Honour, Consult with me (*Ibid.*) (HK). You can't in honour refuse to carry him a challenge (*Old Bachelor*, V.2, p. 79).

Recognizing the claims of friendship:

Comedy: my lord's opinion of my honour and honesty (*Double Dealer*, III.1, p. 135).

Protecting a woman's reputation:

Comedy: You look as if you had more honour (*Old Bachelor*, IV.3, p. 58). well, but your honour too (*Double Dealer*, II.1, p. 128). whether I can in honour discover 'em all (*Ibid.*, III.1, p. 137). I have more honour than to tell first (*Love for Love*, I.2, p. 212). you bankrupt in honour, as indigent of wealth (*Way of the World*, II.1, p. 340).

Tragedy: provoke/ A man of honour to expose their fame (*Cleomenes*, V.2, p. 356).

Good manners:

Comedy: a well bred Man, and a Man of honour (*Volunteers*, I.2, p. 175).

Not accepting payment:

Comedy: to imitate our betters in their honour (*Constant Couple*, I.2, p. 146). leave honour to nobility that can support it (*Ibid.*). your honour should be cashiered (*Ibid.*).

Miscellaneous:

Comedy: have too much Honour to do any thing under-hand (*Relapse*, II.1, p. 42) (not concealing one's love-intrigues). thought myself piqu'd in Honour to debauch her (*Ibid.*, III.1, p. 47) (debauching a woman of "an Insolent Vertue"). Virtue consists in Goodness, Honour, Gratitude (*Provoked Wife*, III.1, p. 143) (not clearly specified, but not inconsistent with adultery). That Phantome of Honour (*Ibid.*) (the same).

(b) *The m Group*

Comedy: Honour Madam, Honour must be obey'd (*Volunteers*, II.1, p. 181) (two examples, both HK). What? set aside my Honour (*Ibid.*, IV.1, p. 210). should I quit my honour you'd despise me (*Ibid.*, IV.1, p. 211). I wont quit my Honour for the World (*Ibid.*, V.1, p. 215). for being a Man of Honour (*Ibid.*). she will not suffer me to satisfy my Honour (*Ibid.*). whose Courage dwells more in their Honour, than their Nature (*Provoked Wife*, IV.2, p. 155).

(c) *The v Group*

Keeping one's word:

Comedy: what Love and Honour oblige me to (*Volunteers*, V.1, p. 224) (also not withdrawing from a marriage-contract).

Sexual continence:

Comedy: a thing, our Honour and Religion have forbid us (*Provoked Wife*, I.1, p. 118). to make them look like honour (*Constant Couple*, V.1, p. 207).

Tragedy: Came to the verge of honour, and there stopped (*Love Triumphant*, V.1, p. 471) (incest).

Not being ungrateful:

Comedy: I pleaded honour and nearness of blood (*Double Dealer*, I.1, p. 108).

Miscellaneous:

Comedy: breaches in woman's honour (*Constant Couple*, V.3, p. 220) (not being guilty of lying, perjury, dissembling, etc.).

Tragedy: Still in the paths of honour persevere (*Mourning Bride*, V.3, p. 485) ("virtuous deeds", not "crimes").

(d) *The x Group*

Comedy: well tempered, of great Honour (*Volunteers*, I.1, p. 167). You are a Man of honour (*Ibid.*, II.1, p. 180). He Honour (*Ibid.*, III.1, p. 194). a brave Fellow, and a Fellow of honour (*Ibid.*, III.1, p. 195). He's a man of honour and of sense (*Ibid.*, III.1, p. 196). I am a Person of Honour (*Ibid.*, III.1, p. 198). The same Honour ever shines in all your Actions (*Ibid.*, IV.1, p. 210). his worth, his Honour, and his Fame (*Ibid.*, V.1, p. 216). to doubt the honour of Sir Joseph Wittol (*Old Bachelor*, II.1, p. 24). you are flinging conscience and honour in my face (*Double Dealer*, I.3, p. 115). you may in honour betray her (*Ibid.*, III.1, p. 137). my daughter can in conscience or honour (*Ibid.*, IV.2, p. 155). the least spark, either of Honour or good Nature (*Provoked Wife*, V.2, p. 169). a man of honour, wit, and breeding (*Constant Couple*, III.3, p. 176). there's something of honour in his temper (*Ibid.*, III.5, p. 188). You have too much honour (*Ibid.*, IV.1, p. 191). I rely on your word and honour (*Ibid.*, IV.1, p. 194). If you have love and honour in your soul (*Ibid.*, V.3, p. 226).

Tragedy: Trust my honour (*Love Triumphant*, III.1, p. 419).

(e) *Summary, H 1691—1700*

Table 47 gives a summary of the k/m/v/x classification of H for the decade 1691—1700. The figures are rather small, but it can at any rate be noticed that the k group is the largest, with 39% of the examples; v and m are about the same size, between 10 and 15%, and the x group is rather large, with 35%; there are no examples of km. The percentage of m examples is considerably greater than in the previous decade, and the difference is in fact significant. It should be noticed, however, that seven out of the eight examples of m occur in one play, *The Volunteers*, which is perhaps not characteristic of the decade (cf. p. 199 above); if these examples are neglected, the figure for m becomes comparable with those for the previous two decades. The figures for tragedy are too small for any comparison to be possible between comedy and tragedy.

TABLE 47. *Numbers of k, m, v, and x: H material, 1691—1700.*

	k	m	v	x	Total
Comedy	20	8	5	18	51
Tragedy	1	0	2	1	4
All Plays	21	8	7	19	55

J. Summary, H 1591—1700

As in the R and RH groups, there is an obvious tendency for the k group to grow at the expense of the m and v groups; the tendency is much more strongly marked in comedy than in tragedy. The v group, however, is consistently larger than it is in RH (and *a fortiori* than in R). In the large k groups of the second half of the century, a big part is played by examples connected with the rules of duelling and with sexual libertinism (e. g. protecting the reputation of a woman with whom one commits adultery). There is no significant change in the percentage of examples with joint head-meanings; if, however, the cases of HK are left out of account, then there is a decline of joint head-meanings from about 5.3% in the first half of the century to about 1.7% in the second half, and this is significant. The explanation for this is probably the same as that offered in the case of R (p. 200 above).

CHAPTER 10

Virtue and Convention:
(V) Summary

A. The Changes during the Century

It is unlikely that all the classifications of individual examples given in the last three chapters will meet with universal approval: indeed, it would be impossible to produce a classification that would satisfy everybody. However, there is a solid body of examples where there is not likely to be serious dispute, and it will probably be agreed that my tables provide a sufficiently good working basis for my purposes.

Tables 48 to 51 give a summary of the k/m/v/x classification decade by decade, with columns for the half-centuries and for the grand total. First R, RH, and H are shown separately, and then in the fourth table the figures are given for R, RH, and H combined. In each table, comedy and tragedy are shown separately, and then the combined figures given for all plays together. In each line, the upper figure, (a), gives the number of examples, while the lower figure, (b), gives this as a percentage for that head-meaning and period. A statistical analysis of these tables has been carried out at the Statistical Institute of the University of Gothenburg. In nearly all cases, the k/m/v/x pattern was found to change significantly from one half of the century to the other (period 1591 to 1640 compared with period 1661 to 1700). In each half of the century, moreover, comedy was compared with tragedy, and the three head-meanings were compared with each other, and in these cases too the differences were found to be significant in most cases.[1]

---

[1] The comparison between the two halves of the century gave the following results: Comedy, R significant change, RH just significant change, H significant change; Tragedy, R no significant change, RH significant change, H just significant change. Since all the trends are in the same direction, it is probable that the change in R tragedy is also real. The comparison between comedy and tragedy gave the

TABLE 48. *Frequencies of k, m, v, and x: R material.*

Period from to	1591 1600	1601 1610	1611 1620	1621 1630	1631 1640	1591 1640	1661 1670	1671 1680	1681 1690	1691 1700	1661 1700	Grand Total
Comedy.. k (a)	6	9	23	43	46	127	40	82	31	14	167	294
(b)	16	23	48	51	60	44	68	71	76	47	68	55
m (a)	18	11	11	10	12	62	8	8	6	9	31	93
(b)	49	28	23	12	16	22	14	7	15	30	13	17
v (a)	7	10	2	12	4	35	3	9	0	3	15	50
(b)	19	26	4	14	5	12	5	8	0	10	6	9
x (a)	6	9	12	20	15	62	8	17	4	4	33	95
(b)	16	23	25	24	19	22	14	15	10	13	14	18
Tragedy.. k (a)	19	27	44	27	44	161	12	46	13	3	74	235
(b)	29	35	31	29	44	34	32	46	41	19	40	35
m (a)	30	22	59	26	26	163	16	28	4	6	54	217
(b)	45	29	41	28	26	34	42	28	13	38	29	33
v (a)	9	6	15	11	13	54	4	8	3	3	18	72
(b)	14	8	10	12	13	11	11	8	9	19	10	11
x (a)	8	21	25	29	17	100	6	19	12	4	41	141
(b)	12	28	17	31	17	21	16	19	38	25	22	21
All Plays. k (a)	25	36	67	70	90	288	52	128	44	17	241	529
(b)	24	31	35	39	51	38	54	59	60	37	56	44
m (a)	48	33	70	36	38	225	24	36	10	15	85	310
(b)	47	29	37	20	21	29	25	17	14	33	20	26
v (a)	16	16	17	23	17	89	7	17	3	6	33	122
(b)	16	14	9	13	10	12	7	8	4	13	8	10
x (a)	14	30	37	49	32	162	14	36	16	8	74	236
(b)	14	26	19	28	18	21	14	17	22	17	17	20

(a) Number of examples.
(b) Percentage.

following results: period 1591 to 1640, R significant difference, RH almost significant difference, H no significant difference; period 1661 to 1700, R significant difference, RH no significant difference, H significant difference. In the comparison between R, RH, and H, the differences in k/m/v/x pattern were found to be significant both in the first half of the century and in the second, both in comedy and in tragedy.

TABLE 49. *Frequencies of k, m, v, and x: RH material.*

Period from to			1591 1600	1601 1610	1611 1620	1621 1630	1631 1640	1591 1640	1661 1670	1671 1680	1681 1690	1691 1700	1661 1700	Grand Total
Comedy	k	(a)	1	2	7	6	9	25	12	16	9	4	41	66
		(b)	13	14	50	25	47	32	60	46	47	31	47	40
	m	(a)	1	3	3	2	1	10	3	4	4	3	14	24
		(b)	13	21	21	8	5	13	15	11	21	23	16	14
	v	(a)	3	3	0	8	4	18	1	6	0	0	7	25
		(b)	38	21	0	33	21	23	5	15	0	0	8	15
	x	(a)	3	6	4	8	5	26	4	9	6	6	25	51
		(b)	38	43	29	33	26	33	20	26	32	46	29	31
Tragedy	k	(a)	1	6	3	3	8	21	16	17	8	4	45	66
		(b)	6	32	10	14	30	18	47	33	40	33	38	28
	m	(a)	1	5	12	4	6	28	2	11	0	3	16	44
		(b)	6	26	39	19	22	24	6	21	0	25	14	19
	v	(a)	8	3	4	8	9	32	5	5	4	0	14	46
		(b)	47	16	13	38	33	28	15	10	20	0	12	20
	x	(a)	7	5	12	6	4	34	11	19	8	5	43	77
		(b)	41	26	39	29	15	30	32	37	40	42	36	33
All Plays	k	(a)	2	8	10	9	17	46	28	33	17	8	86	132
		(b)	8	24	22	20	37	23	52	38	44	32	42	33
	m	(a)	2	8	15	6	7	38	5	15	4	6	30	68
		(b)	8	24	33	13	15	20	9	17	10	24	15	17
	v	(a)	11	6	4	16	13	50	6	11	4	0	21	71
		(b)	44	18	9	36	28	26	11	13	10	0	10	18
	x	(a)	10	11	16	14	9	60	15	28	14	11	68	128
		(b)	40	33	36	31	20	31	28	32	36	44	33	32

(a) Number of examples.
(b) Percentage.

If we confine ourselves for the moment to comparisons between the two halves of the century, we shall immediately notice the way in which k increases in frequency and v decreases in frequency during the century: in every single section of the tables, the percentage of k goes up and the percentage of v goes down. This is shown in a different form in Table 52, which gives the k/v ratio (i. e. the quotient of k divided by v) for each half of the century.

TABLE 50. *Frequencies of k, m, v, and x: H material.*

Period from to			1591 1600	1601 1610	1611 1620	1621 1630	1631 1640	1591 1640	1661 1670	1671 1680	1681 1690	1691 1700	1661 1700	Grand Total
Comedy..	k	(a)	1	3	4	3	9	20	47	71	34	20	172	192
		(b)	13	17	19	15	32	21	56	64	45	39	54	46
	m	(a)	0	3	4	1	0	8	0	1	0	8	9	17
		(b)	0	17	19	5	0	8	0	1	0	16	3	4
	v	(a)	3	8	9	10	8	38	19	15	15	5	54	92
		(b)	38	44	43	50	29	40	23	14	20	10	17	22
	x	(a)	4	4	4	6	11	29	18	24	26	18	86	115
		(b)	50	22	19	30	39	31	21	22	35	35	27	28
Tragedy..	k	(a)	2	9	5	1	8	25	14	17	7	1	39	64
		(b)	15	20	9	5	23	15	33	26	24	25	28	21
	m	(a)	0	8	3	3	2	16	1	3	1	0	5	21
		(b)	0	17	6	14	6	9	2	5	3	0	4	7
	v	(a)	6	20	22	11	8	67	18	20	5	2	45	112
		(b)	46	43	42	50	23	40	43	31	17	50	32	36
	x	(a)	5	9	23	7	17	61	9	25	16	1	51	112
		(b)	38	20	43	32	49	36	21	38	55	25	36	36
All Plays.	k	(a)	3	12	9	4	17	45	61	88	41	21	211	256
		(b)	14	19	12	10	27	17	48	50	39	38	46	35
	m	(a)	0	11	7	4	2	24	1	4	1	8	14	38
		(b)	0	17	9	10	3	9	1	2	1	15	3	5
	v	(a)	9	28	31	21	16	105	37	35	20	7	99	204
		(b)	43	44	42	50	25	40	29	20	19	13	21	28
	x	(a)	9	13	27	13	28	90	27	49	42	19	137	227
		(b)	43	20	36	31	44	34	21	28	40	35	30	31

(a) Number of examples.
(b) Percentage.

This growth of k at the expense of v means that the code of honour, as depicted in the drama, moves further away from the Christian ideals of the time. Even in the first half of the century, k is more frequent than v (total k/v ratio 1.55), but in the second half of the century it becomes very much more frequent (total k/v ratio 3.5); so a code that was only partly consonant with Christianity (as interpreted by the age) became very much less consonant with it. The change is much more

VIRTUE AND CONVENTION: SUMMARY

TABLE 51. *Frequencies of k, m, v, and x: combined R, RH, and H material.*

Period from to	1591–1600	1601–1610	1611–1620	1621–1630	1631–1640	1591–1640	1661–1670	1671–1680	1681–1690	1691–1700	1661–1700	Grand Total
Comedy .. k (a)	8	14	34	52	64	172	99	169	74	38	380	552
(b)	15	20	41	40	52	37	61	64	55	40	58	50
m (a)	19	17	18	13	13	80	11	13	10	20	54	134
(b)	36	24	22	10	10	17	7	5	7	21	8	12
v (a)	13	21	11	30	16	91	23	30	15	8	76	167
(b)	25	30	13	23	13	20	14	11	11	9	12	15
x (a)	13	19	20	34	31	117	30	50	36	28	144	261
(b)	25	27	24	26	25	25	18	19	27	30	22	23
Tragedy .. k (a)	22	42	52	31	60	207	42	80	28	8	158	365
(b)	23	30	23	23	37	27	37	37	35	25	36	30
m (a)	31	35	74	33	34	207	19	42	5	9	75	282
(b)	32	25	33	24	21	27	17	19	6	28	17	23
v (a)	23	29	41	30	30	153	27	33	12	5	77	230
(b)	24	21	18	22	19	20	24	15	15	16	17	19
x (a)	20	35	60	42	38	195	26	63	36	10	135	330
(b)	21	25	26	31	25	26	23	29	44	31	30	27
All Plays. k (a)	30	56	86	83	124	379	141	249	102	46	538	917
(b)	20	26	28	31	43	31	51	52	47	37	49	40
m (a)	50	52	92	46	47	287	30	55	15	29	129	416
(b)	34	24	30	17	16	23	11	11	7	23	12	18
v (a)	36	50	52	60	46	244	50	63	27	13	153	397
(b)	24	23	17	23	16	20	18	13	13	10	14	17
x (a)	33	54	80	76	69	312	56	113	72	38	279	591
(b)	22	25	26	29	24	26	20	24	33	30	25	25

(a) Number of examples.
(b) Percentage.

marked in comedy than in tragedy; in total, the change in comedy is from 1.9 to 5.0, while in tragedy it is from 1.35 to 2.1, i. e. an increase of about 160% compared with one of about 55%. I take this to indicate an increased discrepancy between people as they really were, and as they liked to imagine themselves. Their idealized self-portrait became more remote from the Christian ideal (more remote even than the *reality* of the earlier period), but their true code changed even more

TABLE 52. *The k/v ratio in the two halves of the century.*

		1591—1640	1661—1700
Comedy	R	3.6	11.1
	RH	1.4	5.9
	H	0.53	3.2
Tragedy	R	3.0	4.1
	RH	0.66	3.2
	H	0.37	0.87

rapidly, and the points at which it overlapped with Christian morality became almost negligible. I take the findings to support the view advanced earlier, namely that the increased emphasis on honour as a code of conduct, and the rise of the head-meaning H, were part of a process whereby the gentry (or a part of them) developed a distinctive code of behaviour to mark themselves off from the rest of society, and especially from the professional and commercial classes (lawyers, merchants, tradesmen) and from those with puritanical leanings. If this is so, it may be thought strange that the percentage of v is consistently higher in H than in R (while RH, as might be expected, is intermediate). Part at least of the explanation for this lies in the fact that there are certain types of k content in R which are not found in H, because they are contents to which H, by the very nature of things, does not lend itself. Two especially are prominent: R arising from high rank, and reflected R, the first of which is fairly common in the first half of the century, and the second of which is extremely common in the second half. There is no quality of character corresponding to the R arising from high rank or to the R lost when a female relative is unchaste.

It will be seen from the tables that k does not grow only at the expense of v; there is also a marked decline in m. With only one exception (RH comedy), the percentage of m everywhere falls in the second half of the century; the exception is not a very compelling one, for the amount of material involved is small, and in any case it is to be observed that even here the k/m ratio increases, even though the percentage of m rises. If we take the overall figures (Table 51), it is seen that the percentage of m falls from 23% in the first half of the century to 12% in the second — almost to half. The fall is greater in comedy (from 17%

to 8%) than in tragedy (from 27% to 17%), and m is also considerably more frequent in tragedy than in comedy. The decline of m must mean that the upper-class ideal came to place less emphasis on military qualities; honour became less concerned with warfare, and more concerned with personal and family matters (duelling, chastity, love-intrigues). I suggest that this is, at least in part, a reflection of a change in the nature and the occupations of the aristocracy, a change that went on from the end of the Middle Ages and which can be considered complete by the end of the 17th century: the change from the feudal magnate, whose castle was his home, and whose occupation and recreation was war, to the pleasure-loving town aristocrat, who might if he wished play a part in public life, but who had no *necessary* social function. Admittedly the old feudal aristocracy hardly existed in its medieval form at the end of the 16th century, and Kelso (among others) has emphasized the change in the gentlemanly ideal in the 16th century, and the importance of the new humanist education for the Tudor administrator;[1]) but even the Tudor nobleman, with his retinue of followers, his large household, and the essential part he played in public life,[2]) was very different from the idle rich of the Restoration period; and interest in the military art may have declined in sixteenth-century England, but young blades still went off jauntily to war "in search of honor".[3]) During the seventeenth century, moreover, warfare became professionalized, and armies became, much more than previously, the highly drilled machines of the state;[4]) by the end of the century, therefore, there must have been considerably less scope for a gentleman's personal military initiative, and for personal military glory.

The fact that the decline of m is greater in comedy than in tragedy presumably means, once again, that the gap widened between people as they really were and as they would have liked to imagine themselves: the ideal hero of Restoration tragedy attached greater importance to military honour than did the Restoration gentleman who admired him. The percentage of m in Restoration tragedy is the same as that in the comedy of the earlier period: the idealized portrait of the second half of the century approximates to the reality of the first half. The decline

---

[1]) *Op. cit.*, Chapters I and IV.
[2]) See Salingar, "The Social Setting", pp. 28—9.
[3]) Kelso, *op. cit.*, pp. 44—9.
[4]) See Clark, *The Seventeenth Century*, pp. 102—114.

in m cannot simply be explained in terms of change of subject-matter; this may play a part in comedy, but hardly in tragedy, where warfare continues to be a prominent subject. Dryden, for example, considered that[1])

> an heroic play ought to be an imitation, in little, of an heroic poem; and consequently that love and valour ought to be the subject of it.

This represents the view of his age in general; love, indeed, tends to be the dominant theme, but nearly always there is at least a background of war and military heroism; in fact tragedies without a military background are probably commoner in the first half of the century than in the second (e. g. *The Changeling, The White Devil, Romeo and Juliet, 'Tis Pity She's a Whore*). Nevertheless the percentage of m sinks, so it seems reasonable to conclude that military qualities and achievements came to play a smaller part in the ideal of honour. Not much can be said about km, as there are only 35 examples. As a fraction of the R/RH/H group, km is more frequent in the first half of the century than in the second, and for comedy the difference is significant. It is commonest in the period 1611—1640, when "duelling k" is on the upswing but m has not yet much declined.

The tendency, then, is for k to increase in frequency, and for v and m to decrease. No such clear tendency is shown by x; its percentage rises in some sections, and falls in others, and the change is usually small compared to that in the other groups; only in one place (R comedy) is the change in x at all considerable. Most of the changes are probably mere random fluctuations.

So far we have been considering only the differences between the totals for the two halves of the century, but it is also worth looking at the figures for the separate decades. A study of these suggests very strongly that the changes that we have discovered between the two halves of the century took place during the earlier period, not during the later; they can usually be seen going on more or less continuously from 1591 to 1640, but not after 1660. The curves, of course, are not always very smooth, but this is not to be expected: the figures are much smaller than when we were considering the two half-centuries, and random fluctuations obviously play a bigger part. Moreover, there are at least two factors at work to interfere with the smoothness of

---

[1]) *Conquest of Granada.1*, Preface.

the curve; the first is an element of uncertainty in the dating of some of the plays, especially in the first half of the century: plays with extremely disputed dates have not been admitted, but even so there are a number of plays which ought perhaps to be moved a decade one way or the other, or which may have been submitted to revision before publication; the second factor is the operation of temporary factors (local or topical interest) which may in a given decade be sufficient to counteract the current trend; the startling increase of m in the decade 1691—1700 may be a case of this type: interest in a military campaign, and perhaps an attempt to rouse enthusiasm for it, lead to an emphasis on the military elements in honour; there is a similar case in the early 1620's, when the war hysteria against Spain which marked those years is clearly reflected in some of the plays, especially Massinger's *Maid of Honour* and *Bondman* (in the former play Massinger very closely reproduces the situation of James I and his nephew Frederick, the Elector Palatine, in a thin Sicilian disguise, and in effect incites England to go to war on behalf of Frederick and his lost Bohemian kingdom); in this case, however, the crop of m examples thus produced is insufficient to countervail the general falling trend. If these disturbing factors are remembered, it will be seen that in many cases the trends of the first half of the century are remarkably clear; in some cases these trends can also be seen continuing in the Restoration period, at least for the first two decades. For example, the rise of k in comedy gives an extremely smooth curve in the R material, with the percentages 16, 23, 48, 51, and 60, continuing in the Restoration period with 68, 71, and 76 (but showing the characteristic reversal of the trend in the final decade, with 47); the curve is less smooth in the RH and H material, where there are fewer examples, but in the total material there is again a smooth curve, with percentages of 15, 20, 41, 40, and 52, continuing in the Restoration period with 61 and 64. Similar trends (rising for k, falling for v and m) can be found in other sections, and in cases where the trend does not emerge clearly from the figures for the separate decades, it can often be demonstrated by comparing the period 1591 to 1610 with the period 1611 to 1640. It therefore seems reasonable to conclude that the differences seen between the two halves of the century are not something that happened suddenly during the Commonwealth, or on the return of the cavalier exiles from France, but are the product of a continuous process going on throughout the first half of the century. The figures suggest that the most rapid change went on round about 1610—1620, though for m it may have been earlier, round about 1600.[1])

The trends in the second half of the century are not so well marked, and in many ways we seem to have reached a plateau. In some cases the decade 1661—1670 shows a continuation of the trends of the first half of the century, but in other cases it is at about the same level as the decade 1631—1640 (as though the curve had flattened off during the Commonwealth period). Sometimes the trend of the first half of the century continues through two or even three decades of the Restoration period, and then flattens off. The general impression one gets is that the trends seen in the first half of the century continue up to about 1660 or 1670, and that stabilization then takes place at about the level which has been reached. There is even a suggestion of a reversal of the trends in the last two decades of the century, and this is especially strongly marked in the last decade; the apparent change, however, may be largely illusory (see Appendix E). In any case the apparent reversal of trends does not affect v, which continues to decline.

B. The k Group

It can be seen from Chapters 7 to 9 that a large part is played in the k group by duelling honour. In this I include the group that I have called "sensitivity to insult", the non-toleration of rivals in love, and the observance of the various rules of duelling. If a gentleman is insulted or injured in any way, honour demands that he shall take revenge; if the wronger is a gentleman, he must challenge him to a duel; if he is not a gentleman, or if he refuses to fight, the injured party may resort to cudgelling him (no gentleman with a sense of honour will of course tolerate this, but will fight). In some cases reconciliation may be

---

[1]) The analysis by the Statistical Institute also included a comparison of the period 1591 to 1610 with the period 1611 to 1640. R, RH, and H were considered separately, and so were comedy and tragedy. A significant change in the k/m/v/x pattern was found for R in comedy, and a nearly significant change for H in tragedy; in the remaining sections the change was not significant. Since the material for the comparison was small, especially for RH and H, it is not surprising that so many of the results were negative. However, since similar trends are seen in R, RH, and H, both in comedy and in tragedy, it seems legitimate to argue from R comedy and H tragedy to the other sections, and assume that there too the changes seen in the first half of the century are real.

achieved, for example by apology, or by the righting of the wrong done; but these matters are extremely delicate, because neither party is willing to appear to be frightened or to be yielding under pressure, and when things have reached a certain stage a duel is often more or less inevitable, because neither side can cry off without fear of loss of honour; the situation is seen in parody in *Twelfth Night*, in the duel between Viola and Ague-cheek ("the Gentleman will for his honors sake haue one bowt with you: he cannot by the Duello auoide it"); but it occurs often enough in deadly earnest. Revenge of course sometimes takes other forms than duelling; an insult from one monarch to another may be avenged by war; and a man who has been wronged by his sovereign or by a man of great power may resort to murder; however, it should be noted that it is rare for secret revenge of this kind to be carried out in the name of honour: the villain-heroes of Revenge Tragedy do not usually have honour on their lips as a motive for their deeds; still less is it normal (as it apparently was in Spain)[1] for secret vengeance for honour to be carried out on a rival who is not in a position of power. Nor is it normal to hire banditti to do your fighting for you, in the Italian style. The English gentleman whose honour is wronged tends to demand satisfaction from his wronger with the sword; and the non-English heroes of the English drama usually do the same.

The other groups have been commented on earlier: being a rival in love is sometimes in itself sufficient motive for duelling; and a gentleman must observe certain rules about duelling (accepting and carrying challenges, acting as a second when asked, not evading the duty of duelling, fighting under fair conditions, etc.). If all these types of duelling honour are taken together (roughly, the first three items on the list on pp. 140—143 above), the examples concerned are found to amount to no less than 37% of all the examples of k. There is not much difference between R, RH, and H. Nearly everywhere, the percentage is higher in comedy than in tragedy, in total 42% against 30%. In total there is no appreciable change (as a percentage of k) with time: there is a rise from 37% in the first half-century to 37.4% in the second, but this is negligible statistically. But on the other hand the k group itself grows considerably during the century, from 31% of

---

[1] See E. M. Wilson, "Family Honour", pp. 19—20; Castro, *op. cit.*, pp. 25—6.

all examples of the R/RH/H group in the first half-century to 49%
in the second; simultaneously, it will be remembered, the R/RH/H
group itself increases in frequency from 9.6 examples per play to 13.9.
While, therefore, the percentage of duelling examples remains stationary
with respect to the k group, this in fact means that they increase considerably in relation to the R/RH/H group, and increase even more in
absolute frequency (number of examples per play): in absolute terms,
in fact, they more than double.

This suggests that, among the theatre-going classes, there was an
increased interest in duelling during the 17th century, and this accords
with the evidence produced by Bowers,[1]) who shows that there was
a great increase in duelling in England after the accession of James I.
Bowers suggests several possible reasons for this, but takes the view
that it was mainly due to the influx of Scots into London with the new
sovereign; the Scots were a more primitive people, among whom the
traditions of the blood-feud were still strongly rooted, and moreover
the inevitable jealousy between Scots and English increased the number
of quarrels. This may well have been an aggravating circumstance,
but it is not a convincing explanation of the great popularity of duelling
throughout the century; it can only have been a transient influence,
but Bowers himself points out that even Cromwell had to issue a proclamation against duelling, that Charles II wrote two orders against it,
and that it continued without abatement into the eighteenth century;
if my own material can be trusted, the upper classes were even more
interested in duelling in the Restoration period than they had been
in the reign of James I. Other causes suggested by Bowers are the
inability of James I, compared with Elizabeth, to control his courtiers
(another transient influence), the influence of French and Italian practice, and the increased emphasis on court life, with courtiers competing
for favour and jealous of their prerogatives. To these I would add
another possible cause: an upper-class desire to have a kind of classjustice outside the law-courts, which were in the hands of people who
were not always of gentle birth. I have already suggested that the upper
classes had good reasons for wishing to mark themselves off from the
rest of society by their own moral code; it is not strange, therefore,
that in their dealings with one another they should also disregard the

---

[1]) *Op. cit.*, pp. 30—34. See also Clark, *The Later Stuarts*, pp. 403—4.

legal code of the rest of society as something beneath their notice. Upholders of the duel often maintain that it is a kind of justice, and Bowers cites one of them as writing:[1])

> Since no one shall judge of honour but him who has it, the judges of civil courts (who are base in their origin) are unfitted for the duty.

In other words, members of the aristocracy are unwilling to submit themselves to law-courts run by people of plebeian origin. Perhaps the political conflicts of the century are behind this once again: the more the courtier feels himself in opposition to other parts of society, the less willing he will be to have his actions judged by anybody outside his own circle. I therefore suggest that the increased emphasis on duelling-honour is another aspect of the process of isolation of the courtier class, and their development of a group morality opposed to that of the rest of society.

Another prominent group of examples, which is closely related to duelling honour, is that where reputation is lost by the unchastity of a wife or female relative; it is also lost if one's fiancée is unchaste (with another man) or if one's wife is discovered to have been unchaste before marriage. The man's conduct may have been quite beyond reproach, but he nevertheless loses honour (R) on these occasions. It is not always easy to distinguish this "reflected honour" from duelling-honour (sensitivity to affront, willingness to take revenge, etc.), since the seduction of a female relative is an imperative ground for challenging the seducer. The difference between the two types lies in the point of view from which the matter is considered; in the "reflected" type, attention is concentrated on the disgrace which accrues to the man simply from the fact of the relative's unchastity, quite apart from any action which he may feel called upon to take in the matter; in the "duelling" type, attention is concentrated on the fact that the man has suffered an affront or injury, and must take revenge in order to maintain his reputation. In both types, honour may be regained or "repaired" by the marriage of the woman to the seducer, and in this case a duel may be avoided; when it is a wife who is unchaste, however, there is no such possibility, and for a man of honour there is no alternative to challenging the seducer. It is not common in the English drama,

---

[1]) *Op. cit.*, p. 33.

as apparently it was in the Spanish,[1]) for revenge also to be taken upon the unchaste woman; in my material, there are only half a dozen places where honour is said to demand the killing of an unchaste wife or female relative, and even fewer where she is in fact killed; the faithless wife may be sent to a nunnery, she may be divorced, she may commit suicide, she may perhaps be forgiven, or even continue to carry out her wifely duties unforgiven, but she is not usually murdered; Othello is the exception, not the rule, in English drama.

Most of these examples of reflected honour are classified as R; there are a few RH, and one example of H (meaning "concern about this kind of R"). There is a marked increase in the frequency of the type in the second half of the century. If we consider only R, which is the meaning most concerned, we find that they rise from 11% of the k group in the first half of the century to 29% in the second half. If we take the figures for the whole R/RH/H material, the rise does not look so striking, but it is still substantial, from 10% of the k group to 14%; and here again we must remember that the k group itself expands considerably during the century, and that the R/RH/H group increases greatly in absolute frequency, so that in absolute terms this type of "reflected" honour increases very greatly. There are no great differences between comedy and tragedy.

The expansion of this type of "reflected R", like that of duelling honour, is part of the shift of interest in the code of honour from public matters to private and family matters, and may be related to the tendency in the 17th century for the aristocracy to lose the obvious public and political functions that they still had under the Tudors.[2]) In the growth of "reflected R", a part is also obviously played by Restoration libertinism; with so many wolves on the prowl, men developed a ferocious defensive attitude about their wives and sisters; the ridiculous thing is that the outraged gallant challenging the seducer of his sister is often busily engaged in the seduction of other men's sisters; the contradiction arises from the double standard of morality, one for men and another for women. The Restoration cult of libertinism may itself be due in part to the decline of the public function of the aristocracy; the ideal

---

[1]) See E. M. Wilson, "Family Honour", pp. 19—20; Castro, *op. cit.*, pp. 25—9.

[2]) See Knights, *Drama and Society*, pp. 111—17. It has been remarked by G. N. Clark that, in the Restoration period, the gentry lost enthusiasm for the work of local government (*The Later Stuarts*, p. 16).

of a "life of pleasure" is obviously a suitable one for a class lacking a social function but possessed of a good deal of money.

Another group that is much larger in the second half of the century than in the first is that connected with sexual libertinism: sexual virility, constancy to an adulterous mistress, keeping illicit assignations, etc.. Some of these usages probably arose from the meaning "keeping one's word", especially in the phrase "man of honour"; in the Restoration period, gallants often say "You will find me a man of honour", meaning "I will keep my promise — to give you sexual satisfaction, to keep my assignation with you, etc."; often this is intended to sound witty, but it nevertheless reflects faithfully enough the ethos of the gallants who say it. Since a man of honour can also be one who does *not* seduce, an ambiguity arises which is useful to women who attach more importance to reputation than to chastity; a married woman being courted by a Restoration rake sometimes says in effect, "I don't really know whether I ought to come into this arbour with you, as you suggest; are you a man of honour?"; the rake replies, "I assure you that I am a man of honour, madam; come in and I will demonstrate the fact to you". This enables the woman to seem to refuse (thus keeping up appearances) while in reality accepting and even encouraging the man's advances.[1]) This favourite use of the phrase "man of honour" (where honour is obviously H, not R) perhaps explains why the increase in this usage is greater in H than in R and RH. In total, the group increases from 1.3% of k in the first half of the century to 6.5% in the second, but if H is considered alone the increase is from 0% to 13%. As could be expected, nearly all the examples are in comedy, and the usage is rare in tragedy.

A related content is the protecting of the reputation of a woman with whom you have an illicit affair, especially if she is a gentlewoman; a man of honour never talks or boasts about his conquests, and does everything in his power to prevent the woman from being exposed and losing her reputation. This type is not found at all in R, which is very natural, since secrecy is the essence of the thing; there is one example classified as RH, and 25 as H. It is interesting that every single one of these 26 examples is in the second half of the century, and there is not one in the pre-Commonwealth period; one might almost, therefore,

---

[1]) For a clear example, see *The Virtuoso,* Act III Sc. 1.

regard this as the rise of a new meaning. The causes of this development are obviously the same as those of the "sexual virility" group. Only two of the examples are in tragedy, but the number of examples of H in tragedy is very small, and the difference between comedy and tragedy is in fact not here significant. (This means of course that the material available is not sufficient in quantity for the question to be decided.)

Another content that increases in importance inside the k group is that relating to the claims of friendship. It is not a particularly large group, accounting in total only for about 3% of the k examples, but there may in fact be other examples which ought to be classified here (including some in the v group), since it is a somewhat difficult content to detect. The examples I have in fact classified under this heading are found in R, in RH, and in H, but are least frequent in R and most frequent in H. They occur both in comedy and in tragedy, but are rather more frequent in the former. Only three of the examples are found in the first half of the century, while 24 are found in the second half; this means an increase from 0.8% to 4.5% of the total k group; the increase is most strongly marked in H. The friendship group is another example of the increase in frequency of contents related to private and personal matters, as contrasted with public ones.

All the k contents so far considered have either increased in importance during the century or remained stationary (which also means a net increase in importance owing to the expansion of the k group itself); there is one group, however, which clearly declines in importance: reputation for high rank, and some related types. The "high rank" content occurs only in R; in the first half of the century, it constitutes quite an important part of the Rk group, in fact 15% of it, with 44 examples, but there is a catastrophic decline in the second half of the century to 1.7% (only four examples). It is considerably more frequent in tragedy than in comedy, and the decline takes place in both. The decline is so great that it far outweighs the increase caused by the expansion of the k group, and the decline is in fact an absolute one. It may seem strange that this group should decline, since the Restoration aristocracy certainly attached great importance to social rank; it should be noted, however, that this content is not one which is directly a determinant of behaviour, and the great expansion of the R/RH/H group during the century is primarily in contents which are: the increased emphasis on honour is on honour as a code of conduct; secondly, it should be noted that this content is one that is connected with public and political life, and not with the personal and family matters which honour comes increasingly to be concerned with during the century. These are not explanations, of course, but rather restatements of what happened in other terms: but they will perhaps make it clear that the decline of the "high rank" group is consistent with the other trends we have seen in the century, and not as surprising as might seem at first sight.

There are also declines in two related groups: ostentation, and making socially good marriages. Both occur mainly in R, and mainly in comedy, and decline considerably during the century. Ostentation includes living up to one's income and to one's position, and is closely related to the idea of rank; it can be considered as another of the more public and political contents. The making of "good" marriages is obviously more of a family affair, but it too has political aspects, and is also closely related to the idea of social rank. I take the decline in these two groups, and the decline in the "high rank" group, to be caused, at any rate in part, by the declining part in public life played by the nobility and their followers. The Tudor magnate was very much a public figure, and the greater part of his life was lived in public; his housekeeping, his liberality, his ostentation, were part of his public life, and largely political in aim. The Restoration nobleman often lived lavishly, had an eye for effect, and perhaps played a part in public life (though not as inevitably as his Tudor ancestor); but "housekeeping" in the 16th century sense had disappeared, and the great man no longer felt obliged to maintain enormous bands of followers or to indulge in "magnificence" as an essential part of his career.[1]

C. The v Group

Less can be said about the v group, because the number of examples is considerably smaller than in the k group, and it is therefore much harder to draw any safe conclusions. A few points may be noted about its composition, however.

---

[1] Moreover, he could no longer afford such display; see Tawney, *op. cit.*, pp. 8—10. But for a different view, see Trevor-Roper, *The Gentry 1540—1640*, pp. 4—8, 33.

The "truthfulness" group constitutes about 8% of the v group, and shows no change with time. The group concerned with keeping promises, vows, and oaths is about the same size in total (or slightly larger), but this group shows a considerable change with time, being about three times as large in the second half of the century as in the first (considered as a fraction of the v group); this increase is more than enough to outweigh the shrinking of the v group itself; it seems that it became commoner to strengthen or confirm a promise by solemnly affirming it on one's honour; and it will be remembered that it is in the second half of the century that the head-meaning W first appears. The type is fairly evenly distributed among the three head-meanings, and between comedy and tragedy.

The group connected with loyalty to civil governors (not committing treason, not rebelling, serving the best interests of your sovereign, etc.) accounts for about 14% of the v group, and is rather commoner in tragedy than in comedy. There is no change with time. A content that is often linked with this one, "not murdering", shows a decline from about 6% to about 4% of the v group; this content is also commoner in tragedy than in comedy.

The group "not conniving at unchastity" falls from about 8% to about 5% of the v group; it is found in all three head-meanings and in both comedy and tragedy. On the other hand, the group labelled "sexual continence" increases from about 15% of the v group in the first half of the century to about 20% in the second half. This may seem rather surprising, especially as the group is as well represented in comedy as in tragedy. However, it should be noticed that the group includes "not raping" and "not committing incest", and even the Restoration rake does not normally view rape and incest with favour; moreover, a large number of the examples (nearly half of those in the Restoration period) are spoken by women: at a time when there is a double standard of sexual morality (being a man of honour can mean either "being a good wencher" or "not attempting to seduce, courting with the intention of marrying") the women will obviously attempt to enforce the interpretation which is consistent with their interests and with their own code (C). Finally, it should be remembered that the increase of the group as a percentage of the v group does not constitute an absolute increase, since the v group itself declines; in terms of the R/RH/H group, the "sexual continence" group in fact shows no appreciable change with time.

It may be thought that there is no very clear distinction between this sexual continence group and another head-meaning, C. I do not normally include examples under C when the possessor is a man; when a man is concerned, the main emphasis is not in fact usually on chastity, but on (for example) keeping one's word, acting in good faith, etc.; often the man of honour is one who courts a girl with the genuine intention of marrying her, and not simply in the hope of seducing her, and he may attach no importance to male chastity as such, may in fact have mistresses. Similarly, he may feel that honour forbids him to commit rape or incest, without feeling that honour demands complete male chastity. All these types would come under my "sexual continence" heading. It will be noticed, however, that there are also a few cases in the group where a woman is the possessor; these are cases where, although the behaviour demanded in fact includes sexual continence, the content is considerably wider (including, perhaps, gratitude, obedience to a husband, etc.), or where it seems clear that "honour" does not mean "chastity" as such. An example can be given from *The Virtuoso*; Lady Gimcrack, a married woman, is making very obvious advances to Bruce, a young gallant:

> your perfections are so prevalent, that were I not in honour engag'd unto Sir *Nicholas* (and Honour has the greatest Ascendent in the World upon me) I assure you I would not venture my self alone with such a person: But honour's a great matter, a great thing, I'll vow and swear.
> (III.1, p. 135)

Sir Nicholas is her husband, and it is extremely difficult to interpret the first example of honour ("in honour engag'd") as "chastity", even though chastity is the conduct demanded; she means rather, "By marrying Sir Nicholas I have undertaken to reserve myself for him, and it wouldn't be fair to him to give away his property". The other two examples lend themselves more easily to the C interpretation, but even here it seems more natural to give them a wider interpretation, as they are inevitably influenced by the foregoing example; Lady Gimcrack, moreover, certainly does not intend to give Bruce the impression that she attaches overmuch importance to chastity.

There are no other sub-groups of any size in the v group. It is perhaps worth noticing that there are two contents that occur only in the first half of the century, and not in the second: "not being revengeful", and "piety"; but the numbers involved are too small for much emphasis to be given to this.

D. The growth of n

It was seen in chapter 5 that, in both R and RH, there is an increase during the century of the percentage of examples with n, and a decrease of those with g; the possessors of honour became more defensive, more concerned with good name and less with glory. In the material given in Chapters 7 and 8 it will have become obvious that this rise of n is closely correlated with the rise of k; the large k group that appears in the second half of the century consists predominantly of examples of Rnk, while Rgk is relatively rare. It seems interesting to enquire whether the increase in n is solely due to the k group, or whether there is a parallel change in the other groups. To answer this question, I have examined the percentages of n, g and u in the two halves of the century for m, v, and x separately. In the RH material, there is in every case an increase in the percentage of n and a decrease in the percentage of

TABLE 53. *Numbers and frequencies of n, g, and u in the m, v, and x groups. R and RH material combined, All Plays.*

	1591 to 1640			1661 to 1700		
	n	g	u	n	g	u
m (a)	24	174	65	13	82	20
(b)	9.1	66	25	11	71	17
v (a)	102	13	24	49	2	3
(b)	73	9.4	17	91	3.7	5.6
x (a)	78	55	89	73	16	53
(b)	35	25	40	51	11	37
Total (a)	204	242	178	135	100	76
(b)	33	39	29	43	32	24

(a) Number of examples.
(b) Percentage.

g during the century; this is also true of the R material as far as v and x are concerned, but in the Rm group the reverse is true (i. e. the percentage of n falls and of g increases); if the R material and the RH material are combined, then the m group too is found to give a net increase in the n/g ratio, although both n and g in fact increase at the expense of u. I shall not reproduce the figures for R and RH separately (all the material is in any case available in the tables in Chapters 7 and 8), but in Table 53 I give the figures for the combined R and RH material.

It will be seen that, in total, the n/g ratio changes from 0.85 in the first half of the century to 1.34 in the second; this change is not very large compared with that in the k group (which is actually from 3.9 in the first half of the century to 20.2 in the second), but is nevertheless significant. It can therefore be concluded that the increasingly defensive attitude towards honour that developes during the century, and the reduced emphasis on glory, are not confined to the k group, but are characteristic of R and RH as a whole.

E. Contemporary Comments

The changes surveyed in this chapter constitute a considerable modification of honour as a code of conduct; during the century, the behaviour demanded by honour came to overlap less with Christian virtue; greater emphasis was placed on revenge and duelling; "reflected" reputation was accorded greater importance, i. e. reputation not primarily dependent on the behaviour of the man himself, but on the behaviour of others, especially his womenfolk; military qualities and military glory receded into the background; the attitude to reputation became more defensive, the preservation of good name being given much greater emphasis than the acquiring of glory; and in general honour came to be more concerned with private and family matters and less with public and political matters. These changes are found both in comedy and in tragedy, but to a greater extent in the former; I interpret this as meaning that the idealized self-portrait and real practice both changed, but that practice changed more. If this is correct, and the behaviour demanded by honour really did change in English society in the ways suggested (at least among the theatre-going classes), then one might well expect to find some comment on this fact in the drama of the time. There are of course many discussions of honour in the drama I have used as material; for example, there is the long lecture by the King to Bertram in *All's Well*, on the relation between high rank and honourableness, between inherited and acquired honour; the honour appropriate to women is often deliberately contrasted with the honour appropriate to men, especially when a woman is resisting seduction; and so on. The comment we should expect on these changes would be of a somewhat different type, however; one would rather expect it to be a protest, asserting that nowadays so-and-so is commonly believed to constitute honour, but of course honour is *really* so-and-so — it would in fact be a definition of "true honour"; the points it would make would cover the kind of changes we have seen — for example the increased prominence of duelling and private revenge and the diminished emphasis on war and public service; and it would not be surprising if it compared the good old days with the degenerate present. One would expect the protest to take place at a time when the changes were proceeding sufficiently fast and had gone sufficiently far to be quite obvious, but when the earlier conditions were still sufficiently close to be remembered; we have seen that the changes in the k/m/v/x groups probably proceeded continuously throughout the first half of the century (cf. pp. 270—272 above); by about 1630 the change must have been quite considerable, but the reign of Elizabeth was still in living memory, and this would not be at all an unlikely time for protest to occur. The protest could be expected to come from an older man, who could remember and who admired the ideals of the earlier part of the century, whereas the young would only be likely to know what they had been brought up in.

It is a remarkable fact that, in my material, I have found, not one, but no less than three protests that come very close to the conditions sketched above; they are all quite large-scale set-pieces, so that their purpose is unmistakable; they all occur within a period of a few years; and I have found nothing comparable to them in other periods in my material. The plays in which they occur are *The Broken Heart, The New Inn*, and *A Very Woman*, probably to be dated 1629, 1629, and 1634.[1]) The authors are Ford, Jonson, and Massinger; the last two

---

[1]) It is interesting that 1630 is the date of Richard Brathwaite's *The English Gentleman*, which emphasizes Christian ideals for the gentleman, and opposes duelling; see Ustick, *op. cit.*, pp. 154—6. Ustick, however, looks on this as something new, and seems to underestimate the Christian elements in the Tudor ideal.

had both grown up in the reign of Elizabeth, and were in their fifties when they wrote these plays; Ford was younger, but he was probably in his 'teens when Elizabeth died, and in his forties when he wrote *The Broken Heart*.

The passage in *The Broken Heart* consists of a lecture by Tecnicus, a philosopher, to Orgilus, a young nobleman, on the nature of true honour. Tecnicus suspects, rightly, that Orgilus is meditating a violent revenge on his enemies, and questions him closely; Orgilus protests the innocence of his intentions, and asserts that he has no single thought or inclination inconsistent with his honour; whereupon Tecnicus launches into his homily:

>   I beleeue it.
> But know then *Orgilus* what honour is:
> Honour consists not in a bare opinion
> By doing any act that feeds content;
> Braue in appearance, 'cause we thinke it braue:
> Such honour comes by accident, not nature
> Proceeding from the vices of our passion
> Which makes our reason drunke. But reall Honour
> Is the reward of vertue, and acquir'd
> By Iustice or by valour, which for Bases
> Hath Iustice to vphold it. He then failes
> In honour, who for lucre of Reuenge
> Commits thefts, murthers, Treasons and Adulteries,
> With such like, by intrenching on iust Lawes,
> Whose sou'raignty is best preseru'd by Iustice.
> Thus as you see how honour must be grounded
> On knowledge, not opinion: For opinion
> Relyes on probability and Accident,
> But knowledge on Necessity and Truth:
> I leaue thee to the fit consideration
> Of what becomes the grace of reall Honour,
> Wishing successe to all thy vertuous meanings.
>   (1068—89)

This speech in effect denies that Rk and Hk are "real honour"; true honour does not lead men to desire revenge, or to commit murders, adulteries, etc.; as in Ashley, it is the "reward of vertue". Military glory is permitted, however, for honour can be acquired by valour, provided it is exercised in a just cause. The speech then is a manifesto for the v and m element in honour, and against the k element, written against the current of the age; and in particular it condemns revenge and the committing of crimes in the name of honour. It is not a very long passage, but it calls attention to itself by its quality as a set-piece, and it is clearly intended as the dramatist's comment on the action; Tecnicus, indeed, hardly has any function except to act as a commenting chorus on the events of the play. Orgilus, of course, disregards his warnings, and goes on down the path to murder and death.

The passage from *The New Inn* is Lovel's long and eloquent definition of True Valour before the Court of Love (Act IV Scene 4). It is not directly on the subject of honour, but honour comes into it, and it is extremely relevant to the rise of duelling. In Lovel's view, true valour is always consistent with reason and virtue, never proceeds out of passion, and is always exercised in a lawful cause:

> Lov<el>. A certaine meane 'twixt feare, and confidence:
> No inconsiderate rashnesse, or vaine appetite
> Of false encountring formidable things;
> But a true science of distinguishing
> What's good or euill. It springs out of reason,
> And tends to perfect honesty, the scope
> Is always honour, and the publique good:
> It is no valour for a priuate cause.
> Bea<ufort>. No? not for reputation?
> Lov.   That's man's Idoll,
> Set vp 'gainst God, the maker of all lawes,
> Who hath commanded vs we should not kill;
> And yet we say, we must for reputation.
>   (IV.4.40—51)

It is noticeable here that Lovel uses "honour" for what he approves of, and "reputation" for what he does not (and Jonson makes Beaufort help him). This is no accident, for Lovel is made to continue in the same way in the rest of the scene; he only uses the word "honour" twice in his long harangue, and both times with approval; in situations where he disapproves, he uses words like "reputation", "infamy", and "opinion". The disapproval is mainly for duelling, and what Jonson is in effect doing is to deny that honour has anything to do with duelling, by refusing to use the word about it; like Ford, he is defining "true honour", but is doing it by his usage, not by theorizing, and the absence of the word "honour" is here as important as its presence in other contexts. The greater part of Lovel's oration is in fact a long and scathing attack on the pettiness and the egocentric sensibility about reputation that cause duelling, and in many passages we can almost see him skirting his way round the contemporary idea of duelling-honour while carefully refraining himself from using the word:

> What honest man can either feare his owne,
> Or else will hurt anothers reputation?
> Feare to doe base, vnworthy things, is valour,
> If they be done to vs, to suffer them,
> Is valour too.
> . . . .
>
> But we are, now, come to that delicacie,
> And tendernesse of sense, we thinke an insolence
> Worse then an injury, beare words worse then deeds;
> We are not so much troubled with the wrong,
> As with the opinion of the wrong!
> . . . .
>
> He laugh'd at me!
> He broke a iest! a third tooke place of me!
> How most ridiculous quarrels are all these?
> Notes of a queasie, and sick stomack, labouring
> With want of a true iniury!
> (IV.4.52—6, 160—4, 170—4)

It is impossible to believe that the absence of the word "honour" from passages like these is just an accident, especially if we look at the kind of things his contemporaries were writing; and we should notice that this passage is not a short one — the scene of Lovel's oration goes on for some 200 lines, without the word *honour* once being used in its duelling-sense. Lovel's definition of the scope of true valour does not exclude war, and he insists that its object must be the public good; we may therefore read his oration as a protest against the decline of the v and m elements in honour, and the rise of the k elements, the decline of the public elements and the rise of the private ones.

The passage in *The New Inn* is a set-piece on a large scale, but in *A Very Woman* the theme is given even more prominence: no less than one of the main themes of the play is a character's re-education and his redefinition of the word *honour*. At the beginning of the play, which takes place in Palermo, the Prince of Tarent, Don John Antonio, has just been an unsuccessful suitor for the hand of Almira, the viceroy's daughter, having been defeated in love by a less famous rival, a nobleman called Cardenes. Don John accepts his defeat gracefully, but Cardenes goes out of his way to taunt him, to suggest that he has lost honour by his defeat, and to insult him generally; Don John answers mildly and reasonably, but Cardenes persists, and finally succeeds in provoking him into fighting a duel, in which Cardenes is seriously wounded. Cardenes' life is saved by a skilful physician, Paulo, but while convalescing he falls into a profound melancholy, caused by his realization that he has wronged Antonio; he meditates on the nature of honour, and decides that, since honour "clasps / All-perfect justice in her arms", and never does to others what she is not willing to suffer herself, therefore he must do to himself what he would have done to Antonio had Antonio wronged him instead of *vice versa*: in other words he must kill himself. His suicide is prevented, however, by his attendants, and Paulo sets about curing him by methods that must place Massinger high among the ranks of the early exponents of psychiatry; in a series of impersonations, characters come and tell him about their lives, with the object of teaching him something about the art of living. One of the important contributions is from Paulo himself, who comes disguised as a soldier to talk to Cardenes about honour:

> *Car.* Now speak, old soldier,
> The height of HONOUR?
> *Paul.* No man to offend,
> Ne'er to reveal the secrets of a friend;
> Rather to suffer than to do wrong;
> To make the heart no stranger to the tongue;
> Provoked, not to betray an enemy,
> Nor eat his meat I choke with flattery;
> Blushless to tell wherefore I wear my scars
> Or for my conscience, or my country's wars;
> To aim at just things; if we have wildly run
> Into offences, wish them all undone:
> 'Tis poor, in grief for a wrong done, to die,
> Honour, to dare to live, and satisfy.
>
> (IV.1, p. 457)

The key points for Cardenes are not fighting in an unjust cause, and having the courage to live and make amends for wrongs that one has done. By such methods Paulo succeeds in curing Cardenes of his melancholy. Don Antonio, who has disguised himself during Cardenes' recovery, now reappears, and Cardenes enquires about him:

> Car. Is he in health, strong, vigorous, and as able
> As when he left me dead?
> Captain. Your own eyes, sir,
> Shall make good my report.
> Car. I am glad of it,
> And take you comfort in it, sir, there's hope,
> Fair hope left for me, to repair mine honour.
> Duke. What's that?
> Car. I will do something that shall speak me Messina's son.
> (V.6, p. 465)

The audience is deliberately kept uninformed about Cardenes' intentions, but the people round him are obviously meant to get the impression that he intends to fight Don John again.[1]) This impression is maintained when Cardenes and Antonio meet:

> Sir, 'tis best known to you, on what strict terms
> The reputation of men's fame and honours
> Depends in this so punctual age, in which
> A word that may receive a harsh construction
> Is answer'd and defended by the sword:
> (V.6, p. 465)

This is obviously leading up to a challenge, but the climax that Cardenes finally brings us to is a different one:

> I have received from your hands wounds and deep ones,
> My honour in the general report
> Tainted and soil'd, for which I will demand
> This satisfaction — that you would forgive
> My contumelious words and blow, my rash
> And unadvised wildness first threw on you.
> Thus I would teach the world a better way,
> For the recovery of a wounded honour,
> Than with a savage fury, not true courage,
> Still to run headlong on.
> (*Ibid.*)

Cardenes' view of honour has changed since the beginning of the play, and the audience is plainly intended to approve. All duelling is not

---

[1]) In my material, I have classified this example, and some later ones, as Rnk, even though that is not Cardenes' meaning in his heart; however, both the audience and his stage-hearers are obviously expected to take them in this meaning (sensitivity to injury, etc.), which is the natural one in the context, and it seems best to disregard Cardenes' secret intentions.

explicitly condemned, but fighting in a wrong cause is condemned, and Cardenes adds the moral:

> I'll add this, he that does wrong, not alone
> Draws, but makes sharp, his enemy's sword against
> His own life and his honour. I have paid for't;
> And wish that they who dare most, would learn from me,
> Not to maintain a wrong, but to repent it.
>
> *(Ibid.)*

This incident, together with the earlier duel and Paulo's definition of honour, can be seen as a protest against the growth of the k element in honour; Paulo's speech emphasizes military qualities ("my country's wars") and v elements (not lying, not flattering, being just, repenting and redressing wrongs); and even if duelling is not condemned in so many words, it can hardly be said to receive an unqualified approval.

It is interesting to compare these passages with one written over fifty years later, in Shadwell's *The Scowrers*. In this play, Sir Will Rant is leader of a band of "scowrers", practitioners of a kind of upper-class hooliganism which was especially common in the seventeenth and eighteenth centuries. Out of sheer high spirits and a sense of glorious irresponsibility, they go round drinking, fighting, breaking windows, abducting women, beating up the watch, etc., in other words "scowring". At the end of the play, Sir Will is made to see the folly of his behaviour, in a long lecture given him by his father, Mr Rant. Shadwell was a great admirer of Ben Jonson, whom he closely imitated (in all but essentials), and Mr Rant's speech is clearly reminiscent of Lovel's oration on true valour in *The New Inn*. However, there are differences between Lovel's attitude and Mr Rant's, as can be seen from the following passage:

> You're all meer Sops in Wine, your Brains are Bogs;
> A Toast is equal to a common Drunkard:
> You'll say you have Courage, No, it is not Valour;
> Valour is joyn'd with Vertue, never prostitute,
> But sacred, and employ'd to just Defence,
> Of Prince and Country, and the best of Friends,
> With necessary vindication of our Honour:
>
> *(The Scowrers, V.1, p. 139)*

Lovel had argued that it is not true valour in a private cause, i. e. that one should only fight for one's country, and should not duel. Mr

Rant condemns meaningless brawling, but he permits fighting for one's country, and fighting in a private cause for one's friends or in vindication of one's own honour, i. e. duelling; in fact his attitude is really exactly the reverse of Lovel's, for he permits precisely the kind of private fighting that Lovel is most insistent to condemn; and with this kind of private fighting he explicitly couples the word "honour", which Lovel carefully refrains from using of it. Mr Rant's speech is also an elaborate set-piece, and obviously intended as a homily to the audience, setting them a high standard to imitate; and incorporated in the ideal put forward is the idea that private duelling is justified in defence of your friends and in vindication of your own honour — precisely the kind of attitude that Jonson, Massinger, and Ford were protesting against.

F. The Possibility of Foreign Influence

In some of the developments that took place, foreign influence may have played a part; in the Romance languages there were words (such as French *honneur*) which an Englishman would immediately have identified with *honour*; and the idea of a code of honour as a regulator of behaviour was widespread in Europe.[1]) So, for example, the development of phrases like "man of honour" may have been encouraged by foreign example: the French phrase "Dames de Honeur" occurs in my material earlier than any English phrase of the same type, and at a time when, to judge from my material, such expressions were relatively rare in English.[2]) English ideals of conduct, too, may well have been influenced by those of the Mediterranean countries, which were such a constant source of inspiration to Renaissance England. It has already been remarked that the vogue of duelling owed something to continental influence, and the details of duelling-etiquette were certainly borrowed from continental handbooks. Such continental influence would naturally be reflected in the drama, which owed so much to Mediterranean sources for its stories, and often for a good deal more.[3]) However, I have not attempted to investigate the nature

---

[1]) See Kelso, *op. cit.*, pp. 96 sqq., and bibliography; Bryson, *op. cit.*, p. 1.

[2]) See pp. 327—329 below.

[3]) See for example Schelling, *op. cit.*, I, pp. xxix, 208—11, 408—10, etc.; Nicoll, *op. cit.*, p. 20; M. Hume, *Spanish Influence on English Literature*, pp. 265—9, 291—8. On the other hand, we must not underestimate the independence of the

or the extent of any such influence on the usage of the English word *honour*, as this would have taken me too far afield. The important point to remember is, however, that the possible existence of foreign influence in no way invalidates what I have said about the social causes of many of the changes. To be influenced by ideas or attitudes presupposes a sympathy with them; no man will begin, for example, to hold up sexual promiscuity as an ideal of behaviour simply because dramatists in another country do so; in cases of this kind the foreign influence is simply a catalyst.

However, this does not dispose of the other type of case discussed in Chapter 1: the case where the dramatist reproduces the manners, customs, and attitudes of another country in his play and intends them to be understood as such, to be seen as something foreign, a piece of local colour. In a case like this, the usage of *honour* in the play cannot necessarily be taken as reflecting normal English usage or ideals. It is clear from references in the drama that writers were aware, throughout the seventeenth century, that the code of honour was somewhat different in other countries; the references I have found are especially to Spain, France, and Italy, and in nearly every case it is said or implied that the code of honour is more strictly defined and observed in these countries, that men are more jealous, more easily affronted, more suspicious of their womenfolk; in Holland, on the other hand, it is said (at any rate after 1660) that men have no sense of honour, are cowards, will not duel, etc. . The simplest way of discovering whether any such differences were incorporated in the drama as "local colour" is to compare plays set in England with plays set abroad. It seems best to choose the Restoration period for this purpose, since, if any of the changes of the 17th Century are due to this local colour, they should appear most clearly here, when the change has gone furthest. Obviously one must not mix up tragedy and comedy, since there are such large differences between them with respect to honour-usage; the tragedies of the Restoration period are hopelessly unlocalized, all in the same ideal world of heroic fantasy, so it is practically inevitable that the

---

English dramatists; even the Restoration period, which used to be thought of as a new start under French influence, is now being seen more and more as a native development of pre-Commonwealth drama. This theme has been elaborated especially by Hotson, Lynch, and Harbage, but also by many other writers; for a list of some of them, and of their opponents, see Nicoll, *op. cit.*, p. 380.

comedies should be chosen. Here, in Restoration comedy, if anywhere, we ought to be able to see "local colour" if it exists at all in seventeenth century drama: the plays are realistic, and they are performed for a sophisticated upper-class audience (and a travelled audience), who would be more likely to scorn anachronisms and lack of local colour than the earlier audiences would. The only difficulty is that the vast majority of the comedies are set in England. However, there is one country, Spain, that provides a setting for six of them, and I have chosen these for the comparison, although the number of examples is still regrettably small. Spain is a good country to have, however, because there are frequent references in Restoration drama to the strictness of Spanish manners, the formality of Spanish life, and the punctilios of Spanish honour. The six plays are *An Evening's Love* (1668), *The Man's the Master* (1668), *The Dutch Lover* (1673), *The Spanish Friar* (1680), *The False Count* (1681), and *The Amorous Bigot* (1690). The authors are Dryden (2), Aphra Behn (2), Davenant, and Shadwell. I have studied the examples in these six plays, and compared them with those for Restoration comedy as a whole. I have studied only the examples of R, RH, and H, as these are the head-meanings where foreign differences in the code of honour would appear most clearly. In the six plays, there are 40 examples of R, 18 examples of RH, and 41 examples of H; the number per play therefore comes out at 6.7, 3.0, and 6.8 respectively, compared with 4.9, 1.8, and 6.4 respectively for all Restoration comedy.[1]) They are therefore more frequent in the six plays with Spanish settings, and for R and RH the difference is significant. Table 54 shows the k/m/v/x classification of the examples. In each case, the upper row, (a), shows the number of examples, the second row, (b), this number as a percentage, and the third row, (c), the corresponding percentage in the Restoration-comedy group as a whole (cf. Tables 48 to 51).

It will be seen from the table that there are no very striking differences between the percentages for these six plays and for Restoration comedy as a whole. In total, the percentages are very much the same, except that in the Spanish plays the x group is smaller and the other three groups have all increased somewhat at its expense; the difference in x

---

[1]) In the classical Spanish drama, the words corresponding to *honour* nearly always mean R, not H; see Castro, *op. cit.*, passim; J. L. Brooks, *"La Estrella de Sevilla"*, pp. 11—12.

TABLE 54. *Numbers and percentages of k, m, v, and x in six Restoration Comedies with Spanish settings.*

		k	m	v	x	Total
R	(a)	29	6	1	4	40
	(b)	72%	15%	2.5%	10%	—
	(c)	68%	13%	6%	14%	—
RH	(a)	11	5	0	2	18
	(b)	61%	28%	0.0%	11%	—
	(c)	46%	16%	8%	30%	—
H	(a)	22	0	14	5	41
	(b)	54%	0.0%	34%	12%	—
	(c)	54%	3%	17%	27%	—
All	(a)	62	11	15	11	99
	(b)	63%	11%	15%	11%	—
	(c)	58%	8%	12%	22%	—

(a) Number of examples.
(b) Percentage.
(c) Corresponding percentage for all Restoration Comedy.

is in fact the only significant difference in the combined percentages, and this can hardly be held up as a characteristic of "Spanish honour". Naturally enough the fluctuations are rather wider for the head-meanings separately, where the number of examples is smaller, but the differences between the Spanish plays and all plays with respect to k, v, and m are not significant, with the exception of v in the head-meaning H. On the whole, the table does not encourage the idea that the dramatists were trying to depict a view of honour different from that in the other plays. Nor does a study of the individual examples in the six plays reveal any obvious difference; the contents are of much the same kind as those found in the other comedies. I have also compared the n/g/u classification for R and RH; in the six plays, the figures are as follows: R, n 33, g 7, u 0; RH, n 12, g 4, u 2. These give percentages which for n and g are not significantly different from those for all Restoration comedy, though for u the difference is just significant.

The outcome seems to be that there are rather more examples of *honour* (R/RH/H) in the six Spanish plays than in the average Restoration comedy, but that in type and content the examples show no significant differences of any importance from those of Restoration comedy as a whole. This may mean that, when the authors were using a Spanish setting, they tended to make the characters more sensitive about their honour than the characters in English plays, since they knew that Spaniards were very punctilious about their honour, but depicted the demands of honour as being the same as in England. This is a plausible view, but it rests on the evidence of six plays only, and of course the *absence* of significant differences is a negative criterion, and might conceivably fail if a larger number of plays were studied. But it does at any rate seem likely that there are no very *large* differences with respect to honour between plays set in England and plays set in other countries; and this is the important thing from our point of view. And what is true of Restoration comedy is probably *a fortiori* true of other seventeenth century plays.

One's impressions from the plays as a whole certainly confirm this impression. In general, the demands of honour are depicted as being very much the same wherever the scene is set, due allowances being made for the idealizing and exaggerating tendencies of the heroic drama as compared with comedy. I have been struck by only one exception to this, and this only on a small scale. As we have seen earlier, secret wife-murder was a typically Spanish custom, not found in England. I have found very few cases in my material where honour is said to demand the killing of an unchaste wife or sister, but in the second half of the century the few examples that occur are all in Spanish contexts. There are only two or three such references in the first half of the century, and they show no particular geographical trend; in the second half, there are seven references, four plays being involved, and three of the plays are set in Spain (*The Dutch Lover, Don Carlos,* and *Abdelazer*); the fourth play (*The Gentleman Dancing Master*) is set in England, but the character referred to is "Don Diego", the Spaniardized Englishman. This may have been one of the peculiarities of the Spanish code of honour that people in England knew about (it is certainly a memorable one).

G. Public Theatre and Private Theatre

In discussing the changes in the requirements of the code of honour which we find in the drama during the century, I have assumed that we are witnessing changes in upper-class attitudes with time. Theoretically, however, a different explanation is possible: since the audience changes in composition during the century, it could be argued that the differences are solely due to the different demands of an upper class audience and a broad audience, without any changes taking place in the ideas and attitudes of the upper classes; in other words, if in 1600 the theatre-audience had been composed solely of courtly gentry, the demands of honour would have been represented on the stage exactly as they were in the Restoration period. This is not a very plausible theory to anyone who has studied the history and literature of both periods, and perhaps the simplest answer is to point to the sheer fact that there *was* a broad theatre audience in Shakespeare's day, which in itself shows that the attitudes of the aristocracy were different from those of the Restoration aristocracy; theatrical history is not something that can be viewed in isolation from cultural history as a whole. However, a further test is possible. At the beginning of the century there were in fact theatres in London which catered for a more aristocratic and exclusive audience than the Globe and the Fortune and similar public theatres; these were the so-called "private theatres",[1] the indoor theatres where the boys' companies performed, which charged higher prices than the ordinary public theatres; these charges were sufficiently high for it to be certain that the private theatres were more or less the preserve of the gentry.[2] Certain plays were first performed in the private theatres, and (in view of the normal theatrical practice of the time) were presumably commissioned for them. A comparison between these plays and the plays written for the public theatre should therefore be able to decide the question at issue; if the changes in *honour*-usage in the drama during the century are due *solely* to the change in the social composition of the audience, without any simultaneous change in the attitudes of the theatre-going upper classes, then the plays written for the private theatres at the beginning of the century ought to show us an *honour*-usage like that of the Restoration period, not like that of the early seventeenth-century public theatre; or at the very least the plays written for the private theatre ought to show some trend in the Restoration direction.

---

[1] See Chambers, *Elizabethan Stage*, II, pp. 355—6, 474—517, 522—4.

[2] For theatre-prices and wages, see Harbage, *Shakespeare's Audience*, pp. 55—65.

My material for the decade 1601—1610 includes ten plays that were first performed by boys' companies;[1]) one is a pastoral (Fletcher's *Faithful Shepherdess*), and the remaining nine are comedies. It will therefore be convenient to compare the nine comedies with the comedies as a whole in the same decade (sixteen in all). The nine comedies are the following: *Blurt Master Constable* (1601), *Poetaster* (1601), *The Phoenix* (1604), *Eastward Ho* (1605), *A Trick to Catch the Old One* (1605), *A Mad World, My Masters* (1606), *Michaelmas Term* (1606), *Your Five Gallants* (1607), and *Epicoene* (1609). The first is by Dekker and Middleton (probably mostly Dekker), the second and the last by Jonson, the fourth by Jonson, Chapman, and Marston, and the remainder by Middleton. In these nine comedies, there are 15 examples of R, 4 examples of RH, and 4 examples of H; in each case the number per play is lower than for comedy as a whole in the decade (whereas in Restoration comedy it is higher). Of the 23 examples, 6 are classified as k, 7 as m, 5 as v, and 5 as x, giving percentages of 26, 30, 22, and 22 respectively; these are not significantly different from the percentages for all comedy in the decade (20, 24, 30, and 27 respectively). On the other hand, the k/m/v/x pattern of these nine private-theatre comedies does differ significantly from that of Restoration comedy as a whole; for k the difference is significant, and for m highly significant. I have not troubled to calculate whether these nine plays differ significantly from comedy as a whole for the period 1591—1640, since the differences are in any case in a direction *opposite* to those of Restoration comedy (i. e. the private-theatre plays are less like Restoration comedy than are other comedies of the first half-century). In the 19 examples of R and RH, there are 7 examples of n, 6 of g, and 6 of u; here again the proportions differ from those for comedy 1591—1640 in a direction opposite to that of Restoration comedy.[2])

These nine plays, therefore, offer evidence against the argument that the change in the code of honour depicted in the drama resulted only from the change in the class-composition of the audience, and not

---

[1]) I follow the attributions of first performances given in Harbage's *Annals of English Drama*; I do not count *The Family of Love* as a private-theatre play, as it is a doubtful case. For boys' companies and adult companies, see Chambers, *Elizabethan Stage* II, pp. 3—260.

[2]) These findings have been strengthened by the study of a further eight comedies written for the private theatres. See Appendix E.

from an actual change in the code as apprehended by the theatre-going upper classes. I do not wish to minimize the importance of the change that took place in the composition of the audience; the great age of English drama began in the late 1580's when the popular tradition and the learned tradition came together — which implies that their audiences came together; and when the audience began to narrow into a class audience, the drama began to decline: the debility of Restoration drama, plainly, was to some extent due to one of the things on which it prided itself, its remoteness from the popular. The point I want to make is that the change in the audience cannot be viewed as an event in itself; it was part of a much wider social process, and during that process the attitudes of the upper classes in England changed a good deal. Part of this change, I contend, is seen in the changes in the use of the word *honour* in the drama. In the later part of the century especially, the social group concerned was small: we must not confuse the theatre-audience with the nation. But the theatre-audience had a life outside the theatre, and the changes in the drama cannot be fully understood unless we take that life into account.

CHAPTER 11

Chastity

The group of meanings concerned with chastity (Rc/RcC/C) has already been discussed in a number of contexts. The total number of examples is 736, rather less than a third the size of the R/RH/H group. In the first half of the century, it is about equally frequent in comedy and in tragedy (2.6 and 2.8 examples per play respectively), but in the second half it is much more frequent in comedy (6.2 examples per play against 2.8 in tragedy). We have also seen that it is usually only attributed to women, and that in the second half of the century there is a great increase (in comedy) in the frequency of examples of "mere reputation" (Rco).

Table 55 shows the proportions between the various head-meanings of the group for each decade; in each row, the upper line, (a), shows the number of examples found, and the lower line, (b), shows this as a percentage. Comedy and tragedy are shown separately, but the sum of these two would not be very helpful, since the trends are in opposite directions: the Rc/C ratio increases with time in comedy, but decreases in tragedy. In comedy, Rc increases from 31% in the first half-century to 47% in the second, while C falls from 48% to 28%; so their proportions are almost exactly reversed. These changes are highly significant. In tragedy, on the other hand, Rc falls from 41% in the first half of the century to 22% in the second, while C rises from 43% to 54%; the change in the Rc/C ratio is significant. In both comedy and tragedy, the percentage of the equivocal type, RcC, increases slightly, but these increases are not significant; if, however, the figures for tragedy and comedy are combined, then the increase in RcC is just significant. No clear trends can be seen in the individual decades: the number of examples is probably too small for the curves to emerge from the random fluctuations and the disturbing influences.

It will be seen that the development in the Rc/RcC/C group is different from that in the R/RH/H group; in the latter group, there is a great

TABLE 55. *Number and percentage of examples of Rc, RcC, and C.*

Period from to	1591 1600	1601 1610	1611 1620	1621 1630	1631 1640	1591 1640	1661 1670	1671 1680	1681 1690	1691 1700	1661 1700	Grand Total
Comedy Rc (a)	1	7	12	10	24	54	35	70	26	15	146	200
(b)	13	19	26	29	49	31	61	48	33	50	47	41
RcC (a)	4	12	7	4	9	36	13	42	21	3	79	115
(b)	50	33	15	12	18	21	23	29	27	10	25	24
C (a)	3	17	27	20	16	83	9	34	31	12	86	169
(b)	38	47	59	59	33	48	16	23	41	40	28	35
Tragedy Rc (a)	5	9	14	28	14	70	3	13	1	1	18	88
(b)	100	26	36	54	35	41	43	28	5	14	22	35
RcC (a)	0	9	3	7	8	27	2	12	4	2	20	47
(b)	0	26	8	13	20	16	29	26	19	26	24	19
C (a)	0	16	22	17	18	73	2	22	16	4	44	117
(b)	0	47	56	33	45	43	29	47	76	57	54	46

(a) Number of examples.
(b) Percentage of Rc/RcC/C group for the given period.

increase in H, while R remains stationary or even declines a little, the net result being an increase in the H/R ratio, both in comedy and in tragedy; in the Rc/RcC/C group, on the other hand, the C/Rc ratio increases in tragedy but decreases in comedy; there is nothing in the Rc/RcC/C group corresponding to the spectacular expansion of H during the 17th century. A key point for understanding this difference is the fact that, during the century, the conduct demanded by the R/RH/H group changed, while that demanded by the Rc/RcC/C group did not; the most important single point of conduct for a woman was and remained the preservation of her chastity, and the honour-code in this respect remained identical with the Christian code. In the R/RH/H group, a code of conduct was elaborated which was different from the one current in the rest of society, and the rise of H is one of the reflections of this fact; no such deviation from the norms of the time took place in the Rc/RcC/C group. It is not difficult to see why chastity remained a major requirement for the women of the upper classes: in a society where both high rank and property are inherited through the male, and where men are the dominant sex, legitimacy is of great importance for men of wealth and title, and they will therefore insist on strict chastity for their womenfolk, whatever they may do themselves; in the seventeenth century, this idea of inheritance by legitimate heirs was so strong that it would obviously outweigh the kind of forces that we have seen at work in the R/RH/H group; for upper class women, chastity was bound to remain the ideal, at any rate officially.

It is against this background that we must see the change in the Rc/C ratio. It then seems natural to interpret the expansion of Rc in comedy as a sign that appearances became more important than reality, that more emphasis was placed on seeming chaste and less on being chaste; legitimate heirs were no doubt important, but the woman could always take the view that "what the eye don't see, the heart don't grieve over"; and this attitude is in fact occasionally expressed in Restoration comedy. This view of the expansion of Rc in comedy is supported by the great increase in the number of examples of "mere reputation", which has already been dealt with (Chapter 5, Rco). This means in fact that the growth of libertinism in the Restoration period is not limited to men; women fail to see why there should be a double standard of morality (sexual freedom for men, sexual captivity for women), and imitate the men; but, because of the official demand for chastity, their libertinism has to be secret, while the men's is openly avowed. This situation is bound to arise, because of the inconsistency in the men's position: the Restoration gallant demands absolute chastity from his own womenfolk, but at the same time does his best to persuade other men's wives and sisters to be unchaste. It is also interesting to notice that it is not only the unchaste women who attach great importance to appearances; the chaste heroines of Restoration comedy often strike one as being chaste simply because that is the easiest way of keeping up appearances, the easiest way of preserving one's Rc; one would not dream of attributing religious motives to them for their chastity — it is simply that the worldly inconveniences and dangers of unchastity are too great; honour and Christian virtue are not the same thing, even when the conduct demanded is the same. As a clear example of this attitude, we can take a scene from Shadwell's *A True Widow*; in Act II Scene 1, an upper-class bawd, Lady Busy, tries to persuade the chaste heroine, Isabella, to become the mistress of a nobleman in return for a handsome settlement; Isabella firmly resists, but she never argues on grounds of conscience or religion; what she stresses is the loss of reputation, the inconvenience, the way in which she would cut herself off from fashionable society:

> *Isab<ella>.* A very Comfortable thing, for a Gentlewoman to bring her self into a Condition of never conversing with a Woman of Quality, who has Wit, and Honour, again; but must sort with those Tawdry painted things of the Town.
> *Gart<rude>.* Can't you keep Company with my Mother and me.
> *L. Busy.* Look you Madam, you are under a great mistake, for do not Ladies of Wit and Honour, keep dayly Company with those things as you call them?
> (II.1, p. 304)

We are a long way indeed from the attitude of an earlier Isabella:

> *Ang<elo>.* Beleeue me on mine Honor,
> My words express my purpose.
> *Isa<bella>.* Ha? Little honor, to be much beleeu'd,
> And most pernitious purpose: Seeming, seeming.
> (*Measure for Measure*, II.4.46—9)

In Restoration comedy, one often feels that the "seeming" has become the most important thing for the characters. This is perhaps another of the ways in which the Beaumont and Fletcher plays anticipate the Restoration period; Coleridge says of Beaumont and Fletcher:[1])

> It is too plain that the authors had no one idea of chastity as a virtue, but only such a conception as a blind man might have of the power of seeing, by handling an ox's eye. In the Queen of Corinth, indeed, they talk differently; but it is all talk, and nothing is real in it but the dread of losing a reputation.

The opposite change in Restoration tragedy, the increase of C at the expense of Rc, may perhaps be seen as a compensation in the ideal sphere for what was happening in the real world, an increased assertion of the ideal which was being so blatantly violated in reality. The situation is different from that in the R/RH/H group, because of the social necessity for the upper classes to maintain female chastity as an ideal. As in so many things, the writer of Restoration tragedy shouts loudly because nobody really believes him.

We have seen that the changes in the R/RH/H group provoked protest from three dramatists round about 1630; it is interesting that there is a play that might be interpreted as a similar protest at the increasing importance of Rc as compared with C. This play occurs at about the

---

[1]) *Essays and Lectures on Shakespeare*, p. 204.

same time (1638), but is by a younger man, Davenant. A great part of his tragicomedy *The Fair Favourite* deals with the relationship between the king of Naples (a married man) and a young unmarried woman, Eumena. Their friendship is a perfectly innocent one, but it is misinterpreted by the world, and especially by Eumena's brother Oramont, who assumes that Eumena is the king's mistress. Eumena tells the king that his behaviour towards her has caused her chastity to be suspected, and begins to regret the unconventionality of her behaviour:

> 'Tis equal, sure,
> To have no honour, and to have the world
> Believe that it is lost. Honour's a rich,
> A glorious upper vestment, which we wear
> To please the lookers on, as well as to
> Delight our selves.
>
> (II.1, p. 230)

The first *honour* here is C: having people believe that you are unchaste is as bad as actually being unchaste. And so she naturally moves on to the meaning Rc in her second sentence; a woman's chastity, obviously, is not a "glorious upper vestment", but her reputation can be considered as one. The king urges her to keep up her courage, and hold by her earlier resolve to despise the opinion of the world, and value only inner worth irrespective of reputation:

> Where is the courage of thy virtue fled,
> When, valiant with thine own integrity,
> Thou didst resolve to slight opinion as
> The vulgar doom? Oft hast thou said, honour
> Doth dwell within, and cannot live abroad;
> For, like extracted spirits in
> A viol shut, it keeps its vigour whilst
> 'Tis close retain'd, but, when dispers'd and mix'd
> With open air, the virtue so evaporates,
> That all its value is for ever lost.
>
> (II.1, pp. 230—1)

The king here goes so far as to assert that honour (C or H) is actually weakened by reputation; or perhaps that true worth is never recognized and that reputation should therefore be despised. Eumena does not deny these sentiments that he attributes to her, but continues to regret the way in which women's actions are misinterpreted, and the great importance that is attached to reputation:

> O that the world cou'd be instructed thus!
> But the severe mistake on women's honours,
> Must last like other heresies, and be
> Too strong for truth or reason's force, because
> 'Tis popular and old.
>
> (II.1, p. 231)

It is true that she says that this mistake is "old", but nevertheless it may be that the whole theme is a protest against, or at any rate a comment on, an increasing tendency to emphasize Rc at the expense of C, especially as this particular form of unconventional behaviour is extremely uncommon in seventeenth century drama — indeed I have found no exact parallel to it in the rest of my material.

There is a change within Rc during the century which is a pointer in the same direction, although the number of examples is too small for decisive conclusions to be drawn from it alone; this is the development of what I shall call "circumstantial loss of Rc". Of course, almost all loss of Rc is based on circumstantial evidence, as Iago cleverly points out to Othello; but in the seventeenth century Rc is often lost on circumstantial evidence which to us seems quite inadequate, or perhaps conventional (certain behaviour is conventionally considered immodest which to us does not seem especially so), and it is examples of this kind that I include under this heading. The following are examples of behaviour that, in certain plays, are said to cause loss of Rc, and which I class as circumstantial: talking to a man out of a window; having a private meeting with a man; being wooed by two men at once, especially if they quarrel or fight about you; having a lover or a husband who shows jealousy; writing an indiscreet letter to a man (not a letter that reveals an intrigue, but one that reveals affection for him); making the first advances to a man, instead of waiting passively to be wooed; indulging in such escapades as disguising yourself as a boy. Naturally such behaviour is not always said to cause loss of Rc; Shakespeare's heroines, for example, do not usually seem worried by the possibility when they dress up as men; and that is what makes it interesting to see if the frequency of the type changes. As circumstantial I do not count loss of Rc caused by eloping with a man, allowing a married man to woo you, allowing any man to woo you if you are yourself married, or being found in bed with a man; nor do I count loss of Rc caused by slander. With the term thus defined, I have found that the frequency of circumstantial loss of Rc increases in comedy (from about 12.5% in the first half of the century to about 17% in the second) and decreases in tragedy (from about 12% to about 2.5%). (The percentages are of the total number of Rc plus RcC in the period concerned, since "circumstantial loss" can occur in both of these.) For comedy, the change is not significant; for tragedy, it is nearly significant. The trend in comedy fits well with the tendency (shown in the increase of the Rc/C ratio) to put increased emphasis on appearances, and the change may be real (though obviously we are not entitled to assert that it is on the strength of my material). It may perhaps be argued that, on the contrary, a large number of cases of "circumstantial loss" shows great delicacy in the users, a very high standard of modesty; I cannot agree with this view; I think it rather shows that society has a very low opinion of the morals of its women, and is prepared to think the worst of them; it is not much of a compliment to a woman to assume that, if she is left alone in a room with a man, she will immediately commit adultery with him or make arrangements to do so at some future time.

It will be remembered that the head-meaning C can refer either to a mental state (purity of mind, modesty) or to a physical state (physical chastity, virginity, physical faithfulness to husband); for convenience I shall call these Cm and Cb respectively (mnemonic for "mind" and "body"). It seems interesting to enquire whether there was any change in the ratio between these two during the century, especially as this is another of the points on which Coleridge contrasts Beaumont and Fletcher with Shakespeare, asserting of Beaumont and Fletcher that "all their women are represented with the minds of strumpets".[1]) I have examined my material from this point of view, but have not been able to come to absolutely definite conclusions; a majority of the examples mean both Cm and Cb, or could mean either, so the material available is rather small. In comedy, there is an increase in the percentage of Cm (from about 11% in the first half of the century to about 16% in the second half), but this is not significant; at the same time, there is a fall in the percentage of Cb (35% to 22%) and this is just significant. (Percentages are in terms of the combined C and RcC material for the period in question.) In tragedy, there is an increase in the percentage of both Cm and Cb (17% to 23% and 30% to 44% respectively)

---

[1]) *Ibid.*

but neither change is significant, though the change in Cb approaches the just-significant level. No information can be obtained from comedy and tragedy combined, because the trends cancel one another out. The only information that really seems to emerge from all this is that the percentage of Cb falls in comedy, and perhaps increases in tragedy; and it is difficult to know what interpretation to attach to this.

However this may be, a reading of the plays does suggest that, in the Restoration period, writers were more keenly aware of the co-existence of the two meanings than they had been earlier; the percentage of examples in which one of the meanings is predominant remains substantially unchanged, but in the second half of the century one sometimes meets examples where both meanings are used simultaneously, in conflict, for grotesque or comic effect. For example, in a scene from *The Virtuoso* (which has already been referred to earlier), Lady Gimcrack successfully makes advances to Bruce, a gallant, while maintaining a pretence of modesty; finally she agrees to go into a grotto with him:

> L. Gim. I will not try if you be not sure of your Honor. I'll not venture, I protest.
> Bruce. What ever you are of mine, you are sure of your own.
> L. Gim. Right, that will defend me. Now tempt what you will though we go in, nay, though we shut the door too: I fear nothing; it's all one to me as long as I have my Honour about me. Come.
>
> (III.1, p. 136)

The grotesque contrast between Cm and Cb is produced by the use of the phrase "have my Honour about me", which suggests the kind of small physical object that one carries about in one's pocket, like a handkerchief. It continues Lady Gimcrack's technique of using the word to accept while pretending to refuse: her Cm will prevent her from yielding to Bruce, but fortunately she has her Cb "about her" so that she can give it to him. This level of vulgarity is not particularly unusual for Shadwell. There is a similar example in *The Double Dealer*; Lady Plyant, another lady of the same type, mistakenly believes that Mellefont has designs on her, and is fluttering at him, asserting her honour and her impregnability, but at the same time hinting that if anybody could make her weaken it might be he:

> Hear you! no, no; I'll deny you first, and hear you afterward. For one does not know how one's mind may change upon hearing. —

Hearing is one of the senses, and all the senses are fallible; my honour is infallible and uncomeatable.

(II.1, p. 127)

The effect is produced here by the two discrepant adjectives, infallible referring to Cm and uncomeatable to Cb. In both these examples, it will be noticed that the Cb element can well be interpreted in the unusual sense "physical organ" (*N. E. D.* meaning 3 b); in my material, this sense only occurs in would-be humorous effects of this kind, and only in the second half of the century; the first example quoted by the *N. E. D.* is from 1688.

Members of the Rc/RcC/C group do not seem to enter very readily into combinations with other head-meanings; altogether I have found a total of 21 examples with joint head-meanings, 9 in the first half of the century and 12 in the second half, i. e. only 2.6% and 3.1% respectively. There are also, of course, quite a number of cases where there is a shift of meaning; this especially occurs when the word *honour* is applied successively to two or more different persons; if one of these is a woman and another a man, it sometimes happens that the honour attributed to the woman is Rc/RcC/C, while that attributed to the man is R/RH/H or M/T/P, so that the meaning of the word alters in the course of the sentence; as explained earlier, cases of this kind are not counted as joint head-meanings, but only the first head-meaning is counted, for purely practical reasons.

While, however, the members of the Rc/RcC/C group are not often found in combination with other head-meanings, they are often deliberately contrasted with them. This technique of throwing different meanings of the word *honour* into deliberate contrast with one another for theatrical effect is quite common in the seventeenth century drama; it especially occurs with members of the Rc/RcC/C group when women's morality is contrasted with men's, and is most often pitted against examples either of the R/RH/H group or of the M/T/P group. There is a well-known example in *All's Well*; Bertram, a married man, is wooing Diana, who is resisting him; suddenly, as if capriciously, she asks him to give her a ring that he is wearing, but he replies that it is not in his power to do so:

It is an honour longing to our house,
Bequeathed downe from manie Ancestors,

> Which were the greatest obloquie i'th world
> In me to loose.
>
> (IV.2.42—5)

This gives Diana the opening she wants, and she flings the word back at him with a different meaning:

> Mine Honors such a Ring,
> My chastities the Iewell of our house,
> Bequeathed downe from many Ancestors,
> Which were the greatest obloquie i'th world,
> In mee to loose. Thus your owne proper wisedome
> Brings in the Champion honor on my part,
> Against your vaine assault.
>
> (IV.2.45—51)

Shakespeare's use of the device here is concentrated and economical; Shirley takes it in *The Lady of Pleasure* and expands it into forty or fifty lines; Lord A. asks Celestina to be his mistress, and she replies in a parable; she tells him that she knows an extremely wealthy man who is of base descent, and wishes to buy a coat-of-arms; Lord A. replies contemptuously that of course that is easy, but Celestina has an objection:

> But these (viz. the arms) will want antiquity, my lord,
> The seal of honour. What's a coat cut out
> But yesterday, to make a man a gentleman?
>
> (V.1, p. 96).

He therefore wishes (she says) to buy Lord A.'s coat-of-arms and title (which are very ancient), and will pay as much for them as Lord A. likes. Lord A. (rather wooden-headedly, one feels) produces the indignant reaction that Celestina expects, and enables her to make her point by the contrast of TP ("The seal of honour") with C:

> *Lord.* I'll sooner give these arms to the hangman's axe,
> My head, my heart, to twenty executions,
> Than sell one atom from my name.
> *Cel.* Change that,
> And answer him would buy my honour from me;
> Honour, that is not worn upon a flag,
> Or pennon, that, without the owner's dangers,
> An enemy may ravish, and bear from me;
> But that which grows and withers with my soul,
> Beside the body's stain: think, think, my lord,

CHASTITY 309

> To what you would unworthily betray me,
> If you would not, for price of gold, or pleasure,
> (If that be more your idol) lose the glory
> And painted honour of your house.
>
> (V.i, p. 97)

Not content with the contrast with TP, she throws in military glory for good measure. It is not often that the theme is given as much elaboration as here, but the basic idea is fairly common. An example where the contrast is with the R/RH/H group can be given from *A True Widow*; Lord Bellamour is trying to persuade Isabella to become his mistress, and she is resisting:

> Can you pretend to love, and tempt me from my Honour? ....
> ... When a Man of Honour can turn Coward, you may prevail on me; the case is equal.
>
> (III.1, p. 319)

The contrast here is between RcC and H; for me to be unchaste, Isabella is saying, would be equivalent to your being a coward; the man's "proper virtue" is courage, and the woman's chastity. She does not argue, it will be noticed, on grounds of conscience or religion; instead she compares the demands that honour makes on a man and on a woman.

Contrasts of this kind arise because there are two standards of morality, one for men and one for women: honour demands that a woman should be chaste, but not usually that a man should. However, we have already seen that, in the R/RH/H group, there are examples where the demands of honour include sexual continence for men, and in a few of these it could be plausibly argued that the meaning is C (occasionally Rc) although the owner is a man. Most of these occur in the first half of the century, and the clearest cases concern the following characters: Postumus (*Cymbeline*), Florizel (*Winter's Tale*), Ferdinand (*The Tempest*), Arnoldo (*The Custom of the Country*), Lisander (*The Lover's Progress*), Charles (*The Elder Brother*, two examples), Lorenzo (*The Bashful Lover*), and Alonzo (*The Bashful Lover*). I have in fact classified these nine examples as H (except for the last two, which are RH and R respectively), but they might well have been put in the Rc/RcC/C group. These nine examples are entirely serious, but of course there are also a number of cases which are not serious, or where the idea of male chastity is treated with contempt. In the second half of the century there are no serious examples; the most likely candidates for the male-chastity group are five examples in *The Gentleman Dancing Master*, which are completely farcical (classified Rnvo), an example in *The Virtuoso*, which is hypocritical and deliberately ambiguous (classified Hv), and an example in *The Double Dealer*, concerning Mellefont, which probably refers to gratitude rather than chastity (classified Hv). Moreover, of the nine examples in the first half of the century, by far the clearest candidates for the C classification are the first four, which all fall within the first three decades of our period. The only clear examples of male chastity being held up as part of the ideal of the code of honour, therefore, occur very early in the period, and such examples are entirely absent from the second half of the century.

CHAPTER 12

Other Head-Meanings

A. The MTP Group

It has already been seen that the MTP group is the second-largest main group of head-meanings, rather less than half the size of the R/RH/H group. Tables 56 and 57, which are for comedy and for tragedy respectively, show the numbers and frequencies of the three head-meanings of the group, and also of the combinations MT, TP and MTP. In each row of the tables, the upper line, (a), gives the number of examples, and the lower line, (b), the number per play. The figures given in these tables are not for ultimate frequencies; the figures for M, for example, are for all examples in which M occurs, and therefore include the figures for MT and for MTP given lower down; similarly, the figures for MT include those for MTP. To find the total number of examples of M, therefore, one consults only the M line; the MT and MTP lines must not be added to it.

It will be seen from the tables that, if the two halves of the century are compared, M increases in frequency in comedy, but decreases in tragedy; in fact it doubles in comedy and drops to half in tragedy (both changes highly significant). T, on the other hand, declines considerably in both comedy and tragedy (both highly significant). P shows no change in comedy, but falls to half in tragedy (highly significant). The groups MT, TP, and MTP all decrease in frequency, in both comedy and tragedy, and most of these changes are significant. The figures are too small for the separate decades to tell us much, but it is curious to observe a tendency inside the first half of the century for the frequency of all groups to increase with time, even those that show a decline in the second half of the century; this is especially noticeable in comedy.[1]

---

[1] A number of examples of phrases of the type "man of honour" have been left unclassified, because they are used so vaguely. It is likely that quite a few of these were intended to carry a P element, and some of them also a T element

TABLE 56. *Numbers and frequencies of the members of the M/T/P group. Comedy.*

Period from to	1591 1600	1601 1610	1611 1620	1621 1630	1631 1640	1591 1640	1661 1670	1671 1680	1681 1690	1691 1700	1661 1700	Grand Total
M .... (a)	12	30	36	47	48	173	44	108	86	29	267	440
(b)	1.1	1.9	3.0	2.9	4.0	2.6	4.4	5.4	7.2	3.6	5.3	3.8
T .... (a)	9	23	15	31	31	109	11	12	20	2	45	154
(b)	0.8	1.4	1.3	1.9	2.6	1.6	1.1	0.6	1.7	0.3	0.9	1.3
P .... (a)	8	20	12	23	26	89	20	23	20	3	66	155
(b)	0.7	1.3	1.0	1.4	2.2	1.3	2.0	1.2	1.7	0.4	1.3	1.3
MT .... (a)	3	7	5	13	13	41	0	2	3	0	5	46
(b)	0.3	0.4	0.4	0.8	1.1	0.6	0	0.1	0.3	0	0.1	0.4
TP .... (a)	7	19	9	18	20	73	7	11	17	2	37	110
(b)	0.6	1.2	0.8	1.1	1.7	1.1	0.7	0.6	1.4	0.3	0.7	0.9
MTP .... (a)	1	3	1	3	2	10	0	1	1	0	2	12
(b)	0.1	0.2	0.1	0.2	0.2	0.15	0	0.1	0.1	0	0·04	0.1

(a) Number of examples.
(b) Number of examples per play.

The opposite trends in M for comedy and for tragedy result from a process in which M loses intensity and becomes part of a mere courtesy-phrase; it will be noticed that the MT group declines in both comedy and tragedy, so the increase of M in comedy is caused by examples of M unconnected with T. An examination of the examples has shown that it is not only MT that declines, but also M referring to any public distinction conferred by the sovereign (or other ruling power). We can denote by Mt all examples of M which refer to public distinctions of this kind — orders, decorations, the erection of statues, etc. — including titles; it is then found that, in comedy, there are 55 examples of Mt in the first half of the century, but only 9 in the second, which means

("man of honour" meaning, among other things, "member of the gentry" and "member of the nobility"). Of these unclassified examples, 9 occur in the first half of the century (6 in comedy, 3 in tragedy), and 29 in the second half (20 in comedy and 9 in tragedy). It is possible, therefore, that the decline of T and P is not quite as great as Tables 56 and 57 suggest.

TABLE 57. *Numbers and frequencies of the members of the M/T/P group. Tragedy.*

Period from to	1591 1600	1601 1610	1611 1620	1621 1630	1631 1640	1591 1640	1661 1670	1671 1680	1681 1690	1691 1700	1661 1700	Grand Total
M .... (a)	19	54	95	62	48	278	25	25	14	3	67	345
(b)	1.9	3.9	6.8	6.2	4.0	4.6	3.1	2.1	2.8	0.8	2.3	3.9
T .... (a)	27	18	56	43	19	163	1	16	3	1	21	184
(b)	2.7	1.3	4.0	4.3	1.6	2.7	0.1	1.3	0.3	0.3	0.7	2.1
P .... (a)	22	13	35	22	28	120	6	17	4	1	28	148
(b)	2.2	0.9	2.5	2.2	2.3	2.0	0.8	1.4	0.3	0.3	1.0	1.7
MT .... (a)	9	10	33	22	5	79	1	7	0	0	8	87
(b)	0.9	0.7	2.4	2.2	0.4	1.3	0.1	0.6	0	0	0.1	1.0
TP .... (a)	15	8	26	22	13	84	4	11	3	1	19	103
(b)	1.5	0.6	1.9	2.2	1.1	1.4	0.5	0.9	0.6	0.3	0.7	1.2
MTP .... (a)	0	1	7	1	0	9	0	2	0	0	2	11
(b)	0	0.1	0.5	0.1	0	0.15	0	0.2	0	0	0.07	0.12

(a) Number of examples.
(b) Number of examples per play.

that Mt as a percentage of M falls from 29% to only 3.3%; even if we allow for the absolute doubling of frequency that occurs for M in comedy, the fall is very heavy. In tragedy, on the other hand, there are 138 examples of Mt in the first half of the century, and 32 in the second half, and the fall in percentage in this case is only from 50% to 48%; but it should be remembered that in tragedy the M group shrinks to half its former size, so that even in tragedy there is a considerable decline of Mt absolutely speaking. Examination of the non-Mt examples of M shows that, while some of them refer to something which is in fact a considerable distinction to the receiver, others refer to mere trivialities, and the word *honour* is used either out of exaggeration or as a conventional politeness. To give some idea of this development, I have classified all examples of M into one of four groups, according to the degree of loss of intensity: (1) No loss of intensity; (2) Slight loss of intensity; (3) Moderate loss of intensity; (4) Great loss of intensity. I have judged the degree of intensity from the point of view of Mt,

i. e. M considered as a public mark of distinction conferred by the sovereign, not from the private point of view; for example, when the young hero says that he would prefer the honour of the heroine's hand to any title the sovereign could bestow on him, he is no doubt telling the truth, and one may agree with his scale of values, but nevertheless from the public point of view there is a loss of intensity when her hand is called "an honour"; to obtain the hand of a social equal cannot be considered as bestowing public distinction, whatever the man may feel about it personally. A few examples will be given to show the kind of classifications adopted: (1) No loss of intensity: Here are included all examples of Mt, and also a number of other examples where the award does in fact bring considerable public distinction; (2) Slight loss of intensity: Here are included such things as marrying or wishing to marry a social equal, the friendship of a social equal (or superior), entertaining or being entertained by somebody of much higher rank (e. g. the sovereign), and being presented with an elaborate entertainment (e. g. a masque); (3) Moderate loss of intensity: This includes such things as entertaining or being entertained by somebody of rather higher rank, being introduced to somebody of high rank or great distinction, being the servant or follower of a great prince, being praised, having outward signs of respect paid to one (e. g. curtsies), being in the company of a lady (for a man), being presented with a less elaborate entertainment (e. g. music); (4) Great loss of intensity: Here I include things which confer no distinction at all (e. g. the company and the acquaintance of social equals); things which just happen to be so, and where no intention of conferring can possibly be involved (e. g. being related so somebody, lodging in the same house as somebody); things where the conferring is really the other way round, but where the conferrer out of politeness says that *he* is receiving an honour; and things which are positively undesirable and unpleasant, and which are called honours to show contempt for the receiver (the honour of being hanged, of being killed by such a fine fellow as the speaker, etc.). Of course a lot depends on the circumstances, and on the relative social ranks of the giver and receiver; praise, for example, may under some circumstances not constitute loss of intensity at all, if formally and publicly performed as an official reward. Table 58 shows the numbers and percentages of examples in each of these four grades of intensity; figures are given for each half of the century, and for comedy and

TABLE 58. *Loss of intensity of M.*

		Comedy		Tragedy	
		1591 to 1640	1661 to 1700	1591 to 1640	1661 to 1700
No loss of intensity	(a)	86	17	187	46
	(b)	50%	6%	67%	69%
Slight loss of	(a)	19	66	34	8
intensity	(b)	11%	25%	12%	12%
Moderate loss of	(a)	51	69	37	7
intensity	(b)	29%	26%	13%	10%
Great loss of	(a)	17	115	20	6
intensity	(b)	10%	43%	7%	9%

(a) Number of examples.
(b) Percentage of M.

tragedy separately; in every row, the upper line, (a), shows the number of examples, and the lower line, (b), shows these as a percentage of M for the period and type of play in question.

The picture here is similar to that found for Mt. In comedy, the loss of intensity in the second half of the century is overwhelming, the examples with no loss dropping from 50% to 6% and those with great loss rising from 10% to 43%; but in tragedy there is no significant difference at all between the two halves of the century. I suggest that the difference between comedy and tragedy is a stylistic matter; in real life, M loses intensity and comes to be used very commonly in courtesy-phrases, and this development is reflected in comedy; in tragedy, however, this relatively new usage is felt to be too colloquial and undignified for the "noble" style that was practised (and taken so seriously) in the heroic plays.[1]

Loss of intensity or "fading" or this kind is of course a common enough semasiological event, arising from the very human tendency to exaggerate in order to produce effect on the hearer, or from the

---

[1] This cult of a "noble" style is no doubt itself connected with the restriction of the drama to an upper-class audience, and with the development of an exclusive sphere of "polite letters".

simulation of emotion that does not really exist in the speaker;[1]) and it does not seem necessary to invoke any specially profound or important cultural causes for the loss of intensity in this particular case. It is possible, however, that the process was facilitated by some of the other developments going on in the word *honour*; for example, we have already seen that the head-meaning R tended during the century to lose its earlier application to high rank and the ceremonies due to high rank, and that this may have had fairly direct social causes; this weakening of the associative link between "honour" and "rank" may have made it easier for M to fade in intensity; moreover, as we shall see shortly, there was a further weakening of the association between "rank" and "honour", since there was a decline of the head-meaning P. The fading of M may also have been facilitated by an increased emphasis in upper-class society on the minor points of compliment and courtesy, a natural result of the rise of a cliquey town-set after the Restoration.[2])

The extensive use of the weakened M in courtesy-phrases is usually treated quite unironically in Restoration comedy, and all the best people use it quite naturally and unselfconsciously. Occasionally, however, there are indications that its use, or at any rate its excessive use, could sound affected or gushing. This is not surprising, of course: any conventional courtesy-phrase, if overdone, can become the mark of affectation or of floweriness of speech. The clearest example of this that I have found in my material occurs in *Bury Fair* (1689); in this play there are a number of gushing and affected characters — Lady Fantast, Mrs Fantast, and Trim — who frequently have honour on their lips, and there are no less than 19 examples of M in the play, all with some degree of loss of intensity. In one scene, Lady Fantast feels impelled to correct the speech of her younger daughter, Gertrude, who is a sensible and unaffected gentlewoman; Gertrude comes into the room where Mrs Fantast, her elder sister, is waiting for her, so that they can go to the fair together:

> Mrs. Fan. Sweet Madam *Gatty*, I have some Minutes impatiently expected your arrival, that I might do my self the great Honour to kiss your Hands, and enjoy the favour of your Company into the Fair.

---

[1]) See Stern, *op. cit.*, pp. 390—400.
[2]) See Harbage, *Cavalier Drama*, pp. 79—80.

Gert.   I got ready as soon as e're I cou'd, and am now come to wait on you.

L. Fan.   O, fye, Daughter! will you never attain, by mine, and my dear Daughters Examples, to a more Polite way of Expression, and a Nicer form of Breeding? Fye, fye, I come to wait on you! You shou'd have said; I assure you, Madam, the honour is all on my side, and I cannot be ambitious of a greater, than the enjoyment of the sweet Society of so excellent a Person. This is Breeding.

(II.1, p. 314)

There follows a dispute about natural and affected conversation, in which Shadwell is plainly on Gertrude's side. However, it is clear that the exaggerated use of courtesy-phrases with "honour", which is part of Lady Fantast's "breeding", did not discredit them entirely; in this very play, some of the examples of weakened M are used by sympathetic characters, and are quite unironical; and of course both Mt and the weakened courtesy-M have survived into present-day English side by side.

Parallel with the decline in Mt is a decline in frequency of T and P. The decline of T is extremely marked, which is not surprising, since it shares the decline of Mt, and the group MT naturally shows a heavy fall in the second half of the century. The decline of P is less marked, since, although there is a fall in tragedy, there is none in comedy, which is a little curious. It is probable that we are here witnessing, in the second half of the seventeenth century, the beginning of the process which was to lead to the disappearance of the head-meanings T and P from the word *honour*; for these two meanings can hardly be said to belong to *honour* in present-day English; it is true that "an honour" can be a title, but this is always in the combination MT, and it is hardly possible today to use the head-meaning T alone, as for example Ben Jonson does in the passages from *The Devil is an Ass* cited on p. 66 above; and the head-meaning P has completely disappeared, so that today, for example, "a man of honour" cannot possibly mean "a man of high rank", as it could in the seventeenth century. There may be both social and linguistic causes at work in producing this loss of meaning. We have already seen that there is a weakening, during the century, of the association between *honour* and the ideas related to high rank, as seen for example in the change in the content of R; this may be due, at least in part, to the tendency for breeding to become more important as a mark of gentry than birth (it will be remembered that, in comedy, the possessors of honour R/RH/H in the Restoration period were drawn more from the ordinary gentry and less from the nobility than in the first half of the century), and also to the tendency for the nobility to be less immediately involved in public affairs, with the result that the R/RH/H group came to refer more to private and personal conduct than to the rank and display connected with public life. Beside this, however, it is possible to see a good linguistic reason for the disappearance of the head-meanings P and T: semantic clash with the head-meaning H. This latter head-meaning, we have already seen, expanded enormously in the seventeenth century, probably because of the need of the upper classes to denote their code of conduct by a word distinct from those used by other classes; in the second half of the century, too, there is a great spread of the phrase "man of honour" (and similar types), probably for similar reasons (perhaps assisted by foreign influence).[1] In the second half of the century, the phrase "man of honour" sometimes certainly means "man of P (or TP)", and sometimes it certainly means "man of H (or RH)"; in many contexts, however, it is impossible to tell which it means, and there are many examples where I have classified it RHTP (or perhaps HP, or something similar); there are even some examples (twenty or so) which I have put under the U group, because they are very vague and really tell us little. I suggest that the ambiguity of the phrase "man of honour" probably contributed to the decline of the head-meanings P and T; there would be a tendency to replace it by phrases like "man of rank" and "man of birth" when T and P were intended, and to reserve "man of honour" for the H (or RH) meaning. There is a similar ambiguity in the present-day word "gentleman", which seems to be losing its sense of "man of gentle birth" while retaining that of "man of refinement and delicacy, man who shows courtesy and consideration to others", which is exactly parallel to the retention by *honour* of H and its loss of T and P.[2]

Rank and title can be either inherited from ancestors or acquired by one's own deeds (or misdeeds); in the Renaissance, there was often

---

[1] On phrases like "man of honour", see pp. 327—9 below.

[2] In the case of "gentleman", too, it is probable that there are both linguistic factors (semantic conflict) and social factors (spread of democratic sentiment, decline of the gentry as a class). At the same time, of course, *gentleman* is coming in some circles to mean simply "man".

discussion of the relative merits of the two types, called respectively "nobility native" and "nobility dative".[1]) It would therefore be interesting to know whether the word *honour* in my material, when used in the senses T and P, most often refers to inherited or acquired honour, and whether there is any change during the century. I have examined my examples from this point of view, accepting only information which is immediately obvious from the plays themselves (i. e. not embarking on research into the play-sources or into history). In many cases, of course, it is impossible to tell whether the honour is inherited or acquired, so the material is rather small. I have arrived at the conclusion that in the first half of the century there are 149 acquired to 51 inherited, and in the second half 35 acquired to 6 inherited. In both periods, then, acquired honour is much more often referred to than inherited honour, in those cases of T and P where a distinction is possible; the difference appears to become greater with time, since the ratio of acquired to inherited is 2.9 to 1 in the first half of the century and 5.8 to 1 in the second half, but unfortunately the number of examples is too small for any conclusion to be drawn from this — the difference is not significant.

B. The Head-Meaning E

The head-meaning E, "esteem, respect, reverence", is a rare one in my material. I have found a total of 70 examples, 38 in comedy and 32 in tragedy; 47 are in the first half of the century (28 in tragedy and 19 in comedy) and 23 in the second half (4 in tragedy and 19 in comedy). Somewhat different figures are obtained if we take only those examples where E is the sole head-meaning, and leave out of account those where E is part of a joint head-meaning; these figures may be more reliable, since it is often difficult to decide whether or not there is an E element in a complex head-meaning, whereas the examples of E alone are usually fairly clear. Table 59 shows the number of examples of E in each decade, comedy and tragedy being given separately; in each case, the upper line, (a), shows the number of examples of E alone (i. e. as sole head-meaning), and the lower line, (b), the total number of examples of E (i. e. both as sole head-meaning and as part of joint head-meanings). It can be seen from this table that, of the 70 examples,

---

[1]) See Kelso, *op. cit.*, pp. 22—5. For examples of discussions of this in the drama, see *All's Well*, Act II Sc. 3, and *Merchant of Venice* II.8.36—48.

TABLE 59. *Number of examples of E.*

Period from to	1591 1600	1601 1610	1611 1620	1621 1630	1631 1640	1591 1640	1661 1670	1671 1680	1681 1690	1691 1700	1661 1700	Grand Total
Comedy .... (a)	1	0	2	3	1	7	5	3	5	5	18	25
(b)	5	2	5	5	2	19	5	3	6	5	19	38
Tragedy .... (a)	2	2	4	1	2	11	1	3	0	0	4	15
(b)	5	10	7	3	3	28	1	3	0	0	4	32
All Plays ... (a)	3	2	6	4	3	18	6	6	5	5	22	40
(b)	10	12	12	8	5	47	6	6	6	5	23	70

(a) E as sole head-meaning.
(b) All examples of E.

no less than thirty occur as part of a joint head-meaning, and that all but one of these occur in the first half of the century; nearly two-thirds of the examples of E in the first half of the century occur as part of a joint head-meaning, while in the second half this is true of only about 4%. This may be a real difference, part of the tendency for writers in the second half of the century to write in a less complex way than their grandfathers, to place more reliance on statement and less on suggestion;[1]) but it is admittedly a rather difficult and subjective business to select those examples which contain an E element in a joint head-meaning, and I should not like to put much emphasis on this finding.

C. The Head-Meaning S

Examples of the head-meaning S, "something that confers honour", are not very frequent in my material, about as frequent as examples of E. There are quite a few examples in the material which could be equally well read as, say, R or as S (conferring R); I do not classify these examples as S, however, but as R (etc.), reserving S for those cases where the alternative reading is impossible or unlikely. In other words, I adopt the principle of classifying an example as "X" in preference to "S (conferring X)", if the former reading is equally possible.

---

[1]) See for example Eliot's essay on Dryden — "Dryden's words ... are precise, they state immensely, but their suggestiveness is often nothing" (*Selected Essays*, p. 315).

In these cases one is not in fact confronted with two different meanings so much as with two different syntactical ways of looking at the same meaning. This principle of classification is no doubt one of the reasons why I have found very few examples of S as part of a joint head-meaning; there are only four such examples (CS twice, HS once, MS once), all in the first half of the century, i. e. about 5.25% of the examples of S. Table 60 shows the number of examples of S found in each decade,

TABLE 60. *Number of examples of S.*

Period from to	1591 1600	1601 1610	1611 1620	1621 1630	1631 1640	1591 1640	1661 1670	1671 1680	1681 1690	1691 1700	1661 1700	Grand Total
Comedy	3	8	3	8	5	27	0	1	0	2	3	30
Tragedy	2	9	10	9	8	38	2	5	0	1	8	46
Total	5	17	13	17	13	65	2	6	0	3	11	76

comedy and tragedy being given separately. In total, it will be seen that the frequency of S falls during the century (actually from 0.51 examples per play in the first half of the century to 0.14 in the second half, which is significant).

What is conferred in the examples of S is most often Rg and/or D, or occasionally E, though E occurs only in the first half of the century (in 9 examples). Among the examples of R conferred, there are 8 examples of Rk (7 of them in the first half of the century), 13 examples of Rm (10 of them in the first half of the century), and 9 examples of Rv (all in the first half of the century); Rg occurs 54 times (45 in the first half-century), Ru 12 times (all in the first half-century), and Rn only once (first half-century). It will be seen that, if these examples were added to the examples of the head-meaning R, they would by no means reverse the trends found there.

D. The Head-Meaning W

The head-meaning W, "a promise, word of honour", arises in the second half of the seventeenth century, the first example recorded by the *N. E. D.* being from 1658—59. My own first indisputable example is from 1672. I have found twelve examples altogether, three in the decade 1671 to 1680, six in the decade 1681 to 1690, and three in the decade 1691 to 1700. There is another example that looks rather like W, but it is in the year 1607, which makes it rather difficult to accept. It occurs in *Timon of Athens*, when the senators on the walls of Athens agree to surrender the city to Alcibiades on conditions:

> Throw thy Gloue,
> Or any Token of thine Honour else,
> That thou wilt vse the warres as thy redresse,
> And not as our Confusion:
>
> (V.4.60—3)

There are other examples in the drama of a glove being thrown down as a token or, more often, a "pawn", of a man's honour, especially in challenges; usually *honour* can be interpreted R in these cases, the glove being the evidence that will cause loss of reputation if he fails to fight. In the example from *Timon* it is the word "That" which makes it difficult to read "Honour" either as R or as H, and which makes it very natural to read it as "promise". It is possible, of course, that the construction is confused or elliptical, but the W interpretation cannot be lightly dismissed, for at the date in question there was already a type of construction in use which probably led to the rise of the W usage. The usage which probably led to W is the pledging or binding of R in a promise; a man says in effect, "If I don't do as I say, may I lose my reputation (for truthfulness)", in other words "I pledge my honour". The idea that reputation is lost by failing to keep a promise is not uncommon; it is seen very clearly, for example, in the passage from *Love's Labour's Lost* from which I took the second example of R in Chapter 2 (p. 47 above). And so we often find expressions like the following:

> My Lord, I clayme the gift, my due by promise,
> For which your Honor and your Faith is pawn'd,
> Th'Earledome of Hertford, and the moueables,
> Which you haue promised I shall possesse.
>
> (*Richard III*, IV.2.89—92)

There is not much temptation to interpret "Honor" as W in this example, but it only needs a slight change of construction to make the temptation considerable. One can consider, for example, the following cases in *The Duchess of Malfi*; the Cardinal is making Pescara, Grisolan, and others, promise not to go to his brother that night if he is delirious, even if they hear shouts for help:

Card.　　　　　　Nay, I must have you promise
　　　　　　　Upon your honors, for I was enjoyn'd to't
　　　　　　　By himselfe; and he seem'd to urge it sencibly.
Pescara. Let our honors bind this trifle.
$$(V.4.10—13)$$

Here the first example cannot be interpreted as W, but the second one very easily can; the condition of equivocality exists which makes the emergence of the new head-meaning possible. In the following scene of the play, the Cardinal is being murdered, and shouting for help, but Pescara and the rest do not go to help him, because they think he is only testing them, to see if they will keep their promises; Grisolan says:

　　　　He doth this pretty well:
　　　　But it will not serve; to laugh me out of mine honour!
$$(V.5.34—5)$$

Here again the example is equivocal, and the meaning W is possible, and, now that we are further away from the Cardinal's original "promise / Upon your honours", the W interpretation is even easier. I have not in fact attributed the meaning W to these examples, but it does seem plausible that some people may have apprehended such cases as W quite early in the century, and the *Timon* example may be a genuine early case of the new meaning.

It is interesting to compare the fate of W with that of H; they were both new meanings of *honour*, and probably produced by a similar mechanism; but whereas, within a century of its origin, H became one of the most widespread and important meanings of the word, W never became more than an occasional usage, and died out again within a couple of centuries of its inception. The difference is obviously due to the fact that H fulfilled a need, while W did not.

E. The Head-Meaning D

The head-meaning D, "distinction, the quality of being distinctive or distinguished", is rare in my material. Once again, this is due in part to the fact that I have only used the D classification when there was no other reasonable head-meaning possible; this usually means M. I do not use the classification MD, but classify an example as M unless D forces itself as the meaning instead. However, even if one took the borderline cases and moved them from M to D, the D group would still be extremely small.

As it is, I am left with only 9 examples of D as a sole head-meaning, of which five are in the first half of the century, and four in the second.

F. The Head-Meaning K

The status of K as an independent head-meaning is a little doubtful. It means "the code of honour (considered as a set of laws)", and obviously it is not far removed from H, from which it is not easy to distinguish. I have found only two examples which I have found it necessary to classify as K alone; they both occur in the second half of the century. Otherwise K only occurs in the combinations HK and RHK (just occasionally RK). In total, K occurs ten times in the first half of the century, and 38 times in the second half. This increase may be a reflection of the increasing tendency to make honour into the distinctive code of behaviour for gentlemen; but the boundary between H and HK is not easy to draw, and I should not like to put much emphasis on this finding. The increase in H would in any case lead one to expect an increase in the number of examples interpretable as K.

G. The Head-Meaning L

The head-meaning L, the legal meaning "a seigniory of several manors held under one baron or lord paramount", is extremely rare in my material. I have found no examples at all where it is the sole head-meaning, but have found a few where it may be present as a joint head-meaning or perhaps as a subsidiary one. There are eight cases where I think I feel its presence, three in the decade 1591 to 1600, one in the decade 1601 to 1610, two in the decade 1611 to 1620, and two in the decade 1621 to 1630; all of them are earlier than 1627, and the meaning, a feudal technical one, may have been dying out. It is possible, however, that the men of the early part of the century, with their passionate interest in litigation, felt the meaning as present in many examples where it is lost to us.

H. The Head-Meaning O

Of the examples of O, i. e. *honour* used in oaths and asseverations like "on my honour", some half-dozen are also classified under other head-meanings, since the context gives a clear and emphatic meaning to them in these cases; the vast majority, however, are classified only under O, since it is hardly possible to assign a meaning to the separate parts of the phrase "on my honour", but only to the phrase as a whole;

originally the word *honour* may here have meant R, and may still have been felt as such in solemn asseverations, but when the phrase was used simply as a petty oath or exclamation it is doubtful whether any meaning at all was attached to the word *honour* as such; this can be seen from some of the strange phrases that occasionally crop up under O: "by the unblemish'd Honour of my beard" (*Amorous Bigot*, II.1, p. 37); "by the honour of all mustachios, and of all the beards in Spain" (*The Man's the Master*, V.1, p. 97).

The numbers of examples of O in each decade have already been given in Tables 4 to 6. It will be seen that in tragedy the frequency is substantially unchanged (the small decline in the second half of the century is not significant), but in comedy the frequency trebles in the second half of the century (significant). The increase is largely accounted for by an expansion of the phrase as a petty oath, which is often almost meaningless; it was probably felt too undignified for frequent use in tragedy, just like the weakened M (see p. 315 above). As in the case of M, too, there are occasional hints that it was used to excess by affected or (in the case of O) eccentric characters; thus all the 13 examples of O that occur in *The Humorists* are from characters of this type, and so are the 10 in *The Sullen Lovers*; but, again as in the case of M, O also continues to be used by serious and sympathetic characters; and it continues to be used in solemn assertions, not only as a petty exclamation. A study of the figures for the individual decades suggests that O may actually have become less fashionable during the course of the first half of the century, but come into fashion again after the Commonwealth period.

The users of O are substantially the same as the possessors of R/RH/H, i. e. they are almost exclusively gentry or pretenders to gentry, and they are more often men than women. I have found only one clear case of the serious use of O by a non-gentle character without any suggestion of pretentiousness or affectation (a servant in *The Relapse*, 1696). Naturally enough it is sometimes used by bullies, pretentious whores, comic conceited servants, affected wives of city knights, and other such pretenders to gentry or to the manners of the gentry. There is an interesting case in 1635 where the rich widow of a sea-captain uses it while conversing with a noblewoman, but immediately retracts it and apologizes, obviously realizing that it is an expression not fitting her social rank:

on mine honour,
I should have said my credit, I cry you mercy,
Heartily mercy!

(*News from Plymouth*, I.2, p. 120)

As in the case of R/RH/H, there is a tendency for the users in Restoration comedy to come more from the ordinary gentry and less from the nobility than in the first half of the century.

I. The Head-Meaning Y

This nearly always occurs in the second-person form, "your honour", and is very often addressed to a person of higher rank than the speaker. It is not uncommon, however, for noblemen of equal rank to use it as a formal mode of address to one another, and it is sometimes even used to a nobleman of lower rank than the speaker, as for example by Reignier (Duke of Anjou and titular King of Naples) to the Earl of Suffolk (*Henry VI.1*, V.3.147), or by the Duke of Buckingham to the Lord Hastings (*Richard III*, III.2.114). Addressees below noble rank amount only to some dozen in the first half of the century, and to about three times that number in the second half; in practically all these cases the addressees are of gentle rank (the only exceptions being of the Caliban/Stephano type) and the speaker is of much lower rank than the person addressed.

The numbers of examples of Y have already been shown in Tables 4 to 6. In comedy, there is no significant difference between the two halves of the century. In tragedy, the untypical play *The Widow Ranter* should be left out of account, and there is then a significant decrease in Y in the second half of the century. I suggest the same explanation as in the case of weakened M and O, namely that the usage was beginning to seem too undignified for the decorum and high style of Restoration heroic drama. This may have been because the phrase was being increasingly addressed to people of non-noble rank, for there is a statistically significant increase in the number of non-noble addressees in the second half of the century. This loss of intensity probably continued later, for an eighteenth-century dictionary says that Y was a title given to gentlefolk who were *not* noble, and was mainly used by their servants or by people of low rank.[1]

---

[1] "Your honour, en titel som gifwes Herrar och Fruer i England som icke äro adel, men eliest af förnäm börd eller wärdighet, dock sker det mäst af deras huus-

J. "Man of Honour" and Similar Expressions

Phrases of the type "man of honour" do not constitute a head-meaning of their own, but this seems a convenient place to say a few words about them. The word *honour* in these expressions is of course classified under one or other of the head-meanings in the usual way (even if only under U), so all the examples mentioned here have already been counted in the tables somewhere or other; but the phrase is sufficiently important to deserve a little attention on its own.

The commonest phrase of the type is "man of honour" itself; both "woman of honour" and "person of honour" are quite common, the latter being used of both men and women; less frequent are "lady of honour" and "gentleman of honour"; and there are a whole lot of nouns that give rise to occasional phrases of the type — squire, cavalier, fellow, page, child, people, minister, daughter, waiting-woman, and even friar and whore. Sometimes there is a qualifiying adjective ("man of shining honour") or a second noun ("man of wealth and honour"), but these types form only a small minority of the cases. There is one usage which I do not include among these, and which can be dismissed at once: this is "maid of honour"; this has its special technical meaning, "woman of high rank attendant upon a royal personage", and has very little resemblance to the "man of honour" type; I have found the phrase "maid of honour" 3 times in the first half of the century, and 15 times in the second; I usually put it in the U category, though occasionally it is deliberately used with a pun on the meaning H (there is an example in *The City Heiress*); the expression "maid of honour" is sometimes used as a type of exalted female rank, and it is possible that originally the word *honour* in the expression bore the meaning P.

The most striking thing about "man of honour" and similar phrases in my material is the change of frequency they show with time; this can be seen from Table 61, which gives the numbers of examples for each decade. The phrase "man of honour" is given separately, and then the sum of other phrases of the type ("person of honour", "woman of honour", etc.), but excluding "maid of honour". Figures are given for tragedy and comedy separately, then for the two combined.

It can be seen from this table that there is an enormous expansion in the second half of the century; the expressions are really rather rare in

---

folk och andra af ringare stånd" (Jacobus Serenius, *Dictionarium Anglo-Svethico-Latinum*, Hamburg 1734, s. v. *honour*).

TABLE 61. *Number of examples of "Man of Honour" and similar expressions.*

Period from to	1591 1600	1601 1610	1611 1620	1621 1630	1631 1640	1591 1640	1661 1670	1671 1680	1681 1690	1691 1700	1661 1700	Grand Total
"Man of (a)	0	1	1	2	1	5	19	44	40	9	112	117
Honour" (b)	0	0	0	4	1	5	2	11	1	4	18	23
Total	0	1	1	6	2	10	21	55	41	13	130	140
Other (a)	0	3	1	3	3	10	20	34	11	4	69	79
Phrases (b)	0	1	5	0	0	6	0	0	3	1	4	10
Total	0	4	6	3	3	16	20	34	14	5	73	89

(a) Comedy.
(b) Tragedy.

the first half of the century (in total only 0.2 examples per play),[1] while in the second half they are quite frequent (in total 2.6 examples per play). The increase is by a factor of about thirteen; it is considerably greater in "man of honour" than in the other phrases, and very much greater in comedy than in tragedy. The increase in tragedy is perhaps even less than appears from the table; in the second half of the century, no less than 13 of the examples in tragedy (12 "man of honour" and one other) occur in two plays, *The Libertine* and *The Widow Ranter*; these two plays both contain considerable naturalistic elements, and have long passages which are closer to typical Restoration comedy than to typical Restoration tragedy; if these two plays are left out of account, the increase in tragedy becomes much reduced for "man of honour" and quite negligible for the other expressions. The explanation I offer for the difference between comedy and tragedy is the same as in the case of weakened M, and O, and Y; the expressions probably sounded too colloquial and undignified to be used much in Restoration tragedy, which cultivated an exalted style. The enormous development in comedy is probably to be taken as a direct reflection of what was happening in the speech of the theatre-going classes.

Such expressions as "man of honour", then, first become widely used round about the middle of the seventeenth century, and are relatively

---

[1] This rarity of the phrase at the beginning of the century is an objection to Empson's suggestion that *Othello* may be "an attempt to isolate a racial or national type of the Man of Honour" (*op. cit.*, p. 245).

uncommon at the opening of the century. They do not occur at all in Shakespeare, the nearest he gets being the French phrase "Dames de Honeur" in *Henry V* (which is not included in my table, because I count only phrases containing the English word *honour*). The first example in my material is in Middleton's *A Mad World* (1606). It is not easy to decide what the phrases most often meant when used early in the century. In the second half of the century, there are various meanings; "man of honour" can mean "man of H", "man of P", man of "TP", and occasionally "man of R", together with the various combinations of these; there are quite a number of equivocal cases classified RHP or RHTP, and even a number classified as U. In the expressions for women, the same elements are found, plus Rc and C. The H element can be either v or k, though k is the commoner, but of course it is often impossible to tell. The P element is often found without T, meaning "of gentle rank", but it is often difficult to be sure whether "man of honour" is referring primarily to the status of gentleman or to the qualities considered appropriate to that status.

In the first half of the century the number of examples is rather small; it can be said, however, that (in contrast to the later period) there are no examples where *honour* certainly means H, though there are a few where H is a possible element in a joint head-meaning. On the whole, T and P seem to be the commonest elements, R and H occurring only as possible combiners with them. Originally, then, it seems likely that in phrases like "man of honour" the *honour* meant mostly TP or P, and that it was only in the second half of the century that it often came to mean H or RH. Whether this was so or not, we can probably see the great expansion of these phrases as yet another facet of the aristocratic development of a group ethos; "man of honour" became the upper-class equivalent to the "virtuous man" of the middle classes, and a counterblast to it.[1]

---

[1] The suddenness of the expansion after the Commonwealth suggests that French influence may have been a contributory factor, but an expansion on this scale must surely indicate that the phrase was felt to fulfil some need such as that I have suggested. The returning Cavaliers may have adopted certain gallicisms in their speech, but it remains to be explained why they chose to adopt some and not others. Phrases of the type certainly existed in France: Littré records "homme d'honneur", "gens d'honneur", and "femme d'honneur" from the seventeenth century, and attributes to "honneur" meanings corresponding to my H and C (*Dictionnaire de la langue française*, s. v. honneur, 4 and 5).

CHAPTER 13

Summary and Conclusions

A. Summary of Changes

The use of the noun *honour* has been studied in 235 plays (206 in the main material, 29 in the supplementary) from the periods 1591 to 1640 and 1661 to 1700. Tragedy and comedy have been considered separately, plays of other types being put into whichever of the two groups they most resembled. During the periods studied, considerable changes have been found to occur in the use of the noun *honour*; when the material is large enough, these changes can usually be seen going on as a continuous process during the period 1591 to 1640, the difference between the first decade and the fifth often being very considerable; when the threads are picked up again in 1661, the changes are usually found to have gone even further in the same direction; in general, however, the curves level off early in the Restoration period, though sometimes the trend continues for a couple of decades before this happens. Most of the changes, therefore, seem to take place during the first half of the seventeenth century, and to be completed by 1660 or soon after.

An account is given of the meanings of *honour* found in the material (Chapter 2), and of the changes in frequency of these meanings with time (Chapter 3). There are three groups of meanings which are extremely frequent: (1) a group concerned with the regulation of the behaviour of the gentry ("reputation" and "honourableness of character"); (2) a group connected with social rank ("mark of distinction", "title of rank", "high rank"); and (3) a group concerned specifically with the conduct of women ("chastity", "reputation for chastity"). The word is used more frequently in the second half of the century than in the first, though this increase is limited to comedy, where the increase (in terms of number of usages per play) is about 100%. Many individual meanings increase in frequency; the most notable increase is in the use of the meaning "honourableness of character" (H), which is rare at the beginning of the century, but very common in the Restoration period, both in comedy and in tragedy. Some meanings, however, do not increase; among these are the meanings "high rank" (P) and "title of rank" (T), which both decrease in frequency.

Most attention has been devoted to the meanings concerned with the regulation of the conduct of the gentry ("reputation", "honourableness of character", and the equivocal case that can mean either, denoted R, H, and RH respectively). In Chapters 6 to 10, an analysis is carried out of the conduct demanded by honour in these senses, and changes are found to occur during the century: less emphasis comes to be placed on military qualities and military achievements; at the same time, the code of conduct prescribed comes to overlap less with the morality of Christianity (as interpreted by the seventeenth century). Increased emphasis is given to duelling-honour (the requirement that insult and injury shall be avenged by duel, and that the etiquette of the duelling encounter shall be observed), to the loss of prestige caused to a man by the behaviour of other members of his family (especially by the unchastity of the female members) even when he himself is blameless, and to the requirements of honour in the matter of sexual libertinism (e. g. protecting the reputation of an adulterous mistress). Less emphasis, however, comes to be given to the reputation arising from high rank and its attendant ostentation. All these changes are found both in comedy and in tragedy, but are much more marked in comedy. In comedy, especially, there is an increasing tendency for *honour* to prescribe behaviour that is not only different from that prescribed by Christian morality, but is in fact utterly opposed to it (e. g. sexual libertinism). Round about the year 1630, passages are found in three plays which can be interpreted as a comment on these changes in the demands of honour, and as a condemnation of them (Chapter 10, E).

The meanings "chastity" (C) and "reputation for chastity" (Rc) are normally used only of women, though there are a few possible examples of their serious application to men, all early in the century (Chapter 11). In comedy, there is during the century an increase in the frequency of the meaning "reputation for chastity" at the expense of the meaning "chastity", while in tragedy the opposite change takes place. There is also an increasing tendency, in comedy, for the meaning "reputation for chastity" (Rc) to carry the implication "but not in fact chaste" (Rco), a tendency which is shared in a lesser degree by the meaning "reputation" in general (R) (Chapter 5, B).

In the meaning "reputation" (R, and also in RH), there is an increase during the century in usages which are defensive in attitude ("good name") at the expense of ones which are expansive in attitude ("glory"): negative reputation becomes more important than positive reputation (Chapter 5, A). However, in the meaning "reputation for chastity" (Rc), the usage is almost invariably of the negative type.

In some meanings, there is a loss of intensity during the century; this is especially true of the meaning "something conferred as a mark of respect or distinction" (M), which in the first half of the century refers mainly to titles, orders, etc. publicly conferred by the sovereign, but which in the second half of the century is most often used of private and often trivial conferments (the honour of somebody's company, acquaintance, etc.). Other usages which show some loss of intensity are oaths and asseverations in which honour is invoked (O), which increasingly tend to be mere meaningless exclamations, and forms like "your honour" as a respectful mode of address (Y), which increasingly tend to be used to ordinary gentry (by their inferiors) and not merely to the nobility (Chapter 12).

The century witnesses the rise of the phrase "man of honour" and similar types, which are rare at the beginning of the period and common at the end; "man of honour" sometimes means "man of high rank", sometimes "man of honourable character or principles", and sometimes both (Chapter 12, J).

At the beginning of the century, there are differences between comedy and tragedy; in tragedy, for example, there is greater emphasis on military achievements and military reputation, and a greater overlap of the code of honour with Christian morals. In nearly all respects, the result of the changes during the century is to widen the gap between comedy and tragedy; in other words, the changes are greater in comedy than in tragedy. However, the changes in tragedy are often by no means insignificant, and the overall changes cannot be simply explained away as a redistribution of usages between comedy and tragedy.

The meanings of *honour* relating directly to the regulation of conduct, when used seriously, are used only of the gentry, or of people who claim gentry;[1] there are only a handful of exceptions to this rule, and the quite certain ones all relate to women's chastity or reputation for

---

[1] I use "the gentry" in the wide sense, to include the nobility and royalty; gentry of lower rank than the nobility I call "the ordinary gentry".

chastity. Not only do the vast majority of examples relate to people of gentle birth, but a very large proportion of these relate to people of noble or royal rank. In comedy, there is an increase during the century in the proportion of ordinary gentry, at the expense of the higher ranks, but in tragedy the trend is the other way, with an increase in the proportion of characters of royal rank. Knights are not often depicted as possessors of honour, perhaps because they were regarded as types of the parvenu, but in Restoration comedy honour (chastity, reputation for chastity) is attributed to large numbers of knights' ladies, perhaps because of the habit of the gallant heroes of carrying on intrigues with the wives of the parvenus. There are some indications that honour could be possessed by all soldiers, even common soldiers; it is not clear whether this is an exception to the rule about gentry, or whether it shows that all soldiers tended to claim gentry. Honour is occasionally attributed to members of the professional and commercial classes (lawyers, merchants, etc.), and when this is done seriously it seems that we are expected to regard these characters as members of the gentry; such attributions are commoner in the first half of the century than in the second. (Chapter 4.)

B. Possible Causes of the Changes

My main concern has been to discover and exhibit the usage, and especially the changes in the usage, but in the course of doing so I have also put forward a number of suggestions about the causes of the changes that I have found. The causes that I have suggested have been of two kinds: (1) social causes, arising from the particular historical development of English society in the period in question; (2) linguistic causes, arising from human psychology and the nature of language (or at any rate the English language) in general, which might well have operated even if the social history of England in the seventeenth century had followed a very different path.[1]) I have emphasized the change in

---

[1]) I am not suggesting that there is anything eternal or immutable either in human nature or in language; it is simply a question of the time-scale on which changes operate; common semantic changes of the "loss of intensity" type occur in widely separated societies and at widely separated times, and for similar reasons, and will no doubt continue to do so; in comparison with the period of a mere century covered by this study, semantic changes of this type are caused by factors which can be considered as relatively stable and permanent. Cf. L. Bloomfield, *Language*, p. 20.

the theatre-audience during the seventeenth century, the way in which the middle classes fell out of it during the first half of the century, and the way in which it became an almost exclusively aristocratic audience after the Restoration (Chapter 1, E); but I include this under causes of the first type, since I see the change in the theatre as a result of the changes in society outside, especially the growing hostility between court and city, between king and parliament, between cavalier and puritan. I have suggested that the general increase in interest in honour as a theme in English drama is a result of the change in the audience, since honour is a prerogative of the upper classes, and the theatre increasingly caters for upper-class taste. However, I take the development in comedy (which is relatively realistic) to show that the increasing interest in honour was also a real fact in society outside the theatre, and that courtly circles became especially interested in honour as a determinant of conduct, as a code of behaviour; this interest is seen in the enormous increase in frequency of the meaning "honourableness of character" (H) and of the phrase "man of honour". I have suggested that both the spread of these, and also the changes in the conduct demanded by the code of honour, reflect the process whereby the upper classes (or a section of them) develop a class-ethos different from that of the rest of society, and especially different from that of the puritans, as they become increasingly cut off from the rest of society, and increasingly hostile to the middle classes. The growing connection between honour and sexual libertinism is part of the anti-puritan movement, and the increased frequency of duelling-honour perhaps reflects the desire of the courtier to have a class-justice outside the ordinary law-courts, which were often run by people of non-gentle origins. The decline in the military element in the ideal of honour may be due to the decline of the military function of the nobleman, as the feudal castle gives way to the gentleman's country-house, and as warfare becomes increasingly professionalized. At the same time, the nobility come to play a less automatic part in public affairs, and to be less obviously public persons than in the sixteenth century; I have suggested that this may have encouraged the tendency for more emphasis to be placed on the personal and private elements in the code of honour (e. g. duelling, and the chastity of female relatives) and less on the public and political elements (e. g. ostentation, "magnificence", the reputation arising from high rank, and warfare).

The development in the women's particular form of honour (chastity) is, in comedy (and therefore probably in real life too), towards a greater emphasis on appearances and reputation, and a smaller emphasis on chastity itself. I have suggested that this is caused by the discrepancy between two desires on the part of the Restoration town-gentleman: first, to have legitimate heirs to inherit his wealth and titles (which demands the upholding of chastity as an ideal for women), and second to live the life of a gentleman of pleasure dictated by his anti-puritan code of morals (which requires a supply of willing women). The ideal of a life of pleasure (normal in Restoration comedy) is perhaps another result of the loss by the upper classes of any obvious public and political function.

The increasing differences between comedy and tragedy I take to indicate an increasing discrepancy between the gentry as they liked to imagine themselves, and as they really were: as life became less noble and less heroic, the aristocratic ideal became more so, indeed impossibly so. This was presumably a kind of compensation, and perhaps also an attempt to maintain their self-esteem; the less admirable their lives were in practice, the more vociferously they had to assert a hyper-magnanimous ideal.

On the other hand, it is not necessary to invoke any such special social causes to explain some of the changes, such as the loss of intensity in M, and the decline of T and P; the former is type of fading which is common enough everywhere, and the latter is probably due to semantic conflict. However, I do not wish to draw too sharp a line between these "linguistic" causes and the "social" causes; in all semantic change, a key part is played by the needs of the speaker, and in the last analysis, presumably, there is no real distinction between "social needs" and "psychological needs". Nor need one always assume a single cause for a change; it has been seen that two new meanings of *honour* arise within a century of one another, "honourableness of character", and "word of honour, promise", both probably by a similar linguistic mechanism; the former develops into one of the most important meanings of the word, while the other is never very common and dies out after a couple of centuries of shadowy life; here, linguistic mechanisms produce two new meanings, but extra-linguistic needs probably play the largest part in determining the difference between their histories. Moreover, the new expanding meaning (H) probably contributes to the decay of an established meaning, "high rank" (P), through semantic conflict, though that decay may have been assisted by an extra-linguistic factor, the decline of ostentation as a necessary part of a nobleman's public life. Here we have "linguistic" and "social" factors intertwined.

I realize, of course, that the various influences may have worked more indirectly than my formulations suggest, and naturally I do not exclude the possibility of other influences, such as foreign influence. I have argued, however, that foreign influence cannot in any case be considered as more than a catalyst: there must have been something in the situation and in the attitudes of those influenced that made them susceptible to the influence (Chapter 1, D). I have also discussed the question whether English dramatists attempted to reproduce a foreign code of honour in plays with a foreign setting; an examination of Restoration comedies set in Spain has led me to the view that they did not do so to any marked extent; the Spanish characters are represented as more sensitive about honour than English characters, but the demands of honour are represented as essentially the same for both (Chapter 10, F).

I have compared the treatment of honour in comedies from the decade 1601 to 1610 written for the public theatres and for the private theatres respectively, but have found no significant differences between them; on the other hand, they both differ significantly from the comedies of the Restoration period (Chapter 10, G). I take this to show that the changes in the use of the word *honour* cannot be explained as solely due to the change from a broad audience to a select upper-class audience; it is also necessary to postulate an actual change in the usage (and consequently in the attitudes) of the theatre-going upper-classes during the century. I have however emphasized the fact that in the second half of the century the theatre-going public was drawn from a small town-set; it represented a narrower section of society, for example, than Addison's Spectator Club some years later, which included a city merchant, a country squire, and a pious clergyman; there can be little doubt that the Restoration dramatists excluded from gentry (and therefore from the possession of honour) many people who would themselves have claimed it, and whose claims would have been generally admitted in the eighteenth century. The set that dominated the Restoration theatre must not be wholly judged by its own pretensions.

With this qualification made, however, it does seem justifiable to claim that the changes in the code of honour seen in the drama during the seventeenth century do represent a real change in the upper-class ideal. The large changes seen in comedy are probably a not too distant reflection of the changes that actually occurred. The changes in tragedy are more probably to be seen as a change in the idealized image of themselves that the upper classes liked to contemplate. The total changes in usage that have been found represent a major change in scale of values, and make it clear that changes in meaning may be intimately bound up with the whole cultural development (in this case one is tempted to say "cultural disintegration") of a social group.

APPENDIX A

Chronological list of plays used as material.

Column (a) date; (b) title; (c) presumed authorship; (d) edition cited, and volume number (for details, see Appendix C); (e) how cited; (f) type of play; (g) number of examples of *honour* (noun) found. In column (f), the letters C and T in brackets show whether the play is classified in the comedy-group or the tragedy-group.

(1) The Main Material

(a)	(b)	(c)	(d)	(e)	(f)	(g)
1591	*Henry VI, Part 2*	Shakespeare	First Folio	Act, sc., line	History (T)	18
1591	*Henry VI, Part 3*	Shakespeare	First Folio	Act, sc., line	History (T)	11
1592	*Henry VI, Part 1*	Shakespeare	First Folio	Act, sc., line	History (T)	20
1592	*Richard III*	Shakespeare	First Folio[1])	Act, sc., line	History (T)	16
1593	*Comedy of Errors*	Shakespeare	First Folio	Act, sc., line	Comedy (C)	3
1593	*Two Gentlemen of Verona*	Shakespeare	First Folio	Act, sc., line	Comedy (C)	9
1594	*Titus Andronicus*	Shakespeare	First Folio	Act, sc., line	Tragedy (T)	24
1594	*Love's Labour's Lost*	Shakespeare	First Folio	Act, sc., line	Comedy (C)	8
1594	*Taming of the Shrew*	Shakespeare	First Folio	Act, sc., line	Comedy (C)	12
1595	*Romeo and Juliet*	Shakespeare	First Folio	Act, sc., line	Tragedy (T)	3
1595	*Midsummer Night's Dream*	Shakespeare	First Folio	Act, sc., line	Comedy (C)	0
1595	*Richard II*	Shakespeare	First Folio[2])	Act, sc., line	History (T)	22
1596	*King John*	Shakespeare	First Folio	Act, sc., line	History (T)	16
1596	*Merchant of Venice*	Shakespeare	First Folio	Act, sc., line	Comedy (C)	12
1597	*Henry IV, Part 1*	Shakespeare	First Folio	Act, sc., line	History (C)	25
1597	*Henry IV, Part 2*	Shakespeare	First Folio	Act, sc., line	History (C)	20
1598	*Much Ado About Nothing*	Shakespeare	First Folio	Act, sc., line	Comedy (C)	10
1599	*Henry V*	Shakespeare	First Folio	Act, sc., line	History (T)	22
1599	*Julius Caesar*	Shakespeare	First Folio	Act, sc., line	Tragedy (T)	15

[1]) Two of the examples are not in the folio, and are taken from the 1597 quarto.
[2]) Two of the examples are not in F, and are taken from the first quarto (1597).

APPENDIX A

(a)	(b)	(c)	(d)	(e)	(f)	(g)
1600	Merry Wives of Windsor	Shakespeare	First Folio	Act, sc., line	Comedy (C)	10
1600	As You Like It	Shakespeare	First Folio	Act, sc., line	Comedy (C)	12
1601	Twelfth Night	Shakespeare	First Folio	Act, sc., line	Comedy (C)	9
1601	Hamlet	Shakespeare	First Folio[1])	Act, sc., line	Tragedy (T)	11
1601	Blurt, Master Constable	Middleton and Dekker	Middleton Vol. 1	Act, sc., line	Comedy (C)	21
1601	Poetaster	Jonson	Jonson Vol. IV	Act, sc., line	Comedy (C)	14
1602	Troilus and Cressida	Shakespeare	First Folio[2])	Act, sc., line	Tragedy (T)	26
1602	Family of Love	Middleton	Vol. 3	Act, sc., line	Comedy (C)	2
1603	All's Well that Ends Well	Shakespeare	First Folio	Act, sc., line	Comedy (C)	44
1603	Sejanus	Jonson	Vol. IV	Act, sc., line	Tragedy (T)	28
1604	Measure for Measure	Shakespeare	First Folio	Act, sc., line	Comedy (C)	45
1604	Othello	Shakespeare	First Folio	Act, sc., line	Tragedy (T)	11
1604	The Phoenix	Middleton	Vol. 1	Act, sc., line	Comedy (C)	16
1605	King Lear	Shakespeare	First Folio	Act, sc., line	Tragedy (T)	11
1605	Eastward Ho	Chapman, Jonson, and Marston	Jonson, Vol. IV	Act, sc., line	Comedy (C)	8
1605	A Trick to Catch the Old One	Middleton	Vol. 2	Act, sc., line	Comedy	2
1605	Volpone	Jonson	Vol. V	Act, sc., line	Comedy (C)	16
1606	Macbeth	Shakespeare	First Folio	Act, sc., line	Tragedy (T)	15
1606	Michaelmas Term	Middleton	Vol. 1	Act, sc., line	Comedy (C)	2
1606	A Mad World, my Masters	Middleton	Vol. 3	Act, sc., line	Comedy (C)	20
1607	Timon of Athens	Middleton, Shakespeare and Day?	Shakespeare First Folio	Act, sc., line	Tragedy (T)	25
1607	Antony and Cleopatra	Shakespeare	First Folio	Act, sc., line	Tragedy (T)	21
1607	Your Five Gallants	Middleton	Vol. 3	Act, sc., line	Comedy (C)	5
1608	Pericles	Shakespeare and ?	Shakespeare Quarto 1609	Act, sc., line	Tragicomedy (T)	23

[1]) One of the examples is not in F, and is taken from the second quarto (1604—5).
[2]) One of the examples is from the quarto (1609), where F reads *honour'd*.

(a)	(b)	(c)	(d)	(e)	(f)	(g)
1608	The Faithful Shepherdess	Fletcher	B. & F., Vol. 2	Act, sc., page	Pastoral (T)	7
1609	Coriolanus	Shakespeare	First Folio	Act, sc., line	Tragedy (T)	37
1609	Epicoene	Jonson	Vol. V	Act, sc., line	Comedy (C)	12
1609	Philaster	Beaumont & Fletcher	B. & F., Vol. 1	Act, sc., page	Tragicomedy (T)	17
1610	Cymbeline	Shakespeare	First Folio	Act, sc., line	Tragicomedy (T)	30
1610	Maid's Tragedy	Beaumont & Fletcher	B. & F.,[1]) Vol. 1	Act, sc., page	Tragedy (T)	33
1610	The Alchemist	Jonson	Vol. V	Act, sc., line	Comedy (C)	8
1610	The Roaring Girl	Middleton & Dekker	Middleton, Vol. 4	Act, sc., line	Comedy (C)	5
1611	Winter's Tale	Shakespeare	First Folio	Act, sc., line	Tragicomedy (T)	29
1611	Catiline	Jonson	Vol. V	Act, sc., line	Tragedy (T)	30
1611	A King and No King	Beaumont & Fletcher	B. & F., Vol. 1	Act, sc., page	Tragicomedy (T)	12
1611	The Tempest	Shakespeare	First Folio	Act, sc., line	Comedy (C)	8
1612	A Chaste Maid in Cheapside	Middleton	Vol. 5	Act, sc., line	Comedy (C)	1
1612	The Captain	Beaumont & Fletcher?	B. and F., Vol. 5	Act, sc., page	Comedy (C)	10
1612	White Devil	Webster	Vol. 1	Act, sc., line	Tragedy (T)	7
1613	Henry VIII	Shakespeare & Fletcher	Shakespeare First Folio	Act, sc., line	History (T)	53
1613	Scornful Lady	Beaumont & Fletcher	B. & F., Vol. 1	Act, sc., page	Comedy (C)	8
1613	Duchess of Malfi	Webster	Vol. 2	Act, sc., line	Tragedy (T)	19
1614	Valentinian	Fletcher	B. & F., Vol. 4	Act, sc., page	Tragedy (T)	53
1614	Bartholomew Fair	Jonson	Vol. VI	Act, sc., line	Comedy (C)	2
1614	Wit without Money	Fletcher	B. & F., Vol. 2	Act, sc., page	Comedy (C)	9
1615	Monsieur Thomas	Fletcher	B. & F., Vol. 4	Act, sc., page	Comedy (C)	4
1615	The Witch	Middleton	Vol. 5	Act, sc., line	Tragicomedy (T)	15
1616	The Devil is an Ass	Jonson	Vol. VI	Act, sc., line	Comedy (C)	16

[1]) One example (on p. 69) is omitted, as it seems to be a misprint in the Folio for *houre* (which is the reading of Qq 1 to 4).

APPENDIX A

(a)	(b)	(c)	(d)	(e)	(f)	(g)
1617	A Fair Quarrel	Middleton & Rowley	Middleton Vol. 4	Act, sc., line	Comedy (C)	27
1617	The Mad Lover	Fletcher	B. & F., Vol. 3	Act, sc., page	Tragicomedy (T)	24
1618	The Loyal Subject	Fletcher	B. & F., Vol. 3	Act, sc., page	Tragicomedy (T)	51
1619	The Humorous Lieutenant	Fletcher	B. & F., Vol. 2	Act, sc., page	Tragicomedy (T)	44
1619	The Laws of Candy	Massinger and Ford?	B. & F., Vol. 3	Act, sc., page	Tragicomedy (T)	26
1619	The Little French Lawyer	Fletcher & Massinger	B. & F., Vol. 3	Act, sc., page	Comedy (C)	76
1619	The Bloody Brother	Massinger, Fletcher, and Jonson.	B. & F., Vol. 4	Act, sc., page	Tragedy (T)	24
1620	The Devil's Law Case	Webster	Vol. 2	Act, sc., line	Comedy (C)	10
1620	The False One	Fletcher & Massinger	B. & F., Vol. 3	Act, sc., page	Tragedy (T)	34
1620	The Custom of the Country	Fletcher & Massinger	B. & F., Vol. 1	Act, sc., page	Comedy (C)	38
1621	The Wild Goose Chase	Fletcher	B. & F., Vol. 4	Act, sc., page	Comedy (C)	19
1621	The Pilgrim	Fletcher	B. & F., Vol. 5	Act, sc., page	Comedy (C)	19
1621	Anything for a Quiet Life	Webster & Middleton	Webster, Vol. 4	Act, sc., line	Comedy (C)	6
1621	The Maid of Honour	Massinger	Massinger	Act, sc., page	Tragicomedy (T)	26
1622	Beggars' Bush	Fletcher & Massinger	B. & F., Vol. 2	Act, sc., page	Comedy (C)	7
1622	The Spanish Curate	Fletcher & Massinger	B. & F., Vol. 2	Act, sc., page	Comedy (C)	8
1622	The Prophetess	Fletcher & Massinger	B. & F., Vol. 5	Act, sc., page	Tragicomedy (T)	48
1622	The Changeling	Middleton & Rowley	Middleton, Vol. 6	Act, sc., line	Tragedy (T)	18
1623	The Lover's Progress	Fletcher & Massinger	B. & F., Vol. 5	Act, sc., page	Tragedy (T)	40
1623	The Bondman	Massinger	Massinger	Act, sc., page	Tragicomedy (T)	49

(a)	(b)	(c)	(d)	(e)	(f)	(g)
1623	The Spanish Gipsy	Middleton & Rowley	Middleton, Vol. 6	Act, sc., line	Comedy (C)	12
1624	Rule a Wife, and have a Wife	Fletcher	B. & F., Vol. 3	Act, sc., page	Comedy (C)	25
1624	Wife for a Month	Fletcher	B. & F., Vol. 5	Act, sc., page	Tragicomedy (T)	44
1624	The Renegado	Massinger	Massinger	Act, sc., page	Tragicomedy (T)	16
1624	A Game at Chess	Middleton	Vol. 7	Act, sc., line	Morality (C)	28
1625	The Chances	Fletcher	B. & F., Vol. 4	Act, sc., page	Comedy (C)	27
1625	A Cure for a Cuckold	Webster & Rowley	Webster, Vol. 3	Act, sc., line	Comedy (C)	11
1625	The Elder Brother	Fletcher & Massinger	B. & F., Vol. 2	Act, sc., page	Comedy (C)	16
1625	A New Way to Pay Old Debts	Massinger	Massinger	Act, sc., page	Comedy (C)	28
1625	The Staple of News	Jonson	Vol. VI	Act, sc., line	Comedy (C)	11
1626	The Fair Maid of the Inn	Massinger, Webster, & Ford?	Webster, Vol. 4	Act, sc., line	Comedy (C)	26
1627	The Great Duke of Florence	Massinger	Massinger	Act, sc., page	Tragicomedy (T)	17
1627	'Tis Pity She's a Whore	Ford	Materials, N. S., Vol. 1	Line	Tragedy (T)	11
1628	The Witty Fair One	Shirley	Vol. 1	Act, sc., page	Comedy (C)	7
1629	The Broken Heart	Ford	Materials, N. S., Vol. 1	Line	Tragedy (T)	27
1629	The New Inn	Jonson	Vol. VI	Act, sc., line	Comedy (C)	13
1631	The Traitor	Shirley	Vol. 2	Act, sc., page	Tragedy (T)	33
1631	The Emperor of the East	Massinger	Massinger	Act, sc., page	Tragicomedy (T)	24
1632	Hyde Park	Shirley	Vol. 2	Act, sc., page	Comedy (C)	29
1632	The City Madam	Massinger	Massinger	Act, sc., page	Comedy (C)	16
1632	The Magnetic Lady	Jonson	Vol. VI	Act, sc., line	Comedy (C)	12
1633	Perkin Warbeck	Ford	Materials, N. S., Vol. 1	Line	History (T)	24
1633	The Guardian	Massinger	Massinger	Act, sc., page	Comedy (C)	26
1634	A Very Woman	Massinger	Massinger	Act sc., page	Tragicomedy (T)	30
1634	The Wits	Davenant	Vol. 2	Act, sc., page	Comedy (C)	6

APPENDIX A

(a)	(b)	(c)	(d)	(e)	(f)	(g)
1634	Love and Honour	Davenant	Vol. 3	Act, sc., page	Tragicomedy (T)	11
1635	The Lady of Pleasure	Shirley	Vol. 4	Act, sc., page	Comedy (C)	36
1635	The Platonic Lovers	Davenant	Vol. 2	Act, sc., page	Tragicomedy[1] (T)	5
1635	News from Plymouth	Davenant	Vol. 4	Act, sc., page	Comedy (C)	23
1636	The Fancies	Ford	Materials, N. S., Vol. 1	Line	Comedy (C)	24
1636	The Bashful Lover	Massinger	Massinger	Act, sc., page	Tragicomedy (T)	39
1637	The Royal Master	Shirley	Vol. 4	Act, sc., page	Comedy (C)	42
1638	The Lady's Trial	Ford	Materials, N. S., Vol. 1	Line	Comedy (C)	26
1638	The Unfortunate Lovers	Davenant	Vol. 3	Act, sc., page	Tragedy (T)	10
1638	The Fair Favourite	Davenant	Vol. 4	Act, sc., page	Tragicomedy (T)	21
1638	The Constant Maid	Shirley	Vol. 4	Act, sc., page	Comedy (C)	9
1639	The Distresses	Davenant	Vol. 4	Act, sc., page	Comedy (C)	30
1639	The Politician	Shirley	Vol. 5	Act, sc., page	Tragedy (T)	21
1640	The Imposture	Shirley	Vol. 5	Act, sc., page	Tragicomedy (T)	50
1641	The Cardinal[2])	Shirley	Vol. 5	Act, sc., page	Tragedy (T)	36
1662	The Law against Lovers	Davenant	Vol. 5	Act, sc., page	Comedy (C)	22
1663	The Wild Gallant	Dryden	Vol. 2	Act, sc., page	Comedy (C)	8
1663	The Rival Ladies	Dryden	Vol. 2	Act, sc., page	Tragicomedy (T)	17
1664	The Indian Queen	Howard & Dryden	Dryden, Vol. 2	Act, sc., page	Tragicomedy (T)	20
1664	The Comical Revenge	Etherege	Vol. 1	Act, sc., line	Comedy (C)	40
1665	The Indian Emperor	Dryden	Vol. 2	Act, sc., page	Tragicomedy (T)	35

[1]) Both by its editors and by Harbage, *The Platonic Lovers* is called a comedy; on its title-page, however, it is called a tragicomedy, and this seems to me to be the juster classification.

[2]) Although *The Cardinal* falls outside the decade 1631 to 1640, I have included it in preference to some other of Shirley's plays because it is one of his best known, and one of the few available to the general reader (in the Mermaid edition).

(a)	(b)	(c)	(d)	(e)	(f)	(g)
1667	Secret Love	Dryden	Vol. 2	Act, sc., page	Tragicomedy (T)	12
1667	Sir Martin Mar-all	Dryden & Cavendish	Dryden, Vol. 3	Act, sc., page	Comedy (C)	5
1667	The Tempest[1]	Dryden & Davenant	Dryden, Vol. 3	Act, sc., page	Comedy (C)	7
1668	An Evening's Love	Dryden	Vol. 3	Act, sc., page	Comedy (C)	23
1668	The Sullen Lovers	Shadwell	Vol. 1	Act, sc., page	Comedy (C)	53
1668	She Would if She Could	Etherege	Vol. 2	Act, sc., line	Comedy (C)	56
1668	The Man's the Master	Davenant	Vol. 5	Act, sc., page	Comedy (C)	43
1669	Tyrannic Love	Dryden	Vol. 3	Act, sc., page	Tragedy (T)	15
1669	The Royal Shepherdess	Shadwell & Fountain	Shadwell, Vol. 1	Act, sc., page	Tragicomedy (T)	29
1670	Conquest of Granada, the First Part	Dryden	Vol. 4	Act, sc., page	Tragicomedy (T)	9
1670	The Humorists	Shadwell	Vol. 1	Act, sc., page	Comedy (C)	71
1670	The Forced Marriage	Behn	Vol. 3	Act, sc., page	Tragicomedy (T)	28
1671	Love in a Wood	Wycherley	Wycherley	Act, sc., page	Comedy (C)	32
1671	The Conquest of Granada, the Second Part	Dryden	Vol. 4	Act, sc., page	Tragicomedy (T)	45
1671	Marriage à la Mode	Dryden	Vol. 4	Act, sc., page	Comedy (C)	19
1671	The Amorous Prince	Behn	Vol. 4	Act, sc., page	Comedy (C)	24
1672	The Gentleman Dancing-Master	Wycherley	Wycherley	Act, sc., page	Comedy (C)	46
1672	The Assignation	Dryden	Vol. 4	Act, sc., page	Comedy (C)	11
1672	Amboyna	Dryden	Vol. 5	Act, sc., page	Tragedy (T)	15
1672	Epsom Wells	Shadwell	Vol. 2	Act, sc., page	Comedy (C)	66
1673	The Dutch Lover	Behn	Vol. 1	Act, sc., page	Comedy (C)	21

[1]) Mr Montague Summers says in his edition of Shadwell (Vol. 1, p. cvi) that all Dryden editors have printed Shadwell's operatic version of *The Tempest* of 1674, not the non-operatic Dryden/Davenant version of 1670, which he himself first published in 1922. I have therefore checked Saintsbury's version against the one edited by Summers in the Nonesuch Dryden; as far as *honour* is concerned there is no difference between the two versions (except for minor differences of spelling and punctuation).

APPENDIX A

(a)	(b)	(c)	(d)	(e)	(f)	(g)
1675	Alcibiades	Otway	Vo. 1	Act, sc., line	Tragedy (T)	50
1675	The Country Wife	Wycherley	Wycherley	Act, sc., page	Comedy (C)	86
1675	Aureng-Zebe	Dryden	Vol. 5	Act, sc., page	Tragicomedy (T)	19
1675	The Libertine	Shadwell	Vol. 3	Act, sc., page	Tragedy (T)	40
1676	Don Carlos	Otway	Vol. 1	Act, sc., line	Tragedy (T)	20
1676	The Plain Dealer	Wycherley	Wycherley	Act, sc., page	Comedy (C)	63
1676	The Virtuoso	Shadwell	Vol. 3	Act, sc., page	Comedy (C)	61
1676	The Man of Mode	Etherege	Vol. 2	Act, sc., line	Comedy (C)	8
1676	Abdelazer	Behn	Vol. 2	Act, sc., page	Tragedy (T)	38
1676	The Town Fop	Behn	Vol. 3	Act, sc., page	Comedy (C)	24
1677	All for Love	Dryden	Vol. 5	Act, sc., page	Tragedy (T)	21
1677	The Rover, Part 1	Behn	Vol. 1	Act, sc., page	Comedy (C)	19
1678	Friendship in Fashion	Otway	Vol. 1	Act, sc., line	Comedy (C)	40
1678	The Kind Keeper	Dryden	Vol. 6	Act, sc., page	Comedy (C)	10
1678	Oedipus	Lee and Dryden	Dryden, Vol. 6	Act, sc., page	Tragedy (T)	7
1678	A True Widow	Shadwell	Vol. 3	Act, sc., page	Comedy (C)	24
1678	Sir Patient Fancy	Behn	Vol. 4	Act, sc., page	Comedy (C)	13
1679	Caius Marius	Otway	Vol. 1	Act, sc., line	Tragedy (T)	18
1679	Troilus and Cressida	Dryden	Vol. 6	Act, sc., page	Tragedy (T)	24
1679	The Woman-Captain	Shadwell	Vol. 4	Act, sc., page	Comedy (C)	15
1680	The Orphan	Otway	Vol. 2	Act, sc., line	Tragedy (T)	29
1680	The Soldier's Fortune	Otway	Vol. 2	Act, sc., line	Comedy (C)	29
1680	The Spanish Friar	Dryden	Vol. 6	Act, sc., page	Comedy (C)	18
1681	The Lancashire Witches	Shadwell	Vol. 4	Act, sc., page	Comedy (C)	24
1681	The Roundheads	Behn	Vol. 1	Act, sc., page	Comedy (C)	34
1681	The False Count	Behn	Vol. 3	Act, sc., page	Comedy (C)	46
1682	Venice Preserved	Otway	Vol. 2	Act, sc., line	Tragedy (T)	31
1682	The Duke of Guise	Lee and Dryden	Dryden, Vol. 7	Act, sc., page	Tragedy (T)	24
1682	The City Heiress	Behn	Vol. 2	Act, sc., page	Comedy (C)	33
1683	The Atheist	Otway	Vol. 2	Act, sc., line	Comedy (C)	27
1683	Constantine the Great	Lee	Vol. 2	Act, sc., page	Tragedy (T)	8
1686	The Lucky Chance	Behn	Vol. 3	Act, sc., page	Comedy (C)	12
1688	The Squire of Alsatia	Shadwell	Vol. 4	Act, sc., page	Comedy (C)	29

(a)	(b)	(c)	(d)	(e)	(f)	(g)
1689	Don Sebastian	Dryden	Vol. 7	Act, sc., page	Tragedy (T)	26
1689	Bury Fair	Shadwell	Vol. 4	Act, sc., page	Comedy (C)	54
1689	The Widow Ranter	Behn	Vol. 4	Act, sc., page	Tragicomedy (T)	75
1689	The Younger[1]) Brother	Behn	Vol. 4	Act, sc., page	Comedy (C)	13
1690	Amphitryon	Dryden	Vol. 8	Act, sc., page	Comedy (C)	24
1690	The Amorous Bigot	Shadwell	Vol. 5	Act, sc., page	Comedy (C)	54
1690	The Scowrers	Shadwell	Vol. 5	Act, sc., page	Comedy (C)	42
1691	King Arthur	Dryden	Vol. 8	Act, sc., page	Dramatic Opera (T)	14
1692	Cleomenes	Dryden	Vol. 8	Act, sc., page	Tragedy (T)	11
1692	The Volunteers	Shadwell	Vol. 5	Act, sc., page	Comedy (C)	65
1693	The Old Bachelor	Congreve	Congreve	Act, sc., page	Comedy (C)	9
1693	The Double Dealer	Congreve	Congreve	Act, sc., page	Comedy (C)	31
1694	Love Triumphant	Dryden	Vol. 8	Act, sc., page	Tragicomedy (T)	23
1695	Love for Love	Congreve	Congreve	Act, sc., page	Comedy (C)	10
1696	The Relapse	Vanbrugh	Vol. 1	Act, sc., page	Comedy (C)	28
1697	The Provoked Wife	Vanbrugh	Vol. 1	Act, sc., page	Comedy (C)	14
1697	The Mourning Bride	Congreve	Congreve	Act, sc., page	Tragicomedy (T)	6
1699	The Constant Couple	Farquhar	Farquhar	Act, sc., page	Comedy (C)	38
1700	The Way of the World	Congreve	Congreve	Act, sc., page	Comedy (C)	10

[1]) The date given by Harbage for *The Younger Brother*, 1696, is that of first production, which was posthumous. As it seems possible that Behn may have been working intermittently on the play throughout the 1680's, I have dated it 1689, the year of her death. The alterations made in it by Charles Gildon when he produced it in 1696 do not seem to have been very great, to judge from his Epistle Dedicatory.

APPENDIX A 347

(2) *The Supplementary Material*

(a)	(b)	(c)	(d)	(e)	(f)	(g)
1591	Edward I	Peele	Malone Society Reprint	—	History (T)	40
1591	Orlando Furioso	Greene	Vol. 1	—	Comedy (C)	12
1592	Dr Faustus	Marlowe	Marlowe	—	Tragedy (T)	5
1592	Summer's Last Will and Testament	Nashe	Vol. 3	—	Comedy (C)	9
1592	Edward II	Marlowe	Marlowe	—	History (T)	24
1593	Massacre at Paris	Marlowe	Marlowe	—	Tragedy (T)	6
1594	Alphonsus Emperor of Germany	Peele?	Chapman's Tragedies	—	Tragedy (T)	16
1596	Blind Beggar of Alexandria	Chapman	Chapman's Comedies	—	Comedy (C)	10
1597	An Humourous Day's Mirth	Chapman	Chapman's Comedies	—	Comedy (C)	10
1598	Every Man in his Humour	Jonson	Materialien Vol. 10	—	Comedy (C)	7
1599	Every Man out of his Humour	Jonson	1600 Quarto	—	Comedy (C)	3
1599	Antonio and Mellida	Marston	Vol. 1	—	Tragicomedy (T)	19
1599	Antonio's Revenge	Marston	Vol. 1	—	Tragedy (T)	15
1600	Jack Drum's Entertainment	Marston	Vol. 3	—	Comedy (C)	5
1601	Cynthia's Revels	Jonson	Vol. 4	—	Comedy (C)	26
1601	What You Will	Marston	Vol. 2	—	Comedy (C)	5
1602	The Gentleman Usher	Chapman	Chapman's Comedies	—	Comedy (C)	13
1602	May-Day	Chapman	Chapman's Comedies	—	Comedy (C)	11
1603	Sir Giles Goosecap	Chapman	Chapman's Comedies	—	Comedy (C)	16
1604	Westward Ho	Dekker and Webster	Dekker Vol. 2	—	Comedy (C)	8
1605	Northward Ho	Dekker and Webster	Dekker Vol. 2	—	Comedy (C)	0
1606	The Woman-Hater	Beaumont	B. & F., Vol. 10	—	Comedy (C)	14
1694	The Married Beau	Crowne	Vol. 4	—	Comedy (C)	37

(a)	(b)	(c)	(d)	(e)	(f)	(g)
1695	*Oroonoko*	Southerne	*Five Restoration Tragedies*	—	Tragedy (T)	17
1696	*Aesop Part 1*	Vanbrugh	Vol. 2	—	Comedy (C)	20
1698	*Love and a Bottle*	Farquhar	Vol. 1	—	Comedy (C)	26
1698	*Caligula*	Crowne	Vol. 4	—	Tragedy (T)	32
1700	*The Pilgrim*	Vanbrugh	Vol. 2	—	Comedy (C)	8
1700	*Richard III*	Cibber	Vol. 2	—	History (T)	2

APPENDIX B

Alphabetical list of plays used as material, with dates.

The 29 plays of the supplementary material are not included in this appendix. In the alphabetical arrangement, the definite and indefinite articles have not been taken into account, nor has the word "King" when it immediately precedes a proper name; for example, *The Chances* should be sought under C, and *King Lear* under L.

Abdelazer, or The Moor's Revenge. 1676.
Alchemist, The. 1610.
Alcibiades. 1675.
All for Love, or The World Well Lost. 1677.
All's Well that Ends Well. 1603.
Amboyna, or The Cruelty of the Dutch to the English Merchants. 1672.
Amorous Bigot, The. 1690.
Amorous Prince, The, or The Curious Husband. 1671.
Amphitryon, or The Two Socias. 1690.
Antony and Cleopatra. 1607.
Anything for a Quiet Life. 1621.
Arthur, King, or The British Worthy. 1691.
As You Like It. 1600.
Assignation, The, or Love in a Nunnery. 1672.
Atheist, The, or The Second Part of the Soldier's Fortune. 1683.
Aureng-Zebe. 1675.
Bartholomew Fair. 1614.
Bashful Lover, The. 1636.
Beggars' Bush. 1622.
Bloody Brother, The, or Rollo Duke of Normandy. 1619.
Blurt, Master-Constable, or the Spaniard's Night-walk. 1601.
Bondman, The. 1623.

Broken Heart, The. 1629.
Bury Fair. 1689.
Caius Marius, The History and Fall of. 1679.
Captain, The. 1612.
Cardinal, The. 1641.
Catiline his Conspiracy. 1611.
Chances, The. 1625.
Changeling, The. 1622.
Chaste Maid in Cheapside, A. 1612.
City Heiress, The, or Sir Timothy Treat-all. 1682.
City Madam, The. 1632.
Cleomenes the Spartan Hero. 1692.
Comedy of Errors, The. 1593.
Comical Revenge, The, or Love in a Tub. 1664.
Conquest of Granada, The, the First Part, or Almanzor and Almahide. 1670.
Conquest of Granada, The, the Second Part, or Almanzor and Almahide. 1671.
Constant Couple, The, or A Trip to the Jubilee. 1699.
Constant Maid, The. 1638.
Constantine the Great. 1683.
Coriolanus, The Tragedy of. 1609.
Country Wife, The. 1675.
Cure for a Cuckold, A. 1625.

Custom of the Country, The. 1620.
Cymbeline King of Britain. 1610.
Devil is an Ass, The. 1616.
Devil's Law Case, The. 1620.
Distresses, The. 1639.
Don Carlos Prince of Spain. 1676.
Don Sebastian. 1689.
Double Dealer, The. 1693.
Duchess of Malfi, The. 1613.
Duke of Guise, The. 1682.
Dutch Lover, The. 1673.
Eastward Ho. 1605.
Elder Brother, The. 1625.
Emperor of the East, The. 1631.
Epicoene, or The Silent Woman. 1609.
Epsom Wells. 1672.
Evening's Love, An, or The Mock Astrologer. 1668.
Fair Favourite, The. 1638.
Fair Maid of the Inn, The. 1626.
Fair Quarrel, A. 1617.
Faithful Shepherdess, The. 1608.
False Count, The, or A New Way to Play an Old Game. 1681.
False One, The. 1620.
Family of Love, The. 1602.
Fancies Chaste and Noble, The. 1636.
Forced Marriage, The, or The Jealous Bridegroom. 1670.
Friendship in Fashion. 1678.
Game at Chess, A. 1624.
Gentleman Dancing-Master, The. 1672.
Great Duke of Florence, The. 1627.
Guardian, The. 1633.
Hamlet, The Tragedy of. 1601.
Henry IV, The First Part of King. 1597.
Henry IV, The Second Part of King. 1597.
Henry V, The Life of King. 1599.
Henry VI, The First Part of King. 1592.
Henry VI, The Second Part of King. 1591.
Henry VI, The Third Part of King. 1591.
Henry VIII, The Life of King. 1613.

Humorists, The. 1670.
Humorous Lieutenant, The. 1619.
Hyde Park. 1632.
Imposture, The. 1640.
Indian Emperor, The, or The Conquest of Mexico by the Spaniards. 1665.
Indian Queen, The. 1664.
John, The Life and Death of King. 1596.
Julius Caesar, The Life and Death of. 1599.
Kind Keeper, The, or Mr Limberham. 1678.
King and No King, A. 1611.
Lady of Pleasure, The. 1635.
Lady's Trial, The. 1638.
Lancashire Witches, The. 1681.
Law against Lovers, The. 1662.
Laws of Candy, The. 1619.
Lear, King. 1605.
Libertine, The. 1675.
Little French Lawyer, The. 1619.
Love and Honour. 1634.
Love for Love. 1695.
Love in a Wood, or St James's Park. 1671.
Love Triumphant, or Nature Will Prevail. 1694.
Love's Labour's Lost. 1594.
Lover's Progress, The. 1623.
Loyal Subject, The. 1618.
Lucky Chance, The, or An Alderman's Bargain. 1686.
Macbeth, The Tragedy of. 1606.
Mad Lover, The. 1617.
Mad World, my Masters, A. 1606.
Magnetic Lady, The, or Humours Reconciled. 1632.
Maid of Honour, The. 1621.
Maid's Tragedy, The. 1610.
Man of Mode, The, or Sir Fopling Flutter. 1676.
Man's the Master, The. 1668.
Marriage à la Mode. 1671.
Measure for Measure. 1604.

APPENDIX B

Merchant of Venice, The. 1596.
Merry Wives of Windsor, The. 1600.
Michaelmas Term. 1606.
Midsummer Night's Dream, A. 1595.
Monsieur Thomas. 1615.
Mourning Bride, The. 1697.
Much Ado about Nothing. 1598.
New Inn, The, or The Light Heart. 1629.
New Way to Pay Old Debts, A. 1625.
News from Plymouth. 1635.
Oedipus. 1678.
Old Bachelor, The. 1693.
Orphan, The, or The Unhappy Marriage. 1680.
Othello, the Moor of Venice. 1604.
Pericles, Prince of Tyre. 1608.
Perkin Warbeck. 1633.
Philaster, or Love Lies a-Bleeding. 1609.
Phoenix, The. 1604.
Pilgrim, The. 1621.
Plain Dealer, The. 1676.
Platonic Lovers, The. 1635.
Poetaster, or The Arraignment. 1601.
Politician, The. 1639.
Prophetess, The, or The History of Diocletian. 1622.
Provoked Wife, The. 1697.
Relapse, The, or Virtue in Danger. 1696.
Renegado, The. 1624.
Richard II, The Life and Death of. 1595.
Richard III, The Life and Death of. 1592.
Rival Ladies, The. 1663.
Roaring Girl, The, or Moll Cutpurse. 1610.
Romeo and Juliet. 1595.
Roundheads, The, or The Good Old Cause. 1681.
Rover, The, or The Banished Cavaliers. 1677.
Royal Master, The. 1637.

Royal Shepherdess, The. 1669.
Rule a Wife and Have a Wife. 1624.
Scornful Lady, The. 1613.
Scowrers, The. 1690.
Secret Love, or The Maiden Queen. 1667.
Sejanus his Fall. 1603.
She Would if She Could. 1668.
Sir Martin Mar-all, or The Feigned Innocence. 1667.
Sir Patient Fancy. 1678.
Soldier's Fortune, The. 1680.
Spanish Curate, The. 1622.
Spanish Friar, The, or The Double Discovery. 1680.
Spanish Gipsy, The. 1623.
Squire of Alsatia, The. 1688.
Staple of News, The. 1625.
Sullen Lovers, The, or The Impertinents. 1668.
Taming of the Shrew, The. 1594.
Tempest, The. 1611.
Tempest, The, or The Enchanted Island. 1667.
Timon of Athens. 1607.
'Tis Pity She's a Whore. 1627.
Titus Andronicus. 1594.
Town Fop, The, or Sir Timothy Tawdrey. 1676.
Traitor, The. 1631.
Trick to Catch the Old One, A. 1605.
Troilus and Cressida, The Tragedy of. 1602.
Troilus and Cressida, or Truth Found too Late. 1679.
True Widow, A. 1678.
Twelfth Night, or What You Will. 1601.
Two Gentlemen of Verona, The. 1593.
Tyrannic Love, or The Royal Martyr. 1669.
Unfortunate Lovers, The. 1638.
Valentinian. 1614.
Venice Preserved, or A Plot Discovered. 1682.

Very Woman, A. 1634.
Virtuoso, The. 1676.
Volpone, or The Fox. 1605.
Volunteers, The, or The Stock Jobbers. 1692.
Way of the World, The. 1700.
White Devil, The, or Vittoria Corombona. 1612.
Widow Ranter, The, or The History of Bacon in Virginia. 1689.
Wife for a Month, A. 1624.
Wild Gallant, The. 1663.
Wild-Goose-Chase, The. 1621.
Winter's Tale, The. 1611.
Wit Without Money. 1614.
Witch, The. 1615.
Wits, The. 1634.
Witty Fair One, The. 1628.
Woman Captain, The. 1679.
Younger Brother, The, or The Amorous Jilt. 1689.
Your Five Gallants. 1607.

APPENDIX C

Editions of plays used as material.

Beaumont, F., and Fletcher, J., *The Works of Francis Beaumont and John Fletcher*, ed. A. Glover and A. R. Waller, 10 vols (Cambridge, 1905—12).
Behn, A., *The Works of Aphra Behn*, ed. Montague Summers, 6 vols (London and Stratford-on-Avon, 1915).
Chapman, G., *The Comedies of George Chapman*, ed. T. M. Parrott (London and New York, 1914).
— — *The Tragedies of George Chapman*, ed. T. M. Parrott (London and New York, 1910).
Cibber, C., *The Dramatic Works of Colley Cibber, Esq.*, Vol. 2 (London, 1777).
Congreve, W., *The Best Plays of the Old Dramatists. William Congreve*, ed. A. C. Ewald (Mermaid Series) (London, 1887).
Crowne, J., *The Dramatic Works of John Crowne*, Vol. 4 (Dramatists of the Restoration) (Edinburgh and London, 1874).
Davenant, W., *The Dramatic Works of Sir William D'Avenant*, ed. J. Maidment and W. H. Logan, 5 vols (Dramatists of the Restoration) (Edinburgh and London, 1872—74).
Dekker, T., *Dramatic Works*, ed. Fredson Bowers, Vols 1—2 (Cambridge, 1953—55).
Dryden, J., *The Works of John Dryden*, ed. Sir Walter Scott, revised by G. Saintsbury, Vols I—VIII (Edinburgh, 1882—84).
Etherege, G., *The Dramatic Works of Sir George Etherege*, ed. H. F. P. Brett-Smith, 2 vols (Oxford, 1927).
Farquhar, G., *The Dramatic Works*, ed. A. C. Ewald, Vol. 1 (London, 1892).
Five Restoration Tragedies, ed. Bonamy Dobrée (World's Classics) (Oxford, 1928). (Contains Thomas Southerne's *Oroonoko*.)
Fletcher, J., see Beaumont, F.
Ford, J., see *Materials*.
Greene, R., *The Plays and Poems of Robert Greene*, ed. J. Churton Collins, 2 vols (Oxford, 1905).
Jonson, B., *Ben Jonson*, ed. C. H. Herford and P. Simpson, Vols I—VI (Oxford, 1925—38).
— — *Every Man Out of his Humour 1600*, ed. Wilson and Greg (Malone Society Reprints) (Oxford, 1920).
Lee, N., *The Dramatick Works of Mr. Nathanael Lee*, Vol. 2 (London, 1734).
Marlowe, C., *The Works of Christopher Marlowe*, ed. C. F. Tucker Brooke (Oxford, 1910).
Marston, J., *The Plays of John Marston*, ed. H. Harvey Wood, 3 vols (Edinburgh, 1934—39).

Massinger, P., *The Plays of Philip Massinger*, ed. W. Gifford, third edition (New York, 1860).
Materialien zur Kunde des älteren Englischen Dramas, ed. W. Bang, Vol. 10 (Louvain, 1905). (Contains 1601 Quarto of *Every Man in his Humour*.)
Materials for the Study of the Old English Drama, ed. Henry de Vocht, New Series, Vol. 1 (Louvain, 1927). (Contains five plays by John Ford.)
Middleton, T., *The Works of Thomas Middleton*, ed. A. H. Bullen, 8 vols (London, 1885—86).
Nashe, T., *Works of Thomas Nashe*, ed. R. B. McKerrow, 5 vols (London, 1904—10).
Otway, T., *The Works of Thomas Otway. Plays, Poems, and Love-Letters*, ed. J. C. Ghosh, 2 vols (Oxford, 1932).
Peele, G., *King Edward the First*, ed. W. W. Greg (Malone Society Reprints) (Oxford, 1911).
Shadwell, T., *The Complete Works*, ed. M. Summers, 5 vols (London, 1927).
Shakespeare, W., *Mr. William Shakespeares Comedies, Histories, & Tragedies. A facsimile edition prepared by Helge Kökeritz. With an introduction by Charles Tyler Prouty* (New Haven, 1954).
— — *Shakespeare Quartos in Collotype Facsimile*, with introductory notes by W. W. Greg, Numbers 1—8 (Shakespeare Association) (London, 1939—52).
— — *Shakespeare Quarto Facsimiles*, issued under the superintendence of Dr F. J. Furnivall, with photo-lithography by William Griggs (Nos 1—17) and Charles Praetorius (Nos 18—43) (London, 1880—90).
— — *The Works of William Shakespeare gathered into One Volume* (A. H. Bullen's text, Shakespeare Head Press) (Oxford, 1934).
Shirley, J., *The Dramatic Works and Poems of James Shirley*, ed. W. Gifford and A. Dyce, 6 vols (London, 1833).
Southerne, T., see *Five Restoration Tragedies*.
Vanbrugh, J., *The Complete Works of Sir John Vanbrugh*, the plays ed. Bonamy Dobrée, Vols 1—2 (London, 1927).
Webster, J., *The Complete Works of John Webster*, ed. F. L. Lucas, 4 vols (London, 1927).
Wycherley, W., *The Complete Plays of William Wycherley*, ed. W. C. Ward (Mermaid Series) (London, 1948).

APPENDIX D

Other works referred to.

Adams, J. C., *The Globe Playhouse* (Cambridge U. S. A. 1943).
Ashley, R., *Of Honour*, ed. V. B. Heltzel (San Marino 1947).
Barber, C., "A Rare Use of the Word *Honour* as a Criterion of Middleton's Authorship", in *English Studies* (Amsterdam), XXXVIII pp. 161—8 (1957).
Beljame, A., *Le public et les hommes de lettres en Angleterre au dix-huitième siècle* (Paris 1881).
Bentley, G. E., *The Jacobean and Caroline Stage*, Vols 1—5 (Oxford 1941—56).
Bethell, S. L., *The Cultural Revolution of the Seventeenth Century* (London 1951).
Bloomfield, L., *Language* (New York 1933).
Bowers, F. T., *Elizabethan Revenge Tragedy 1587—1642* (Princeton 1940).
Bradbrook, M. C., *Themes and Conventions of Elizabethan Tragedy* (Cambridge 1935).
Brennan, E. M., *The Theme of Revenge in Elizabethan Life and Drama 1580—1605*, unpublished M. A. thesis of the Queen's University, Belfast (1955).
Brooks, J. L., "*La Estrella de Sevilla:* 'Admirable y famosa tragedia'", in *Bulletin of Hispanic Studies*, XXXII No. 1, pp. 8—20 (Liverpool 1955).
Bryson, F. R., *The Point of Honor in Sixteenth-Century Italy* (New York 1935).
Buckingham, Duke of, see Villiers.
Bush, D., *English Literature in the Earlier Seventeenth Century* (Oxford 1945).
Butterfield, H., *The Origins of Modern Science 1300—1800* (London 1949).
Cambridge History of English Literature, The, ed. A. W. Ward and A. R. Waller, Vols V, VI, VIII (Cambridge 1910—12).
Campbell, L. B., "Theories of Revenge in Renaissance England", in *Modern Philology*, Vol. XXVIII No. 3 (1931).
Castro, A, "Algunas observaciones acerca del concepto del honor en los siglos XVI y XVII", in *Revista de Filología Española*, Vol. III (1916), pp. 1—50, 357—86.
Chambers, E. K., *William Shakespeare*, 2 vols (Oxford 1930).
—— *The Elizabethan Stage*, 4 vols, corrected reprint (Oxford 1945).
Chase, L. N., *The English Heroic Play* (New York 1903).
Clark, G. N., *The Later Stuarts 1660—1714* (Oxford 1934).
—— *The Seventeenth Century*, second edition (Oxford 1947).
Coleridge, S. T., *Essays and Lectures on Shakespeare and some other Old Poets and Dramatists* (Everyman) (London 1907).
Danby, J. F., *Shakespeare's Doctrine of Nature. A Study of King Lear* (London 1949).

— — *Poets on Fortune's Hill* (London 1952).
Davies, G., *The Early Stuarts 1603—1660* (Oxford 1937).
Dobrée, B., *Restoration Comedy 1660—1720* (Oxford 1924).
— — *Restoration Tragedy 1660—1720* (Oxford 1929).
Draper, J. W., "Desdemona: a Compound of Two Cultures", in *Révue de littérature comparée*, 13 (1933).
Dunkel, W. D., *The Dramatic Technique of Thomas Middleton in his Comedies of London Life* (Chicago 1925).
Eliot, T. S., *Selected Essays*, second edition revised and enlarged (London 1934).
Ellehauge, M., *English Restoration Drama* (Copenhagen 1933).
Ellis-Fermor, U. M., *The Jacobean Drama* (London 1936).
Empson, W., *The Structure of Complex Words* (London 1951).
Harbage, A., *Cavalier Drama* (New York 1936).
— — *Annals of English Drama 975—1700* (Philadelphia 1940).
— — *Shakespeare's Audience* (New York 1941).
Hotson, L., *The Commonwealth and Restoration Stage* (Cambridge U. S. A. 1928).
Hume, M., *Spanish Influence on English Literature* (London 1905).
Humphreys, A. R., *The Augustan World* (London 1954).
Hutchinson, L., *Memoirs of the Life of Colonel Hutchinson*, ed. by the Rev. Julius Hutchinson, fifth edition (London 1846).
Johnson, S., *The Poems of Samuel Johnson*, ed. D. N. Smith and E. C. McAdam (Oxford 1941).
Joseph, B., *Conscience and the King* (London 1953).
Kelso, R., *The Doctrine of the English Gentleman in the Sixteenth Century* (University of Illinois Studies in Language and Literature, Vol. XIV Nos. 1—2) (Urbana Illinois 1929).
Knight, G. W., *The Olive and the Sword* (London 1944).
Knights, L. C., "Notes on Comedy", in *Determinations. Critical Essays*, ed. F. R. Leavis (London 1934).
— — *Drama and Society in the Age of Jonson* (London 1937).
— — "Shakespeare and Political Wisdom", in *The Sewanee Review*, Vol. LXI No. 1 (1953).
Krutch, K. W., *Comedy and Conscience after the Restoration*, revised edition (New York 1949).
Laski, H. J., *The Rise of European Liberalism* (London 1936).
Leavis, F. R., *The Common Pursuit* (London 1952).
Lewis, C. S., *De Descriptione Temporum* (Cambridge 1955).
Littré, E., *Dictionnaire de la langue française*, four vols (Paris 1885—9).
Lynch, K., *The Social Mode of Restoration Comedy* (University of Michigan Publications in Language and Literature, III) (New York 1926).
MacCallum, M. W., *Shakespeare's Roman Plays and their Background* (London 1910).
Matoré, G., *La méthode en lexicologie* (Paris 1953).
New English Dictionary, A, on Historical Principles, ed. J. A. H. Murray and others (Oxford 1888—1933).

Nicoll, A., *A History of Restoration Drama 1660 to 1700*, third edition (revised) (Cambridge 1940).
North, Sir Thomas, *Plutarch's Lives of the Noble Grecians and Romans*, ed. G.Wyndham, Vols 2, 5, and 6 (The Tudor Translations) (London 1895—6).
Oliphant, E. H. C., *The Plays of Beaumont and Fletcher* (New Haven 1927).
Onions, C. T., *A Shakespeare Glossary*, corrected edition (Oxford 1946).
Palmer, J., *The Comedy of Manners* (London 1913).
Peacham, H., *Peacham's Compleat Gentleman 1634*, with an introduction by G. S. Gordon (Tudor and Stuart Library Vol. 5) (Oxford 1906).
Praz, M., "Shakespeare's Italy", in *Shakespeare Survey 7*, ed. A. Nicoll (Cambridge 1954).
Rudskoger, A., *Fair, Foul, Nice, Proper. A Contribution to the Study of Polysemy* (Gothenburg Studies in English, I) (Stockholm 1952).
Salingar, L. G., "The Social Setting" and "The Decline of Tragedy", in *A Guide to English Literature: 2 The Age of Shakespeare*, ed. B. Ford (London 1955).
Saussure, F. de, *Cours de linguistique générale*, ed. C. Bally and A. Sechehaye, second edition (Paris 1922).
Schelling, F. E., *Elizabethan Drama 1558—1642*, 2 vols (London, Boston, and New York 1911).
Serenius, Jacobus, *Dictionarium Anglo-Svethico-Latinum* (Hamburg 1734).
Stern, G., *Meaning and Change of Meaning* (Gothenburg 1931).
Stone, L., "The Anatomy of the Elizabethan Aristocracy", in *The Economic History Review* Vol. XVIII Nos 1 & 2 (1948).
— — "The Elizabethan Aristocracy — A Restatement", in *The Economic History Review* Second Series, Vol. IV No. 3 (1952).
Talon, H. A., *John Bunyan, l'homme et l'oeuvre* (Paris 1948).
Tawney, R. H., "The Rise of the Gentry, 1558—1640", in *The Economic History Review* Vol. XI (1941).
— — "The Rise of the Gentry: a Postscript", in *The Economic History Review* Second Series, Vol. VII No. 1 (1954).
Thorndike, A. H., *English Comedy* (New York 1929).
Tillyard, E. M. W., *The Elizabethan World Picture* (London 1943).
— — *Shakespeare's History Plays* (London 1944).
Trevelyan, G. M., *England under the Stuarts*, 16th edition (London 1933).
Trevor-Roper, H. R., "The Elizabethan Aristocracy: an Anatomy Anatomized", in *The Economic History Review* Second Series, Vol. III No. 3 (1951).
— — *The Gentry 1540—1640*, Economic History Review Supplements No. 1 (London 1953).
Ullmann, S., *The Principles of Semantics* (Glasgow 1951).
Ustick, W. L., "Changing Ideals of Aristocratic Character and Conduct in Seventeenth-Century England", in *Modern Philology*, Vol. XXX No. 2 (1932).
Villiers, G., Duke of Buckingham, *The Rehearsal*, ed. M. Summers (Stratford-on-Avon 1914).
Whole Duty of Man, The, revised and corrected edition (Belfast 1772).

Wiggin, P. G., *An Inquiry into the Authorship of the Middleton-Rowley Plays* (Boston 1897).
Willey, B., *The Seventeenth Century Background* (London 1934).
—— *The Eighteenth Century Background* (London 1940).
Wilson, E. M., "'Othello', a Tragedy of Honour", in *The Listener* Vol. XLVII No. 1214 (June 5th 1952).
—— "Family Honour in the Plays of Shakespeare's Predecessors and Contemporaries", in *Essays and Studies 1953*, ed. G. Bullough for the English Association (London 1953).
Wilson, J. D., *The Fortunes of Falstaff* (Cambridge 1943).
Wilson, J. H., *The Influence of Beaumont and Fletcher on Restoration Drama* (Columbus 1928).
Wright, L. B., *Middle-Class Culture in Elizabethan England* (Chapel Hill 1935).
Wyld, H. C., *The Universal English Dictionary* (London 1946).
Zeeveld, W. G., "'Food for Powder'—'Food for Worms'", in *Shakespeare Quarterly*, Vol. III No. 3 (1952).

APPENDIX E

Supplementary Material

When the main material used in this book had been collected and analysed, material was collected from a further 29 plays, to give additional information on a number of specific points. Particulars of the plays concerned are given at the end of Appendix A, pp. 347—348, and the editions consulted are included in Appendix C. Excerpts from these plays are not included in Chapters 7—9, nor are the findings from them incorporated in the various statistical tables throughout the book. Instead, a summary of the findings from this supplementary material will be given here. The material falls into three groups, in three different decades, and each group will be considered in turn; then, in a fourth section, something will be said about the effects of all three groups on the statistical tables as a whole. It can be said at once that, at almost every point, the supplementary material confirms and corroborates the conclusions already drawn from the main material.

(a) *Supplementary Material, 1591—1600*

Since, in the original material, the decade 1591—1600 was represented by Shakespeare alone, it seemed desirable to collect material by other authors as a check. I have therefore examined 14 plays (7 in the comedy-group and 7 in the tragedy-group) by Marlowe, Greene, Peele, Nashe, Chapman, Marston, and Jonson.

The new material contains a total of 8 examples per play for comedy, and 17.9 per play for tragedy, compared with 11 and 16.7 in the old material. The frequencies of the main groups of head-meanings are very similar to those found in the original material (Tables 4—6). The R/RH/H group becomes a little smaller: if the old material and the new are combined, the figures become 4.2 per play in comedy, and 8.9 in tragedy (compared with original 4.8 and 9.6); it will be seen that this brings out even more strongly the rising tendency already found during the first half-century. Similarly, it is confirmed that the Rc/RcC/C group is very small in this decade. The same is true of the breakdown into R, RH, and H, and of the proportions of n, g, and u: insofar as there is any change in the figures, it is one that reinforces the trends already found in the century. In some respects the material is too small to add significantly to what has already been discovered, but at any rate it does not contradict earlier findings; there are no examples of Ro or of Rco; there are only four examples of the Rc/RcC/C group, and no examples of Cm or Cb; there are eight examples of acquired TP, and one example of inherited, but this does not increase the material sufficiently to make the position any clearer (cf. p. 319).

There is only one respect in which the new material reduces the steepness of the curves found for the whole century, and this is in the k/m/v/x ratios, but even

TABLE 62. *Supplementary material 1591—1600. Percentages of k, m, v, and x.*

Comedy	Original material	New material	Combined	Tragedy	Original material	New material	Combined
k	15%	36%	21%	k	23%	27%	24%
m	36%	18%	31%	m	32%	13%	25%
v	25%	9%	20%	v	24%	27%	25%
x	25%	36%	28%	x	21%	33%	25%

here the significant differences remain, although slightly reduced. Table 62 shows the percentages of k, v, m, and x in the old material, the new material, and the two combined; as the number of examples is not very great, R, RH, and H are not shown separately.

It will be seen that the addition of the new material reduces the percentage of m and increases the percentage of k; but if the new combined figures are inserted in Table 51 in place of the old, no essential difference is made to the pattern of the century. The lower percentage of m in the new plays is perhaps a result of the large popular elements in these plays; not only comedies like *Orlando Furioso* and *Jack Drum's Entertainment*, but also histories like *Edward I* are strikingly popular in tone and content; by contrast, Shakespeare's plays of the same period are positively aristocratic in tone, despite their large popular elements and their popular success. A considerable number of the examples of k in the new material are connected with high rank and its attendant ostentation.

(b) *Supplementary Material, 1601—1610*

In Chapter 10 (pp. 295—298), I examined for this decade the honour-usage in the comedies which were written for the private theatre, and compared them with the comedies of the decade as a whole. I concluded that the comedies written for the private theatres did not at all anticipate the usage of Restoration comedy, and indeed that if they differed at all from the other comedies of the decade it was in the direction away from Restoration comedy. Since this comparison was based on only nine plays, and as one author (Middleton) was strongly represented, I have examined a further eight comedies written for the private theatre. The authors are Jonson, Marston, Chapman, Dekker, Webster, and Beaumont.

The new material confirms the findings of pp. 297—298. The frequency of the R/RH/H group in the new material is 2.9 per play, compared with 2.6 in the original nine comedies (both figures lower than that for all comedy in the decade). The k/m/v/x ratios are found to be practically identical with those for all comedy in the decade: the figures for the private-theatre plays (old and new material combined) are k 22%, m 22%, v 26%, x 30%; the figures for all comedy in the decade (Table 51) are k 20%, m 24%, v 30%, x 27%. The n/g ratio still differs from that for all comedy in the decade in a direction opposite to Restoration comedy; the figures for all seventeen private-theatre plays are n 29%, g 37%, u 34%. It is therefore clear that the usage in the private theatres in this decade does not anticipate the usage in Restoration comedy, but that it does on the other hand closely resemble usage in the public theatres of the time.

(c) *Supplementary Material, 1691—1700*

In the original material, the decade 1691—1700 was represented by only twelve plays. This might not have mattered, had not the decade departed from the norm for the rest of the half-century. There were in fact signs suggesting that the hitherto prevailing trends in the century were being halted or even reversed. There is in fact little material available in this decade, but I have succeeded in finding another seven plays (four comedies and three tragedies) which were for various reasons not available to me when I collected the original material.

The simplest way to summarize the effects of the new material will be to consider the main tables of the book in turn:

Table 3: The overall decline in frequency in the last decade of the century is supported by the new material. The number of examples per play in the combined material is for comedy 24.7, for tragedy 15.0, total 21.2.

Tables 4—6: The new material brings no appreciable change, except in MTP tragedy, where the figure now goes up to 3.6, which is comparable with the other decades of the half-century. The new combined figures for the R/RH/H group are 10.9 (comedy), and 7.4 (tragedy), so the decline in this decade is confirmed.

Tables 7—9: The new figures are almost identical with the old; where they differ, they are slightly lower. The fall of H in tragedy is confirmed, the new combined figure still being 1.0.

Tables 16—18: No appreciable change.

Table 19: No change.

Table 20: In comedy, there are 6 examples of Rco out of a total of 13 examples of Rc and RcC. The percentage of Rco for the second half of the century thus goes up from 35.6 to 36.2. There are no new examples of Rco in tragedy, out of a total of four new examples of Rc and RcC.

Tables 48—51: When the new material is added, the figures become more like those of the other decades of the half-century, but still show a slight tendency to reverse earlier trends. In comedy the figures become (for R, RH, and H combined, Table 51): k 43.5%, m 19.1%, v 12.2%, and x 25.2%; in tragedy they become: k 34.6%, m 23.1%, v 17.3%, and x 25.0%. The figures for tragedy are now reasonably similar to those for the other decades of the half-century, but in comedy there is still a sharp rise in m and a fairly sharp drop in k, reversing previous trends. If, however, one play is left out of the material, the picture for comedy becomes quite different; the play to be omitted is *The Volunteers*, and then the combined figures for old and new material (comedy) become: k 51%, m 9%, v 16%, and x 24%. The figures now differ hardly at all from immediately preceding decades. So far we have been considering R, RH, and H combined, but the same is found to be true of each separately, in those cases where the material is large enough to give a clear picture. It seems likely, therefore, that the apparent reversing of trends in the k/m/v/x ratios in this last decade is illusory; the greater part of the change is obviously due to one play, and this may be a freak.

Table 55: The new material causes no appreciable change.

In general, the new material for this decade confirms the findings already made, except that great doubt is cast on the apparent reversing of trends in the k/m/v/x ratios.

(d) *Supplementary Material, General*

While collecting the special information required from the extra plays in the decade 1601—1610, I also collected from them the full information required in the various tables in the book. The total available material for the decades 1591—1600 and 1601—1610 was thus increased very considerably. The new material confirmed all the earlier conclusions, and often made the change much clearer within the first half-century; it strengthened the impression that the rate of change was rapid in the decade 1610—20. Occasionally, however, the new material reduces the apparent size of a change: in the decade 1601—1610, as in 1591—1600, the new material reduces the size of the m group slightly; however, the falling tendency in m remains clear, and the fact that the change is attested by an even larger body of material makes it more certain.

On some points the new material gives no further clarity: it provides insufficient extra examples to clear up the question of Cm and Cb (see pp. 305—306) or the question of inherited and acquired rank (see pp. 318—319). On most points, however, it confirms the conclusions already reached on all three decades in question, and the only place where it throws doubt on the picture given by the original material is in the apparent change of trends in the k/m/v/x ratio in the decade 1691—1700.

APPENDIX F

Statistical Methods

Since I have studied only a sample of the usage of the century, it is necessary to apply statistical techniques to my various tables before we can be certain what they tell us. If the tables show a change in a ratio with time (for example a change in the k/v ratio between the first half of the century and the second), we still have to discover whether the change is greater than could have been expected from chance alone, i. e. we have to discover whether the change is statistically significant.

The statistical analysis of Tables 48 to 51 (which I consider the most important tables in the book) was carried out at the Statistical Institute of Gothenburg University, by courtesy of the head of the institute, Dr Hannes Hyrenius. For the remaining tables, I carried out the statistical analysis myself, using the chi-square method, and I must take the responsibility for any errors either in methods or in calculation. As will be seen from my comments on the various tables, my method has usually been to examine one variable at a time, though occasionally I examine the ratio between two variables. When a change is significant at the 99% level (i. e. when there is only one chance in a hundred that it is a random fluctuation) I denote it "significant"; at the 99.9% level, "highly significant"; at the 95% level, "just significant". Occasionally I make use of the 90% level, and this I denote "nearly significant".

In some tables, I am interested in the absolute frequency with which a usage occurs, not with the ratio between different usages; this is so, for example, in Tables 3 to 9. The method I have used in such cases is to consider the number of examples as a percentage of the estimated total number of nouns in the material in question. For this purpose I have made sample counts in different plays and estimated the approximate number of nouns per play in my material (about 3,500). More refined techniques would have been possible for these tables, but I did not consider the amount of work involved to be justifiable, and the results given by my method are sufficient for my purposes.

The statistical methods assume that the examples are a true random sample of the material being assessed; this will presumably be the case if the plays selected give balanced representation to different authors and different genres. It is obvious that the plays I have studied are not representative of the drama as a whole in the century: I have excluded plays which aim specifically at a middle-class audience and I have tried to choose the best writers and the most representative writers in each period. It does seem fair to claim, however, that the plays I have used as my material provide a good random sample of *the type of play I wish to study*, i. e. the play that represents upper-class attitudes in its period.

APPENDIX G

List of Minor Symbols

A list of symbols for head-meanings (capital letters) has already been given as an appendix to Chapter 2 (p. 87 above). Below is given a list of the minor symbols (small letters) which are attached to the symbols for head-meanings to denote various sub-classes.

b = used with C to indicate that the chastity referred to is a physical state, not a mental one; contrasted with m.

c = part of the composite symbol Rc for the head-meaning "reputation for chastity".

g = used with R (and RH) to indicate positive reputation, "glory"; contrasted with n.

k = used with R, RH, and H to indicate that the behaviour and the attitudes involved are not consistent with Christian morals (as interpreted by the age); contrasted with v (and with m).

km = a sub-group of m, to indicate that the military reputation or military qualities are won or exercised in duel or private brawl, not in war.

m = used with R, RH, and H to indicate a military content (military reputation, martial qualities of character).

m = used with C to indicate that the chastity referred to is purity of mind, a mental state not a physical one; contrasted with b.

n = used with R (and RH) to indicate negative reputation, "good name"; contrasted with g.

o = used with R and Rc (also RH and RcC) to indicate that the speaker assumes in the possessor of the reputation the absence of the relevant qualities, and takes his hearer to understand this.

(o) = used with R and Rc (also RH and RcC) to show that the possessor of the reputation lacks the relevant qualities, but that this fact is concealed from the hearer, or is not known to the speaker.

t = used with M to indicate that the mark of distinction conferred is not something trivial, but constitutes a considerable public distinction.

u = unclassified with respect to n and g.

v = used with R, RH, and H to indicate that the behaviour and the attitudes involved are in accordance with Christian morals (as interpreted by the age); contrasted with k (and with m).

x = unclassified with respect to k, v, and m.

APPENDIX TO CHAPTER 2
Summary of Symbols for Head-Meanings

C	=	chastity.
D	=	distinction, eminence.
E	=	esteem, veneration, respect.
K	=	the code of honour (considered as a set of laws).
L	=	legal meaning, "a seigniory of several manors held under one baron or lord paramount".
M	=	something conferred or done as a mark or token of respect or distinction (including the special usages "praise" and "a bow, obeisance, curtsey").
H	=	honourableness of character, honourable behaviour.
O	=	use in oaths and asseverations.
P	=	high position, rank, high birth.
R	=	reputation.
Rc	=	reputation for chastity.
RcC	=	equivocal Rc/C.
RH	=	equivocal R/H.
S	=	a source or cause of honour, something or somebody that does honour (to).
T	=	title of rank.
U	=	unclassified.
W	=	word of honour, statement or promise made on one's honour.
Y	=	respectful form of address or reference, "your honour", etc.

APPENDIX G

List of Minor Symbols

A list of symbols for head-meanings (capital letters) has already been given as an appendix to Chapter 2 (p. 87 above). Below is given a list of the minor symbols (small letters) which are attached to the symbols for head-meanings to denote various sub-classes.

b = used with C to indicate that the chastity referred to is a physical state, not a mental one; contrasted with m.

c = part of the composite symbol Rc for the head-meaning "reputation for chastity".

g = used with R (and RH) to indicate positive reputation, "glory"; contrasted with n.

k = used with R, RH, and H to indicate that the behaviour and the attitudes involved are not consistent with Christian morals (as interpreted by the age); contrasted with v (and with m).

km = a sub-group of m, to indicate that the military reputation or military qualities are won or exercised in duel or private brawl, not in war.

m = used with R, RH, and H to indicate a military content (military reputation, martial qualities of character).

m = used with C to indicate that the chastity referred to is purity of mind, a mental state not a physical one; contrasted with b.

n = used with R (and RH) to indicate negative reputation, "good name"; contrasted with g.

o = used with R and Rc (also RH and RcC) to indicate that the speaker assumes in the possessor of the reputation the absence of the relevant qualities, and takes his hearer to understand this.

(o) = used with R and Rc (also RH and RcC) to show that the possessor of the reputation lacks the relevant qualities, but that this fact is concealed from the hearer, or is not known to the speaker.

t = used with M to indicate that the mark of distinction conferred is not something trivial, but constitutes a considerable public distinction.

u = unclassified with respect to n and g.

v = used with R, RH, and H to indicate that the behaviour and the attitudes involved are in accordance with Christian morals (as interpreted by the age); contrasted with k (and with m).

x = unclassified with respect to k, v, and m.